Edward Stirling Rivett Carnac

The Presidential Armies of India

Edward Stirling Rivett Carnac

The Presidential Armies of India

ISBN/EAN: 9783743325159

Manufactured in Europe, USA, Canada, Australia, Japa

Cover: Foto ©ninafisch / pixelio.de

Manufactured and distributed by brebook publishing software (www.brebook.com)

Edward Stirling Rivett Carnac

The Presidential Armies of India

THE
PRESIDENTIAL ARMIES
OF INDIA.

BY THE LATE

COLONEL S. RIVETT-CARNAC,

FORMERLY 11TH HUSSARS.

WITH A CONTINUATION AND GENERAL REMARKS
ON INDIA.

BY

THE AUTHOR OF "OUR BURMESE WARS AND RELATIONS WITH BURMA,"
"DISTINGUISHED ANGLO-INDIANS," ETC.

LONDON:
W. H. ALLEN & CO., 13 WATERLOO PLACE. S.W.
AND AT CALCUTTA.

1890.

(All Rights Reserved.)

LONDON:
PRINTED BY W. H. ALLEN AND CO., 13 WATERLOO PLACE,
PALL MALL. S.W.

PREFACE.

PROBABLY few literary men would ever think of attempting to write, after Gibbon, another *History of the Decline and Fall of the Roman Empire*, or give to the world a second brilliant *History of England*, treading the same ground as Lord Macaulay; so, turning to the East, or India, it may safely be affirmed, after the histories of Abbé Raynal, Orme, Mill, Auber, and, as especially regards the great Bengal Sepoy Mutiny, Kaye, Malleson, and Holmes—to say nothing of the *Decisive Battles of India* with, as the famous *Edinburgh* reviewer says of Boswell's *Life of Johnson*, "Eclipse first, and the rest nowhere"—there are few authors who would venture, even conducted by "historic truth," to tread again, over the same fields, "the long extent of backward time." And yet, without such full and graphic details as abound in the works of the above writers, it would not be possible to do ample justice to the Presidential Armies of India. By liberal quotation, and the rather unfair, but common mode of transposing their language, the subject might easily have been extended to two or three volumes instead of one, which would have simply wearied the reader, instead of attracting his attention; so the author of this "Continuation," though at the risk of not carrying out Colonel Rivett-Carnac's original plan, has preferred chiefly to confine himself—as there are well-known published works on the subjects omitted—to a few historical and other sketches, supplementing the work with various useful details, and, it is to be hoped, somewhat valuable Appendices, in order to give the British public—who appear to have so little time for reading aught save the ever-welcome newspaper—some idea of what has been performed by our Presidential Armies during the one hundred and fifty years of British military glory, wonderful civil administration, and mercantile success in the East.

Under Governors or Presidents Clive and Verelst, in Calcutta—and, doubtless, also in Madras and Bombay—there were a few local growls, as in our time. The Civil and Military officers were, to the horror of the East India Company and their "heaven-born general," both luxurious and extravagant; in the opinion of Clive, as will hereafter be seen, they had become "far gone in luxury and debauchery"; while the cool, calculating, hard-working, and enterprising "Interloper," against whom war had been waged since the days of Sir Josiah Child, the model East India Director, or from the very end of the seventeenth century, was in nearly as anomalous a position as the zealous and most deserving Uncovenanted official in the nineteenth. Lord Clive was most anxious to check the growth of luxury and extravagance in the Indian Army; and now, at the end of the present century, while this preface is being written, Europe is astonished at the new Emperor William of Germany taking such a vast interest in the welfare of the working man, and resolving at the same time, with a decision of character of which Frederick the Great might have been proud, that " the alarming increase of luxury in the Army must be resisted with all seriousness and energy." There is a decided smack of the Clive language in this wise resolution of the independent Emperor William which cannot fail to be pleasing to Englishmen.

Under the able rule of Clive, Calcutta rose " like a phœnix from its ashes." One hundred years after India's severest trial, the great Bengal Sepoy Mutiny, had a similar effect on the entire dominion, as, from our putting down the rebellion by the most decisive measures—so materially assisted by the Presidency Armies, and even patriotic "Interloping" Volunteers, with such mighty men as Venables, the noble-hearted, who equipped a force and held a district, and the Calcutta Volunteer Guards, who were ready, with their Interlopers' corps of cavalry, infantry, and artillery, to defend the city against any number of rebel sepoys—as was also the case at Arrah, in Rajshahye, Pubna, Kishnaghur, and other stations—the thunder passed away; the air was cleared; and the Englishman's "loved," but too much neglected, India was saved.

By September 1858, when the Government had been taken over by the Crown, even such an anomaly as a genuine Anglo-Indian interloper became almost impossible.

Doubtless, in time of need, our Presidential Armies will yet have, as of yore, the assistance of a splendid reserve force, chiefly recruited from the strong Uncovenanted ranks—"Siva's* Own"—in Calcutta, Madras, and Bombay. As Clive declared that India must be kept by the sword, every European in the country should have some military training about him; and nothing can be better than the Volunteer system, conducted on fair and liberal principles. We cannot be entirely civil until the chief opposing forces—say, over two hundred millions of Hindus and fifty millions of Mahomedans —are reconciled to each other.

To meet " coming events," then, to complete our great schemes of civilisation, whatever they may be, every European in India should be half a soldier. The great Parsi community in Bombay evidently cherished some views of the sort, or they would not, as has recently been the case, have felt so pleased at being allowed

* Siva, the Hindu Satan, or Destroying Power.

by the Viceroy to join the Volunteer movement. It is quite refreshing to read, regarding the high-souled sons of Zoroaster, that Government has sanctioned their enrolment in the "local battalion of Volunteers." There can be no doubt that well-trained Parsís would form, in the event of future rebellion or commotion, safe and valuable auxiliaries to the Presidential Armies. This, and many other matters, should be thoroughly understood by the Englishman at home, especially should he have any position in the Home Government of India. But the question ever comes to the Anglo-Indian mind, or to the servant, civil or military, who has passed his best years in the country, When are the English people going to understand India? Echo answers, When? They have been told scores of times that "India is the largest appendage of a great empire which the world ever saw"; and again, as if a libel on the general intelligence of the renowned British Senate—although written forty years ago, yet true in part now—"that the ignorance and the indifference of both Houses of Parliament upon matters connected with India is deplorable." To say that things have not greatly improved in these respects would be wrong. But how is it possible for the British Parliament to do justice to India when so much of its time is given to Ireland, with a population of fifty or sixty times less than that of our greatest Dependency? With one or two exceptions, for many years, there has been scarcely any instance of an honourable member of the House of Commons throwing his whole heart and soul into an Indian question, with the energy (to say nothing of the eloquence) of a Burke or a Sheridan, so as to place his auditors for the time actually in India, while redressing the wrongs of its people, or, it may be, of those who form a portion of the machinery of its government. In this spring of 1890, public attention will have been directed to the remarkable confessions of two distinguished Members of Parliament regarding their Indian experiences. There are now some hopes of a stronger British interest being created in India and Indian affairs, when we read that the impression left on Professor Bryce's mind by his visit to India was that of "the extraordinary solidity and safety of our government." Not such a great chance at present, as in the days of Sir John Malcolm, of our, as he quaintly said, "getting up in the morning with our throats cut!" And, again, Mr. Childers after his visit to India was fain to confess how little he had learnt about India after months of almost continuous travelling, study, and conversation. There is nothing of the frivolous "globe-trotter" about such admirably modest and shrewd remarks of the M.P. travellers, who may yet take a trip into "Darkest Africa" with the greatest traveller of our time, who is now rivalling Burnes, when, to throw a line of light over Asia fifty years ago, he came to London with the manuscript of his famous travels into Bokhara. Nor is there aught save downright earnestness in the energetic and philanthropic action of Mr. H. S. King, M.P., who during a brief visit to India not only powerfully advocated the claims of the "Uncovenanted," but found time to visit the city of the Nizam at Hyderabad, taking an interest in a local educational institute, and also to bring back in his pocket a grand scheme for the establishment of an Indian Institute in England. It is only such well-timed energy, in a variety of ways, that can make our great Indian Empire really worth possessing, and cause the Englishman, with reference to Carlyle's remark, to be as loth to eradicate India from his country's history as to take away his own loved Shakspeare from our literature. The Chelsea philosopher leans to the immortality of Shakspeare; for he thinks "Indian Empire will go, at any rate, some day." This is sadly prophetic for the Presidential Armies. The chain of historical narrative in this work disappears purposely after the conquest of Mysore—the importance of which can never be fully appreciated; and which it required the foresight, vigour, and determination of three of our most famous Governors-General—Warren Hastings, and the Marquesses Cornwallis and Wellesley—and the tact as well as the strategy of our ablest generals to accomplish.

Mysore may be styled the first grand field of combination for display of prowess by the three Presidency armies. Now (April 1890), instead of the expensive "pride, pomp, and circumstance of glorious war," we read that Peace is also having her triumphs—one of them being a subscription of £1,000 sterling to Mr. H. S. King's fund for establishing an Indian Institute in England for the convenience and welfare of Indian gentlemen, generously given by His Highness the Maharajah of Mysore.

It may now be stated that the first six chapters of this work, written by the late Colonel Rivett-Carnac, appeared in the *Army and Navy Magazine*, the last in the number for June 1888. Of these six chapters alone, it might be said that there are few contributions to Indian history which give so much information in so small a space; and hence the utility of this work for schools and private students may become apparent.

As to the twelfth chapter, a considerable portion of it originally appeared in *The Indian Magazine* for March and April 1889, under the title of "Ava, City of the new Marquisate: the old 'City of Gems,' and Capital of the Jewels' Kingdom." The larger part of the second paper referred chiefly and briefly to the minerals of Burma and the now well-known ruby mines, which, of course, have nothing to do with the Presidential Armies further than had they not conquered Pegu and Upper Burma there would now have been no "Ruby Mines Company, Limited."

Two of the greatest living authorities on Indian military affairs —both distinguished Anglo-Indians—have kindly furnished replies to a few brief queries submitted to them, with a view to give more completeness to the present work.

"Had you asked me your questions some fifty years ago, or

when I first knew India, I should have replied, Leave the commanders-in-chief as they are: let not the centralization (or any other) system in Bengal be applied to Bombay or Madras; and the Volunteer system is impolitic for India. But British India is no longer 'Oriental'; and having clothed herself in Western garments, must adapt herself to Western ways. Whether we have done well to transform her, so far as transformation has already gone, I am not prepared to say; but rulers in India are as liable to form erroneous conclusions and make erroneous forecasts as rulers in other parts, and Government at home will naturally support their nominees. For the present day, my impression is that:—

"1. Commanders-in-chief may well be abolished at Presidencies.

"2. A centralization system bringing all troops in India under the immediate ken of the one commander-in-chief (but not necessarily assimilating their organization) might act healthily, if the commander-in-chief and his staff were the men for their places.

"3. The Volunteer assistance should be purely tentative and confined to localities."

From such a great authority on the subject of an Indian mutiny, the following information would seem to be especially valuable. It is the opinion of this eminent Anglo-Indian :—

"1st. That I don't think there can be another mutiny, as now we man all the guns, hold all the forts, and occupy all the dominating positions in India; and the natives know it.

"2nd. I am in favour of abolishing the commands-in-chief in Madras and Bombay.

"3rd. Volunteers in India should be treated precisely as Volunteers in England are treated. You must recollect that when the first mutiny broke out in 1857 we had only 30,000 English troops in India to about 240,000 natives (I write from memory); whereas now we have 60,000 to 120,000. Then the natives manned more than half the guns, whereas now they man none, or next to none. The natives held the arsenals, the magazines, and, to a large extent, the fortresses; now they hold none of these. There was great discontent throughout the country and the army; now there is not. The natives were awake; the English were asleep. Yet, in spite of these drawbacks, we prevailed! How could they have a chance of success now?"

There can be no doubt that, as stated by the first authority, "British India is no longer 'Oriental.'" A new organization of the Indian Presidency armies will, however, require skill as well as caution; and it is highly pleasing to read that Sir Frederick Roberts is to be detained in India to direct or aid in such a noble purpose. But well organized and highly effective local armies—which can only be effective if kept up to the full strength of officers—should ever be backed up by impregnable defences, which, unfortunately, has been far from generally the case in the Presidencies of India. We have not, as a rule, been so foolish as to despise our enemy in the field; but we have for a long series of years despised him in the matter of local defence; and, although not fearing another mutiny, we have for long quite closed our eyes to the possibility of some strong naval European Power one day attacking India, while our own navy might be fully employed elsewhere.

The question now is, Have either of the three Presidency cities strong support? There is one thing quite certain that, in addition to neglecting other measures of strategy, or "grand tactics," we have neither in Calcutta, Madras, or Bombay, ordinary maxim though it be, assured to the artillery "all its defensive effect." The uselessness and neglect of the defences of Bombay occupied the zealous attention of the Duke of Connaught before leaving India and his high command in the Bombay Presidency. It is to be hoped that serious charges of a similar nature will never be brought against those who are responsible for the complete efficiency of the defences of Calcutta, Madras, and Rangoon. With strong local defences, powerful guns ready to be manned at a moment's warning, and Clive's absolute necessity, " a strong and commanding military force," National Congresses, possible elective systems—the elective principle, founded, as Sir Erskine Perry said of certain land tenures in Oudh, on an "imperfect theory"—antagonistic Mahomedans and Hindus, caste prejudices, and Russian designs on our Eastern Empire, need cause us no anxiety; and the chance of a good Indian Budget—like that which is said to exist in the present year*—will be more probable than hitherto. If the sword cannot be sheathed in highly-civilised Europe, how is it possible that it can, for a long time to come, with so many opposing forces and such a vast, overwhelming population, be sheathed in India?

W. F. B. L.

London, April 1890.

---

* Presented to the Legislative Council on March 21, and considered the most satisfactory Budget of the last seven or eight years. About the middle of April it was announced that Sir David Barbour's Budget gave a surplus of two and three-quarters crores (millions), "achieved without extra taxation or impost."

CONTENTS.

	PAGE
SKETCH OF THE AUTHOR'S CAREER AND SERVICES . . .	xvii

CHAPTER I.
A SHORT CHAPTER ON VERY EARLY ANGLO-INDIAN HISTORY . . 1

CHAPTER II.
THE EARLY HISTORY OF THE BOMBAY AND MADRAS PRESIDENCIES 30

CHAPTER III.
THE EARLY HISTORY OF THE BENGAL PRESIDENCY . . . 60

CHAPTER IV.
PROGRESS OF THE ENGLISH IN INDIA FROM 1700 TO THE PEACE OF AIX-LA-CHAPELLE, 1748 93

CHAPTER V.
PROGRESS OF THE BRITISH ARMS IN INDIA FROM THE PEACE OF AIX-LA-CHAPELLE, 1748, TO THE FALL OF DUPLEIX, 1754 . 125

CHAPTER VI.
THE PRESIDENTIAL ARMIES 159

CHAPTER VII.
CHANDERNAGORE—PLASSEY—CHINSURAH—OPERATIONS IN BENGAL 188

CHAPTER VIII.

Origin and Progress of our Indian Artillery—Lord Clive and the Army 237

CHAPTER IX.

Lally in the Carnatic—Colonel Forde in the Northern Circars — Successes and Reverses of Lally — Bussy —Bombay 264

CHAPTER X.

War with, and Conquest of, Mysore—Brief Record of a Distinguished Bombay Infantry Regiment . 299

CHAPTER XI.

The Bengal Artillery—Astonishing March to Bamian—The Madras Sappers and Miners 329

CHAPTER XII.

Ava, City of the New Marquisate 351

NOTES.

I.—Amalgamation.—Bengal European Regiment.—A Fusilier Anecdote 370
II.—Fourth "Prince of Wales' Own" Regiment Madras Light Cavalry 372
Indian Regiments of Cavalry 376

APPENDICES.

A.—Lord Napier of Magdala 379
B.—Field Operations in Upper Burma 388
C.—"The Native Armies of India" 416

SKETCH OF
THE AUTHOR'S CAREER AND SERVICES.

COLONEL EDWARD STIRLING RIVETT-CARNAC, son of Rear-Admiral Rivett-Carnac, born at Broadstairs, Kent, 14th September 1841, died 28th February 1888, at Southsea. Entered the service as Cornet, 1st Bengal Cavalry, 4th January 1858. Lieutenant, 18th May 1858; 19th Hussars, 18th May 1858; Captain, 19th Hussars, 25th January 1871. Exchanged to 11th Hussars, 14th February 1872; Major (local India), 4th January 1878; Major, (Brevet), 31st January 1880; Lieutenant-Colonel, July 1881; Colonel, July 1885.

Service.

1858.—March to July 1858. Indian Mutiny Campaign, attached to 7th Hussars. Officer Chief in Command, Lieutenant-General Sir Colin Campbell. *Medal.*

1860.—China War, in Fane's Horse. Sinho: Siege of Taku Forts; Chinkia Whan; Tangchow. Chief in command, Lieutenant-General Sir Hope Grant, G.C.B. *Medal,* with clasps for Taku Forts and Pekin; mentioned by Brigadier Pattle after Sinho and Tangchow in his despatches; mentioned in G.O. letter of Right Honourable Secretary of State for India, No. 50, of 24th January 1861.

1867.—Brigade-Major, and A.D.C. to Major-General W. F. Beatson, Allahabad.

1868.—Abyssinian Campaign, Transport Corps. Chief in command, Lieutenant-General Sir Robert Napier. Present at taking of Magdala. Mentioned as having received the approbation of his superiors for zeal and ability; Military Department's letter, 10th December 1868, from Secretary of State for India. *Medal.*

1875.—December. Delhi, Assistant Quartermaster - General Cavalry Division. Major - General Honourable A. Hardinge's force.

1876.—Delhi Imperial Assemblage, Assistant Quartermaster-General Artillery Division.

1877.—January to May. Special Famine Duty, Madras. Under Sir Richard Temple (now Baronet and M.P.). Favourably mentioned in despatch of India Office, 19th August 1877.

May. Military Secretary to H.E. the Governor of Bombay, Sir Richard Temple.

1878.—Thanked by H.E. for services in despatching Malta expedition.

1880.—Also for services in connection with the Kandahar railway, and completion of Jacobabad-Sibi section, commenced 5th October 1879, and completed 14th January 1880, representing the construction of $133\frac{1}{2}$ miles of surface broad-gauge railway in 101 days, showing an average of $1\frac{1}{3}$ miles.

Brevet-Major, for connection with Afghan Campaign, and general services in India. Afghan *medal.*

1880.—Military Secretary to General Warre, Commander-in-Chief, Bombay.
1881.—Military Secretary to General the Honourable A. Hardinge, Commander-in-Chief, Bombay.
1886.—Half Pay; returned home.

We may, therefore, remark that Colonel Carnac was taken into "the silent land" prematurely, or the marching orders—which none of us can ever gainsay—were put in force long before his life's work of usefulness might be considered near an honourable close.

The name of Carnac occupies an important place in Indian history. We have already alluded to the Major in our brief historical sketch, when he was in command of the Bengal army, and defeated that of the Emperor of Delhi in the days of Clive. He then took M. Law and his French followers prisoners; commanded the army at the defence of Patna; and eventually accompanied Clive to England, January 1767. He had now attained the rank of General, and Clive was anxious to get his friend a seat among the Court of Directors. And then, at an earlier date, there is a Lieutenant Jacob Carnac, who volunteered for service with the Bengal European Regiment from H.M. 84th.

Running down the years, and coming nearer our own time, we arrive at James Rivett-Carnac, whose period of service as Director of the East India Company extended from 1827 to 1839. He was made a baronet in 1839, and appointed Governor of Bombay in the same year. Colonel Rivett-Carnac, late Military Secretary to the Commander-in-Chief, Bombay Army, it was declared in a highly appreciative tone by a leading Anglo-Indian journal* in London, had left India amidst a flood of eulogy from the Indian press. He was well known and appreciated through three distinguishing

* Allen's *Indian Mail*, March 2, 1886

qualifications: his personal popularity; his humane and well-considered endeavours to improve the position of the Native Sepoy; and his various articles on the great question of Russian advance towards our splendid dominion, which gained him distinction throughout India. He had also paid special attention to the defence of Meshid from Russian aggression, and he was known to be a trustworthy authority on the Persian Gulf region. Still in the prime of life—only forty-five—it was well remarked, in March 1886, Colonel Rivett-Carnac had before him "a fresh career of usefulness" in England; and there was every reason to see his capacity and experience fitly utilised by some appropriate appointment by the Home Authorities on his arrival.

But as is so often the case with our most useful toilers in the Indian land, though not at home meeting with "severest obloquy," he did not receive what he had every right to expect.

Five years before this period, the leading Bombay journal remarked:—11th HUSSARS.—Speaking of Major Rivett-Carnac, who has been selected to fill the office of Military Secretary to General Hardinge, it is saying "something for his reputation, for his knowledge of military affairs, and his experience in business details, that he should have been chosen as Military Secretary by three such different men as Sir Richard Temple, General Warre, and the present Commander-in-Chief. He has served the Queen as a soldier for 23 years in all parts of the world, where there was anything stirring." It is this constant desire for action among our intelligent officers which does so much, not only to render the British name respected wherever they go, but to aid the cause of general civilization and sound policy in a very remarkable degree.

The gallant Colonel was a keen-eyed traveller also. He visited Japan twice, and journeyed across the Great Wall of China and into Thibet over the Himalayas. As will have been seen, his services were various. He served throughout the campaign in Abyssinia, and, as on former occasions, was honourably mentioned in despatches.

After aiding the versatile and accomplished Sir Richard Temple during the Madras famine, he received the acknowledgment of the Secretary of State for India, and the Viceroy's congratulation upon this recognition of his services.

As Military Secretary to Sir Richard Temple, during the despatch of the Malta Expedition, he served with great credit to himself and advantage to the public. The same may be said of his work during the expedition to Kandahar. For his services in connection with the successful construction of the railway line from the Indus to Libi, it is written that "Major Rivett-Carnac would assuredly have received a reward, but for the sudden departure of Lord Lytton." While Military Secretary to General Warre, it is said that he applied to join the forces in Natal. Fortunately for himself permission was refused, and he remained to occupy his old position under General Hardinge, to whom his long experience in military affairs was of much assistance, and which would be more so during the completion of expected reforms in the Bombay army.

Always fond of adventure and novelty, it was said that on the expiration of his term of Staff service he would return to England by a new route through Persia.

According to a high military authority,* in an elegant tribute written a few weeks after his death, it is said that Colonel Carnac began to serve his Queen and country at the age of 16 years. He became Sir Richard Temple's Military Secretary when Sir Richard was appointed Governor of Bombay in 1877. "He accompanied his chief in the ride to Candahar, when the railway line was suc-

* *Naval and Military Gazette,* March 24, 1888.

cessfully constructed—141 miles in 101 days—which was justly considered the most remarkable progress made in India during modern times. . . . Colonel Rivett-Carnac's health had suffered much from the climate of India, and it is indeed much to be deplored that the career of this gallant, energetic, and most popular officer should have been cut off in his 47th year." It is the old story of real excellence too frequently having but a brief reign below.

The Times of India wrote, with its usual good taste and good feeling :—

"The death of Colonel Rivett-Carnac will be a personal loss to a large number of Englishmen on this side of India. He was not only a gallant and enthusiastic soldier, passionately fond of his profession, but he was a thorough military student. Excepting, perhaps, General Macgregor, no man knew more of the difficult questions connected with our frontier policy; and while in India, he used to keep himself posted in European opinion by constant correspondence with such experts as M. Vambéry and Mr. Marvin. It was through his instrumentality, and that of his chief, General Hardinge, that the public were at last aroused to the danger of leaving the great Eastern ports undefended; and it is well that this should be recalled, now that we are at last setting our defences in order. When he left India two years ago, we said that the Sepoy owed a debt of gratitude to Colonel Carnac for the earnestness with which he contended that the widows caused by the Afghan War should receive a pension.

"The employment of retired Sepoys as Commissionaires was also a movement which owed its birth and success in a great measure to his zealous advocacy. He was a finished Persian scholar, and, like all our best soldiers, a many-sided man. It is, as we wrote

* March, 1888.

then, not usual to draw aside the veil which covers the Press; but we may be permitted to say that the interesting letters regarding Java and Batavia which were published in our columns, and attracted considerable attention, were written by him. These letters are so graphic and fresh as to be well worth re-publication. They were indeed privately reprinted, and as a simple record of travel in an almost unknown country we scarcely remember anything better. Their author had the unusual knack of cosmopolitan sympathy, and his death will leave a blank in many circles not apt to be moved by sudden changes. He was, in a word, a likeable man. Colonel Carnac's friends in this country had no reason to suppose that he was dangerously ill. When he wrote last he was in the middle of an important work, *The History of the Indian Army*." This is, we believe, the present incomplete, though in many respects valuable, work now given to the world as the *Presidential Armies of India*.

As will be seen at the end of the sixth chapter, the Colonel's devoted wife, when near the "last scene of all," wrote, from his own dictation, an interesting paragraph on the defeat of the French at Chandernagore. Colonel Rivett-Carnac, then, may be said to have taken his farewell of earth while recording the overthrow of the greatest enemies the British ever had in India—the French; conquered by the greatest military captain and statesman India ever saw—Colonel, afterwards Robert Lord Clive.

W. F. B. L.

THE PRESIDENTIAL ARMIES OF INDIA.

CHAPTER I.

A SHORT CHAPTER ON VERY EARLY ANGLO-INDIAN HISTORY.

"No event," says Abbé Raynal in his *History of the Settlement and Trade of the Europeans in the East and West Indies*, "has been so interesting to mankind in general, and to the inhabitants of Europe in particular, as the discovery of the new world and the passage to India by the Cape of Good Hope."

For Europe we may now well substitute England.

When, in 1497, Vasco de Gama doubled the Cape of Good Hope, formerly known as the Cape of Storms, and discovered the sea route to the East, and the Portuguese and Dutch subsequently explored all the coasts of India in the sixteenth and seventeenth centuries, they little thought that they were but preparing the way for the English, the modern Phœnicians, who were destined to oust them from their possessions, and form that Colonial and Indian Empire, the power and greatness of which were lately practically exemplified to a wondering and admiring nation in the Exhibition, opened by their Queen-Empress with a pomp and ceremony worthy of the occasion. Well might the English people point with pride and thankfulness to the great buildings containing specimens of the arts, industries, and products of the mighty Empire that has sprung from the little island, whom her sons, toiling in far-distant lands, proudly call Home, and on whose possessions, extending over more than 9,000,000 square miles, and numbering 305½ million inhabitants, the sun never sets.*

For, like the Phœnicians of old, our habitation is but a small speck of ground; and like as they in their day engrossed all the commerce of the Western world, so now have we, that of the East, retaining, at the same time, a lion's share of Western trade. If it be true, as supposed, that the Phœnicians learnt navigation from the Syrians, they speedily eclipsed their masters in the art, and soon became the the greatest navigators, explorers, and colonists of the ancient world; their Empire was that of the sea. In all these respects the two nations are identical. It is quite possible that the Britons learnt the first rudiments of navigation from the Phœnicians, for it is certain that the latter extended their voyages to Western Britain—indeed, it is the opinion of Bochart, the celebrated orientalist of the seventeenth century, that the name "Britannia" is derived from the Phœnician *Barat Anas*, signifying "the land of tin or lead"; and this belief is strengthened by the fact that the Greek name for the island, given at a later period, was *Cassiterides*, which has the same signification.

The Phœnicians, having learnt the value of the products and fabrics of the Indies from the Syrians, with whom they traded, first introduced them into Europe, and eventually extended their voyages from the Red Sea † to those rich and prosperous countries, enjoy-

---

* The exact numbers furnished by the Commission for the Colonial and Indian Exhibition, 1886, are as follows:—

BRITISH EMPIRE.

Area	9,126,999 square miles.
Population	305,337,924.
Imports	£390,018,569.
Exports	£295,967,583.

† Mr. Robertson, in his work on Ancient India, gives the following origin to the name appropriated, in modern times, for the Arabian Gulf. In ancient days, the ocean extending from the Gulf to India was named the Erythræan Sea, after King Erythras, which, in the Greek, signifies Red.

ing, as they undoubtedly did, even in those early days, a high civilisation. Herodotus says that these bold navigators, setting out from Egypt in the days of Pharaoh Necho, circumnavigated Africa, by way of the Red Sea, returning to Egypt by the Pillars of Hercules (Straits of Gibraltar), and that the voyage took three years. But their sea-borne trade with distant India could have been but small, and it is to the Arabs, who about the middle of the seventh century had established their power in Egypt, that the world, in the days of Charlemagne, owes the foundation of the most extensive commerce that had been known since the times of Athens and Carthage.

At that period the Arabs, masters of Northern Africa, Spain, Asia Minor, Persia, and part of India, introduced from one country to another reciprocal exchange of the commodities of their vast empire, which they gradually extended to China. Alexandria, after the destruction of Tyre, then became the great market for Eastern goods, which were eagerly purchased by the famous merchants of Venice and Genoa, who exchanged them in the marts of Europe. The Arabs themselves introduced some of these commodities into France, Germany, and England, and the Crusades added to the European taste for Eastern luxuries.*

But although India was now well known for the beauty of its fabrics, it had not yet become accessible to Europe.

Marco Polo, the Venetian, in the thirteenth century, following the footsteps of his father in Asian explorations, visited China, India, and Java; but it was not until three centuries after the Crusades that the first attempts were made to reach India by sea. The honour of the discovery of the sea-route belongs to Portugal.

John I. formed a plan of extending his dominions by sea and land, and some expeditions were by him despatched to Barbary. His son Henry, who possessed both ambition and genius of a high order, determined to undertake discoveries in the West. He was

* Abbé Raynal's *History of the European Settlement and Trade in the East and West Indies.*

the first who applied the compass, already known in Europe, to the purposes of navigation.* Madeira was discovered in 1418, and in 1420 he possessed himself of the Canaries and the West Coast of Africa, as far as Congo. In the reign of John II., astronomy was applied to navigation, and the most southern point of Africa was seen by Bartholemy Diaz in 1486, and called by him the Cape of Storms. This name was changed into that of "Good Hope" by the clear-sighted monarch, who foresaw that it would open up the route to the Indies. In A.D. 1497, his successor, Emanuel, equipped a fleet of four ships, which, under the command of Vasco de Gama, rounded the Cape, and, after a voyage of thirteen months, attended with great difficulties, landed in Hindostan.

The great peninsula now known as India extends from N. lat. 7° 27' at Cape Comorin to 35° 40' at the Indian Caucasus north of Peshawar, and long. 67°, where the Beluchistan mountain barrier marks the frontier, to 90° where the line cuts the Brahmaputra river. It forms an immense triangle having its apex in the south, its base to the north; its western shores are bathed by the waves of the Indian Ocean, its eastern shores by those of the Bay of Bengal. The area of this great peninsula is over one million square miles, its greatest length is 1,900 miles, its greatest breadth somewhat less, and its population is 245½ millions. This calculation does not include Burmah, and other territories east of the Brahmaputra river.†

Fable, rather than history, tells the story of ancient Hindostan, the learned men of which claim for their origin an exaggerated antiquity, although, in the opinion of some, the peninsula of India

---

* Abbé Raynal's *History of the European Settlement and Trade in the East and West Indies.*

† The following are the statistics supplied by the Royal Commission, Colonial and Indian Exhibition, 1886 :—

BRITISH EMPIRE IN INDIA (INCLUDING BURMAH).
Area . . . . . 1,574,516 square miles.
Population . . . . 253,982,595.
Trade , , . { £68,156,654 imports.
                £89,098,427 exports.

must, from its geological formation, have been among the earliest inhabited portions of the globe. That this antiquity is great there can be no doubt, for, accepting with caution the statement of the Hindoos that a Prince Bardht was supreme a century after the Deluge, and that a line of Kings, the Chandras, reigned 8,200 years before Christ, it is generally accepted that the Aryan invasion of India took place about B.C. 2,000.* The sacred writings of the Hindoos, the Vedas, are also said to have been written a century and a half B.C. The epic poems, *Mahabarata* and *Ramayna* are of somewhat later date, and full of extravagant myths.† The Laws of Menu possess an uncertain antiquity; some are of opinion that they date from the eleventh or twelfth centuries B.C.; others that they deal with the customs of society 800 years B.C.‡ These laws divide the community into four classes or castes, and lay down the rights and privileges of each. In some instances Menu is reputed to be the son of Brahma, and the first man, and to be identical with Ménès, the first King of Egypt, where the same institution of class division existed. In the seventh century B.C. Buddha, the religious reformer, the Martin Luther of those early days, appears on the scene. He, like Luther, preached against the arrogance of the priestly caste, or Brahmins. His religion travelled far into the East; he died about 540 B.C. His death was the signal for the revival of Brahmanism in a modified form. Those who hesitated between the old and new faiths, formed themselves into a sect known as Jains (about 600 B.C.), whose temples are to-day among the most beautiful and perfect in India.

A portion of India was invaded by the Persians, under Scylax, sent by King Darius Hystaspes, who reigned 522 years before the

* The most eminent Pundits and Brahmins assembled in Calcutta, by the authority and under the inspection of Warren Hastings, to compile a full code of Hindoo laws, stated that some of the writers upon whose authority they founded the decrees which they inserted in the Code, lived several *millions* of years before their time!!—Robertson, vol. xii. (*India*) and see p. xxxviii. of the Code.

† According to the Hindoos, they were written 3,000 years B.C.

‡ The Hindoos themselves suppose the laws to have been revealed by Menu some millions of years ago.—Sir W. Jones' Third Discourse, *Asiatic Research.* p. 428.

Christian era; he drew an annual tribute of 360 talents of gold from the conquered provinces.*

The Greeks are believed to have visited India by land, and by the Red Sea and Persian Gulf, for the purpose of instruction in the industrial arts, before the days of Pythagoras, who died about 470 B.C.; but the first accounts of Indian conquest that come to us with any degree of accuracy, are those of the invasion of the present Punjab by the Macedonian Emperor, Alexander the Great, a full account of which has been left by Arrian (who derived his information from the journals left by Nearchus and others) in his *Anabasis of Alexander*. This invasion was undertaken in the rainy season of 327 B.C., when he defeated Porus, the Indian ruler. The army suffered extraordinary hardships. Alexander's designs to advance to the Ganges were frustrated by his troops, who declined to proceed further to the east in that inclement season. Alexander retraced his steps, leaving his lieutenants to administer the conquered territories, and himself sailed down the Indus to the ocean, reducing to subjection the various tribes he encountered on the way. Having reached the sea with the greater portion of his victorious but long-suffering army, he took the land route, across arid deserts, to Babylon, which he reached after incredible sufferings. About 10,000 men embarked in his best ships under his lieutenant, Nearchus, with orders to explore the coast, their final destination being the Euphrates. This was successfully accomplished. The Greek dominion survived between 100 and 200 years after the great monarch's death, and succeeding dynasties conquered the fertile territories watered by the Ganges and Jumna rivers.† The Edicts of Asoka, written on the rocks with a pen of iron, throw some light on the events of the third century B.C., in which he lived.

---

* The expedition under Scylax, which is described by Herodotus, is not mentioned by Nearchus, Ptolemy, Aristobulus, or Arrian.

† Seleucus, one of Alexander's most able generals, and, after his death, Sovereign of that portion of the Macedonian Empire known under the name of Upper Asia, invaded India. Little, however, is known of his exploits; but he is said to have reached the Ganges, and even the modern Allahabad.

The Greek power in India was overturned by an irruption of Tartar hordes, who, according to Strabo (whose testimony is confirmed by Chinese writers) invaded the country about 126 years B.C., after overrunning Bactria. From this period to the seventh century after Christ, little is known except what is derived from Chinese and Greek sources.

Towards the middle of the seventh century, the west coast of India from Malabar to Scind, was frequently raided by those Arab Mahometans (before-mentioned as introducing Eastern commodities into Europe), but no Mahometan power can be said to have made any impression on Hindostan until the eleventh century of the Christian era.

Mahmood, the son of Sabatagin, better known as Sultan Mahmood, had at this period established himself at Ghuzni, in Afghanistan, and founded the Ghuznividian dynasty. He rose from a humble station, and about A.D. 999 conquered Korasan.

In 1001 he invaded and conquered Lahore, extended his conquests to Guzerat, and his fame is remembered and execrated to this day by Hindoos generally as the destroyer of many monuments of their idolatry, notably the temples of Napakote and Somnaut. His dominions extended from the banks of the Ganges to the shores of the Caspian Sea; but in many of the conquered districts his power was more nominal than real. This nominal supremacy was the cause of frequent inroads into India by successive princes of the dynasty, for the purpose of enforcing tribute due from provinces subdued by former invaders. The successors of Mahmood having been driven from Ghuzni by the Afghan house of Ghoor, their capital was established at Lahore. The last of this line of princes was treacherously murdered by Mahomed Ghoory, with whom began the Gaurian dynasty.

In 1193 Delhi was wrested from its Hindoo ruler by Kotb-od-deen, Mahomed's general. In this reign Ajmere, Guzerat, and Agra fell under the Mahometan rule, and succeeding princes of the dynasty carried their conquests to Bengal.

On the death of Mahomed, Kotb-od-deen proclaimed himself

independent, and with him commenced the Mahometan power at Delhi. This dynasty did not survive many generations, and was succeeded by that of Khilgy. Feroze, the first prince of this house, carried war into the distant Deccan (1294), where immense booty was secured and transferred to Delhi. The last ruler of the Khilgy dynasty, Moobarik by name, was murdered, and his throne usurped, by a trusted servant. This man was, in his turn, slain by Ghazi Khan Toghluk, Governor of the Punjab Province, the founder of the Toghluk dynasty.

During this dynasty the capital of the Mahometan power was transferred to Deoghur, a conquered Hindoo city, afterwards named, by Mahomed Toghluk, Dowlatabad. To this city the inhabitants of Delhi were forced to migrate, and their ancient capital was left to fall into ruin, as is testified to-day by the vast remains of Toghlukabad, near modern Delhi.

But events had been occurring in Europe which, in due course, were destined to place a rival Mahometan power on the throne of Delhi. The Mogols or Mongols, after overrunning Western and Central Asia under their leader, Chengiz Khan, invaded Russia, Poland, Bohemia, and Hungary, and were the terror of Europe. They arrived on the frontiers of India as early as 1219, and frequently raided the adjacent territories, carrying fire and sword wherever they went. In 1398, about ten years after the death of Feroze Toghluk, Timour or Timourlang (commonly written Tamerlane), meaning "Timour the Lame," advanced against Delhi. The Government was at that time in disorder, the throne being disputed and contested by rival princes of the house of Toghluk. The victory gained was an easy one, and Timour was proclaimed Emperor. Contributions were demanded of the inhabitants, but, these not being forthcoming with sufficient celerity to satisfy the savage conqueror and his cruel followers, the city was given to the fire, and its luckless people to the sword. Timour left Delhi almost immediately, and retired to his Central Asian fastnesses with an immense treasure. Thence he invaded Syria, destroyed Bagdad, and, about 1404, turned his victorious arms towards China, which country he invaded at the head of 200,000 followers. He died in the province of Khokand in 1405.

Thus were the first seeds of the mighty Mogul Empire planted in the fertile plains of Hindostan.

The confusion and anarchy consequent on the conquest by Timour and the weak government of Khizr, who shortly after his departure ruled at Delhi, was the signal for revolt in the distant provinces, the governors of which declared their independence, and the Mogul power sank to insignificance, until Mahomed Baber, a descendant of Timour's, who was proclaimed sovereign of the Moguls in Tartary in 1494, after reducing Samarkand which had revolted, turned his attention to India, which he considered his by right of former conquest, and consequently invaded.

At Panipat, near Delhi, in 1526, he conquered the Afghan ruler after a hotly-contested day, and secured possession of the capital. Hoomayoon, his son, pushed on at once and captured Gwalior. Baber secured his power not without difficulty, but at length succeeded in firmly establishing the Mogul Empire in India. He was his own biographer, and left a most curious account of his life and doings, which was translated and published in 1826.

Hoomayoon succeeded Baber, but was forced to vacate the throne of Delhi in favour of Sheer, an Afghan; on the death of Sheer, Hoomayoon again seized the reins of government. His successor was Akbar, his son, who in 1556 was, at an early age, proclaimed Emperor. His reign was stormy and long; he reduced many of the revolted states to subjection, and invaded the Deccan, of which he styled himself Emperor, although his success was but partial, but he firmly established his empire, which included Cabul, Kandahar, the whole of Hindostan, and part of the Deccan. Students of Indian geography will understand the extent of his Indian empire by a perusal of the provinces into which it was divided; they were Delhi, Bengal, Allahabad, Oude, Behar, Berar, Ajmere, Agra, Moltan, Lahore, Cabul, Kandeish, Ahmednagar, Guzerat, and Mahé.

Akbar, who is generally considered to have been a just ruler, was tolerant of religion.* He reigned nearly fifty-one years, and was followed by his son Selim (better known as Jehangir) in 1605. The principal event of this reign, so far as this short chapter of Indian history is concerned, is the reception at the Court of Jehangir of an embassy from England, under Sir Thomas Roe,† sent by James I. to the Mogul Court in 1615, to ask for the protection of the Great Mogul for the English traders, who, under the name of the London East India Company, had, in 1600, established trade at Bantaun in Java, for the Malayan archipelago and China, and later at Surat, for Hindostan.

Having brought the history of India down to the earliest days of the East India Company, and as the exploits of succeeding Emperors will necessarily be touched upon in recording the doings of the English in India, it is time to return to the Portuguese, who, under Vasco de Gama, as before mentioned, reached India in 1497-98, or, in other words, during the period of the poorly-established rule at Delhi, which took place between the conquest of Timour and the triumph of the arms of his descendant, Mahomed Baber, in 1526.‡

Gama first landed at Calicut, on the south-western or Malabar coast; here he was well received and hospitably treated, so much so that an alliance and treaty of commerce was proposed to him by the authorities of the land. Besides the natives, he found many Arab Mahometans established in India. These were mostly the descendants of those Arabs who had made incursions into India, and possessed themselves of the western sea-board extending from the Goa of to-day to the Indus; their numbers had greatly increased,

* Mr. Robertson in his vol. xii. *(India)* says Akbar was "one of the few Sovereigns entitled to the appellation both of 'great and good.'" Again, "Akbar incorporated into one code the purest precepts of the Koran with the institutes of Menu."—Thorn's *Wars in India.*

† He arrived December 1615, accompanied the Emperor to the Deccan, and left at the close of 1618.—Elphinstone.

‡ The reason for entering into somewhat minute details of the conquests of the Portuguese, French, and Dutch in the East, will explain itself further on, when it will be seen that most of the territories mentioned were wrested from one or the other of those nations by the English, and with the aid of native troops of the several Presidential armies.—Author.

for, being polygamists, they contracted marriage in many places, which they visited for purposes of trade; their power was great, and they were the factors for all eastern commodities of which Alexandria was the mart.

Calicut was by no means a safe port; but the Arabs, who were to some extent missionaries, are said to have entertained for it a religious sentiment, as being the place at which a king of Malabar had embarked for Mecca after having embraced the faith of the Prophet.*

Gama soon found Mahometan jealousy too strong for him. The Arabs threw suspicion on the rival power which they feared, and induced the Zamorin, or Prince-Governor of the province, to undertake the massacre of the adventurers. The plot was discovered, and the Admiral with his fleet escaped the threatened danger. Timely reprisals procured a restitution of his merchandise, when he sailed for Europe, carrying with him some of the natives as trophies of his enterprise.

The enthusiasm that attended the return of Gama and his fleet to Portugal was unbounded. Hopes were entertained of establishing the richest commerce in the world, and the Pope, whose authority was in those days supreme in Catholic Europe, gave to the Portuguese all the lands they might discover in the East, together with permission " to trade with infidels."† There was no lack of adventurers ready to embark on board the new fleet fitting out for India, the ambitious for fame, the avaricious greedy of gain, and the superstitious in hopes of propagating their religion by persuasion, or, if necessary, by force of arms.

Alvares Cabral was given command of the expedition, which consisted of thirteen vessels. He arrived safely at Calicut, and restored some of the Indians who had been taken to Europe by Gama. Although these men spoke highly of the treatment they had received, the Zamorin would not be reconciled to the Portuguese, and, at the instigation of the Arabs, massacred a number of

---

* Abbé Raynal.
† Robertson's *India*, vol. xii.

the adventurers. In retaliation, Cabral burnt the town and the Arab fleet in harbour. He then visited and traded with several places on the coast, notably Cochin and Cananor, with the rulers of which, tributaries of the Zamorin his enemy, he entered into alliance.

With their assistance he was soon master of the Malabar coast and destroyed the Arab trade, and rich cargoes were despatched to Lisbon, which speedily became the mart of Europe for Eastern goods.

Alphonso Albuquerque was the first Viceroy sent by Portugal to its growing possessions, and he it was who seized upon Goa, the present capital of Portugal in India.

About this time he saw the necessity of destroying the trade of Egypt with India. The Venetians, equal sufferers with Egypt by the commercial success of Portugal, had formed a confederacy with the Arabs settled in Egypt, on the eastern coast of Africa and scattered over India, to place every obstacle in the way of Portuguese ambition, and had, in 1508, assisted the Egyptian Sultan to equip a fleet of ten vessels for this purpose. The Portuguese having foreseen this confederacy, had the previous year determined to prevent it by establishing their power in the Red Sea, and formed a plan for seizing on the island of Socotra at the mouth of the Gulf of Aden. This scheme was successfully carried out by Tristan d'Acuqhna. The island, however, did not turn out to be of the value expected, as ships from the Red Sea did not touch there on the outward voyages, although it was necessary to sight the island before entering the Gulf of Aden when homeward bound.*
The Egyptian fleet passed in safety, and having encountered the Portuguese armament in the Indian Sea, gained some successes which had no lasting effect, as future fleets from Egypt were constantly beaten and dispersed by the small squadron kept by Portugal to cruise at the entrance of the gulf.

These skirmishes annoyed Albuquerque, who determined to destroy Suez; but this enterprise, although attempted, was aban-

* Abbé Raynal.

doned on account of the immense difficulties that were encountered; effectual measures were, however, taken to prevent hostile vessels reaching the coasts of India.*

But this was not sufficient, as there was another outlet for Indian trade to Europe *viâ* the Persian Gulf, the Euphrates Valley, and Alexandretta on the Mediterranean, opposite the island of Cyprus. Albuquerque, therefore, determined to become master of the gulf.

On an island in the Straits of Mocandon was the city of Ormus, founded by an Arabian conqueror in the eleventh century, the centre of trade between India and Persia. Albuquerque having ravaged the towns on the coast subject to Ormus, suddenly appeared before that city, and with ease conquered the Arab armament sent to oppose him.† Treachery in his own fleet made him abandon his conquest for a time, but shortly after Ormus was again attacked and became subject to the Portuguese, whose power being now completely established at both the outlets of trade, began to cast their eyes further east.

The island of Ceylon would have fallen an easy prey, its conquest having been commenced by his predecessor, d'Almeyda, and subsequently completed, but Albuquerque made no settlement there, nor did he establish himself on the Coromandel coast, but sailed for the coast of Malacca, being of opinion that the latter was of more immediate importance, and that, with it and Ceylon in his possession, the easy conquest of the Coromandel must follow.

Malacca was the emporium for the trade from China, Japan, the Philippines, and Molucca islands, and, after some early ill-success, fell to Albuquerque in 1511. From thence an expedition was despatched to the Moluccas, where the Arab traders were again dispersed, and the valuable trade in cloves and nutmegs fell into the hands of Portugal. In the meanwhile, Albuquerque completed the conquest of the Malabar coast. He died at Goa, in 1515, without wealth, and out of favour at Court.

* Robertson's *India*, vol. xii.
† *Ibid.*, also Abbé Raynal.

He was succeeded by Lopez Soarez, who pursued his designs, and, like him, advocated trade with distant China.

In 1518, a Portuguese ambassador, by name Perez, was despatched from Lisbon, with a squadron, to China. He was well received, and, to his astonishment, found the country enjoying a high state of civilisation, so much so, indeed, that, to use the words of Abbé Raynal, " we shall not wonder at the surprise of the Portuguese ambassador, who had been accustomed to the barbarous and ridiculous manners of Europe " ! !

Perez went to Pekin, and visited many cities of China, and was about to enter into a treaty with the Emperor when, a fresh squadron arrived on the coast, the commander of which, having built a fort without permission on one of the islands off the coast, took every opportunity of pillaging ships bound for Chinese ports.

For these misdeeds Perez was seized and imprisoned, and died in confinement.

For some years the Portuguese were refused admission into China, but eventually were permitted to trade with the port of Saucian. A notorious pirate having seized on the island of Macao, and threatened Canton, was, with Portuguese assistance, vanquished. In gratitude for this timely aid, the Emperor bestowed Macao on the adventurers.

Their hungry eyes were now turned on Japan, the fame of whose trade they well knew; for a Portuguese ship having been wrecked on the coast of those celebrated islands, the crew, who were hospitably entertained, carried the news of the riches of these new lands to Goa. An expedition was, consequently, sent to Japan, and an extensive trade established. The Portuguese allied themselves with the richest of the Japanese heiresses, and, it is said, carried away annually precious metals to the amount of over half a million sterling.*

The power of Portugal was, by this time, established over a vast territory, extending along the coasts of Guinea, Arabia, and Persia,

* Abbé Raynal.

the peninsula of India, Malacca, and Ceylon, whilst Macao ensured their trade with China and Japan. They had also firmly established their influence on the coast of Zanquebar and the Mozambique; their power in the East was supreme; and they enjoyed the monopoly of many articles coming from their numerous dependencies, and regulated their value in Europe at their discretion, and in 1538 destroyed a powerful fleet sent against them by Solyman the Magnificent, ruler of the Ottoman Empire, which in those days owned Egypt and Syria as provinces.

But religious zeal had induced cruelty amounting to ferocity; an Inquisition was established at Goa, where the *auto da fé* flourished. The pagodas on the Malabar coast were destroyed. Faria, leader of an expedition against pirates in the China seas, plundered the sepulchres of the Chinese Emperors. Correa, having terminated a tedious war with the King of Pegu, treacherously broke all his treaty engagements. Nuno D'Acuqhna, having determined to seize the island of Daman, the inhabitants wished to surrender it to him, but he slaughtered the unresisting people. The Portuguese, indeed, were by this time as willing to break faith with each other as with the natives, and the whole community throughout India was broken up into factions.

Don Juan da Castro, an enlightened administrator and a brave soldier, now took the reins of government, and, in some ways, restored the declining power of Portugal. During his administration, an Indian combination attacked the fortress of Diu, on the Kattywar coast, when the place was, in spite of small numbers, successfully defended, and such prodigies of valour displayed, that the Indians, baffled in all their attempts, said of the defenders (according to Raynal), "Happily, Providence has decreed that there should be as few of them as lyons and tygers, lest they should exterminate the human species."

But the courage and energy reanimated by Castro was not to last, and the power of Portugal was on the wane. Success had secured riches, riches had begotten luxury, and luxury effeminacy. The original conquerors of India were no more, and their successors were degenerate. Possibly Portugal had been exhausted by the numbers of her colonies, and had not the capacity to replace the old adventurers with a race of men equally vigorous. Certain it is that they were replaced by the descendants born in Asia, and often of mixed blood, who gave themselves up to all sorts of excesses, and who possessed not the courage that inspires respect or fear. A confederacy was formed to oust them from the East. To counteract this, an expedition was despatched from Lisbon, which consisted of men who had formerly distinguished themselves in Europe. The Portuguese power was attacked on the Malabar coast, at Daman, Malacca, in the Moluccas. Goa itself was besieged. The Portuguese from Europe, under their commander, Ataida, well maintained their old reputation for valour; the siege was raised, the confederacy in all places defeated, and the supremacy of Portugal again restored.

In the reign of Philip II. of Spain, who, in 1580, acquired the throne of Portugal, the Portuguese in India seem to have, to a great extent, cut themselves adrift from the mother country. Some declared themselves independent governors, some enlisted in the service of the Indian princes, whilst others ranged the Eastern seas as pirates. Spain, indignant at the want of submission of her new subjects, the Indo-Portuguese, no longer supplied fleets of merchantmen, and even withdrew the naval squadron which had hitherto guarded the Indian seas. Garrisons were not reinforced, and fortifications fell into a ruinous condition.

That the Portuguese should have enjoyed the monopoly of Eastern trade for nearly a century is, although curious, of easy explanation. Spain, under Charles V. and Philip II., was engaged in ambitious operations in Europe, and in discoveries in America, and, by the acquisition of Portugal in 1580, shared the trade, in some degree, with the Portuguese. France was occupied with wars in Italy and Spain; England was also engaged in Continental wars, after the weary and bloody strife between the Houses of York and Lancaster, and the power of Venice had been humbled. For these reasons the prominent Powers in Europe remained inactive spectators of the transactions of Portugal in the East.*

The Portuguese at length forfeited their former power, when the Dutch, a free and enlightened nation, tolerant in religious matters, appeared in the East to contest with them the Empire of India, which they had so long held, and so systematically misused.

Towards the end of the sixteenth century Holland formed part of the dominions of Philip II. of Spain. This monarch, a religious fanatic, desired, among other innovations, to introduce the Inquisition among a people always celebrated for its independence, and who had accepted the reformed religion introduced by Martin Luther. Under William of Orange they rose in general revolt, and threw off the yoke of Spain, and having, in 1590, more than once humbled the Spanish flag, they settled down into peaceful traders; their ships being employed in the carrying trade of Europe. The trade of Lisbon for Indian goods soon fell into their hands. These commodities they sold to advantage in the different States of Europe with which they dealt.

Philip II., in retaliation for their revolt against his authority, closed the ports against them in 1594, an act which weakened their trade and drove them to new fields of adventure. They resolved to fit out ships for trade with the East, but, the sea-route *viâ* the Cape of Good Hope being in the hands of their enemies, it was determined to find a northern route, by the frozen sea, to China and Japan. In this attempt they failed.

The story† is told how, while engaged in this enterprise, a merchant named Houtman, a man of energy and determination, was kept prisoner in Lisbon for debt. During his detention he managed to worm the secrets of the Portuguese trade with India and China from his captors, and to make himself master of the details of the intricate navigation in the direction of those countries. This knowledge he transferred to Amsterdam; his release was effected by the payment of his debts by his fellow-merchants, who, having

---

* Robertson's *India*, vol. xii.
† Abbé Raynal.

formed themselves into a company, fitted out a fleet of four vessels, of which they gave him the command. His voyage was successful; he coasted Africa, landed in Madagascar, visited the Maldives and the islands of Sunda, and formed an alliance with the principal sovereign of Java. He returned to Holland stocked with information, rather than treasure, and brought away with him specimens of the inhabitants of all the countries he had visited, and, what was of still greater value, a pilot perfectly acquainted with the coasts of India.

The success of this voyage determined the merchant to establish a settlement in Java as a centre of trade with China and Japan, and well removed from the principal Government of Portugal in the East, which was on the Malabar coast of India. The expedition, consisting of ten vessels, was entrusted to Admiral von Neck, who, after some opposition from the settlers in Java, obtained permission to trade. Thence he visited the Moluccas (where he knew the Portuguese to be deservedly hated), established factories, entered into commercial treaties with the chiefs, and finally returned to Holland the bearer of good tidings and much wealth.

Numerous companies were then formed, but these were, in 1602, united into the "Dutch East India Company," and invested by the States-General with immense powers. A fleet of fourteen ships was next despatched, under Admiral Warwyck; he built a factory in Java, which he fortified, and obtained permission to trade with Johore (on the mainland, near the present Singapore), visited India, and entered into a bloody struggle with the Portuguese, over whom he at first gained easy victories. Fresh reinforcements and vessels were constantly arriving from Holland, whereas, as before mentioned, Philip II. sent none to his unruly subjects in India. The Hollanders showed more perseverance than dash in these wars, and, often repulsed, always returned to the attack, with ultimate success.

In 1607 they attempted to open out trade with China, but their object was frustrated by Portuguese jealousy; in 1624, however, they established themselves in the island of Formosa, opposite the

Chinese province of Fokien. Unexpected prosperity attended this venture. The conquest of China by the Tartars induced numbers of Chinese subjects to seek refuge in Formosa. The activity and industry of these new Colonists speedily drew attention to this extensive island, which soon became the centre of all the commerce carried on between the Philippine islands, China, Japan, Siam, and Java.

But the prosperity of the Hollanders in their new possessions was not destined to be of long continuance. In 1662, being attacked by a Chinese rebel against the Tartar power, they, after a determined resistance, were forced to capitulate and retire to Java; from that moment their trade with China suffered a blow from which it never entirely recovered, but Japan still offered them a market.

Ever since 1641 the trade of the Hollanders with that rich country had been carried on under humiliating circumstances. They were confined to an artificial island built by themselves and called Decima, where they suffered a sort of imprisonment, a bridge, their only means of communication with Nagasaki on the main island, being drawn up from the Japanese side.* Their trade soon became insignificant; for this loss they indemnified themselves by the seizure of the Moluccas and the Celebes. They also settled in Sumatra and carried on an extensive trade with Siam.

In 1640 they colonised the Cape of Good Hope, and in 1641 they drove the Portuguese from Malacca. By the possession of Batavia and Malacca the Dutch were masters of the only straits then known by which trade could be carried on with China and Japan, that is to say the Straits of Malacca and Sunda.† In 1658 they dispossessed the Portuguese of their settlements in Ceylon and of Negapatam on the Coramandel Coast; and in 1662

---

* This was still actually the case in 1861, when Japan was visited by the author.

† It will be remembered that the Straits of Sunda were upheaved and rendered unnavigable (for a time) by the terrible eruption of Krakatao in August 1883. The site was visited by the author early in 1884.

they further diminished the tottering power of Portugal in India by the capture of Cochin, on the coast of Malabar.

But the ascendency of Holland in the East was, like that of Portugal, doomed, and was to make way for that of England. Too great prosperity had rendered them avaricious, unjust to their foreign subjects and to themselves. Public spirit died out in Holland. To again quote the words of Abbé Raynal, writing in 1777: "Meanness, baseness, and dishonesty characterise now the conquerors of Philip. They make a traffic of their oath as of their merchandise, and they will soon become the refuse of the universe, which they had astonished by their industry and their victories. Industrious Hollanders! Ye who were formerly so renowned for your bravery, and are at present so distinguished for your wealth, tremble at the idea of being again reduced to crouch under the rod you have broken. Would you learn how the spirit of commerce may be united and preserved with the spirit of liberty? View from your shores that island and those people whom nature presents to you as a model for your imitation. Keep your eyes constantly fixed on England; if the alliance of that Kingdom has been your support, its conduct will soon serve you as an instructor, and its example as a guide."

Having briefly recounted the means by which Portugal and Holland successively became masters of Eastern trade, it is time to draw attention to that mightier power which is now supreme in India, and whose flag is to be found proudly floating in every port in the West to the confines of China in the East; and whose sons for over 250 years, from 1600 to 1857, the date of the great Mutiny, suffering many vicissitudes of fortune, have fought and traded, and have at length firmly established their country's power in the Land of the Sun, to the admiration and envy of Europe, and to the prosperity of millions of subjects, to whom they have at length given the blessings of solid and settled Government.

About the period of the Portuguese power in India, England boasted many bold navigators; among the most illustrious of these were Sir H. Willoughby, Chancellor, Drake, Frobisher, Davis and Hudson. The Cabots (Jean and Sébastian), father and son, Venetians, established themselves at Bristol under Henry VII., and under his auspices attempted the discovery of the north-west passage to India about 1496. Chancellor attempted the north-east passage in 1553, and discovered Archangel. Drake, in 1577-80, circumnavigated the world, and is still more celebrated for his subsequent victory over the Spanish Armada. Davis, Hudson, and Frobisher were Arctic navigators; but the former afterwards made voyages to India in the interest of the East India Company, and lost his life in the Indian Seas.

The repeated attempts of the English and Dutch to reach India by the northern route, and their endeavours to discover a north-west and north-east passage by the Frozen Ocean having utterly failed, in spite of the gallantry of the commanders and the devotion of their crews, a choice of two routes remained open to subsequent adventurers, the first by the well-known track *viâ* the Cape of Good Hope; the second, by rounding the most southerly point of the American continent, the present Cape Horn.

The practicability of the latter route was proved by Magellan, a Portuguese, who, starting from Sanlucar in 1519, reached the Pacific in the following year, and the Ladrones and Philippine Islands in 1521, which latter were afterwards named in honour of Philip II. In this voyage Magellan lost his life, and the journey was brought to a successful conclusion by his lieutenant, Del Cano, who, having doubled the Cape of Good Hope, arrived at Sanlucar in 1522. The south-western route, although thus shown to be possible, was deemed too circuitous for the practical purposes of trade. The impracticability of the northern, and the length and consequent expense of the south-western route having thus been established, for ever set at rest the vexed question of the most advantageous trade passage to the East.

Undeterred by these considerations, Francis Drake sailed from Plymouth in 1577, and arrived at the Straits of Magellan in the following year; coasted America, and thence visited the Moluccas, reaching Plymouth by way of the Cape of Good Hope in 1580.

During this voyage, although war had not openly been declared with Spain, Drake carried on a conflict with the Spanish vessels he met, and made many captures of a decidedly piratical character. In reply to Spanish complaints, his conduct was disavowed by the Court of Elizabeth, who, notwithstanding, did not hesitate to confer on him the honour of knighthood.

Drake's report of this successful voyage, and the capture, some years later, of a Portuguese ship containing a cargo of immense value, drew public attention to the importance of direct trade with the East, and in 1582 an expedition was entrusted to Mr. Edward Fenton for a voyage to " the East Indies and Cathay." To what extent the funds for this adventure were supplied by Government is not clear; but by the instructions conveyed to the Commander, and which are fully quoted in Beveridge's *History of India*, it is evident that the expedition was under the complete control of the English Court.

This expedition, which was the first that entered into direct competition with the Portuguese in trade with India, *viâ* the Cape of Good Hope, proved a failure, and one vessel only out of five originally despatched reached England in safety.

The next voyage worthy of record was undertaken as a private venture by Mr. Thomas Cavendish in 1586. He fitted out three ships at his own expense, and, following the example of Magellan and Drake, circumnavigated the globe by the south-western route, returning to Plymouth by the Cape of Good Hope in 1588, after a prosperous voyage, having visited the coast of America, the Ladrones (so-called by the Portuguese from the thievish practices of the inhabitants), the Philippines, the Moluccas, and St. Helena. Cavendish committed many unjustifiable depredations, and in his letter to Lord Hudson, the then Lord Chamberlain, dated September 1588, says:—

" I navigated alongst the coast of Chili, Peru, and Nueva Espanna, where I made great spoiles ; I burnt and sunk nineteen sailes of ships, small and great. All the villages and towns that ever I landed at I burnt and spoiled, and had I not bene discovered upon the coast, I had taken great quantitie of treasure."*

* Beveridge's *History of India.*

In 1589, the year after the defeat of the Spanish Armada, a body of English merchants petitioned Elizabeth for permission to fit out a fleet for Eastern trade. The request was granted, and the expedition sailed from Plymouth in 1591, under command of Mr. George Raymond, who was lost during the voyage in his ship the *Penelope*, when the command devolved upon Mr. James Lancaster. The venture proved a failure, although some piratical advantages were gained over the Portuguese. Sickness and mutiny adding to the hardships endured from contrary winds and shortness of provisions, Lancaster was abandoned on the coast of Brazil with a small portion of his crew. After many severe trials he managed to reach England after an absence of over three years.

The Dutch successes about this time fully published, induced an association of merchants to again petition the Queen for permission "to set forth on a voyage to the East Indies and other islands and countries thereabouts." This was dated September 1599.

It is not within the province of this paper to detail the difficulties, chiefly of a political nature, that had to be overcome by the Association before their request was granted by the Crown—suffice it to say that the jealousy of Spain was aroused, and, after the Royal approbation had been accorded, permission was withheld in deference to the representations of the Spanish Court.

After many memorials setting forth the advantages to be gained by the country at large, and an exhaustive report by Fulke Greville, afterwards Lord Brooke, which had a favourable effect, the charter was granted on the 31st December 1600 to "the Governor and Company of the Merchants of London, trading unto the East Indies," by which the Company was empowered to trade with "the countries and parts of Asia, Africa, and America, or any of them beyond the Cape of Bona Esperanza to the Streights of Magellan," with this restriction, that such trade should not interfere with the rights of any Christian prince friendly to the British Crown, who might already be in-possession of any of the countries visited.

The capital of the Company was a little in excess of £30,000, divided among 218 individuals. The Company's first venture consisted of five ships, which, after various delays, left the shores of England in April 1601, under the command of Lancaster, and reached Acheen, in Sumatra, in June 1602.

Lancaster met with a friendly reception from the native authorities, and entered into a treaty by which the English were granted perfect freedom of trade, in spite of the endeavours of the Portuguese to prejudice the King against them. These intrigues having been discovered, Lancaster retaliated by setting off on an expedition to the Straits of Malacca, where he captured a Portuguese vessel richly laden, and, having fully stored his ships with the cargo of his prize, he returned to Acheen, and further ingratiated himself with the authorities of the land by a liberal distribution of the "loot" he had so easily acquired.

From Acheen, Lancaster sailed for Bantam, by the Straits of Sunda. Here, as at Acheen, he was well received, and disposed of his prize goods for local commodities. Having established a factory, he, in February 1603, sailed for England with a full cargo.

The homeward voyage was stormy, and nearly disastrous; but eventually all the ships reached England in safety, but with the loss of many members of their crews; they anchored in the Downs in September 1603, after an absence of two years and five months.

The profits of this voyage, including the hardly justifiable capture of the Portuguese prize off Malacca, amounted to nearly 100 per cent., and two factories had been established on a satisfactory footing at Acheen and Bantam.

The second voyage undertaken by the Company was entrusted to the command of Captain Henry Middleton, and sailed from Gravesend in March 1604. The same ships were again employed, and reached Bantam in December of the same year, where friendly intercourse appears to have been entered into with the Dutch. From Bantam Middleton visited the Moluccas, where he met with some opposition from the Dutch, and finally reached England in May 1606 with a very valuable cargo, but with the loss of one of his vessels.

The third voyage was undertaken in 1607, under the command of Captain Keeling, and traded with the Island of Socotra, at the entrance of the Gulf of Aden; one of the ships under Captain Hawkins, who had formerly sailed in the expedition under Captain Fenton in 1582, having separated from the rest of the fleet, touched at Surat. To Captain Hawkins and his ship, the *Hector*, belongs the honour of being the first to plant the seeds of English trade direct with India. After some opposition from the Portuguese settlers at Surat, the *Hector* sailed for Bantam under the command of its first officer, leaving Hawkins, who foresaw fair prospects of trade, ashore at Surat. Thus was established the Company's first factory in India. Captain Hawkins subsequently visited the court of the Emperor Jehangir, with whom he obtained favour, and a promise of permission to trade. These successes were afterwards frustrated by the intrigues of the Portuguese.*

Captain Keeling, having placed the factory at Bantam on a satisfactory footing, sailed for England, which he reached in May 1610.

In the meanwhile two more voyages were undertaken; the fourth being a total loss, both ships being wrecked. The fifth proved more successful; the clear profits on the third and fifth voyages amounting to 234 per cent.

At this time the Dutch made no secret of their intention of keeping the trade with the Islands entirely in their own hands, and the conduct of the Portuguese at Surat showed an equal determination to monopolise the trade of the Malabar coast; facts that made it evident that the Company, to ensure a successful share of the riches of the East, must in future trade on an increased scale, and be prepared, at all risks, to defend their rights.

The exclusive privileges of the Company having been ratified

---

* The exploits and successes of Hawkins are not mentioned by Bruce in his *Annals of the East India Company.*

by James I., the sixth voyage was undertaken, with an increased capital, and consisted of three ships under the command of Sir Henry Middleton, who had successfully conducted the second voyage. His flagship, the *Trade's Increase*, was of 1,000 tons burden, a vessel of great size in those days. Middleton left England in 1610, and shaped his course for Socotra and the Red Sea, leaving one of his ships, the *Peppercorn*, at Aden. At Mocha the *Trade's Increase* was nearly lost on a sandbank, and Middleton and his crew actually suffered captivity at the hands of the Arabs. At the sacrifice of a portion of his cargo he obtained release, and in September 1611 reached Surat, where he found a powerful Portuguese fleet ready to dispute his right to trade. Here, to his disappointment, he heard of Hawkins' ill success at the Mogul Court, and realised that, for the time being, successful trade with Surat, in opposition to the Portuguese, could not be secured.

Having embarked Captain Hawkins and other Englishmen who had remained at Surat, Middleton sailed for the Red Sea with the intention of forcing trade on all the Indian ships he should meet, on the plea that, having brought fitting commodities to India for barter, and not being allowed to trade on shore, " he would do himself some right, and them no wrong," if he insisted on bartering his goods at sea!

During these questionable proceedings a seventh expedition, under Captain Saris, had started from England and made for Socotra. He traded with Mocha with some success, and finally joined forces with Middleton and continued the depredations on the Indian ships. The loss of the *Trade's Increase* caused the death of Middleton, when Saris continued his voyage to Japan, where, in spite of Dutch opposition, he made arrangements for permanent trade. He concluded a successful venture in 1614.

At the time of Captain Saris' departure from England, Captain Hippon was despatched, in a vessel named the *Globe*, for Bantam. He visited Ceylon, and made his way up the Bay of Bengal, and established a factory at Petapoli, on the Coramandel coast, south of Musilipatam. To Captain Hippon belongs the credit of the foundation of the first English settlement on the east coast of India. He also established factories on the coast of Malacca and Siam.*

Although the Company had now gained some pecuniary advantages by their several voyages, these successes were obtained more by force of arms and depredations on the cargoes of other nations than by fair and legitimate trade. No permanent footing had yet been gained in the East, and, although factories had been established at various places, the position of the factors was precarious and dangerous in the extreme. The Dutch were supreme in Java, Sumatra, and Japan; the Spanish in the Philippines, and the Portuguese in India and Malacca; whilst the English, by their piratical proceedings, had engendered distrust in the minds of the native authorities of the countries with which they desired to trade, and had not as yet shown their superiority over their rivals in honesty, diplomacy, or force of arms.

In 1612, the eighth voyage was undertaken on a different model, and a powerful squadron was despatched to the coast of India, under the command of Captain Thomas Best. Having arrived at Surat, he found himself opposed by a formidable Portuguese fleet, which, after a series of actions, lasting several days, he completely discomfited.

This success over an enemy hitherto looked upon as invincible, entirely changed the attitude of the Emperor Jehangir, who now gladly entered into a treaty with Best, whereby the British were allowed free trade with India, on the payment of $3\frac{1}{2}$ per cent. on their imports as custom-duty to the Mogul. This important concession was dated February 1613.

A permanent footing having thus, at length, been secured, its importance was fully recognised by the Company, who, in future, determined to trade on a joint stock, and to send out fleets of such strength as would ensure their success against all foreign oppo-

* For a full account of the several voyages see Bruce's *Annals* and Beveridge's *History of India*.

sition. But the commanders were strictly enjoined to avoid the errors of the Portuguese and Dutch, and to conduct their enterprises with the natives of India with humanity and fair dealing, and to gain thereby, if possible, the love and respect of the people. Several more voyages were undertaken with various success, but with an average profit of $87\frac{1}{2}$ per cent., and in 1615 the power of England in India was further immensely strengthened by a declaration of war between the Great Mogul and the Portuguese, the defeat of their powerful fleet, under command of the Viceroy of Goa in person, by the British in the Surat Roads, and by the arrival of Sir Thomas Roe, as Ambassador to Jehangir from James I.

But not only Indian trade, but that of Persia also, was effected by these successes. The city of Ormuz was wrested from the Portuguese, and a commercial treaty entered into with the Persian monarch, which brought considerable profit to the coffers of the now, comparatively speaking, prosperous Company.

By this time the power of Portugal in the East was rapidly on the decline, but the Dutch were nearly supreme among the islands (where the English traded almost on sufferance), so much so, that they memorialised James, complaining of British aggression, and founded their claim to the monopoly on the fact that they had by force ousted the Portuguese from their island possessions.

These claims were strenuously resisted by the Company, who brought forward counter claims and charges, which, after protracted negotiations, resulted in a dual control over the Moluccas, Amboyna, and Banda, whereby the Dutch enjoyed two-thirds of the proceeds of the trade, the remaining third being apportioned to the Company.

The arrangement, which took place in 1619, appears to have worked fairly well for a time, but neither of the contracting parties were really contented, and each contrived to render the clauses of the compact to their own advantage, and the scheme eventually suffered the fate of houses governed by two masters. Quarrels and mutual recriminations succeeded, which were destined to have a terrible conclusion in the atrocious massacre at Amboyna, by which, after a mock trial, twelve Englishmen, including the British Agent and his assistants, and one Portuguese, besides several natives, lost their lives, after having been made to confess, under torture, that they had participated in a plot to seize the factory and put the Dutch inhabitants to the sword. The date of this atrocity was February 1623.

Such universal indignation was felt and expressed in England, that James actually *talked* of war, when death put an end to his weak reign; and it was not for years after, during Cromwell's Protectorate, that the massacre and insult were avenged.

The year 1619 sees the infant Company established at Surat, on the west coast of India, and doing a considerable trade with Persia, but, through the intrigues and treachery of the Dutch, powerless in the Spice Islands.

Although a footing had, at last, been established, the power of England in the East was as yet but small, and the position of the Company's agents precarious. Energy, zeal, and a bold defiance of all difficulties and dangers formed the most valuable and principal portion of the Company's stock in trade, and was destined, in future years, to produce the three great Presidencies, whose rise to power on the ruins of Portuguese and Dutch supremacy will form the subject of another chapter.

CHAPTER II.

THE EARLY HISTORY OF THE BOMBAY AND MADRAS PRESIDENCIES.

ALTHOUGH the main object of this book is to deal with the military occupation of India, it has been found impossible to avoid touching on trade matters, carried on with extraordinary zeal and courage, struggling with enormous difficulties, by the civil servants of the Company, who from the earliest times of British Indian history to the anxious days of the Indian Mutiny (when they gained the admiration and esteem of the army, the members of which were proud to fight by their sides against immense odds) have been intimately associated with the military element, which in the early days of the Company consisted solely of the factors themselves and of the officers and crews of the armed trading ships, despatched from England to the Eastern Seas. The training of these crews during the long and dangerous voyages, together with courage and love of adventure, rendered them especially fitted for the task before them, and constituted, perhaps, the best fighting material of the day.

In the first chapter it has been shown how, in 1612, a factory had been established at Surat, on the west coast of India, by Captain Best, commander of the Company's eighth voyage.

To Mr. Kerridge, commander of the ship *Hoseander*, belongs

the credit of opening the first actual commercial transactions between the Company and the natives of India at Surat.*

In spite of the armed opposition of Portugal, the Mogul Emperor's firman, or permission, to the English to establish a factory at Surat, was granted in December 1612, and delivered to Captain Best, with due ceremony, on the 11th January 1613.

In the meanwhile, a ninth voyage had been undertaken, and entrusted to Captain Newport, the profits of which are said by Bruce to have amounted to 160 per cent.

Up to this time the several voyages appear to have been conducted by individuals, partners in the Company, who fitted out the expeditions on their own particular portions of stock. It was therefore resolved that in future all trade with the East should be carried on with a joint stock, only the sum of £429,000 being subscribed for the purpose. With this sum the tenth, eleventh, twelfth, and thirteenth voyages were undertaken with various success. They concluded in 1617, with an average profit, after deducting all expenses, of 87 per cent.†

During this period the Company was already experiencing opposition from the Dutch in the Spice Islands, which laid the foundation of that trade jealousy which in later years produced recrimination and ended in bloody struggles for commercial supremacy between two nations, natural allies.

The assistance given to the Mogul by the English fleet in 1614, whereby the Portuguese were defeated, induced the Emperor Jehanghir to protect the Company's factors and trade, although permission to build a fort to ensure the safety of the Company's goods against Portuguese aggressions does not appear to have been granted. But Mr. Edwardes visited the Imperial Court at Agra, and he and Mr. Kerridge at this time procured a general firman granting permission for perpetual trade in the Mogul's dominions.

A second attempt was made to trade with Persia, Jask being suggested as a suitable position for a factory, and a third experi-

---

* Bruce's *Annals of the East India Company.*
† Bruce's *Annals.*

ment was made to open out trade with Bantam and the Spice Islands.

In 1615 Captain Keelinge obtained permission from the Zamorin, or Prince Governor of the Malabar Coast, to settle a factory at Cranganore, when a treaty was agreed to between them, by which the English were to assist the Zamorin in expelling the Portuguese from Cochin, which was to be ceded to England; the Zamorin and English sharing the expenses of the expedition.

In the same year the Company's agents attempted settlements in several places among the islands, when, although invariably opposed by the forces of the Dutch, Captain Best established a factory at Tekoo, in Sumatra.

It has already been mentioned how the Company's ships had, by assisting the Persians against the Portuguese, established their trade at Ormuz and enjoyed certain advantages on condition of keeping armed ships in the Gulf to counteract the influence of Portugal. To this arrangement Sir Thomas Roe, the King's ambassador at the Mogul's Court, objected, as leading the Company into needless expenses, and possibly because, being on the spot, he noticed signs of jealousy at Court regarding the rising power of the Company.

In 1617 the second joint stock was formed; this amounted to over one million sterling.

At this period the Company had formed factories at Surat, in India; at Acheen, Tekoo, and Jambee in Sumatra; Bantam in Java; and traded with Succadania and Baujarmassin in Borneo, Macassar in the Celebes, Banda, Amboyna, and other Spice Islands, and with Persia, Siam, and Japan.

To conduct this trade they owned thirty-six ships, of from 100 to 1,000 tons, duly armed to resist Dutch and Portuguese aggression, and overcome opposition from the natives and pirates who at that period swarmed at sea.

The above list of countries traded with offers some idea of the vast enterprise of our countrymen nearly 300 years ago, and yet it must be borne in mind that they followed the beaten track of the Portuguese and Dutch, especially of the former. Even in these days of ocean steamers the beautiful islands of the Malay Archipelago are but seldom visited by Englishmen; and although the voyage to India and Japan are holiday trips, a journey from London to Ispahan, and thence to the Persian Gulf and India, is a feat accomplished by few.

The year 1617 dates the establishment of the first Dutch factory at Surat, thus bringing the English merchants face to face with two rivals in the Indian market—that is to say, Portugal and Holland. The Dutch also possessed a factory at Masulipatam, on the Coromandel or east coast of India. Surat was still unfortified, and the Company's goods in constant danger; and the Dutch, supreme in the Malayan Archipelago, seized and destroyed one of the Company's ships, corrupted the crew of another, and captured two French traders. This is the earliest mention of attempts in France to establish an Eastern trade, the French East Indian Company being formed many years later (in 1664.)

In 1618 Sir Thomas Roe entered into a treaty with the Mogul Court to resist the pretensions of Portugal; among the articles of the treaty the following are of interest for the purpose of this narrative:—The native Governor of Surat was to lend armed ships to the English for the better defence of the port, and to permit ten armed men of the Company's ships to land at one time, and the resident merchants to bear arms*; trade was also opened with Mocha, on the Red Sea.

The same year, in retaliation for years of oppression, the English, under Sir Thomas Drake, in treaty with the native authorities, took Batavia from the Dutch. The English, however, did not remain long in possession, for in 1619 the Dutch fortified the position, and made it, as it is to this day, the capital of their East Indian possessions. The same year, in defiance of a treaty entered into between England and Holland, a Dutch fleet of six sail attacked and sank one English ship, and captured three others, after a severe action, in the Port of Tekoo, in Sumatra.

* Bruce's *Annals*.

The year 1620 is interesting for the fact of Saldanha Bay, on the south-east Coast of Africa, being taken possession of by Captain Shillinge, of the Company's service, whereby the right of England to the territory about the Cape of Good Hope was established, years prior to Dutch occupation of that locality.

In the following year Captain Shillinge lost his life in an action off Jask, with the Portuguese, whence he had been despatched with four armed ships from Surat. The action was obstinate, and terminated in favour of the English, whereby their naval renown was raised in Persian estimation, and the Company's trade with that country facilitated.

The Company's attempts during this year to establish trade on the Coromandel coast were frustrated by the Dutch, who owned a fort and garrison at Pullicat.

In 1622 the agents of the Company at Surat suffered greatly by the aggressive conduct of the Dutch, who made prizes of several of the Mogul's ships. The native Powers, being unable or unwilling to distinguish between the several European nations, imprisoned the English factors and agents at Ahmedabad and Surat, the Company having to pay heavy ransoms for the release of their servants. In retaliation it was proposed to seize the Mogul ships carrying pilgrims to Mecca; a course vetoed at the time, but, as will be seen, carried out in future years.

It was in this year that the Company's fleet wrested Ormuz from the Portuguese, and obtained from Persia a portion of the customs of Gombroon.

At the same time the Company's servants in Java were allowed to assume the title of President and Council, a distinction subsequently conferred on their agents in India, from which the great divisions of their future Indian territories derived the designation of Presidencies.

In spite of titles, the English did not flourish in Java, for in this year occurred the atrocious massacre of the Company's servants by the Dutch at Amboyna, by which Captain Towerson, the Agent, and nine factors, besides Portuguese and Japanese, were put to death under incredible tortures, those who survived being handed over to the executioner.

At this time the factories in Japan and Siam were withdrawn, but a ship was sent from Java to try and establish a factory at Tanjore, on the east coast of India; the project was, however, opposed and frustrated by new rivals, the Danes, who are now heard of for the first time in India.

In 1624 the King granted power to the Company's agents and commanders to try their servants by common and martial law.

The news of the Amboyna massacre did not reach England until early in 1624, when it produced an immense sensation. The ambassador at the Hague demanded satisfaction and compensation; and the Lord High Admiral, the Duke of Buckingham, received orders to fit out a fleet to seize the Dutch homeward-bound Indiamen and to keep them until reparation was accorded.

No satisfaction was obtained from the Dutch, who, indeed, a little later had the audacity to appoint Van Speult (their servant who had conducted the massacre) to be the agent at Surat; he appears to have died in an unsuccessful attempt to reduce Mocha, in the Red Sea, in 1626, the expedition having started from Surat. The popular cry was for war; a step not carried out under the varying foreign policy of James, whose weak reign ended by his death in March 1625.

Charles I. now reigned in England, and civil war was, before many years had passed, to distract the nation. The affairs of the Company, no longer receiving the support of the Crown, rapidly fell into serious difficulties. Many stations in the Archipelago were abandoned, and trade generally suffered from the oppression of the Dutch; who, taking advantage of the state of affairs in England, lost no opportunity of insisting on their supremacy; but the Company had too much at stake to meekly give way; they persevered against all difficulties, and as one factory was abandoned another was established.

Thus, in 1625, the example of Captain Hippon was followed, and a factory founded at Armegon, on the east or Coromandel coast of

India. Some time previously trade had been carried on at Masulipatam, on the same coast, but the site was changed to Armegon, where fortifications were allowed to be erected; this is remarkable as the first fortified position occupied by the Company in the peninsula of India. It is mentioned by Bruce that in 1628 it was defended by twelve pieces of cannon and by a guard of twenty-three factors and soldiers. Some years after this event, favourable terms having been offered by the native ruler, the factory was again removed to Masulipatam.

In 1626 the English agent at Surat proposed to the Dutch the advisability of a joint attack on Bombay (then held by the Portuguese), on the understanding that if the island was reduced it should be divided between them and fortified, so as to render them independent of the native powers. From this it will be seen that even in those early days the importance of Bombay was fully recognized.

Up to this time the Company were mere dependants of the Crown; but, Dutch oppression continuing, and no redress being obtainable from Charles, the Company determined to appeal to Parliament direct. This action could not fail to give deep offence at Court.

The Dutch, emboldened by the unsatisfactory condition of affairs in England, became powerful at Surat, and the Portuguese, reinforced with nine ships and 2,000 troops, even threatened the recapture of Ormuz, and the destruction of the Company's trade with Persia; and Bantam, hitherto so important as the emporium of trade with the Spice Islands, sank into insignificance and became dependent on the Surat Agency.

The Company even failed in the management of their own subordinates, and a system of wholesale smuggling, carried on by the crews of their trading vessels, greatly diminished the small profits that remained to the association. For this the Company were alone to blame, as private trading had long been recognized as the right of the humblest of those employed, each seaman and fighting-man being permitted to fill, on his own account, a chest four feet long and one and a half feet wide and deep.*

* Beveridge's *History of India*.

But, in spite of many disadvantages, the Company did not despair, and small grains of comfort helped them to persevere.

In 1631 the third joint stock was subscribed, and the Company's affairs were ordered to be regulated at home by a Governor, Committee, and Court of Adventurers; this is the first mention of what was afterwards known as the Court of Directors.

In the same year the Company's factories were placed under the control of the President and Council at Surat.

In 1632 a firman was obtained from the Persian monarch Shah Sophie, confirming the Company in their trade with Persia, and that of the Coromandel Coast was authorized by the King of Golconda, one of the conditions being that the Company should import Persian horses; thus a trade was established which is now so important as a source of supply of remounts for the British Native Cavalry in India.

In 1634, by firman from the Emperor Shah Jehan, factories were established in Bengal with a port at Piplee. The importance of this concession will be dealt with at length in a future paper.

In 1635 Charles was undertaking the experiment of governing England without the assistance of his Parliament; and—possibly out of ill-feeling arising from the action of the Company in appealing direct to Parliament, in 1628, as before mentioned, or as a means of increasing his own revenues—permitted rival traders, known as Courten's Association, to compete with the established Company, in spite of former charters granted by James and Elizabeth.

It is unnecessary to enter into the particulars of this transaction, which is very fully discussed in Beveridge's *History of India*, vol. i.; and it is sufficient to say that the encroachment of their rivals, and the continued aggressions of the Dutch, served to bring the Company to a very low ebb; while the certainty of a civil war rendered it difficult, if not impossible, to raise the capital necessary for the prosecution of further ventures on a large scale.

The same reasons affected the transactions of the rival traders, who, after some successes and depredations, which subjected them to severe reprisals, disappeared from the field, but not before they had been amalgamated with the old Company under a joint stock arrangement, which was the subject of many quarrels, and was finally settled by Cromwell in favour of the original traders.

In 1685 a factory was established in Scind. In 1640 the Company made a great stride in the acquisition of Madrasapatam, which soon became the first *independent* position of the English in India, which they acquired on very favourable terms from the native ruler of that part of the Coromandel Coast, and where they obtained permission to build a fort, which exists to this day as Fort St. George. Madras was at the same time made subordinate to the President and Council at Bantam.

Difficult as was the position of the Company during the Civil War, its agents in India were not idle, but, exerting themselves in the interest of their employers, succeeded in obtaining permission to establish a fortified factory at Balasore, on the north-west coast of the Bay of Bengal, within reasonable distance of the port of Piplee. The trade with Madras, thanks to the security ensured by its fortifications (which in 1644 had already cost nearly £3,000, and were calculated to cost a further sum of £2,000),* continued to increase, and promised to become even more valuable than Bantam as a factory.

In 1645 the first mention is made of the Company's trade with Suakin, in the Red Sea; for some years after this event the annals of the Company, compiled by Mr. Bruce, deal exclusively with trade matters, which need no notice in these pages. The agents at the various factories continued, however, to be harassed by the Dutch and discredited by the piratical acts of Courten's Association, or the Assada Merchants, as they were now termed.

In 1650 the Company petitioned Parliament for redress of their grievances against the Dutch, and estimated their losses through Dutch hostility at two millions sterling.†

The vigorous rule of Cromwell greatly altered the position of

---

* Bruce's *Annals*
† *Ibid.*

the Company for the better. A fresh petition was presented to Parliament, consisting principally of the old complaint against the Dutch. This was favourably received, not on its merits only, but because Dutch arrogance, in pretending to the sovereignty of the seas, and the encouragement they had given to the House of Stuart, had greatly incensed the Protector. War was declared, which resulted in humbling Holland; but not before she had gained several maritime successes over the Company in Indian waters, notably at the entrance of the Persian Gulf, where four ships were captured and destroyed, and the trade with Persia and Gombroon, for the time being, greatly damaged.

To show how powerless the Company was in India during this period, it may be mentioned that when the news reached Surat of open hostilities between England and the States General, the president at Surat sent an envoy to Delhi to pray for the Mogul's protection against the Dutch, and petitioned the Home Government to despatch four or five large vessels of war and eight or nine smaller ships for the protection of the factories and to act offensively against the common enemy. The Company also petitioned Parliament to allow them to fit out men-of-war for their own protection.

Peace with Holland was concluded in 1654, when satisfaction was demanded and obtained for the massacre of Amboyna, whereby the Dutch Company was to pay to the heirs of the victims the small sum of £3,600, and to the London Company £85,000 for damages sustained; small compensation indeed for so barbarous an act!

Affairs in Bengal were now in a more satisfactory state, a firman having been obtained for free trade from the Emperor Shah Jehan, and Madras was raised to the dignity of a Presidency (1653),* having control over the affairs of the Bengal factories, besides those of the Coromandel Coast; whilst the Persian trade was to be subordinate to Surat. At the same time Bantam was to preside over the affairs of the insular factories. Private trade among the servants of the Company was also prohibited, but without effect.

* Bruce's *Annals*. Beveridge gives the date as 1654.

Pending the signature of the treaty with Holland the Company petitioned Cromwell, pointing out the importance of the Indian trade to the English nation at large, and suggested Bassein and Bombay as the most convenient position for the foundation of factories.

In 1654 the Company was so distressed by the action of private traders (hardly better than pirates) that it was determined to reduce all establishments, and orders were issued for the reduction of the garrison of Fort St. George from twenty-six to ten men! and this command was received at a time when the Dutch were predominant in the Indian Seas, and the armies of Golcondah and Visiapore were waging war against the Nabob of the Carnatic, who had thrown off his allegiance to the former monarch.

In 1656 the Dutch took possession of the Island of Ceylon. This year is also important as being that in which the Marathas, under their great leader Shivaji, invaded the Carnatic.

1657 saw Surat placed at the head of all the Company's Presidencies and factories, Bengal being immediately subordinate to Madras. The death of Shah Jehan also occurred in this year; this event plunged India into civil war, which ended in the accession of Aurungzebe to the Mogul throne. Surat Castle was seized by one of the claimants to Sovereign power, whose general pillaged the town.

In 1658 Cromwell granted to a Mr. Bolt licence to export to India 3 mortars and "20,000 rounds of shells" for Aurungzebe, the Company at the same time exporting large quantities of ordnance stores to counteract Mr. Bolt's proceedings.* Cromwell's death, which occurred the same year, seriously affected the interests of the Company.

In 1659, the Company being embarrassed by the uncertainty of the political situation in England, sent their homeward-bound ships, as a fleet, with orders to touch at St. Helena, and there to await tidings; and should these be unsatisfactory, they were to proceed to Barbadoes, where they were to remain until they

* Bruce's *Annals.*

received intelligence from home. The President at Surat again urged that Bombay should be secured, if necessary by purchase, from Portugal.

The reign of Charles II. opened with important concessions to the Company; a new charter was granted confirming all previous charters, and exclusive privileges *for ever* (instead of for 15 years, as in the charter granted by Elizabeth), and conferring judicial and military power on the Governors* of Presidencies, more especially for the suppression of the private traders now generally known as "Interlopers." Among other matters of importance, the Restoration was the signal for the conclusion of treaties of peace between England, Spain, and the States General, which tended to secure the Company's trade in India.

In 1660 an instance occurred of the Presidency of Surat exercising its power over the Bengal agency; the agent at Hoogly having seized a country vessel in the Ganges, for which act retaliation was threatened by the Mogul's commander, Mir Jumla, orders were issued by the Surat President in Council for its immediate restoration.

In this year pagodas were coined at the mint at Fort St. George, under the agency of Sir Edward Winter, from bullion received from Europe. The Bombay value of the pagoda was £3 10s.

In 1661 Bombay became the property of Charles, ceded by the Crown of Portugal as a portion of the marriage settlement of his queen, the Infanta Catherine, and in the following year a fleet sailed from England under the Earl of Marlborough, having on board an official of high rank from Portugal, who was to arrange the cession of the island, and put the English in possession. A force of 400 soldiers was also embarked, under the command of Sir Abraham Shipman, who was to remain at Bombay as Governor. The affair was not brought to the immediate conclusion anticipated, owing to the claims of the English Governor, who, in 1662,

---

* Although Governors of Presidencies are, according to Bruce, mentioned in the text of the Charter, the first Governor (Sir George Oxinden) was not appointed until 1668.

demanded, with Bombay, the cession of the neighbouring island of Salsette. This demand was resisted, and the English, not being in a position to force an occupation, applied to the then President of Surat, Sir George Oxinden,* for permission to land the troops at that station. The fear of giving offence to the Mogul Emperor by the disembarkation of so considerable a force, produced a refusal which forced Sir Abraham Shipman to disembark on the Island of Anjedivah, south of Goa.

In the meanwhile the admiral, with his fleet, had sailed for England, much to the disappointment of the Company's agents in India, who had, by the presence of the ships of war on the Indian seas, hoped to intimidate the Dutch, who still aspired to supremacy on the coast.

In 1662 another event occurred of importance to the Company. It will be remembered that in association with Courten's Company or Assada Merchants, the India Company had obtained certain possessions on the coast of Africa. Charles II., in spite of the Company's right, granted to his brother, the Duke of York, a charter to form a new African Company. The Directors of the original Company being under obligations to the Crown, and perhaps not being particularly anxious to keep their position in Africa (the Cape of Good Hope at this period being in the possession of the Dutch), made over its rights on the Gold Coast to the new African Company, and so confined their trade exclusively to the Eastern Seas; but they still retained St. Helena, which they had colonized since 1657, and possession of which had been granted to them by Charles II. in 1661.

In 1663 the Company was much alarmed at the equipment of a considerable French fleet, reported to be destined to proceed to the East Indies. Fort St. George was ordered to be placed in the best possible position for defence, and the Portuguese soldiers

---

* He was appointed with a salary of £300 a year, and a gratuity of £200 a year, "for the purpose of removing all temptation to engage in private trade." He was granted a warrant under the privy seal authorizing him to seize all private traders and send them to England.—Bruce's *Annals*.

lately employed, but distrusted, were to be discharged on the receipt of a re-inforcement of thirty English recruits.*

In 1663 Surat was invested by the Marathas. It was in those days surrounded by a mud wall, but was in no position to repulse a determined assault. The native inhabitants were plundered, but the English and Dutch defended their factories with such determined gallantry that the siege was abandoned. Aurungzebe, who then reigned at Delhi, was so impressed with the power of the British that he granted a firman exempting them for ever from transit charges, and a portion of the usual custom duties. At the defence of the Surat factory the Company employed no regular troops, the defending force consisting of the president and his subordinates, assisted by the European crews of the ships.

In the same year Sir Abraham Shipman, finding the accommodation for his troops on the island of Anjedivah insufficient, and seeing little hope of settling the dispute with the Portuguese regarding the cession of Bombay, offered to cede the Crown rights to that island to the Company.

The President and Council at Surat declined the offer, for the following valid reasons: first, it was doubtful whether the Viceroy of Goa would consent; second, they were unprovided with sufficient force for the occupation; third, no one but the King himself had power to transfer the rights of the Crown to the Company.

It is now time to turn to another illustrious nation, an aspirant for power in the East, whose intrigues were one of the prominent causes by which the Company rose, from an association of merchants, to the position of conquerors. It is true that up to the time now brought under notice, the commerce of the Company had not been carried on without bloodshed, but it had been in defence of their trade—even then not always excusable—and not with a view to territorial conquest in India; but the arrival of the French, and their rise to power, in a very few years completely changed the

---

* This order was not carried out, as the Portuguese (known as Topasses) proved their fidelity when Fort St. George was threatened by the King of Golconda, before the order was received.

peaceful occupations of the English Company to one of bitter and incessant war, which ended in the overthrow of France in India.

In 1642 France had established its power in the island of Bourbon (which had been discovered by the Portuguese in 1545) and named it in honour of Louis XIV. Having thus acquired a footing in the Indian Seas, the French, following the example of Portugal, Holland, and England, turned their eyes to the commercial riches of the East.*

Colbert, one of the most able ministers of Louis XIV, obtained the permission of that sovereign, in 1664, for the establishment of a French East India Company, to which exclusive privilege for fifty years was granted, and never renewed. The King not only sanctioned, but supported the Company by a contribution of six millions of francs to its funds, and invited the co-operation of the wealthy. The Queen and Court subscribed 200,000 francs, the merchants 650,000 francs, and various financiers 2,000,000 francs. The nation generally seconded the efforts of its master.†

The year 1664 is moreover eventful for the British occupation of Bombay. The troops under Sir Abraham Shipman had suffered greatly since their occupation of the island of Anjedivah, the commander himself falling a victim to disease. To save the lives of the survivors, numbering about 100 men out of the original 400, the little territory of Bombay was accepted by Mr. Cooke, Sir Abraham's Secretary, on the original terms offered by the Portuguese.‡

In 1665 England was at war with both Holland and France, to the grave detriment of the Company's trade. Agents of the French East India Company arrived in India through Persia, and sent an envoy to the Mogul. This is the first recorded appearance of the French in India.

---

* Voltaire's *Le Siècle de Louis XIV.*
† *Ibid.*
‡ The original numbers embarked for occupation of Bombay was 4 companies of 100 men each, exclusive of officers, at a cost of £13,166. The survivors landed at Bombay were: Mr. Cooke (Governor), 1 ensign, 4 sergeants, 6 corporals, 4 drummers, 1 surgeon, 1 surgeon's mate, 2 gunners, 1 gunner's mate, 1 gun-smith, 97 privates 22 cannon.—Bruce's *Annals.*

The year is also memorable for the extraordinary conduct of Sir Edward Winter, the agent at Fort St. George, who, having forfeited the confidence of the Directors at home, was superseded by Mr. Foxcroft; on the arrival of that gentleman at Madras, Sir Edward Winter seized him and his son, and, having accused them of sedition and treason, placed them in confinement and himself retained the command of the Agency, and, instead of referring his grievances to his superior, the President at Surat, confided in Mr. Cooke, the King's Governor at Bombay, and addressed a letter direct to His Majesty, professing loyalty. These matters were the more serious as Fort St. George was at the time threatened by the King of Golcondah.

In 1666 Sir Gervase Lucas arrived at Bombay as Governor, appointed by the Crown. Inducements were held out to native merchants to settle in the town, and preparations were made to fortify the position. The cost of maintaining the island as a dependency of the Crown was soon found to be excessive, the profits little or nothing, and the claim advanced by Sir Gervase Lucas for precedence, as an officer of the King, over the Company's president at Surat, was the cause of violent disputes; these circumstances combined, determined Charles to offer Bombay to the Company. The offer was accepted, and the island was made over by regular charter on the 27th March 1668, on condition that a yearly rent of £10 in gold should be paid regularly on the 30th of each September, for ever. Sir George Oxinden was appointed Governor and Commander-in-Chief, with a deputy governor, who was to reside in Bombay.

On these remarkably easy terms the Company became possessors of the finest, and, if Karachi is now excepted, the only seaport on the west coast of India. The garrison of Bombay consisted of some 285 men, mostly French, Portuguese, and natives, there being only 93 English, including officers. This is the first mention of *native* troops.*

Shortly before this event twenty recruits were sent to Fort St.

* Bruce's *Annals*.

George, and a small detachment to re-inforce the King's troops at Bombay. Aurungzebe also made a demand on the Governor of Surat for artillerymen and engineers to assist him in his wars in the Deccan. This demand could not be complied with, for the reason that the Governor did not possess any troops, even for his own protection.

For some time after its first occupation Bombay was subordinate to Surat, which still continued the residence of the Governor, a member of his council being appointed as deputy governor, to administer the affairs of the island; the Fort, or Castle, was strengthened for the protection of the rapidly-growing town, and inducements were held out to settlers, who were permitted the free exercise of their respective religions; the harbour was greatly improved, and docks were ordered to be constructed.

Having brought the history of the rise of the Presidencies down to the Company's occupation of Bombay, it becomes necessary to make a short digression, to go back a few years, and give a brief sketch of the rise of the great Maratha Power under Shivaji—this is the more necessary as it will hereafter be seen how, in future years, the destinies of Bombay were to be intimately connected with the Marathas.

The possessions of this great native power were studded over the whole of India, and, says Thornton,* "required compactness only to constitute them a mighty empire." Their rise from a tribe of barbarous hillmen, whose origin is lost in the obscurity of Hindoo antiquity, to a position so powerful as to rule the destinies of the Great Mogul himself, is sufficiently remarkable, and it may be truly affirmed that the Presidency of Bombay owes its present greatness to the wars with the Marathas, which subsequently caused the overthrow of the Rajas of Satara, and their ministers, the Peshwas, and brought the whole of the Konkan and Deccan under the sway of the Government of Bombay.†

* Thornton's *British Empire in India*.
† This short account of Shivaji is taken from a native source, published by Professor Forrest in his *Bombay State Papers*, printed for the Bombay Government in 1885.

EARLY HISTORY OF BOMBAY AND MADRAS. 47

The Maratha power owes it rise to Shahaji, and his son Shivaji. The father of Shahaji was a man of no consequence, but of good family, who took service with the Nizam Shahi. He managed, by stratagem, to marry his son Shahaji to the daughter of an officer of rank in the service of the Mogul. The progeny of this marriage was Shivaji, the founder of the Maratha Empire, who was born in 1626.

Shahaji, after some vicissitudes, became a man of consequence under the King of Bijapur, who bestowed on him the territories of Junnar and Poona, with the villages of Wai and Serol, so well-known to all travellers visiting Mahableshwar, the sanitorium and summer retreat of the Bombay Government. He afterwards held other properties in the districts of Bállápur and Kolar, in the Carnatic, and gained possession of the fortress and district of Tanjore.

Shivaji was brought up on his father's property at Poona, and was trained in military exercises, in which he excelled; on the death of his guardian and tutor, Dádoji Pant, his father being then absent in the Carnatic, Shivaji seized on the Poona estates and provided himself with troops from among the Mavális, or hill people, to the number of 25,000 men.

Shahaji, far from being incensed at this conduct, expressed his warm approval, bestowed upon Shivaji full powers for the government of the country, and sent him assurances of his regard.

At this time Aurungzebe (1653) had been sent by his father, Shah Jehan, the Mogul Emperor, with an army to conquer Bijapur; he was unsuccessful, but succeeded in capturing Dáolatabad, and founded the city of Aurungabad.

Aurungzebe greatly resented the growing power of Shivaji, and determined to chastise and humble him. This ill-feeling is said by native historians to have been the origin of the wars carried on between the Mogul Emperor and the Marathas.

Shivaji seized on the strong fortress of Purandhar by treachery, and possessed himself of the hill forts of Singhur (which overlooks Poona), Torna, Chandraghur, Rajghur, Raighur, and others, and by this time had 60,000 Marathas in his service. Now, conscious of his power, he attacked and seized Jaival from the King of Bijapur. The King complained of this conduct to Shahaji, who replied that he possessed no power over his son Shivaji, but recommended that an army should be sent to punish him. This was accordingly done, the command being given to a Mahometan noble, Afzul Khan, in 1652.

The story of how Afzul Khan[*] was treacherously murdered by Shivaji on the slopes of Prátapghur, and his army cut to pieces, is too well known to require repetition here. In revenge for this defeat another army was sent from Bijapur, under the command of Fazil Khan, Afzul's son, to invest Shivaji in the fortress of Panala, near Kholapur; but although some slight successes were gained, the difficulties of hurting Shivaji in his hill fastnesses were so great that Fazil Khan reluctantly gave up the attempt and retired to Bijapur.

Shivaji now built many forts, and constantly raided the outlying territories of the Mogul Empire. Aurungzebe at once despatched an army to destroy him, but Shivaji gained a complete victory over the Imperial forces, at a place between Poona and Aurungabad.

After this victory Shivaji constructed many strong forts on the coast, notably Savarndurg (afterwards the pirate Angria's stronghold), built vessels to keep "the Feranges" in order, and possessed himself of the Konkan, from Kalyán to Sondáh.

Aurungzebe sent another army, consisting of 80,000 men, against Shivaji; after investing and taking the fort of Chakan, the Mogul commander-in-chief, Shahisti Khan, installed himself in Shivaji's palace at Poona, from whence he sent him a message calling him a "hill-monkey," incapable of fighting a fair battle in the open field. Such, indeed, was not the Maratha mode of warfare. Shivaji replied in person by coming to Poona in disguise, by night, for the purpose of assassinating the Mogul chief. Having gained an

---

[*] For a full account of the life of Shivaji, and the murder of Afzul Khan, see *Tara*, by Meadows Taylor.

entrance into his palace, he, by mistake, murdered the chief's son, whom he found asleep. In the fight that ensued he cut off the thumb of the father and made good his escape.

After this Shahisti Khan was recalled, and Mirza Raja was by Aurungzebe appointed Subhédar of the Deccan. After many unsuccessful attempts to reduce Shivaji's fastnesses, Mirza requested an armistice, and a treaty was ratified. Among other things it was agreed that Shivaji, accompanied by his son Sambhāji, should visit the Emperor at Delhi. Shivaji remained ten months a guest, or rather a state prisoner, at Delhi, after which he made his escape disguised as a religious mendicant, and visited Allahabad and Benares. Shortly after Shivaji's return to his own country, where he was received with every demonstration of joy, the Prince Shah Alum was appointed to the subhédarship of the Deccan. Shivaji sent a deputation to him at Aurungabad, and concluded a peace on the following terms:—Shivaji was to give up twenty-seven forts and receive in exchange the territory of Birar, Bálápur, and other districts. This peace lasted three years, after which all the forts were wrested from the Imperial troops.

In 1667 Shivaji again threatened Surat, and in 1670 he attacked and plundered the town and factories, from which he obtained much treasure, to which the East India Company probably contributed, although they defended their factory with a spirit worthy of the national character.*

In the meanwhile Shahaji had managed to gain possession of most of the Bijapur fortresses, when, his power being dreaded, he was seized by stratagem; but his life was spared, and he was permitted to retire to Tanjore, from whence he wrote to Shivaji to avenge him, which he immediately did by laying waste the territory of Mudhol, in the Deccan.

After the death of Shahaji, which occurred from an accident out hunting, Shivaji attacked and plundered the territories of Haiderabad and Bijapur, from whose rulers he received a yearly tribute

---

* Thornton's *British Empire in India*. Shivaji used to call Surat his " treasury."

of nine and seven lacs of pagodas† respectively. From these facts some idea of his enormous power and influence may be gained.

After the death of his father, Shahaji, he invaded the Carnatic, seized Vellore and forced his half-brother Venkaji to share with him his father's Carnatic possessions. He took the title of Raja in 1674, and died in 1680.

Shivaji was succeeded by his son, who possessed none of his father's talents; he was captured and put to death by Aurungzebe, who seized nearly all the Maratha strongholds. By these means the Maratha power was sorely crippled, but not crushed.

On the death of the Mogul Emperor, Shahu Raja assumed the Maratha sceptre; he was a weak young man, and allowed all his power to be wielded by his Minister, the Peshwa Balaji, which office then became hereditary.

Balaji was succeded as Peshwa by his son Bajirav, who deprived Shahu Raja of every sign of power, and even detained him a state prisoner.

The usurpation of Bajirav set the example of independence to several of the great officers of state, who, rising from insignificant and even menial offices, became the founders of regal dynasties. The commander-in-chief, Raghoji Bhonsla, declared himself master of the province of Berar and settlement at Nagpur; in the same manner Mulhaji Holkar (Raghoji's lieutenant), a cavalry officer, Nanoji Sindia, the slipper-bearer, and Pilaji Gaekarwar, the cowherd, set up independent governments of provinces,* and their descendants are, to this day, established at Indore, Gwalior, and Baroda respectively. They held commissions in name from the Peshwa, and bound themselves to keep up armies for the support of the Maratha Empire; but, their Government being far removed from central control, they soon commenced conquests on their own account.

To return to Bombay: the bargain concluded between the King and the Company, by which the island was transferred to the

---

* Bombay State Papers, Professor Forrest

latter for the payment of £10 annually, was eminently favourable to the Company. Sir Gervase Lucas, who died in 1667, had, by his wise administration, greatly improved the revenues of the island, which his successor, Mr. Gary, reported to the King and Secretary of State as amounting to £6,490 a year, or 75,000 xeraphins, at the rate of 13 xeraphins to twenty-two shillings and sixpence.*

Sir Edward Winter still kept possession of Fort St. George, and held Mr. Foxcroft and his son prisoners; he was supported in his usurpation by Mr. Gary. Sir George Oxinden, however, appears to have taken a very different view of the conduct of the Madras ex-agent; for he withheld the stock originally intended for investment at Madras, fearing that it might be seized by Sir Edward Winter and used for purposes detrimental to the interests of the Company.

With troubles in Bengal and Madras, and war raging between the Mogul Emperor and Shivaji, which rendered Surat liable to attack at any moment, Sir George Oxinden must have had an anxious command; he was, moreover, engaged in carrying out the regulations framed by the Court of Directors at home, for the administration of Bombay, the most interesting of which are briefly as follows: The fort was to be strengthened, and the town built on a regular plan, under its guns. Europeans were to be encouraged to settle, and were exempted for five years from the payment of customs. Religious freedom was to be permitted; docks were to be constructed, and the harbour improved; recruits, with their wives, were to be sent regularly from England; and an armed ship was to be specially detached for the protection of the trade of the island, and to assist in its defence.† The Commissioners, sent by Sir George Oxinden to take over the island, received from Mr. Gary property, including plate, jewels, and ready money, to the amount of nearly £5,000. The King's troops were offered service under the Company, retaining their rank and pay—those who declined being

---

* Bruce's *Annals*. † *Ibid*.

accommodated with passages to England. Bruce says that the offer was generally accepted. The force consisted of two companies, commanded by captains; the first company was composed of 2 commissioned officers, 66 non-commissioned officers and privates, and 28 Topasses;* and the 2nd company was made up of 3 commissioned officers, 73 non-commissioned officers and privates, and 26 Topasses; there were also 21 pieces of cannon, and two gunners, with ordnance stores in proportion. This small force formed the nucleus of the present Bombay army. It was considered inadequate to the duties required of it, as the commissioners informed Sir George Oxinden, that 300 additional men with 30 pieces of cannon were necessary to form a reliable garrison. They also requested that Engineers might be sent from home, to superintend the construction of the fortifications, and that a Judge Advocate might be appointed.

Sir George Oxinden personally visited the island early in 1668, to establish a system of civil government and to draw up a code of military regulations; the senior captain was appointed to the command of the troops, and obedience was enjoined to the orders of the Civil Government, breach of duty in the inferior ranks being punishable with death, the commissioned officers, for a like offence, being liable to deprivation of rank only. This code was the foundation of the existing regulations, which, however, were much modified on the subsequent arrival of the King's troops in India.

Although matters were progressing favourably, the condition of Bombay was not altogether happy, supplies being obtainable with difficulty; the Portuguese, who placed every possible obstacle in the way, being in possession of Salsette, whilst the opposite coast was under the rule of Shivaji. The trade, also, was exposed to

---

* The Topasses were Christians, generally of mixed blood, but claiming Portuguese origin. Orme, in his *Military Proceedings of the East India Company*, says that they were armed, clad, and disciplined after the European style, and incorporated among the English Companies. From wearing a hat (topie), instead of the turban, as generally used by the natives, these half-caste troops acquired the nickname of "Topasses," and were generally considered inferior in courage to the higher caste of natives and the Mahometans of India.

the depredations of the Malabar pirates; so much so, that the Deputy Governor and Council applied to the Court at home for three armed ships for its protection.

During these proceedings in Bombay, the state of affairs in Madras was becoming more settled; for on the 22nd of August 1668, Sir Edward Winter handed over Fort St. George to Commissioners appointed by the Court of Directors, on condition that his personal safety should be assured to him; these terms were agreed to, and bore bitter fruit in the future. The Commissioners at once released Mr. Foxcroft from the confinement that he had suffered for nearly two years, and placed him in possession of the fort and agency. On his release Mr. Foxcroft acted with great moderation, and Sir Edward Winter was permitted to retire to Pullicat, and subsequently to reside at Masulipatam. The following year he returned to England: no punishment appears to have followed his extraordinary behaviour, and breach of discipline and duty.

It may be of interest to mention that in 1668 the Company ordered its Bantam Agency "to send home 100. lbs weight of the best tey that you can gett." Beveridge, in his *History of India*, remarks that the language used implies that the plant was already understood, but that this is the first public order for an article that subsequently proved of such enormous value as an investment.*

The application of Sir George Oxinden for engineers and armed ships was, in 1669, agreed to by the Directors, and they appointed a Mr. Pett, a practical ship-builder, to construct two vessels for the defence of the island, and the two captains commanding the companies at Bombay were detailed to act as engineers for the construction of fortifications, which were to overawe the Portu-

---

* Within a century of the first order the Company imported nearly three millions of pounds of tea, and in 1834 (the last year of the Company's monopoly) the imports exceeded twenty-three millions of pounds, and paid duty to Government in the sum of £3,589,361 (Beveridge). Since then the importation of this article to England has more than doubled, the consumption in 1885 being computed at 182,455,000 lbs, or at the rate of 4·98 lbs per head of the population.

guese in Salsette and the Marathas on the opposite coast, £1,500 being authorized for the purchase of land in the immediate vicinity of the existing fort. At the same time, the Governor was instructed to exact customs from the Portuguese " till they could bring them to a reasonable accommodation of trade."*

Sir George Oxinden, who had proved himself so valuable as an administrator, died on the 14th July 1669, and was succeeded by Mr. Aungier, afterwards eulogised by Orme for his bearing during a threatened attack by the Dutch on Bombay, when he acted with " the calmness of a philosopher and the courage of a centurion." One of Mr. Aungier's first applications to the Court at home was for recruits to fill existing vacancies at Bombay, and for accommodation for the European troops and their families.

The Siddee of Rajahpore (the Mogul's admiral), greatly embarrassed the Governor by asking for an asylum in Bombay, in the event of his being obliged to abandon that stronghold (described as impregnable except from an attack by sea) to Shivaji. Compliance with this demand might offend Shivaji, and non-compliance the Mogul. Mr. Aungier, therefore, suggested that it might be advisable to gain possession of Rajahpore, which could easily be held by a small garrison.

The Governor's next act was to form two courts at Bombay for the administration of justice,† and to reduce the small garrison from two companies to one; he also formed a court, consisting of a civilian and three military officers, for the administration of martial law.

Fort St. George was in this year besieged by the Nabob of the Carnatic, but the force was shortly after withdrawn without inflicting any serious damage.

The following year sees the garrison of Bombay again increased to two companies, and two brigantines were sanctioned to strengthen the ships already constructed for the defence of the Island, and the

---

* Bruce's *Annals*.

† Trial by jury was ordered to be introduced into the courts in Bombay in 1670. —*Bruce's Annals*.

Malabar trade. Captain Shaxton was appointed to command the troops, he was also given rank as Factor, and was to combine his civil with his military duties; the court also sanctioned the establishment of a Mint, and despatched two vessels to trade with Japan.

Shivaji's attack on Surat has already been alluded to. Although the English defended themselves gallantly, the French factors compounded with the Mahratta Chief, and by their co-operation enabled him to plunder the Mogul's Persian factory. The Dutch do not appear to have been attacked.

The fortifications of Bombay in these troublous times are thus described by Bruce: "The bastions and curtains of the fort towards the land had been raised to within nine feet of their intended height, but towards the sea batteries only had been constructed, as bastions would be the work of a subsequent year." Mr. Bake was appointed Engineer and Surveyor-General of Bombay; a re-inforcement of 300 recruits was demanded, and it was suggested that they should be enlisted for a term of years, "that being under martial law their discipline and services, in case of attack, might be relied on." In answer to this suggestion, 150 recruits were sent from England.

At the same time, the authorities at Fort St. George were desired to fill the existing vacancies in its garrison by volunteers from the Company's ships. The Court of Directors also determined to fix factories at Tywan, Tonquin, and in Japan, where the agents were directed to wear dresses of English cloth, with gold or silver lace, whereby it was hoped to impress on the native authorities an idea of their rank and importance. Negotiations were begun with Shivaji for re-opening trade with Rajahpore, and at Bombay the Governor reported that he had divided the old soldiers between the two companies, that their example might have an effect on the discipline of the recruits; but that as the mortality in the ranks had been great, it would be necessary to send at least 50 men annually to supply vacancies, and, moreover, that additional armed vessels were required for the protection of trade. All these events occurred in 1671.

The alliance entered into between Charles II. and Louis XIV. against Holland, induced the Company to invest Mr. Aungier with discretionary powers to remove the factory from Surat to Bombay, and the trading fleet was greatly strengthened. It consisted of ten ships, of about 4,000 tons in all, carrying from 30 to 36 guns each, and fully manned, commanded by an admiral, assisted by a vice, and rear-admirals.

In anticipation of an attack from the Dutch fleet, the fortifications of Bombay were strengthened, and the inhabitants enrolled as a militia, to assist the troops in defence of the fort and town; this militia consisted of some 1,500 men, armed with muskets and lances. An attempt was made at the same time to increase the two existing companies to 130 men each, by the addition of natives, but even this force was justly considered inadequate to defend the position against a disciplined European enemy. Consequently, an immediate reinforcement was demanded of 500 men, with an annual supply of 100 recruits.*

The necessity of these precautions was soon exemplified by the appearance of a Dutch fleet under Van Goens; the alarm at Bombay was very great, and many of the inhabitants took refuge in flight, some seeking protection in the Portuguese settlements. The Governor in this crisis of affairs endeavoured to secure the assistance of 500 Rajpoots. The firm attitude of Mr. Aungier averted an attack, and the Dutch fleet disappeared from the vicinity of Bombay and Surat.

The same year (1672), the French, then in alliance with England, sent Monsieur de la Haye to India with a considerable force, which although of value in reducing Dutch pretensions, raised a dangerous rival to the Company. De la Haye, after establishing himself at Trincomalee, in Ceylon, landed 300 men and took St. Thomé (now known as St. Thomas' Mount), near Madras, by storm. This is the first recorded appearance of the French on the Coromandel Coast, an event full of future trouble to the Company.

* Bruce's *Annals*.

A few words regarding the early efforts of our great rivals in India, the French, may prove of interest, and be useful for the better understanding of events about to be noticed.

The French Company's first factor in India, at Surat, was a Monsieur Caron, a merchant of French extraction, and a former servant of the Dutch. He had served that Company in Japan, where, having given offence to the native authorities by secretly fortifying his factory, he was expelled the country. His cold reception by the Dutch in Java, after this event, filled him with disgust for his former masters, and induced him to offer his services to the French, who gladly availed themselves of his experience.

Caron justly objected to Surat as the chief centre of French trade, the place being already in English and Dutch occupation, whose trade was established, and with whose riches the young French company could not compete; and wishing to find an independent port, he fixed on the Bay of Trincomalee in Ceylon—which, to-day, is the head-quarters of Her Majesty's ships forming the naval command in the Indian Seas—as a position in every way suitable to his purpose. On the arrival of De la Haye's squadron in India, which was placed under Caron's orders, he proceeded to Trincomalee, then in possession of the Dutch, which surrendered after some resistance.

Here the French occupied a small fort, but their acquisition cost them dear, for the greater part of the crews of the ships and of the land forces perished by want and sickness. This compelled them in turn to surrender to the Dutch. With the remains of what was once a fine force, De la Haye, in 1672, as before-mentioned, attacked and took St. Thomas, which had been built and fortified by the Portuguese a century before. The French retained this position for two years only, when it was wrested from them by the Nabob of the Carnatic, assisted by the Dutch.

After this reverse the French, under Martin, a merchant who had joined De la Haye's expedition, settled at Pondicherry, south of Madras, which place became theirs by purchase in 1683, and which they retain to this day as the head-quarters of France in India.

From this position, more than half a century after its first occupation, the celebrated French Governor, Dupleix, became, for years, a thorn in the side of England.

Although it is outside the objects of this work, it is interesting to follow the movements of the French soon after their arrival in India, as throwing light on their Eastern Foreign Policy of to-day. No sooner were they firmly established at Pondicherry than they opened trade with Siam, in those early days almost absolutely governed by a Greek adventurer, one Constantine Faulkon, who had become Prime Minister to the King, at whose invitation the French visited the country. They soon became possessed of the fortress of Bankok at the mouth of the River Menan, and of the Port of Mergui, from which they opened trade with Pegu, Ava, and Arracan.*

From Siam the French endeavoured to establish themselves at Tonquin, in which they followed the footsteps of the Portuguese and the Dutch, than whom they were not more successful; they also turned their attention to Cochin China. Their success in Siam was not destined to be of long duration, for with the fall of Faulkon from power they lost both Bankok and Mergui, which, although defended by French troops, fell to the attack of the outraged Siamese, described by Abbé Raynal, "as the most cowardly of all people."

Driven from Siam the French concentrated their energies for a time on the fortifications of Pondicherry; but Martin, ambitious for his country's honour, aspired to establish a great French power in Madagascar, proclaimed a French possession by Louis XIII. in 1642. He despatched from Pondicherry an expedition consisting of 1,600 troops and settlers, who, expecting fortune, found death.†

To summarise. The year 1672 sees the Portuguese power much

---

* Abbé Raynal.

† Cochin China (a province of Annam) was ceded to France in 1862 and 1867; its capital is Saigon. Annam fell under her Protectorate in 1884 (the northern portion of this is Tonquin), Madagascar was declared a French Protectorate in 1885—thus, after a lapse of more than 200 years, France has gained the objects aimed at by Martin.

reduced, but still established at Goa, Surat, Salsette and other places in India; the Dutch at Surat, Tranquebar, and in other positions, but more especially masters of the Malay Archipelago, and of the spice trade. The English at Surat, Bombay, Fort St. George (Madras), Masulipatam, Piplee in Bengal, and other small factories; and the Mogul Empire at war with Shivaji, the great leader of the Maratha Power. Here, for a time, they must be left, and attention invited to the Company's affairs in Bengal, which will form the subject of a future paper.

CHAPTER III.

THE EARLY HISTORY OF THE BENGAL PRESIDENCY.

In a former chapter the infancy of the Honourable East India Company has been lightly touched upon, and the origin of two out of the three great Presidencies has been briefly described. Attention is now invited to the Company's factory in Bengal, which, although the last to be established, was destined before the lapse of many years, in consequence of its favourable position for trade with the rich countries adjoining it, to eclipse both Bombay and Madras, and to become the seat of government for all India, with its capital at Calcutta.

As far back as 1620, an attempt had been made by the Company's agents to fix a factory at Patna. Bengal at that period was ruled by a Native Governor, under the title of Soobah, immediately responsible to the Mogul court, the then Soobah being Sooltan Shoojah, the second son of the Emperor Shah Jehan.

It was not until 1624 that a Firman was granted by the Mogul Emperor permitting trade with Bengal; even then the shipping was restricted to the Port of Piplee; this trade was partly established in 1642, but the factory was made dependent on Madras. From this period to the year 1651, the date of the grant of the famous Firman to Mr. Boughton, the affairs of Bengal, as described by Bruce, were confined entirely to trade matters which were carried on with but small success, as at the time now alluded to, the trade of the Company in Bengal was, owing to restrictions placed upon it from Delhi, so insignificant, and attended by so much difficulty and such small profit, that it was under serious consideration whether the factory should not be abandoned.

Mr. Boughton, the surgeon of the Company's ship *Hopewell*, successfully cured the daughter of Shah Jehan from injuries received from fire, and obtained from the grateful Emperor a Firman to trade on advantageous terms. Mr. Boughton visited the Soobah of Bengal and was again successful in the medical treatment of a Zenana favourite; as a reward for his success he received assistance from Sooltan Shoojah in re-organizing the Company's affairs in Bengal, and in 1651-52* the Firman was confirmed, giving the Company the privilege of trading free of duty in that province, on payment of the nominal sum of Rs.3,000 a year; a factory was established on a sound footing at Hoogly, and an agent appointed to Patna, the factory and the agents being subordinate to that of Madras.†

Factories were also some years later established at Bellasore and Cossimbazar.

Affairs progressed quietly until 1660, when the agent (as mentioned in a former paper) seized a vessel belonging to the Mogul, which was subsequently returned with an apology, by order of the Resident at Surat.

Permission to fortify Hoogly, frequently solicited, was persistently refused by the Mogul Emperor, and the armed force of the agency limited to an ensign and thirty men (Europeans) to do honour to the principal agent.‡ This small body of men may be regarded as the nucleus of the Bengal army. There is no evidence

---

* Various dates are given for the establishment of the Hoogly factory. Stewart says 1640; Mill and Bruce say 1651-52. Professor Wilson agrees with the latter, so that date has been accepted for this work.

† The details of the Firman are recorded by Bruce, but he makes no mention of Mr. Boughton's disinterested conduct, whose magnanimous action in preferring the welfare of his employers to his own aggrandizement is alluded to by Orme, Abbé Raynal, Broome, Stewart, and others.

‡ Orme's *Military Transactions in Hindostan*.

that this force was at the moment increased, but it must have been so, quietly, and unostentatiously in course of time, as in 1663–4 the Soobah is found asking for the assistance of English gunners in a war against the King of Arracan. These gunners must have been those belonging to the armed cruizers of the Company, as many years later the "gunner and his crew"* are referred to as the only artillery in Bengal.

In 1669, Bengal was still subordinate to Madras, but was allowed a chief agent and six members of council, similar to those at the latter agency. Trade was then so flourishing that a pilot service for the intricate navigation of the river Hoogly was established.†

The French made their appearance for the first time, in Bengal, in 1672. The Company's agent, and the investments for the season, were much disturbed by this event, and by an outbreak of hostilities between the Dutch and the Nabob of Dacca. In 1674, it is recorded that the agent at Fort St. George complained of the inattention of the Bengal agent to his orders.

In 1675 the Company placed the three Agencies, Surat, Madras, and Hoogly on an equal footing, and similar gradation was granted to its servants.

Irregularities having been discovered in the affairs of the Agency, Mr. Masters (afterwards himself dismissed the Service for gross irregularities) was sent from Madras to remodel the Bengal factory. This occurred in 1676. The next item of importance in the Bengal annals of the Company, is the fact of the Danes procuring commercial privileges from the Mogul. Nothing of interest as regards the subject of this work occurred for five years.

The importance of the Bengal agency, which, among its other factories, now included Malda and Dacca, rapidly increased, and in 1681 the stock allotted for its trade alone amounted to £230,000. Its agent was dignified by the title of Governor, and it was declared independent of Madras. Mr. Hedges was appointed to the Government and sent out from England, taking with him from

---

* Broome's *History of the Bengal Army*.
† Bruce.

Madras, which place he visited *en route,* "a corporal of proved fidelity and twenty soldiers" as body guard, and to strengthen him against "interlopers and free-traders,"* a term synonymous with that of pirates, the outcome of Charles the Second's breach of faith with the Company, by which individuals were permitted to compete with that association.

The Mogul Emperor now began to oppress the flourishing Company, possibly seeing in its success signs of coming power, and ordered 3½ per cent. to be levied on all the goods as customs; this event, the forerunner of serious complications, occurred in 1682.

The small force at Hoogly, the agency having been advanced to the dignity of a Presidency, was again augmented in 1683, when the successor of Mr. Hedges, a Mr. Gyfford, brought from Madras a whole company of troops, with arms and accoutrements for a second company to be formed from the seamen of the ships serving in Bengal waters.†

The same year saw a further change, for Mr. Gyfford was appointed agent at Fort St. George with the title of President over both the settlements of Madras and Bengal. Thus Bengal became again subordinate to Madras.

Freebooters and interlopers were becoming so troublesome, that, in 1684 the directors at home reiterated their orders to the Government of Bengal, to secure some place of safety (for which the sum of Rs.30,000 was authorized to be expended) like those existing at Bombay and Madras, but permission to raise fortifications was still refused by the Great Mogul; a war ship of 72-guns was consequently despatched from England to cruize the Bay of Bengal.‡

It will be remembered that the Firman secured by Boughton in 1651-52, granted the Company free trade in Bengal, for the payment of the nominal sum of Rs.3,000 annually; a breach of this treaty was destined to bring about a crisis in the affairs of the now prosperous merchants, and involve them in a struggle with the power

---

* Bruce's *Annals.*
† *Ibid.*
‡ Broome.

of the Mogul Empire. Native governments, and especially those subordinate to higher authority, are ever open to corruption, and there can be little doubt but that each succeeding Soobah of Bengal had to be "squared" by the Company's agent or governor established at Hoogly.

Nuzzars, or complimentary presents, are always exchanged on all important occasions; these are supposed to be of equal value, but it need hardly be remarked that the party wishing to obtain a favour always gets the worst of the exchange, and by these means the custom by easy degrees descends to a practice of bribery on a large scale. The nuzzar, moreover, must always be proportionate to the dignity, real or imagined, of the individual sought, and thus becomes a fruitful source of dispute. Whatever may have been the real reason for his action, whether his dignity had been insulted or other cause of enmity given, it is recorded that, in 1685, the Soobah of Bengal imposed an unjust duty on the Company's goods in contravention of the conditions of the Firman of 1651; and on the plea of the Company's agents being in league with an impostor, who at that time laid claim to the throne of Delhi, threw the Patna agent into prison.*

The idea that an association of merchants who, unlike Cortes, Pizarro, and others in the conquest of Mexico and Peru, had landed as traders and not as conquerors, who were absolutely without fortifications, and whose troops did not amount to more than a couple of companies of infantry, should seek to overturn the ruling Emperor of Delhi, was sufficiently preposterous; yet on this baseless supposition they were oppressed, their trade for a time paralyzed, and their ships had to leave India without cargoes. The Company at home, alarmed at these proceedings, which might at any time be renewed at the will of the native ruler, having censured their Bengal agents for the timidity they had shown in dealing with the Nabob, applied to Aurungzebe for permission to occupy certain uninhabited islands in the Hoogly, or at the mouths of the Ganges, and taking the initiative, they ordered the fortification of

* Stewart's *History of Bengal.*

a position at Ingellee, which was immediately carried out without permission being accorded.

This energetic action, necessary as it was, is proof that the Directors of the Company were beginning to be conscious of their growing strength; and if further evidence of this is necessary, it is found in an intimation from the Directors in London to their agents in India, which was as follows, that "a plan had been formed for re-asserting the Company's rights of trade in Bengal, and for preventing in the future the oppression of their agents, either by the Nawab or the Dutch, in the exercise of those rights which they had acquired by Phirmaunds" (Firmans).*

In this order is discovered the first signs of the Company's ambitious design of becoming an *independent Power* in India, a design frustrated by Aurungzebe at the time, and not destined to be carried out until many years later, for, as will be seen further on, the Government of Bombay is found addressing the Maratha Ruler as late as 1734, and describing the Company as merchants only, without any view of conquest, and whose sole business was trade.†

This bold decision to risk the wrath of Aurungzebe, and involve the Company in open war with the Mogul Empire, soon bore fruit; a fleet of ten ships was fitted out in England and placed under the command of Captain Nicholson, of the Company's service, under certain conditions, which in these days appear sufficiently curious. Nicholson was by Royal sanction granted the rank of Vice-Admiral, but on his arrival in India he was to be subordinate to the chief agent or governor, who was to assume command as commander-in-chief *and* admiral.‡

On board these ships were six companies, which, with men added from among the seamen of the fleet, it was intended to augment to ten companies of 100 men, or 1,000 in all. The six companies were duly furnished with subaltern officers, those for the four extra companies were to be provided in India, but the command of the

---

* Bruce's *Annals*.
† *Bombay State Papers*. Professor W. G. Forrest.
‡ Bruce's *Annals*.

companies was to devolve on the members of the Governor's Council, as captains! Application was made to the King (James II.—Charles II. having died in 1685) to transfer a company of King's troops to the service of the East India Company, which was accordingly done from the Marquis of Westminster's Regiment, the company being placed under the command of Captain Clifton, who, together with all the other captains of companies, was to have a seat in the Governor's Council.

Commissions were granted by the King to all the naval commanders, who were, however, to rank as junior to the commanders of the King's ships with which they might come in contact. The point of immediate attack was to be Chittagong, where the disembarkation was to take place, and for the armament of which 200 pieces of cannon were supplied. A treaty was to be entered into with the King of Arracan, and the Government of Bombay was desired to open negotiations with Rajah Sambhaji (the then Maratha ruler, and son of Shivaji), on the West Coast, to assist in annoying the Mogul Emperor, whilst the agent at Fort St. George was directed to assist the King of Golcondah, then at war with the Dutch. This order could scarcely be obeyed, as Madras had furnished every available man, about 400, leaving a slender garrison of about twenty Europeans and a few Portuguese for the defence of Fort St. George;* orders were likewise issued for the fleet to punish the King of Siam for his unfriendly behaviour towards agents who had failed to establish trade with his country, and it was to be used against the Portuguese, for the purpose of seizing Salsette, which the English Court still insisted had been ceded, with Bombay, to Charles II., but never given up; thus the Company boldly entered into war all along the coasts of India.

Sir John Child, the then Governor of Bombay, was appointed Governor General of all the Company's settlements in India, and invested with powers to visit Madras, and, if necessary, Bengal, and carry on war or make peace according to circumstances.

Nicholson, with a portion of his fleet, arrived in the river Hoogly

* Broome's *History of the Bengal Army.*

in October 1686. The Soobah, then better known as the Nawab of Bengal, alarmed at the preparations of the English and their bold attitude, offered terms. Whilst these were under negotiation, an accident caused the first collision between the troops of the Nawab and the English. It originated in a bazaar quarrel, which by degrees assumed large proportions and ended in a fight, in which all the troops on both sides were engaged, leaving the English, in spite of inferiority of numbers, completely victorious, the enemy losing 60 killed, and many wounded, besides a battery of 11 guns. Nicholson also bombarded Hoogly from his ships, and destroyed some 500 houses.

The Foujdar, or native official of Hoogly, requested a cessation of arms; this was granted on the condition of the payment of sixty-six lacs of rupees, about £660,000.*

The Nawab had, however, by this time collected a large force, and ordered the seizure of all the Company's goods and agents in the outlying factories, which consisted of Bellasore, Dacca, Malda, Kossimbazaar and Patna. Seeing his danger, the agent seized upon the village of Chuttanutee (the site of the present Calcutta), where he intrenched himself. This determined front induced the

---

* Bruce & Broome give a detailed list of claims as follows:—

	Rs.
For what Bulchund forced from Mr. Vincent at Cassumbuzar	14,000
,, Sief Cawn plundered out of our factory at Pattana by 1,000 Foot and 500 Horse, and putting Mr. Meverill in irons	80,000
For detaining yᵉ agent with yᵉ silk at Cassumbuzar	400,000
For protecting Haggerston from justice	45,000
For what forced out Dacca factory, account Picars	44,000
,, ,, from our Merchants at Hughly	12,000
For demolishing and plundering Malda factory	150,000
For customs paid at the Mint at Hughly contrary to our Phirmaund	150,000
To demorage of shipping yᵉ last three years	2,000,000
For what extorted from us in presents, &ct.	200,000
For debts remaineing and owing us in the country	800,000
For besieging of Hughly factory, yᵉ death of yᵉ Agent and 4 men	300,000
For burning yᵉ old factory and yᵉ goods in it, in yᵉ latter skirmish	300,000
For charge of 1,000 men and 20 ships for yᵉ war	2,000,000
For yᵉ charges of our factorys and buildings if we leave yᵉ country	130,000
	6,625,000

Nawab to again offer terms, one of the most important of which was the grant of a tract of land, with permission to build a fort.

Having thus lulled the suspicions of the agent-governor, the Nawab busied himself in collecting a more powerful force with which to exterminate the British. Being made aware of his danger, the agent, early in 1687, abandoned Chuttanutee and occupied Ingellee, which was already fortified, and his fleet, taking the initiative, seized many of the Mogul's vessels, destroyed his fort at Tanah on the Hoogly, and, attacking Belasore, captured and burnt forty ships belonging to native merchants.

In the meanwhile hostilities had been declared at Bombay, and carried on with great energy by Sir John Child, by which the Mogul's shipping suffered severely, and his revenues were considerably curtailed.

The native Governor of Surat had, however, in the temporary absence of Sir John Child, at Bombay, imprisoned the English agent, Mr. Harris, and seized all the Company's goods, offering a reward for Sir John Child, alive or dead. Bombay was at the same time attacked by the Mogul fleet, under the Seddee,[*] or Admiral, who, although always repulsed by the European garrison, managed to gain possession of the outlying lands, known as Mazagon, Mahim, and Sion.

Ingellee, frequently attacked, offered a stout resistance, so much so that the siege was abandoned.

The English successes by sea, especially off the coast of Malabar, and the inability of the Nawab's troops to crush the gallant band in Bengal, induced Aurungzebe to order his subordinates to offer terms; a treaty was concluded in August 1687, and early in 1688 the Company's agents re-occupied Chuttanutee, where they were again subjected to the hostility of the disappointed and incensed Nawab.

---

[*] The Seddee was the hereditary title of the Mogul's Admirals. These chiefs were of African origin, and gained their important office by undertaking the safe conduct of the Mahometan pilgrims to Mecca. The principal seat of their power was Jingeerah, on the coast near Bombay. The African stokers employed by the great steamship companies trading with India are to this day known as Seddees or Seddee boys.

By all that has gone before, it will be seen that the English, although able to hold their own, had gained no practical advantage. Their losses had, indeed, been heavy, as the climate of Ingellee was pestilential. The news of Nicholson's want of success in firmly establishing the Company's power in Bengal, and overawing the Emperor's deputy, determined the directors to further strengthen their agent at Hoogly and Chuttanutee; a reinforcement consisting of two ships and 160 men was accordingly despatched under Captain Heath, with orders to carry out the original instructions of the Company, and, should he find himself incapable of so doing, he was, in communication with the Agent-Governor, to retire to Madras.

In October 1688, Heath arrived in Bengal; hostilities were again commenced, which proving useless in re-establishing trade, he, with the Company's servants, embarked with all its wealth in November of the same year; and having taken and pillaged Belasore, where he captured a battery of thirty guns, touched at Chettagong, whence an alliance against the Emperor was again offered to the King of Arracan, and again was rejected. After this failure the fleet sailed for Madras, which place was reached in March 1689. Thus was the Company's trade in Bengal for a time absolutely abandoned.

Aurungzebe, furious at the pillage of Belasore, and other losses he had sustained, ordered, with all the assurance of a despot, the utter extermination of the English in India. He gained some successes on land, notably in the Company's territories of Bombay; but finding his revenues suffer severely from the absence of trade, and seeing the utter impossibility of his Mahometan subjects being able to continue their pilgrimages to Holy Mecca whilst the English were all powerful at sea, he at length agreed to negotiate with the delegates sent by Sir John Child shortly before that energetic Governor-General's death in February 1690, when peace was arranged on moderate terms, considering the despot with whom they had to deal, although accompanied by a firman couched in language most humiliating to the English. This firman was dated February 1690, and among other things demanded a fine of

Rs.150,000 for mischief done, and the dismissal "of Mr. Child, who did the disgrace."* Permission was granted to re-occupy Chuttanutee on the old terms of free trade, for the payment of Rs.3,000 a year, but permission to fortify was again refused. Mr. Charnock (the founder of Calcutta) arrived in the Hoogly with thirty soldiers, which number was by the end of the year increased to 100, and took possession of Chuttanutee; so that, after a war lasting for four years, the Company, in 1690, found themselves in the *status quo ante* of 1686.

Thus was frustrated for a time the Company's ambitious design of becoming an independent power in India.

Having seen the Company firmly established in Bengal, attention is again invited to the Island of Bombay, and the proceedings of the Company's servants on the West Coast of India.

Since the year 1672, Bombay, for many years, had been of but small service to the English, and had acquired an evil reputation for unhealthiness, so much so as to give rise to the proverb, "That at Bombay a man's life did not exceed two monsoons."† The unwholesomeness of the air was attributed to the bad quality of the water, the low marshy ground, and to the offensive smell of the manure used at the roots of its innumerable cocoa-nut trees.

As sanitary precautions prevailed, the inhabitants increased, and the extraordinary value of the harbour, then the finest, if not the only one—except Goa, in possession of the Portuguese—deserving the name in India, soon became acknowledged, and it was utilized by the merchant vessels frequenting the Malabar coast as a place of refreshment, and as a winter station and rendezvous for the armed squadrons sent from England. The Company made it the mart of all their trade with Malabar, Surat, and the Persian and Arabian Gulfs. Its importance was of slow growth; but to-day, after 200 years of varying success, it with justice proudly claims to be the richest city, although not yet the capital, of India. ‡

---

* Bruce's *Annals*.
† Abbé Raynal.
‡ The population of Bombay is about 774,000. It is, next to London, the most populous city in the British Empire.

EARLY HISTORY OF BENGAL. 71

In 1672, and for many years after, the Company's possessions on the West Coast of India consisted of Bombay alone, with a few factories, notably Surat, scattered along the coast. The neighbouring Island of Salsette, with its forts of Bandora and Thanna, and Bassein on the main land, were occupied by the Portuguese. Although frequently called upon to defend themselves, peaceful trade was the sole object of the British, and territorial extension was neither aimed at nor desired ; the only force maintained as yet consisted of but a few European troops, seamen from the fleets, some Portuguese, and a body of peons charged with the care of the valuable merchandise.

But the Company's Governor at Bombay, whilst having no pretensions to strength on shore, was powerful at sea.

Although the Treaty of Westminster, dated February 1673, concluded the war with Holland, Bombay was in this year threatened with invasion by the Dutch. Recruits were sent from home, and orders reiterated to strengthen the fortifications, which now mounted 100 guns, and were defended by two companies of 200 men each, 3 companies of Militia, and about 100 men employed in the Marine service.

Negotiations were also opened with Shivaji, who, whilst promising protection to the English, evaded their just demands for losses sustained by Maratha incursions, especially on the factories of Rajahpore and Hubely.

The position of affairs at Madras was far from satisfactory, as St. Thomé was in French possession, and was threatened by the Dutch ; by whichever side retained, it would always remain a menace to the English, for the French force was estimated at 1,800 men, the Dutch at 4,000, whilst the garrison of Fort St. George consisted of 250 Europeans only, and a few peons; consequently Fort St. George was further strengthened, and the officers of the garrison encouraged by additional allowances according to rank.

An important event occurred in 1674 in the coronation of Shivaji, which establishes the date of the Maratha sovereignty ; Mr. Oxinden attended the coronation on the part of the Company, and obtained trade privileges from the Maratha king, in spite of which, and former promises of protection, Surat was again threatened, and a small English factory at Dungum, was attacked and plundered by Maratha Horse.

Whilst these events were happening a dangerous mutiny occurred among the troops at Bombay, under Captain Shaxton, who appears to have encouraged the mutineers. It is evident that the troops had cause for complaint, as their demand for a month's pay (which they declared had been promised them in lieu of discharge at the end of three years' service, which had expired) was granted by the President, Mr. Aungier, who, however, brought the ringleaders to trial by court-martial, which sentenced three of them to death, a sentence carried out in one case only, by the execution of a Corporal Fake, who was shot on the 21st October 1674. Shaxton was also found guilty and sent to England to await the decision of the Court of Directors and of the King on his case. This is the first instance of the servants of the Company exercising their power of martial law. After this event Mr. Aungier considered it advisable to dismiss the Portuguese portion of the garrison and replace them with recruits at that moment arriving from England. He conferred the vacant command, with a seat in Council, on Captain Langford. The regulations of this year provided that one per cent. of the Company's revenue might be spent on the fortifications.

Mr. Aungier considered it necessary to point out to the Court of Directors, that their European rivals in India, the French, Dutch, Portuguese and Danes, although nominally at peace with England, were their bitter enemies in all trade questions, which might at any moment have to be decided by an appeal to arms, and therefore demanded additional garrisons for all the principal factories, as being a matter of the first and most urgent necessity. Mr. Aungier also suggested that the two companies at Bombay might well be commanded by lieutenants, thus saving the pay of two captains, and recommended that the companies should be called the Governor's and Deputy-Governor's Company respectively.*

* Bruce's *Annals.*

The regulations framed by the Court of Directors in 1675 were of great importance to their servants, civil and military. Seniority was established as the rule of succession to all offices of trust. The chief authority was vested in the civil service, the duties of the military being subservient to the promotion of trade, after attending to the defence of the settlement. At the same time the civil servants were to acquire a knowledge of military discipline, and, if found better suited for the military than the civil service, they were to be granted commissions. These regulations were applicable to all the presidencies. Captain Langford was to be allowed to retain his seat in the Council, but this was not to be considered as a precedent on the occurrence of future vacancies.

Forty additional recruits were received at Bombay, and twenty were sent out for Madras, whose garrison in future, it was determined, should be composed of Europeans only; their pay was fixed at twenty-one shillings a month, including rations and necessaries. The former order for the civil servants to be trained to the use of arms was rescinded, and the removal of any servant from a civil to a military post was prohibited.

About this period the garrisons received German recruits, and as they had behaved with "sobriety and regularity"* it was intended to make a larger use of this nationality, and it was further resolved to raise a troop of horse, and place it under the command of Captain Keigwin (formerly Governor of St. Helena). The Militia of the Island now amounted to 600 men, and it is, perhaps, worth mentioning that in this year orders were received to establish a mint at Bombay, at which "Rupee, pice, and budgrooks" were to be coined.

Although the garrisons of the Company were daily growing in strength of numbers, and more important still, in the power of discipline and system, the directors had always been consistent in enjoining their servants to avoid the errors of the Dutch and Portuguese, and to conduct their enterprise with humanity and fair dealing, and so gain, if possible, the respect and love of the

* Bruce.

people.* These philanthropic intentions were not attended by the success they perhaps deserved, and the foregoing chapters have, it is hoped, tended to show how the Company had been oppressed wherever it had settled; it is, therefore, not surprising to find that in 1677 the directors, although they still recommended temporizing expedients, empowered Mr. Aungier to employ force where necessary to enforce the observation of treaties and grants.

Bruce in his *Annals* takes a harsh view of these discretionary powers, and considers that they were granted by the directors to enable them, in the event of questions arising between the King and the Company, regarding possible hostilities, to throw the blame on their servants. This opinion seems unjust, for when the great distance between England and India is considered, distance rendered far greater by the slow sailing of the ships of the day—it taking eighteen months to two years to receive an answer on questions of importance—the discretionary powers appear to have been absolutely necessary, and to show proper trust in able and deserving servants, who being on the spot, and having a force, although a very limited one, at hand, would be better able to judge of the necessities of the moment, than their masters at home.

The troops at this period were enlisted for a term of seven years, and an order is extant, permitting soldiers of approved character, and whose terms had expired, to be promoted to small posts of civil trust. This was a wise method for keeping tried servants in their service, as at the time the Company had extended their trade to Tonquin and Amoy in China, and were contemplating the establishment of a factory at Canton.†

Mr. Aungier died in 1677, universally regretted, and was succeeded by Mr. Rolt, who at once applied for 150 recruits from England, as he could place no reliance on the Portuguese Topasses or the militia, reporting at the same time the completion of the

---

* Abbé Raynal.
† This system has been again tried in the present day, in England for the British, and in India for Native, troops discharged the service with good characters. The scheme has not yet received the measure of success it deserves.

Fort, except the eastern bastion, which, however was under construction.

The year 1678 opened with orders for unreasonable measures of economy, which shortly after led to unhappy results. Not only were the rank and allowances of the President and Council at Surat, and the Deputy Governor of Bombay, to be reduced, but considerable reduction was ordered in the Military Establishment, which was in future to consist of 2 lieutenants, 2 ensigns, 4 sergeants, 4 corporals, and 180 privates; the troop of horse was to be disbanded, and Captain Keigwin dismissed, and the militia was to be discharged; 2 European and 4 Native gunners only were to be allowed for the batteries; all the armed ships, except one frigate, were to be sold, and no further improvements were to be made in the fortifications. The extra allowance granted to thirty men detached as a guard on the Surat factory, was no longer to be allowed; this is the first recorded mention of "batta," which in after years was a frequent cause of discontent and mutiny among the troops of the Company.

These injunctions conclude, as Beveridge well says, "ludicrously and insultingly," by recommending the Governor to maintain strict discipline, so as to have the garrison always ready for a vigorous defence. These orders do not appear to have been extended to Madras.

The wholesale reductions caused, not unnaturally, immense discontent, civil and military, the former with the greater justice, as the Presidency which had rendered such good service to the Company, was degraded to an agency, and the salary of its highest servant reduced to £300 a year, that of a Member of Council being proportionally diminished, the junior member receiving £40 only; on this pittance, it cannot be a matter for surprise if the Company's servants are found indulging in private trade, greatly to the disadvantage of their masters.

The following year still greater cause of discontent was given to the garrison of Bombay. The Directors at home, possibly alarmed at their dangerous reductions, gave orders that two auxiliary companies should be raised, composed of the principal inhabitants, each to be commanded by a captain; by this means superior rank was granted to the auxiliary or volunteer companies, to that enjoyed by the regular troops, whose companies were commanded by lieutenants. The garrison of Fort St. George was next diminished, by reducing the strength of the companies from 100 to 60 men.

With reduced military establishments Bombay was, in 1679, threatened with imminent danger. Shivaji seized on the island of Kenery, situated at the mouth of Bombay Harbour, and the Siddee, the Mogul's Admiral, occupied the island of Henery. Under these circumstances, the Bombay Agent at once applied for a reinforcement of at least 200 men, with proper officers. This demand was partly complied with the following year, the services of Captain Keigwin being again engaged; he was given the rank of Captain-Lieutenant, with pay at six shillings a day, but with no extra allowances, and proceeded to Bombay with seventy men and eighteen small cannon; the garrison was further strengthened by the arrival of twenty-eight recruits, and by the return of the thirty men detached to Surat. The year was also memorable for the death of Shivaji, which occurred on the 5th of April 1680, and the succession of Sambhaji, his son.

The year 1681 saw Surat again raised to a Presidency, and Mr., afterwards Sir John, Child appointed President.

On the 30th August 1682 the English were ignominiously expelled from Bantam (where they had traded with varying success for eighty years) by the Dutch. Notwithstanding this alarming episode, and the continued threatening attitude of the Marathas (who still held the Island of Kenery) and the Mogul Admiral, the garrison of Bombay consisted of 100 Europeans only, with but one armed ship for the protection of the trade and settlement, and this at a time when Bombay was declared by the Directors to be an independent English settlement, and the seat of power and trade of the English in India. Thirty recruits were this year sent to Madras.

In 1683, the King and Court of Directors determined to avenge the insult put upon them by the Dutch in the seizure of Bantam.

A fleet was consequently fitted out under the command of Sir John Wetwang, as Admiral, and Sir Thomas Grantham, as Vice-Admiral. The Abbé Raynal says that there were 8,000 troops on board, and that the Dutch, alarmed at this evidence of the determination of the English, entered into a compact with Charles II., who, for the sum of about £100,000 undertook to forbid the sailing of the united squadrons of the King and Company, and thus sacrificed the honour and trade of his nation.

The Abbé may have exaggerated in his statement, but be that as it may, an agreement was entered into between the Dutch and English in Europe, by which Bantam was to be restored under certain conditions.

A portion of the Fleet, under Sir Thomas Grantham, actually sailed, and was subsequently employed in suppressing the interlopers in the Bay of Bengal, and by its presence strengthened the hands of the Company on the coasts of India.

It had originally been intended that the troops embarked for Bantam should, after the restoration of that place, proceed to Bombay, and a portion of them be formed into a third company of infantry; this intention does not appear to have been carried out, but forty recruits were sent to Bombay, and it was ordered that two companies of Rajpoots, each of 100 men, should be embodied, to be commanded by officers of their own, and to use their own arms. This is the first mention of the enrolment of regular companies of Natives selected from a warlike race. The fortifications of Fort St. George were likewise strengthened and extended.

Whilst the above-mentioned increase of military establishment at Bombay was being carried out, and whilst discontent was still rife among both the soldiers and civilians, an event occurred, which, under the circumstances, should not have been quite unexpected. Captain Keigwin lately appointed to command the garrison, possibly encouraged by the Company's former leniency to Sir Edward Winter, seized the Government of Bombay, annulled the authority of the Company, and claimed it in the King's name. He imprisoned the Deputy-Governor and other members of the Government, appointed his own officers in their place, and, assisted by the troops, mentioned by Bruce as consisting of 150 Europeans, 2,000 Topasses, and the militia or volunteer companies, he seized on the Company's frigate *Hunter*, the ship *Return*, and treasure to the amount of Rs. 60,000.

Captain Keigwin excused himself in letters to the King for the course he had taken, by complaining of the weakness of the Company's Government, and declaring that the revolt was necessary for the safety of the Island, as, unless strong measures were adopted, it would certainly fall an easy prey to either Sambhaji or the Siddee. Negotiations were opened between Keigwin and President Child, who arrived at Bombay for the purpose, but without effect.

The Company now suffered for former weakness, and found themselves deprived, not only of Bombay, but of Bantam, which, towards the end of the year (1683) was abandoned by the Agents, and the trade of its dependencies Jambee, Tonquin, Siam and Canton consequently lost.

In the meanwhile the news of Keigwin's mutiny had reached the startled Directors at home. Their disappointment and anger were the greater, as at this time they were contemplating the removal of the seat of Government from Surat to Bombay. A petition was presented to the King, praying for a Commission under the Great Seal for the restoration of the Island; this was immediately granted, and the Company empowered to receive Bombay from the mutineers, and to offer a free pardon to all except the ringleaders. The fleet under Sir Thomas Grantham was ordered to assemble at Surat and embark such troops as could be mustered. President Child was appointed Captain-General and Admiral of the Company's forces by sea and land. Keigwin's immediate surrender was to be demanded, and, in case of refusal, he and all his adherents were to be proclaimed traitors, and a reward offered for the apprehension of the ringleaders. His Majesty's ship *Phœnix*, commanded by Captain Tyrrel, was sent as a reinforcement to Sir Thomas Grantham, against Keigwin and the interlopers. It was also determined that on the restoration of Bombay the European force should be augmented to three companies of infantry.

During the time occupied by these arrangements, Captain Keigwin had been active, and his Government, as is often the case with that of usurpers, appears to have been a strong one. He negotiated a commercial treaty with Sambhaji, and actually succeeded in inducing him to pay the compensation for losses sustained by the Company, so often applied for with no success from his father Shivaji; he also raised the strength of the garrison to over 500 men.

On the 19th November 1684, Keigwin delivered over the island to Sir Thomas Grantham, as the King's representative, and by him it was at once restored to the Company, represented by Dr. St. John, as King's Judge, and Mr. Zinzan, the temporary governor. Keigwin was subsequently pardoned, his successful negotiations with Sambhaji, and the fact of the treasure he had seized being intact, having probably influenced this merciful, though weak, decision.

The Court's orders for Madras at this season were, that the fort was to be improved, the garrison strengthened, and a troop of cavalry raised from among such of the European residents as kept horses. The extra expenses for fortifications were to be defrayed by an anchorage tax of one dollar and a barrel of gunpowder on all vessels, and by a tax on the inhabitants. A wall was to be built round the town of Madras, and the land round about, including St. Thomé, was to be purchased.

In February 1685, Charles II. died, and was succeeded by his brother, the Duke of York, as James II. Charles, ever impecunious, doubtless extracted large sums from the Company for the preservation of their trade; but it must be admitted, from a study of the records of the period, that the Company was uniformly protected by that monarch. Some writers, especially Abbé Raynal, say that he secretly encouraged the interlopers. He certainly permitted the Duke of York and others to oust the Company from its African possessions, and his action regarding Bantam is doubtful; but, in spite of these drawbacks, the Company owed the possession of Bombay to him, although His Majesty was probably unaware of the value of the concession, or he would hardly have sold it for the annual payment of £10 in gold.

The Company entertained great hopes of support from James II., who, as Duke of York, had been a holder of Indian Stock; nor were the Directors disappointed in the expectation, for more effectual means were at once adopted for the prosecution of interlopers.

The code of martial law, as used in the Royal Army, was in future to be applied to the Company's forces, and President Child, now created a baronet, was granted a body-guard of thirty men under command of a captain; 200 recruits were embarked for Bombay, and orders were given for the entertainment of Europeans in India willing to enter the Company's military service. The seat of Government was finally transferred from Surat to Bombay, and Sir John Wyborne was appointed deputy-governor, on a salary of £250 a year.* All these events occurred in 1685.

Sir John Child, now Governor and General,† and resident at Bombay, was, in 1687, granted an increased body-guard of fifty Grenadiers: 120 recruits were sent from England, and orders were given to make Bombay as strong as possible. It was, moreover, contemplated to acquire the Island of Salsette from Portugal, an idea not carried out until many years after (1774), when it was wrested from the Marathas, who had ousted the Portuguese. Madras was declared an independent power,‡ the fortifications were again strengthened, and 300 men, drafted from the Royal troops in Ireland, were sent as a reinforcement; and it was ordered that for the future the King's Union Flag should always be hoisted on the walls.§

---

* He was dismissed the service two years later for disputing the authority of the Governor-General, Sir John Child.—Bruce's *Annals*.

† Attention is invited to the fact that the original title of the Company's principal officer in India was that of Governor *and* General, that is, Governor of the Settlements, and General of the Forces, not Governor-General as in the present day; so the title has its origin in the dual duties, civil and military, performed by the Company's chief functionary.

‡ The term Independent Power does not imply that Madras was not still subject to the Governor-General at Bombay; it means that Madras was declared a power on the Coromandel coast, independent of the native rulers, and prepared to defend itself and enforce treaties and grants.

§ Bruce.

The war in Bengal at this period, and events connected with it at Bombay and Madras, have already been described in the short account given of Bengal affairs at the commencement of this chapter.

In February 1689, the Prince of Orange and his consort ascended the English throne as William and Mary, James II. having been deposed, and were proclaimed at Bombay the following year. The accession of a Dutch prince to the English throne was alarming to the Directors of the Company, who could never forget the many calamities they had suffered from Dutch aggression.

In February 1690, as before mentioned, Sir John Child died. In him the Company lost a valued servant. His character is variously described. Bruce extols him for energy and a provident concern for the interests of his masters; Beveridge censures him for duplicity, and for playing unsuccessfully a double game with the Mogul, and his officers, themselves masters in deceit; and in the opinion of Abbé Raynal, nothing can be worse than his character. The Abbé describes him as an "avaricious, turbulent, and savage man," and as one "who was as cowardly in time of danger as he had been daring in his piracies." The chances are that he was bold and utterly unscrupulous in carrying out the tortuous policy of the Court of Directors, then presided over by his brother, President Josiah Child; at any rate, the many details of his work at Bombay and Surat, as given by Bruce in his *Annals*, ascertain the fact of his value as a public servant.

Towards the end of 1689, or early in 1690, Sambhaji, the Maratha King, was captured and put to death by Aurungzebe; he was succeeded by the Ram-Rajah, second son of Shivaji.

The proclamation of the accession of William and Mary was made at Bombay on the 22nd June 1690, and Bruce says the fact is the more memorable from its having taken place on the very day that the Mogul army, in command of the Siddee, evacuated the Island of Bombay, under the provision of the Treaty already mentioned as having been entered into between the English and Aurungzebe, and the Company's forces again took possession of Mahim. Sir John Child had been succeeded by Mr. Harris, but with shorn power and title, he being appointed governor, not governor-general; 150 recruits were sent to him, with orders to render Bombay impregnable; this order was the more necessary as, in alliance with the Dutch, William III. had declared war against France. Instructions were issued to Bombay, Madras, and St. Helena, to seize all French ships, and the garrison of Fort St. George was to attack the French at Pondicherry. The Company had, moreover, to face domestic troubles, for the interlopers, encouraged by the Mogul's attack on Bombay, and the evacuation of Bengal, received the support of Parliament to the formation of a new Company, as a rival to the existing association.

In these early days the position and responsibilities of the Company's servants in India could have been no sinecure, for, with England at war with France, the year 1691 sees the garrison of Madras reduced by one company of infantry, although increased in artillery and a small augmentation of the troop of horse. The fortifications of Bombay were also described as being in a ruinous condition, a fact to which the Governor ascribed the late attack of the Siddee, and the humiliating Firman of Aurungzebe. The garrison he reported as reduced by sickness to 35 Europeans only; and although he had a sufficient force of Topasses, they were not to be depended on. A favourable estimation had been formed of the native (Rajpoot) troops lately raised; but recruits were urgently needed, and permission required for necessary expenses of repairing fortifications and building a defending wall round the town. Mr. Harris also informed the Directors that, suspecting the Portuguese Jesuits resident on the Island of having assisted the Siddee in his late attack, they had been seized and their lands confiscated.

Information was received from Madras, of an indecisive naval action off the coast between the allied English and Dutch fleets and that of the French, which was supposed to have sailed for Bengal. This is the first mention of actual hostilities between the French and English in India.

The attitude of the Mogul at this period appears to have been more conciliatory, as he agreed to pay a sum of Rs.80,000 for damage inflicted at Surat in the late war, and granted the Firman for the reconstruction of the Company's trade in Bengal, although it was couched in humiliating terms.

It is interesting to note that in this year the Company was firmly established at Bencoleen, in Sumatra, and had built Fort York, which was garrisoned by negroes imported from Madagascar.

The following year Captain (afterwards Sir John) Goldesborough was appointed Commissary and Superior over all the Company's affairs in India. He arrived at Madras in November 1692. The infantry of the garrison, now reduced to two companies, commanded by lieutenants, was in future to be commanded by the Governor and the First Member of his Council as captains; they were to receive no pay in time of peace. Land was purchased at Tegnapatam, and Fort St. David erected,* an event which aroused the jealousy of the Dutch. The agent in Bengal was still unprovided with a fortified position, but was allowed a force of 100 European soldiers, whilst orders were issued to Bombay to enlist Armenians, Negroes, and Arabs. It is worthy of notice that in this year great encouragement was given to Armenian merchants, both at Bombay and Madras.

In 1693 a French man-of-war captured the British ship *Elizabeth*, fifty miles from Bombay. The extraordinary want of discipline among the Company's servants at Bombay is exemplified by the fact that Mr. Vaux, the then Deputy-Governor, purchased the prize from the French, and used it for the purpose of carrying on private trade; for this act he was suspended. The Company's good name also suffered from the depredations and outrages committed by pirates, who swarmed at sea. These freebooters sailed under English colours, which made it impossible for the natives whom they plundered, and often massacred, to distinguish the vessels of their captors from those of the Company, on whom they threw the blame of their losses.

A new charter (not a confirmation of existing charters) was granted to the Company by William and Mary, differing little from

* A few miles south of Pondicherry.

that granted by Elizabeth, but with certain trade restrictions that need no notice here. An attempt was made to absorb the interlopers by purchase of their vessels and supposed rights; the hands of these illegitimate traders having been immensely strengthened by a decision of the House of Commons, which declared that "it was the right of all Englishmen to trade to the East Indies, or any part of the world, unless prohibited by Act of Parliament."*

Sir John Goldesborough was appointed Governor and General of all the Company's Indian possessions and trade. Thus Madras superseded Bombay as the head-quarters of Indian Government. Sir John Gayer was appointed Lieutenant-General and Governor of Bombay, and chief of all factories in Northern India; he was to succeed Sir John Goldesborough in the event of that officer's death. 150 recruits were sent to Bombay with orders from the Court that, in future, the native troops were to be enlisted from the same caste. Trade was again opened with China.

The most eventful occurrence of the war with the French that took place in India during this year, was the conquest of Pondicherry by the Dutch.

The following year opened with the death of Sir John Goldesborough, whose action in Bengal will be noticed under the account of the proceedings in that Presidency. In the meanwhile the power of the Mogul Empire in Southern India was on the wane, owing to the great age of the Emperor Aurungzebe. His General, Zulfiker Khan, however, formed a scheme by which the English were to be deprived of their possessions of Forts St. George and St. David, and determined to effect their capture by stratagem. The first attempt was made on Fort St. David, which, it was arranged, should be given into his hands by a Doctor Blackwell, who had been bribed to undertake this ignoble act, by valuable presents and promises of future employment under the Mogul. Dr. Blackwell's treachery was fortunately discovered in time; he was seized and taken to Madras, there to await the decision of the Court at home.

* Bruce.

As regards Bombay, Sir John Gayer arrived to assume his government about the time of the death of Mr. Harris, who was succeeded as President at Surat, by Mr. Annesley.

The French were now conducting the war with activity at sea, and had captured five English ships off Galway. They also equipped a fleet of nine ships, said to carry 1,200 troops, and 800 seamen, with Bengal for its supposed destination. Forts St. George and St. David were at once ordered to be strengthened; Cafres or Blacks from the Mozambique were entertained to augment the garrison, and considerable reinforcements of English and Swiss troops were despatched from home; at the same time orders were reiterated to enlist, if possible, Armenians, as it was found that each English recruit cost the Company £30. The Volunteer Horse of Madras was kept in readiness to scour the coast and bring intelligence of the arrival of the French fleet; the assistance even of the Mogul's General was asked for.

Bombay in this year (1695) having received ten recruits only, and the strength of the small garrison having been again reduced by disease, a lieutenant and 70 men were despatched from home. Sir John Gayer was active in looking after the Bombay defences; the out forts were reduced to five, that is to say, Mahim, Sion, Mazagon, Worlee and Suree, but it was proposed to complete the sea defences by constructing batteries on Malabar Hill,* in those days covered with jungle, but now the abode of fashionable Bombay, and the site of one of the residences of His Excellency the Governor. Whilst these improvements were being carried out, it is curious to find the garrison again reduced; a portion of the auxiliary troops were dismissed, and the native levies reduced to seven subadars and 400 men.

But Sir John Gayer had other anxieties. A piratical ship,

---

* In February 1886, when the writer left Bombay, the defences of Malabar Hill consisted of two 18-ton guns, mounted in battery at Government House, Malabar Point, and two others in battery at Mahaluxmee. These were mounted during, or soon after, the despatch of the Malta Expedition, in 1878. A battery mounting small obsolete guns existed before that date on Malabar Point, but it was of late construction.

under English colours, having captured a Pilgrim vessel belonging to the Mogul, the Governor of Surat seized the President and other servants of the Company, numbering 63 persons, imprisoned and placed them in irons. To effect their release Sir John Gayer proposed to take upon himself the responsibility of the safe conduct of the Pilgrims to Mecca.

The year of 1695 is also memorable in the annals of the Company for the establishment of the Scotch East India Company, in the month of June, under the auspices of the King and the Parliament of Scotland.*

About this time, and when the Company was at low ebb, a general clamour arose in England against the monopoly of Indian trade, which, it was contended, should be thrown open to the whole nation, and not be left at the mercy of a mere company of merchants. The Company defended itself, and maintained that it was not possible to carry on a profitable trade with the East, without exclusive privileges; but their enemies added this to their other arguments, that the charter under which the Company carried on their business was insufficient, as it had been granted by successive monarchs, who had no right to grant or to renew it. Both sides had their partizans, but the national voice was against the Company, which was, however, supported by Court favour. Corruption,† intrigues, and libels were the common tools of each party, the Company offering large sums for the renewal of their charter; their adversaries paying freely for its revocation. The dispute, that had been carried on with great violence, was finally settled by Parliament, which declared in favour of open trade; but the old Company had permission to continue its operations until the expiration of its charter.

* The Scotch Company ceased to exist in 1697.

† The sum expended on bribes or "gratifications" at this period amounted to £234,258, acknowledged by Sir Thomas Cooke before a Parliamentary Committee. It was stated in evidence that £10,000 and £50,000 had been offered to, and had been refused by King William III., and it was explained that the former and smaller sum was "customary," it having been given for many years to the reigning monarch, especially to Charles II The Duke of Leeds, President of the Council, narrowly escaped imprisonment for receiving 5,500 guineas.—Bruce's *Annals*.

The year 1696 witnessed the release of President Annesley and the English factors at Surat. Trade was, however, but partially re-established. The garrison of Bombay was so reduced by continued sickness, that, out of the three companies of infantry, four file only could be mustered to form a guard of honour to receive a Dutch Commissary on his way to Surat.* In this year an indecisive action was fought between seven Dutch and five French ships off Vingorla, on the west coast south of Bombay, by which it will be seen that the French were holding their own at sea. No fewer than eight piratical vessels were known to be cruising off the West Coast of India. The successes and enormous plunder secured by these deep-dyed scoundrels, gave rise to serious disaffection among the Company's troops and seamen, many of whom deserted to join the black flag. But worse was to follow. The crews of the Company's frigate *Mocha*, and of a smaller vessel named the *Josiah*, mutinied, murdered their officers, seized the ships and became pirates. The trade of Bombay, Madras, and Bengal was equally depressed by the united action of these marauders, and the loss to the country commerce was estimated at half a million sterling. The following year the Company lost their ship *Hannibal* by the mutiny of the crew, who turned pirates. Matters had now come to such a pass, that the King's cruisers were ordered to engage all pirates at sea, and the Company offered a reward of £50 for any man captured and brought to justice, and £100 for Captain Amery, a notorious leader.

With trade at a standstill, and garrisons reduced to dangerous weakness, the Government of Bombay, now again supreme in India, Sir John Gayer having succeeded, on the death of Sir John Goldesborough, as Governor and General, was greatly embarrassed by an application of the Shah of Persia for assistance against the Arabs, with whom he was at war. To this appeal "an evasive answer" was given, a term of frequent occurrence in the future annals of the Company.

* Bruce.

Not only were the affairs of the Company depressed, but the peninsula of India generally was in a distracted state. Sultan Akbar, son of Aurungzebe, had invaded Northern India with the assistance of Persia; Zulfiker Khan was waging a relentless war with the Ram Rajah and the Marathas; a Mogul army was invading the Carnatic, and another force had seized and destroyed the fortifications of St. Thomé, thereby alarming and seriously endangering Madras itself; and in Bengal, Rajah Subah Sing had made himself master of Rajmahal, in spite of the resistance offered by the Mogul's Governor.

The French successes by sea still continued, for in 1697 they captured two of the Company's ships, which, among other valuables, were carrying eighty recruits for Bombay. To supply this loss, a full company under a lieutenant was embarked. Fort St. David was in this year strengthened by a redoubt, and Mr. Pitt was appointed Governor of Madras independent of Bombay for one year, to enable him, by summary action, to re-arrange affairs at Fort St. George, which, owing to the distance of the supreme Government at Bombay, and dissensions among its servants, had become dangerously unsettled. Orders from home wisely enjoined strict neutrality in the Civil War between Aurungzebe and his sons, which, already begun, was expected to spread.

The peace of Europe was happily restored this year by the Treaty of Ryswick (signed 20th September 1697); this, of course, concluded the war in the Indian seas. French authority says* that 4,200 English merchant vessels, valued at twenty-nine and a half million sterling, fell into the hands of the war-vessels and privateers of France, and that the greater part of these vessels were returning from India laden with rich cargoes; but the good Abbé fails to enumerate the French losses at the same period, by English and Dutch reprisals. Accepting his statements *cum grano salis*, there can be no doubt that the loss of the Company at sea was considerable, and tended much to cripple its resources.

Peace with France gave leisure for the better suppression of

* Abbé Raynal.

piracies, which were daily increasing in audacity. Captain Kidd, of evil notoriety, may, in 1698, be said to have ruled the Indian seas; he introduced considerable organization among the freebooters, thereby rendering them much more formidable, and told off their vessels into squadrons; the Company's old frigate, *Mocha*, being chosen as consort to his own ship. Besides inflicting enormous damage on the country trade, Kidd, among other prizes, seized two of the Company's and three ships belonging to the Dutch, all richly laden. He established fortified positions in several islands, especially in Madagascar, where he refreshed his crews and stored his ill-gotten gains.

The English, Dutch and French entered into an alliance against the marauders, charge of the Indian seas being entrusted to the English, while France was responsible for the Persian Gulf, and Holland for the Red Sea.

It was in the month of September of this year that the new Company, generally known as the English Company in contradistinction to the old or London Company, obtained its charter. It proved a serious rival to the existing association of merchants. There were now two companies sanctioned by Parliament (besides the Scotch Company sanctioned by the Parliament of Scotland, then a separate kingdom) in the place of one company chartered by royal authority.

The new Company was granted privileges in some respects greater than those enjoyed by the old Company; for instance, its principal officers were permitted to assume the title of King's Consuls, which gave them precedence over the officials of the old Company.

The principal factors of the new association arrived in India in 1699. They were Sir Nicolas Waite, appointed to the Malabar coast; Mr. Pitt* (a notorious interloper), appointed to the Coromandel; and Sir Edward Lyttelton, appointed to Bengal. The two

---

* Not to be confounded with Governor Pitt of Madras, who, according to Dr. Nolan, in his *History of the British Empire in India and the East*, was his cousin, and grandfather of the illustrious statesman, William Pitt, Earl of Chatham. Governor Pitt was also the possessor of the celebrated Pitt diamond.

former immediately claimed superiority over Sir John Gayer at Bombay, and Governor Pitt at Madras. Both these gentlemen and Mr. Colt, lately appointed President of the Old Company at Surat, in place of Mr. Annesley dismissed the service, naturally refused to recognize the so-called superior rank of the new comers. This opposition produced animosity if not actual hostilities, a state of affairs at once taken advantage of by their commercial rivals, the French and Dutch, and very seriously embarrassed the old Company which now found itself responsible in the eyes of the natives (who would not or could not understand that the two associations were trading in separate interests), for the acts of their rivals as well as those of the interlopers sailing under English colours, and the depredations of Kidd and his brother pirates.

It now becomes necessary to revert to affairs in Bengal.

It will be remembered that after the insulting and humiliating Firman of Aurungzebe, Mr. Charnock resumed the Presidentship at Chattanutee in 1690-91. Things appear to have progressed peacefully, and no event of importance from a military point of view occurred until the visit of the Governor and General Sir John Goldesborough, who arrived on a tour of inspection from Madras in 1694. He at once reduced the military establishment to the smallest proportions, and allowed a force of two sergeants, two corporals, and twenty men only. The pay of the rank and file was fixed at Rs. 4 (say eight shillings) a month, with clothing and rations, which Sir John considered to be " a salary more ample than the troops in any other establishment received."* When it is considered that this was the pay of Europeans, and was, presumably from the above quotation, higher than that of the men serving in Bombay or Madras, some idea may be formed of the extraordinary cheapness of the necessaries of life in those early days.

In spite of these wholesale reductions, defensive arrangements generally were strictly enjoined. An anticipated French attack about this period, and trouble with interlopers and pirates, was not

* Broome's *History of the Bengal Army.*

the only cause the Bengal President had for alarm, for a rebellion, the consequences of which it was impossible to foresee, had broken out in the Mogul's Bengal Provinces. The President again applied to the Nawab for permission to fortify his factory; and the latter, alarmed at the state of affairs, and probably anxious to enlist the sympathies of the English in the event of further difficulties, gave the President permission to " defend himself."*

This concession, somewhat vague in itself, was immediately taken advantage of, and masonry walls, with bastions and flanking defences were erected. Thus originated the defences of Calcutta.† At the same time the President ordered the enlistment of native soldiers for the protection of the Company's goods at outlying factories. These men were probably merely peons, or badly armed police, but the fact is mentioned as it is the first recorded mention of native troops in Bengal.

In 1699 Sir Edward Lyttelton, the President and Consul of the New Company, arrived in India and established his factory at Hoogly. He brought with him a company of troops as body-guard. He appears to have been at first conciliatory in his attitude towards the President of the old Company, but animosity from trade rivalry soon took the place of friendly relations.

The fortifications of Calcutta had now assumed some strength, and were named Fort William in honour of William III.

Aurungzebe was at this time very feeble, and disturbances were looked upon as certain for the possession of Delhi in the event of his demise. He, however, survived seven years, but the possibility of his early death gave the Company an excuse for again strengthening the Calcutta defences, where barracks were ordered to be erected for the accommodation of reinforcements expected from England. Orders were also reiterated to look to the defences of all outlying establishments.

---

* Bruce.
† The actual site of the present Calcutta was not acquired by the Company until the following year, when the villages of Govindpore and Kaleeghata (of which Calcutta is a corruption), were purchased from the Nawab for Rs. 16,000.

Space does not admit of any account being here given of the transactions of the new century (1700), so eventful in the annals of the East India Company. They will form the subject of a separate chapter. Suffice it to say that the close of the seventeenth century discovers the hostility between the rival companies to have been so great, that their mutual destruction was only prevented by the distracted state of the Mogul Power, on whose ashes the united companies were destined to raise a mighty empire.

CHAPTER IV.

PROGRESS OF THE ENGLISH IN INDIA FROM 1700 TO THE PEACE OF AIX-LA-CHAPELLE, 1748.

FORMER chapters have described briefly the proceedings of the East India Company from the first landing of its agents at Surat in the beginning of the seventeenth century to the end of 1699, and in the present chapter it is proposed to follow the Company's military enterprises during the first half of the eighteenth century. The various histories of India are strangely silent regarding this period, and what little is known relates chiefly to Bombay, and the factories of the West Coast.

In the course of nearly one hundred years, the Association of Merchants Adventurers had succeeded in firmly establishing their trade in India. This trade was protected at three fortified positions, namely, on the Island of Bombay, at Fort St. George, Madras; and at Fort William, Calcutta; besides minor positions, the most important of which was Fort St. David, south of Madras, and distant only a few miles from the French stronghold of Pondicherry.

Although of the three principal fortresses in the possession of the Company, Madras was the oldest, and of great value as the emporium of trade on the East Coast of India, it yielded to Bombay in point of strength and importance, which the latter owed to its insular position and to its magnificent harbour, whilst both Bombay and Madras had to acknowledge Fort William, Calcutta, their superior in commercial riches.

Bearing in mind these facts, it will be acknowledged that the seventeenth century had borne fruits, the value of which cannot be exaggerated, but the eighteenth century opened pregnant with events of still vaster importance—events which were destined hereafter to raise the Company from its position of peaceful merchants to that of conquerors, rulers of an immense territory, and to bestow on its members a power unparalleled in the history of mercantile adventure.

It will be remembered that in 1699 there were two chartered companies in India, the Old, or London, and the New, or English, and that the agents of the latter having consular powers, arrogated to themselves superior rank and authority over the servants of the old established company, whose original charter would expire in 1701, when the New Company entertained the hope that supreme authority in India would fall into their hands; these aspirations were, however, frustrated, for in 1700 an Act of Parliament was passed, whereby the Old, or London Company, was constituted a corporation, with possession of Bombay and St. Helena for ever.*

The bitter quarrels of the agents of the rival companies were the means of seriously impeding the trade of both, and were carried to such a pitch, that the London Company sent an order to its servants in India not to acknowledge the consular powers of the English Company, whose pretensions they declared should be rejected as illegal; whilst on the other hand the English Company proceeding to extremities, seized the goods of the London Company arriving in England, which produced an action at law, the case being tried by jury, and given in favour of the former, which decision raised the value of its stock to 130 per cent. The hatred of the rival agents was, according to Dr. Nolan,† carried to such an extent, that the rites of Christian burial were denied to the

---

* Bruce's *Annals*.
† The *History of the British Empire in India and the East*.

deceased members of the New Company by the authorities of the London Company, and but for the charity of the Armenian inhabitants of Surat, the dead Englishmen would have remained unburied.

About this period Mr. Davenant was sent from England to establish a Court of Admiralty in Bombay for the trial of pirates, of whom a Captain Gillam and nine others had already been brought to justice and executed in England. Harassed by constant disputes and petty jealousies, although a coalition between the rival companies had been agreed to in December 1700, Sir John Gayer, the able governor of the Old Company, desired to be relieved of his command, but was induced by the Board at home to continue in office, as hopes were entertained that his temperate conduct would go far to counteract the proceedings of Sir Nicolas Waite, the agent of the English Company at Surat, whose illegal acts were tending to widen the breach already existing between the Mogul Emperor and the European traders on account of repeated acts of piracy in the Indian seas, for which acts he demanded eighty lacs of rupees* in compensation from the London Company (which he alone recognized), whose agents were in no way responsible for the depredations complained of, or in a position to pay so heavy a price for piracies, which, they more than suspected, had been encouraged by Sir Nicolas Waite for the purpose of ruining his rivals in commerce.

In November 1700 Sir John Gayer visited Surat in hopes of deciding disputes between the rival agents (Sir Nicholas Waite and Mr. Colt), the former of whom had offered heavy bribes to the Mogul Governor to embarrass the trade of the Old Company. Sir John Gayer's efforts were, however, frustrated by the arrival, in December of the same year, of Sir William Norris, appointed by William III., on the part of the English Company, as Ambassador to the Mogul Court, who, on arrival at Surat, grossly insulted the London Company by striking the union flag on board Sir John Gayer's ship.

* About £800,000.

Sir William Norris had reached Masulipatam, on the Coromandel coast, as early as September 1699, but not being permitted to travel overland to the Mogul Court, *viâ* Golcondah, had been obliged to proceed by sea to Surat. He reached the Mogul camp at Panala, a hill fortress near Kholapur, in the Deccan, in April 1701, accompanied by a large retinue, consisting of 60 Europeans and 300 natives, his object being to obtain for the New Company a firman, granting trading rights and protection. After the usual delays of native courts, he was received with much state, and his negotiations were on the point of success, when news was received of the capture and pillage by English pirates of three Mogul ships on their voyage from Mecca with pilgrims. Aurungzebe immediately demanded a guarantee for the future safety of all Mogul shipping from pirates or other causes. Sir William Norris was in no position to sign any such guarantee, he having no power over the other trading nationalities or the pirates, who might at any moment molest the Mogul's fleets. Consequently, having declined to give any guarantee or promise of compensation, he was informed that " he knew his way back to England."* Considering this as a dismissal, he left the Emperor's camp in November 1701, but was forcibly detained at Brampore until a letter and sword for William III. had been delivered to his safe-keeping. He reached Surat in April 1702, and, having embarked for England, died at sea.

The negotiations entered into by Sir William Norris were subsequently rendered unnecessary by the partial union of the two companies in 1702. The cost of the mission is said to have been immense, a sum of three and a half lacs of rupees, or £35,000, having been expended in bribes alone, the total cost being computed at thirteen and a half lacs of rupees, or about £135,000.†

Shortly after this event, the Mogul Emperor pressing his demands on the London Company for payment of the compensation, mentioned in a preceding paragraph, without success, Sir Nicolas Waite seized two members of the London Company's

---

* Bruce's *Annals*. † *Ibid*.

Council and their Secretary at Surat, and handed them over to the Mogul's Governor with their hands tied; and, subsequently, Sir John Gayer himself and other servants of the Old Company were imprisoned at Surat, by order of the Mogul, for the same reason. At the same time Madras was blockaded; the agents at Patna and Rajmahal, in Bengal, were made prisoners, and Calcutta was threatened.

The probability of this action of the Great Mogul had been partly anticipated, and before his departure for Surat Sir John Gayer had again urged the strengthening of the Bombay defensive works, and local efforts had been made in this direction by additional fortifications at Mahim; but the garrison of Bombay and its outpost were reported as ridiculously weak. Fort St. George, Madras, had already been strengthened by native labour; the labourers being exempted from taxation during the progress of the works of defence; whilst the force at Calcutta was augmented by 120 Europeans, besides seamen from the vessels in harbour, who were engaged for the purpose of working additional guns; these precautions were everywhere the more necessary, the Mogul power not being the only one the Company had to dread at that moment, as the Muscat Arabs had become insolent at sea, and the Marathas, and a fleet of six Portuguese men-of-war, threatened the safety of Bombay.

Shortly after his confinement at Surat, Sir John Gayer was offered his release on the payment of 2½ lacs of rupees;* but justly considering that this payment would be a tacit acknowledgment that compensation was due to the Mogul for acts of piracy, the offer was refused, and the servants of the Old Company continued in captivity. In informing his masters of his decision, Sir John Gayer proposed that the Company's trade should be withdrawn wholly from Surat.

During Sir William Morris' embassy at Panala, the union of the London and English Companies was partially effected; the Old

---

* About £25,000.

Company offered to pay off the stock of the New Company at 5 per cent., when the rival associations were to join hands under the name of " the United Company of Merchants of England trading with the East Indies." The capital of the United Company was proposed at two millions sterling, and the dead stock was valued at £400,000 ; this occurred in January 1702, and the transaction was to be completed in seven years.*

Early in 1702 the Indian Seas were well rid of a pest that had infested them for years. Captain Kidd, the notorious pirate, was seized, and executed at Tilbury.

In March 1702 William III. died, and was succeeded by Queen Anne, shortly after whose accession war was declared with France. Orders were at once despatched to make Bombay and Fort St. George very strong, and to complete the wall round the town of Madras, whose agent demanded additional recruits and a powerful fleet, as he felt convinced that at the first sign of trouble the natives would join the French, who would blockade the coast with the aid of the Arab fleet. Fort William, Calcutta, had already been ordered to be built as a regular pentagon with bastions, and sufficiently increased so as to allow of the reception of all the establishments of out-factories in case of need.

In 1703, shortly after the partial union of the Companies, the New Company's factors, Sir Nicolas Waite at Surat, Sir Edward Lyttelton at Hoogly, and Mr. Pitt at Madras, were deprived of their consular titles, which had been such a source of grievance to the servants of the Old Company. Mr. Pitt, of the Old Company's service, was appointed Governor and President at Madras; and Mr. Pitt, of the New Company's service, was removed to Fort St. David,

---

* Mill's *History of British India*. At the Union of the Companies the following were the principal factories in possession of the Company : 1. *Bombay* had factories at Surat, Swally, Broach, Ahmedabad, Agra, Lucknow, Carwar, Tellicherry, Anjongo, Calicut. In Persia, at Gombroom, Shiraz, Ispahan, 2. *Madras* (Fort St. George) had factories at Gingee, Orixa, Cuddalore, Porto Novo, Petipolee, Masulipatam, Madapollam, Vizagapatam. In Sumatra (Fort York), Bencoloon, Indrapore, Sillebar. In China, Tonquin. 3. *Bengal* (Fort William) had factories at Ballasore, Chuttanutteo, Cossim-bazar, Dacca, Hoogly, Malda, Patna, Rajmahal ; besides the above, there were possessions in Java, Borneo, and Polo Condore

and made subordinate to Madras; he died soon after his appointment. Calcutta was ordered to be the head-quarters of the United Company in Bengal.

Pirates continued their depredations at sea to such an extent, that the Home Government sent two men-of-war, the *Severn* and *Scarborough,* to cruise about the coasts of India; the Marathas and the fleet of the Sidee added to these pests, and the safety of Bombay was constantly threatened; consequently additional Topasses were enlisted, together with sufficient seamen to man a small fleet destined to act against either.

To add to the troubles of Bombay, the Portuguese, who held possession of Salsette, obstructed the importations of necessary provisions, and the Mogul's army being at the moment engaged in the siege of Singhur, the Maratha hill fortress overlooking Poona, was within a few days' march of the coast. A plague broke out in the city, causing the death of hundreds of natives, and reducing the European garrison to 76 men; and a great storm about the same time caused infinite damage to the shipping.

The social condition of the Company's servants in India is described by contemporary writers as truly horrible, and Dr. Nolan, in his *History of the British Empire in India and the East,* says, Surat and Bombay were perfect hells, while, as regards the military discipline of the period, it appears to have existed in name only. Officers and men were rendered insubordinate by vexatious regulations and illiberal treatment. A Captain Carr, even insulted the Deputy-Governor of Bombay in his Council Chamber, and when asked for an explanation of his absence from two successive morning parades, treated his superior to "good mouth-filling oaths," and shook his fist in his face! Such was the general disorganization, that the Governor could not find a man whom he could trust with promotion to non-commissioned rank! The Company's ships were strongly suspected of piracies at sea; the chief factors acted as tyrants and oppressors to the military; the agents cheated the Company and the natives, and all were eager for plunder by sea and by land.

Sir John Gayer was still detained at Surat, and Fort St. George was threatened with an attack by the native powers. Its fortifications were pronounced as sufficient, but additional garrison was urgently needed, and permission was asked for and obtained to raise a troop of 60 horse; mortars were also demanded from home, as the shells terrified the natives; and Fort St. David was strengthened.

In 1703 the Marathas again besieged Surat, and demanded a quarter of the revenue as the price of peace.

In 1704 Sir John Gayer was nominated from home, Governor and General for the united interests of the Company, and the anxieties of his office quickly accumulated, as the Mogul again seized the Company's servants at Surat, and a Mogul army, under General Dond Khan, threatened Fort St. David, but retired on the payment of 300 pagodas. Dond Khan then made a demonstration towards Madras, which induced Mr. Pitt to complete the wall previously ordered round the town. A small detachment of recruits was at the same time received from England, but twelve out of sixteen of the men died soon after landing. The necessity for strong reinforcements was constantly urged, as the war with France was progressing and the French at Pondicherry were well supplied with men and material, their strength being numerically stronger than the garrisons of Forts St. George and St. David together. Application was made to Bencoleen Factory for 50 Buggesses, or Javanese soldiers, in exchange for whose services it was proposed to send an equal number of Topasses.

The progress of the war in Europe prevented the despatch of armed cruisers for the suppression of the pirates, who, in 1705, had it all their own way, and the same reason rendered the filling up of garrison vacancies by fresh troops almost impossible.

During this year the servants of the old associations became regularly engaged in the service of the United Company, and the appointment of Sir Edward Lyttelton, as President in Bengal, was revoked.

Sir John Gayer being still detained by the Mogul's Governor at

Surat, Sir Nicolas Waite represented himself as his successor, insinuating that Sir John Gayer had been superseded. There was a certain amount of truth in his statement, for he had been appointed by the United Company to *act* during Sir John Gayer's detention. Instead of using his powers for his rival's restoration to freedom, he instigated the native Governor to greater severity, and Sir John and the agent of the late London Company were still more closely confined. Sir Nicolas Waite was, in course of time, severely censured for his conduct, but those of the members of the Court of Directors who had lately belonged to the English Company secretly approved his proceedings.

Sir Nicolas Waite visited Bombay and reported the wall round the town as unfinished, and recommended that in future the garrison should consist of 200 Europeans, formed into 3 companies, and 50 gunners.

Forts St. George and St. David were again threatened by native forces, and recruits were urgently demanded, especially for the latter, which had been greatly increased, and a wall had been built round Cuddalore. The absolute necessity for powerful reinforcements was again and again urged, as the French at Pondicherry were now very strong, their supply of troops and recruits having been carried out with the utmost regularity.

It is interesting to note that Exchange fluctuated considerably even in those early days in India, for Mr. Pitt, the Madras President, was severely blamed for having paid certain debts due by the Company, at the rate of 10s. 6d. the pagoda, instead of 9s., the rate formerly current. The value of the pagoda in 1706 was reported as 11s.

The state of the garrison of Bombay at this time was sufficiently hopeless; with the Mogul army within three days' march of its walls, the number of European troops was but 40! The native Governor of Surat was also becoming more troublesome, and threatened the destruction of all the European nationalities trading at Surat. This conduct induced the Dutch factory to take action: the agent blockaded the harbour and seized Mogul shipping to the value of 2,000,000 of rupees. This energetic behaviour brought the native Governor to his senses.

The following year, the Marathas having defeated the Mogul army near Ahmedabad, again attacked Surat, and for nine days plundered the villages in the neighbourhood.*

With all these troubles, 8 recruits only were received in Bombay during 1706, and 3 companies of natives were disbanded for neglect of duty. Sir Nicolas Waite urged the necessity of despatching at once from England 200 Europeans at least, with a double proportion of officers. Madras was no better off, having been reinforced by 3 men only, at a moment when a French attack from Pondicherry was daily expected! At Fort William, Calcutta, 16 recruits had been received, raising the garrison to 129 men, of whom 66 were Europeans, besides the gunner and his crew in charge of the artillery.† By this time the whole of the stock of the united Companies in Bengal had been removed to Fort William. The smallness of the garrisons above mentioned proves how little aggressive were the agents of the Companies; indeed, so modest were the ideas emanating from Fort William regarding its garrison, that the President recommended that the troops for its protection and that of the valuable property of the Company should never be allowed to fall below the strength of 100 men, this very moderate force being considered the smallest number capable of efficiently working the defences in case of attack.

To increase the troubles and anxieties of the Agents in India, news was received of the massacre of the Company's servants at Pulo Condore, near Borneo, by Malays. Trade was everywhere almost at a standstill, that of the Malabar coast being ravaged by the Maratha pirates, of whom more will be said hereafter.

The year 1707 was of immense importance to the Company and to India generally, for it witnessed the death of the Mogul Emperor, Aurungzebe, which took place in February, and was the signal for civil war of the fiercest character.

---

* Bruce's *Annals.*
† Broome's *History of the Bengal Army.*

During the last few years of the reign of Aurungzebe, Hindostan had been fast going to ruin. From his death the fall of the Mogul Empire dates, and the history of modern India may be said to begin.

Although it is not the province of this work to enter into the politics of Hindostan, it may be mentioned, that Aurungzebe, whose imperial title was, by the way, Alumgheer, "the conqueror of the world," had at his death reached the advanced age of ninety-one. He had by will—some, especially Stewart, in his *History of Bengal*, say verbally—divided his Kingdom between his three sons: to Mahomed Muazim, the eldest, he assigned Cabul, and the provinces of Lahore and Multan; to Mahomed Azim, the second son, he gave the central portion of Hindostan; and to the youngest, Khan Bukhsch, the southern provinces, or Deccan.

Immediately after the death of Aurungzebe, Azim seized the royal camp and treasure, and having confirmed all the ministers of the late Emperor in their appointments, marched on Delhi to secure it against his elder brother Muazim, then known as Shah Alum. Muazim had, however, with the assistance of his son Azim Ooshan, the Governor of the Bengal Province, seized upon Agra, where was stored all the treasure of Shah Jehan, besides which, Azim Ooshan supplied him with 9 crores of rupees.* With Agra in his possession, and this great treasure, he raised a powerful army and utterly defeated Azim in an action near Agra in which the latter and his two sons were killed.

Muazim then assumed the title of Bahadur Shah, and mounted the throne of Delhi; his first act was to reward the fidelity of Azim Ooshan by nominating him Governor of Bengal, Behar and Orissa, to which he added the province of Allahabad; but being desirous of keeping him for a time near his person at court, he desired him to nominate Mooshad Cooly Khan, his deputy in Bengal and Orissa, and to appoint his own nominees to the charge

---

* Nine millions sterling; but Stewart values the crore at £1,250,000 in those days, which, if his calculation is correct, would make the value of the 9 crores, £11,250,000.

of Behar and Allahabad. This gave him the opportunity of rewarding two of his most faithful adherents, the brothers Syed Abdullah Khan and Syed Hussein Alli Khan, boasted descendants of the Prophet, and afterwards famous in the political history of Bengal ; to the former he entrusted the province of Allahabad, and to the latter Behar.

On the death of Bahadur Shah in 1712, Azim Ooshan seized the royal treasure, but was defeated and killed in a general action by the sons of the late Emperor, the elder of whom ascended the Mogul throne under the title of Jehandar Shah. Jehandar Shah was in turn defeated and put to death by Ferrokshere, son of Azim Ooshan in an action near Agra. Ferrokshere assumed the imperial title in January 1713.

In an article in the *Nineteenth Century*, May 1887, Sir W. W. Hunter, K.C.S.I., gives some interesting details of the pay of the Native troops in the service of Aurungzebe ; a trooper (one horse silladar) received about £2 10s. a month ; a four-horse silladar * about £16 ; a matchlock man £2 4s. ; a native artilleryman about £3 10s.; a European artilleryman (generally Portuguese) £22 a month ; whilst a commander of 5,000 horse received as much as £15,000 a year. This was high pay in a country where grain food cost about ½d. a pound, although it is said to have risen to 5d. a pound during Aurungzebe's southern campaign in 1705.

In 1707 Sir Nicolas Waite, who still continued in command at Bombay, Sir John Gayer not having up to that time obtained his release, applied for recruits from home, and for twelve commissioned officers, the three regular companies being kept up with the greatest difficulty. Military stores were also urgently needed.

In Madras affairs were even worse. Forts St. George and St. David were menaced by the neighbouring Nabobs, but a Maratha invasion of the Carnatic country, called off the armies. Four recruits only were received where 400 were required.

---

* A four-horse silladar is a cavalry soldier who furnishes four horses and accoutrements, which he lets out to troopers called Bagheers ; the system is, to a modified degree, still carried out in the Native cavalry of India.

Bengal was little affected by the civil war, and Calcutta, now regularly built and under the protection of the guns of Fort William, rapidly grew in importance; but its garrison was still weak, consisting of 125 men only, forty-six of whom were Europeans besides the "gunner and his crew." As the company grew in importance, one of the principal cares was the building of strong factories, capable of withstanding any attack from neighbouring Native powers, and training the Agents, factors, and other inhabitants for self-defence. In all these factories, many of them far distant from Bombay, Madras, and Calcutta, the three great strongholds, regular troops in small numbers were maintained. Whenever permission could be gained, or the apathy of the Native Governors rendered the permission unnecessary, the factories were regularly fortified. Towards the end of the year, however, the most stringent economy was enjoined, and many factories in Western India were withdrawn. Forts and factories were still maintained at Carwar, Tellicherry, Ajengo and Calicut, and factories at Surat, Swally, Broach, Ahmedabad and Cambay. Bombay, besides its principal fortress, Bombay Castle, was further defended by small forts at Worlee, Sion, Mazagon, Mahim, and Sewree.*

In 1708 the complete union of the Companies was carried out, when it was determined that the three Presidencies should be separate and distinct, each being absolute within its limits; the President of each, who was also Commander-in-Chief of the military forces, being responsible to the Directors at home. The forces now consisted of men sent as recruits direct from England, deserters from the French and Dutch factories, Portuguese or Topasses, and Native Sepoys. All the Europeans were dressed and armed after the military fashion of the day; but the Native troops, although drilled in the use of the musket, were chiefly armed with the sword, the spear and shield, wore their native dress, and were commanded by Native officers. It is not known what was the actual number of the Native troops at the period of the amalgamation of the

* Since those early days, Bombay has so extended that all these places form districts of the great city of to-day.

Companies, but Mill, in his *History of British India*, vol. ii., says, that in 1707 an effort was made to raise the Sepoys at Calcutta to 300 men.

An early act of the Court of Directors of the United Company was the dismissal from their service of Sir Nicholas Waite, a Mr. Aislabie being appointed in his place. About the same time Sahoji, the Maratha Chief, applied to the Governor of Bombay for arms, ammunition, money, and European troops, to aid him in his wars against the Mahometan powers which had divided the country between them on the death of Aurungzebe, and had cut themselves adrift from the rule of Khan Bukhsch, the son of the late Emperor, and King of Viziapore and Golcondah. This demand could not be complied with.*

Comparative security had so increased the numbers of the inhabitants of Bombay, that the population, in 1715, was computed by the Rev. Mr. Cobb, in his account of Bombay, at 16,000 souls.

During this year an important event occurred in Bengal; an embassy laden with costly presents to the value of £30,000 was sent to the Imperial Court at Delhi for the purpose of obtaining additional trading privileges from the Emperor Ferokshere.† The mission was completely successful, but it was two years before the patents were despatched, and the embassy returned to Calcutta. The success of the Ambassadors was due mainly to a lucky accident. Ferokshere was suffering from a disease that baffled the skill of the native physicians. Mr. Hamilton, the medical officer, attached to the embassy, was then called in, and succeeded in curing the Royal patient, who conferred on him large presents, and, as a further reward, granted the privileges asked for, which, among other things, included permission to purchase a district con-

* Bruce's *Annals.*

† Some of the presents are enumerated by Dr. Nolan, who quotes a letter from the Ambassadors dated Delhi, or Shah Jehanabad, July 8th, 1715.

" We prepared for our first presents, viz. one hundred gold mohurs; the table clock set with precious stones; the unicorn's horn; the gold scrutoire bought from Tendy Caun; the large piece of ambergris; the aflo and chelumcho manilla work; and the map of the world; these with the honorable the Governor's letter were presented, everyone holding something in his hand as usual."

taining thirty-seven towns and villages, and extending ten miles from Calcutta on either side of the river Hoogly. Thus for a second time, was the Company indebted to its medical officers for important grants, the reward of their skill and self-abnegation.*

In 1716 the low wall was completed round the town of Bombay; this was carried out by voluntary subscription of the inhabitants, who agreed to extra taxation for the completion of this most important work.

In 1717 the Ostend Company came into existence, much to the annoyance of the Court of Directors in England, who, from time to time, obtained Acts of Parliament prohibiting foreign adventure in India under severe penalties. The Ostend Company disappeared in 1726.

In the meanwhile the forces of the Company must have been on the increase, for in 1718 an Act of Parliament was obtained, authorizing the Company to seize the persons of all interlopers found within their limits, and send them to England, where they were to be subject to a penalty of £500 for each offence against the trading rights of the Association.†

Dr. Nolan from contemporary records describes the civil administration of the military department as the worst possible, robbery in every form being perpetrated upon the soldiers, British and Native, by purveyors and others with impunity. Yet they were not inactive, for in 1718 the Dessaree, a rajah whose territory bordered on Carwar, besieged that fort during a period of two months, when reinforcements were received from Bombay. He raised the siege and was afterwards defeated. As the native forces continued to hover about Carwar, a force of nearly 3,000 men was despatched from Bombay, which, according to Alexander Hamilton in his *New Account of the East Indies*, behaved disgracefully,

* The presents given to Hamilton by the Emperor were, as quoted by Dr. Nolan, as follows :—

"The King was pleased to give him in public, viz. a vest, a culgee set with precious stones, two diamond rings, an elephant, a horse, and 5,000 rupees, besides ordering, at the same time, all his small instruments to be made in gold, viz. gold buttons for coat, waistcoat, and breeches, set with jewels."

† Mill's *British India.*

retired in front of an inferior force, and only managed to escape under cover of the guns of the fort.*

The following year saw the English embroiled with the Portuguese, the subject of quarrel being the expulsion of intriguing Portuguese priests from Bombay, and ill treatment of English subjects at Thanna in retaliation. A small force from Bombay on two occasions shelled Bandora and exacted humble apologies from the Portuguese. The troops of the Company, moreover, found their work cut out for them in attempts to suppress the growing power of the Maratha pirates, who constantly threatened the trade of India in general, and Bombay in particular, by sea. A short description of these pirates may prove of interest, as their subsequent overthrow by the British in alliance with the Maratha nation was destined, in the future, to greatly increase the power of the latter, and pave the way to the Maratha wars and the downfall of the Maratha Kingdom.

As far back as the end of the seventeenth century, one Konoji Angria, Admiral of the Maratha fleet, a man of ability, and a courageous soldier, having declared himself independent of the Maratha power, seized the small island of Suvarndurg near the coast, south of Bombay, and built himself swift vessels and rowing boats capable of carrying fifty or sixty armed men, with which he attacked the rich merchant-ships trading along the coast. These piracies were first confined to the native traders, but the fame of his courage and success soon called many daring adventurers to his standard, and enabled him to undertake larger enterprises. His dominions extended from near Bombay to Goa, and penetrated some twenty to thirty miles inland, and included many of the strongholds fortified by the great Shivaji, the founder of the Maratha Empire.

As Angria grew in strength, being master of the coast-line, he attacked the flags of the Dutch, Portuguese, and other European

---

* It is but just to say that Hamilton's statements should be received with caution, as in his writings he is generally inimical to the Company and its servants, he, himself, having been a notorious "Interloper."

nations at sea, and took from the French the *Jupiter*, and at one time three Dutch ships, one of which carried an armament of fifty guns. At first the Government of Bombay viewed these depredations with satisfaction, as—being themselves powerful at sea, and well able to cope with the pirates—the attacks on the weaker European powers tended to throw the carrying trade into English bottoms; but when the thieves became sufficiently audacious to attack and actually capture the Company's ships *Derby* and *Restoration*, their forces were joined with those of Portugal for the overthrow of the Angrias.

In 1719 an attempt was made to seize Cavery, one of the many strongholds of the pirates, but the enterprize failed, probably through treachery. In 1720 the English ship *Charlotte*, was seized and taken as a prize to Gheria, which place it was determined to attack. Mr. Walter Brown was detailed to command the expedition; he reached Gheria without opposition. A number of the pirate ships were destroyed, and some of the pirates were killed; but finding the fortress too strong for the force at his command, Mr. Brown was obliged to re-embark his troops.*

In 1722 a combined expedition against the marauders proved abortive, and the Dutch, two years after, met with no better success. Perhaps one of the most memorable sea fights off the coast of India was the engagement of the English merchant ship *Morning Star* with a pirate fleet of five ships, manned by 2,000 men. The English fighting crew is said to have consisted of seventeen men only, although there were other men on board. With this small force, after being twice boarded, and three times set on fire, her captain and all the crew wounded, she managed to make good her escape to Bombay, leaving the pirates with heavy loss, entangled and in confusion after a final effort to board.

In 1728 Angria captured the Company's ship, *King William*, and held its commander a prisoner until a heavy ransom was paid.

---

* The records of the Royal Bombay Fusiliers say, that in 1720, a Troop of Dragoons was attached to the Infantry force, and was reduced and incorporated into the Grenadier Company in 1727.

Further attempts to reduce the power of Angria were made without effect. In 1730 a treaty was entered into with the Sawant Waré State for the purpose of holding the pirates in check. The death of Konoji Angria the same year did not improve matters; he was succeeded by his two sons, Sukaji and Sambaji; the former ruled in Colaba close to Bombay, and the latter held the Southern coast. Sukaji died in 1733, when Colaba fell into the hands of an illegitimate brother, Toolaji, who formed alliances, and rapidly grew in power. He attacked the Fort of Ageen, and this event led to a treaty between the English and the Sidee of Jingeera;* this proved as abortive as other attempts to suppress these pirate pests. This modern Angria even went so far as to seize the town of Rewaree on the River Pen, which flows into Bombay harbour, and thus commanded the communication between Bombay and the main land.†

A squadron from Bombay managed to intercept the pirate fleet in 1734; but the enemy escaped, owing to the irresolution of the British commanders, the result of a divided command. In 1736 some small successes were gained by Bombay troops in Canara. In 1738 operations were again undertaken against the Angrias under the command of Commodore Bagwell; again the pirates escaped, but suffered some damage from the fire of the English ships. The conduct of the Company's forces, naval and military, in these trying expeditions, always acting against vastly superior numbers, is said to have been excellent. Shortly after these events a fleet of four armed merchant ships of the Company were attacked by a powerful pirate squadron; the attack was repulsed, and is mentioned to show how daring these sea kings had become. Internal dissensions and family quarrels somewhat weakened the powers of the Angrias, and were taken advantage of by the Governor of Bombay, who despatched Captain Inchbird to endeavour to foment disputes between the brothers, and to gain by diplomacy

---

* One hundred Europeans and some Artillery under Capt. Inchbird were sent to strengthen his forces.

† Nolan's *History of the British Empire in India.*

that which Bombay had failed to secure by force of arms. Captain Inchbird, however, soon saw the necessity of again appealing to force, and seized many of the Angrias' ships, in spite of which the latter boldly established a foot-hold on the Island of Elephanta. Here the Angrias must be left for a while, and attention invited to another and more powerful section of the Marathas, the Rajahs of Satara, successors of the celebrated Shivaji.

In a former chapter it has been mentioned how, after the death of Shivaji, the power of the Rajahs of Satara was usurped by the Peshwa Balaji. He was succeeded by his son Bajirav, the most renowned of the Peshwas, who, by his conquests, greatly extended the Maratha Kingdom. In 1724 he conquered the fertile province of Guzerat, and ten years later he gained possession of that of Maldwa. In 1738 he threatened Delhi itself, and actually encamped under its walls, greatly to the alarm of the weak Mogul Emperor, Mahomed Shah, although he did not attempt an assault. The same year he inflicted a series of disasters on the Nizam, whom he forced into a humiliating peace, and among other demands obtained from him the sum of half a million sterling.

The conquests of a brother of Bajirav first attracted the attention of the Government of Bombay. This able commander had seized many of the isolated forts belonging to the Portuguese, and taken by assault the strong fortress of Thanna, on the Island of Salsette, close to Bombay, in spite of the vigorous defence of its European garrison. Greatly alarmed, the Governor and Council of Bombay wrote to Bengal expressing their fears that Bombay itself was in danger. This expectation was shared by the Portuguese Governor of Bassein, who, with some truth, pointed out that Bombay, already celebrated for its riches and prosperity, could not long hope for freedom from molestation, if the Marathas were permitted to establish a firm footing in Salsette. He also suggested an alliance against that power; this the Bombay Government declined, declaring itself neutral, notwithstanding which declaration 50 European troops were sent to the assistance of Bandora; these were, however, withdrawn when a Maratha attack was threatened, a half measure which occasioned future trouble.*

In 1739, Bassein, then in Portuguese possession, was invested; the Governor applied to Bombay for assistance, which, with the exception of 200 barrels of powder and 4,000 projectiles, was refused. An urgent appeal for money was then made; church plate, and even the guns of the fortress were offered as security, but sympathy alone was offered, and "a handsome excuse" sent.† Eventually Rs.15,000 was supplied, but this scanty assistance did not prevent the subsequent capitulation of the garrison (in May,) which was allowed to march away with all the honours of war, so greatly had the Marathas been impressed with the gallant defence. The losses of the Portuguese are said to have been 800 officers and men besides many of the civil inhabitants. The Maratha losses were estimated at 5,000 men at least. Shortly before this event the Portuguese defences at Bandora were destroyed to prevent them falling into the hands of the enemy; the fortress of Versova was also abandoned, and on the 14th of February, 1789, the Marathas were complete masters of Salsette.

These events caused serious anxiety at Bombay. The defences of the Presidency town of Western India were of the slightest; armed boats in the Thanna Creek or river, and in the harbour, formed the outer line, but the town wall (subscribed for by the native merchants among others) was but 11 feet in height, and quite unsuited to resist artillery-fire. With danger of invasion so near at hand, the further strengthening of the defences was taken into urgent consideration, and a petition dated July 1789 is extant, in which the Native merchants offer the Government the sum of Rs.30,000 to be expended in carrying a ditch round the town.‡

Up to this time the Deccan was quite unknown to the European masters of Bombay, and little or no communication, and certainly no commercial treaty had ever been entered into with the Maratha

---

* *Bombay State Papers*, Professor W. G. Forrest.
† *Ibid.*
‡ *Ibid*

Power, except that of Captain Keigwin, in 1684, which was noticed in a former chapter. Envoys were now sent to the Rajah at Poona, and to his commander-in-chief at Bassein, and the non-aggressive character, or indeed the humility, of the Company, and the arrogance of the Peshwa cannot be better set forth, than by quoting extracts from the instructions given by the President in Council to the Envoys, and the Peshwa's reply.

Captain Gordon, who was deputed to the Rajah at Poona and Satara, was instructed to point out "that although we prefer peace and good harmony with our neighbours, we are determined to defend ourselves in the best manner we are able in case we are attacked . . . . Our nation has never meddled with their religion, or had any view of conquest or extending our dominions in these parts, where trade is our sole business and end of residence." *

Captain Inchbird, who was sent to the Commander-in-Chief at the same time, was desired to say : " The real end of our occupation of Bombay is to circulate free trade round us . . . our force now maintained as well by land as sea, is merely intended for our preservation." †

These missions were both despatched in the middle of the year 1739.

The mission to the Rajah was resented by the Peshwa, the real power, who considered himself slighted, but it nevertheless produced the following from Shahu Rajah to Bajirav.

"The procedure or policy of the English is of merchants, and they have always carried it with sincerity to our nation, and their desire is to continue to observe the same in the future, that they may deserve my favour which I likewise very much and without fail desire." ‡

Bajirav's egotistical reply to Bombay was as follows, the tone of which speaks for itself :—

"The contentment which the victorious successes actually

---

* *Bombay State Papers*, Professor W. G. Forrest.
† *Ibid.*
‡ *Ibid.*

obtained by my arms has given your Excellency, and which you congratulate upon, is just. Your Excellency writes me that your island subsists by trade, to the great benefit and advantage of the neighbouring countries, and that in regard to the interest of the subject and the improvement of the good of the country I should concur with the favour of my assistance thereto, and my desire is that the subject should be advantaged, the trade be continued, and that our State have its interests and profits, and your Excellency will, I hope, with the continuance of your friendship, contribute to the above ends more and more every day."*

Twenty years later, as will be seen in its proper place, the tone of the British communications to the Maratha Empire was of a very different character. The result of these several diplomatic notes was the first commercial treaty (with the exception noticed above) dated July 1739, entered into between the English and the Marathas, by which the former gained permission to trade free in the Maratha dominions.

This period is also celebrated for the invasion of India by Thamas Cooly Khan, better known as Nadir Shah, who in 1737 had usurped the throne of Persia. In 1738 he invaded the Punjab at the head of an immense army, and entered Delhi after defeating the Imperial forces, which made but a feeble resistance, in March 1739. The ill-fated city was, two days after its capture, given over to the tender mercies of the veteran Persian army. Orme puts down the number of inhabitants massacred at one hundred thousand, and Beveridge says that "at the most moderate estimate the amount carried off in money, jewels, and plate could not have been less than 30 millions sterling." This included the famous Peacock throne. Nadir Shah remained at Delhi only fifty-six days, after which he returned to Kandahar, laden with treasure, to which, it is said, the Company's President in Bengal was forced to contribute. Mahomed Shah also ceded to the conqueror all his territories to the West of the Indus, which included Sind.

---

* *Bombay State Papers*, Professor W. G. Forrest.

PROGRESS OF THE ENGLISH IN INDIA.

The Mogul Empire was now fast tottering to its fall. Several provinces, including Bengal and Oude, had declared their independence. The Rohillas ruled a free state to the East, and within 100 miles of the walls of Delhi. The Sikhs, a semi-religious sect of adventurers, usurped authority in the West. Prior even to the Persian invasion, the Nizam-ul-Mulk, Regulator of the State, had succeeded in freeing himself from the Court of Delhi, and shared with the Marathas the sovereignty of Southern India.

At this period of Indian history, the Company's territorial possessions in Western India consisted of Bombay alone, together with the ground actually occupied by its outlying trading factories, the neighbouring islands of Salsette being in the hands of the Marathas, and that of Kuranja, immediately opposite Bombay, and between it and the mainland, being a stronghold of the Angria pirates.

These islands, together with those of Elephanta and Hog, in the harbour of Bombay, became the property of the Company by conquest as late as the year 1754, an account of which campaign will be found in a future paper.

In 1741 the Bombay Army began to assume some sort of organization, for in that year is found the first mention of a regular regiment as part of the garrison of the Castle. The *Bombay Quarterly* of 1857 states that the regiment was composed as follows:— 1 captain, 9 lieutenants, 15 ensigns, 1 surgeon, 2 sergeants-major, 82 sergeants, 82 corporals, 26 drummers, 319 European privates, 31 Mustees or half-castes, 900 Topasses, 27 servants, 2 Native paymasters, 1 interpreter, and 1 armourer; in all 1,499 men, divided into seven companies; the pay of this force being 10,314 rupees a month.* In addition to the above there were 700 Sepoys, but neither their arms nor dress were uniform. These latter were largely employed in attendance on the Civil Servants of the Company in the capacity of peons, orderlies, and frequently in more menial offices. Nolan says that it was not until 1752 that this class of

* Nolan.

men was struck off the military roll, and became a charge on the Civil Department of the Government.*

The European officers were, as a rule, uneducated, and of humble origin; they were badly paid, were looked down upon by the Civil Servants, and used curious expedients to fill their pockets, little caring whether the results obtained were contributed by the Native traders or by the European troops they themselves commanded. For instance, a document is extant in the Custom Department of Bombay, prohibiting the officer on guard from dealing in fish at the fort gate, he having obtained his stock in trade by confiscating the tenth fish from each of the Native fishermen licensed to sell that article of food within the precincts of the Fort.

In 1742 the European force in Bombay was augmented from Bengal by the arrival of one ensign, two sergeants, four corporals, and fourteen privates.†

The same year Bengal was invaded by the Marathas, and Hoogly sacked. The authorities at Calcutta now dug a ridiculous ditch as a means of defence against these powerful invaders, and more especially against their numerous cavalry. This ditch, as originally designed, was to have surrounded the town, a circumference of seven miles; but as the Marathas did not advance to Calcutta, the work was discontinued, three miles only being completed at great cost and labour. A more sensible defence was, however, organized in the enrolment, for the first time, of a militia, composed of all the European inhabitants without distinction, together with the Armenian traders, and a body of Lascars was

---

* It is to this day a common occurrence in Bombay to hear the Peon or Putta-wallah called "Sepoy." The writer has never heard the term used in Bengal, where the Peons are known as Putta-wallahs and Chuprassies; both derive their names from a badge they wear, formed of brass or silver, on which is inscribed the office or department to which they belong. These men are fairly paid and clothed, receive a small pension, and may be numbered by many thousands. A scheme has within the last few years been set on foot in all the Presidencies, to recruit this useful class of public servants, often employed in positions of trust, from among the Army pensioners.

† *East India United Service Journal*, January 1838.

enlisted to help work the guns under the "gunner and his crew."

The year 1743 is memorable in the annals of the East India Company for the appearance on the scene of Robert Clive, a young "writer," employed in the Madras Agency, who, in a few years, was destined to expel the French from India, and to reduce the Mogul Empire from its once lofty state to a mere dependency of the Company, his masters, and of whom the great minister, Pitt, spoke in the following terms:—"A heaven-born general, who, without being versed in military affairs, had surpassed all the officers of his time." *

Attention is now invited to events that were occurring in Southern India.

In 1744 war was declared between England and France; at this time Monsieur Dupleix † was the Governor of Pondicherry, the head-quarters of the French power in India, and Monsieur La Bourdonnais was Governor of Mauritius, and independent of India. The lands occupied by the English, at Madras, Fort St. David, Tellicherry, and other places on the coast, and by the French at Pondicherry, were within the territories of the Nabob of the Carnatic, Anwar-oo-deen, who, in 1744, had been appointed by the Nizam-ul-Mulk.

In 1745 a British squadron, under the command of Admiral Barnet, appeared in the Indian seas. Dupleix, alarmed for the safety of the French settlements, induced the Nabob to insist that the force on board the English ships should not seek hostilities within his territories. The Nabob accordingly desired the Company's agent at Madras to arrange that the fleet should confine itself to the sea, and not molest the French at Pondicherry, at the same time promising Madras and other English factories immunity from French aggression. Barnet, being a King's officer, was quite

---

* *Military Journal*, vol. i., 1799.

† Dupleix was appointed a member of the French Council at Pondicherry as early as 1720. La Bourdonnais distinguished himself at the siege of Mahé, near Calicut, in 1727, and became Governor of Mauritius and Bourbon in 1734 (Abbé Raynal).

independent of the Madras authorities, but, not wishing to involve the English and French in hostilities on land, complied with the agent's request, refrained from attacking Pondicherry, and left the coast.

In 1746 he returned and encountered the fleet of La Bourdonnais, which had been equipped at Mauritius. The French had the superiority in point of numbers, but this was counterbalanced by the weight of the English armament, its sailing qualities, and skill. After an indecisive action, the English squadron retired, leaving La Bourdonnais free; he at once determined to seize Madras.

The English agent now called on the Nabob to fulfil his promise, and prevent the French attack. The Nabob, although he did not actually encourage the French, took no active precautions to prevent hostilities, and on the 18th August the siege commenced.

Madras, at that period, was, as to-day, divided into White and Black Town; the former was surrounded by a slender wall, with four bastions and 4 light batteries. Black Town was undefended. The English mustered a force of about 300 men, of whom 200 only were soldiers of the garrison, a force which, without the co-operation of Barnet's fleet, which, for some unexplained reason, never appeared, was wholly inadequate to resist the powerful French squadron.

La Bourdonnais landed 1,100 Europeans, 500 Caffres, and 400 natives, disciplined after the European system, and to this overwhelming force, besides the guns of the fleet, Madras surrendered on the 10th September. The French loss was nil, that of the English four or five men only. La Bourdonnais accepted ransom for Madras (afterwards a fruitful source of dissension between him and Dupleix), and the President paid in cash £240,000, and gave hostages for the further payment of £200,000, to be paid in full by October 1749.* Besides the ransom, La Bourdonnais seized £185,000 in stores and material. On the day of the surrender of Madras, the Nabob sent an indignant message to Dupleix at Pon-

---

* Thornton's *History of the British Empire in India.*

dicherry, asking how the French had presumed to enter into open hostilities against his express command? Dupleix appeased the wrath of the Nabob by promising that, in the event of the French being permitted to retain, for the present, the advantage they had gained, Madras should eventually be restored to him. With usual native duplicity, the Nabob was satisfied with these promises, and rendered no assistance to the English in their necessity.

In October the French fleet off Madras suffered severely by a storm, and on the 12th of the same month La Bourdonnais, after quarrelling with Dupleix regarding the terms that had been offered to the English,* returned to his government in the Mauritius, leaving Madras in French occupation.

It is needless to say that Dupleix had no intention of handing over Madras to the Nabob, according to promise, so that potentate decided to wrest it from the French by force. This attempt was unsuccessful, his army being routed by the French under Mons. Paradis.

Dupleix, always dissatisfied with the terms offered to the English by La Bourdonnais, now determined to annul them; this perfidious action was promptly carried out, the property of the merchants was confiscated, and the Governor and leading men of the little community marched as prisoners to Pondicherry.

The English settlement of Fort St. David was situated twelve miles to the south of Pondicherry; its territory was more extensive than that of Madras, and its fort was, of its size, the best in India. The authority of Madras having collapsed, the responsibility of conducting the affairs of the Company on the Coromandel Coast devolved on the Agent at Fort St. David. The garrison, including refugees from Madras, consisted of 200 Europeans and 100 Topasses only; and the Agent, feeling no confidence in the friendship of the Nabob, which had been tendered and accepted

---

* The terms offered by La Bourdonnais were favourable to the English; these Dupleix refused to carry out, on the plea that La Bourdonnais had no right to offer them. La Bourdonnais, not being in a position to coerce Dupleix in this matter, left India in disgust.

after his defeat by the French at Madras, hired 2,000 Peons for the protection of the Company's goods at Cuddalore.

Dupleix now undertook the reduction of the English stronghold, and sent an expedition, under Mons. Bury, consisting of 1,700 men, mostly Europeans, 50 cavalry, and some companies of disciplined Caffre slaves left by La Bourdonnais, to carry out his designs. Bury, by want of caution, allowed himself to be surprised by the Nabob's army, and was forced to retreat with the loss of his baggage and military stores. An attack on Cuddalore was also unsuccessful. As the Nabob had now plainly shown his friendship for the English, and as his army remained in the vicinity of Fort St. David, Dupleix retaliated by invading the Nabob's territories, burning villages, and carrying away all the plunder he could lay hands on.*

The unaccountable non-appearance of the English fleet now raised suspicion in the mind of the Nabob, regarding the courage and power of the English; whereas the well-timed audacity of the French in carrying the war into his territories, served to raise them in his estimation; consequently he laid himself open to the intrigues of Dupleix, who, having been reinforced by the arrival of a small fleet from Acheen, easily detached him from the English by a payment of Rs. 50,000, and presents to the value of Rs. 100,000.†

At this time the garrison of Fort St. David was suffering from want of money and provisions, when, unfortunately, the hands of the French were further strengthened by the seizure of an English ship, laden with a valuable cargo and £60,000 in gold; but in February of the same year (1747), timely aid was rendered by the arrival of another vessel with treasure and a reinforcement of 20 Europeans.‡

In March, another attempt to reduce Fort St. David was undertaken by the French, under Paradis, which was on the point of success, when the English squadron, so long absent, appeared.

---

* Thornton. † *Ibid.* ‡ *Ibid.*

Paradis at once retreated to Pondicherry, fearing an English attack on that place by sea. Thus encouraged, and reinforced by 100 European troops, 150 marines, and 500 seamen from the fleet, the English determined on attacking Pondicherry. The attempt had no greater measure of success than that which attended the French attacks on Fort St. David.

In June 1747 the English were again reinforced by the arrival of 100 Europeans, 200 Topasses, and 100 Sepoys from Bombay, where a force of 2,000 natives had been enrolled in 1746;* 400 Sepoys were received from the settlement of Tellicherry, and during the course of the year an additional 150 Europeans arrived from England.†

In September the fleet visited Madras, and burnt the French ship *Neptune*; but in October, owing to the force of the monsoon, the Admiral was obliged to retire to Trincomalee on the coast of Ceylon, from which harbour he returned in January 1748.

In this year the Company decided to place their artillery on an efficient footing, to do away with the "gunner and his crew," and model it on the European system; the rules promulgated were applied to the three Presidencies, each of which was ordered to maintain one company of artillery with the following complement of officers and men:—

Rank.	Salary.
1 Second Captain	£150 a year.
1 Captain-Lieutenant and Director of Laboratory	100 „
1 First Lieutenant Fireworker	75 „
1 Second „ „	60 „
1 Ensign	50 „
4 Sergeants-Bombardiers	2s. 0d. a day.
4 Corporals „	1s. 6d. „
2 Drummers	1s. 0d. „
100 Gunners	1s. 0d. „

* This is the first mention of native troops being detached on service from their Presidency.
† Thornton.

A captain and chief engineer was appointed to command the three companies on a salary of £200 a year, and was to reside wherever his presence should be most desirable.* These salaries are witness to the cheap living of those days, the salary of the sub-lieutenant of cavalry and infantry of the present day being respectively Rs. 310 and Rs. 256 a month, or, taking them at the value of 2s. the rupee, £372 and £307 a year, against £200 a year received by the chief artillery officer of 1748!

In January 1748 Major Lawrence arrived at Fort St. David, having been appointed from home to command all the Company's forces in India; from this moment the Presidential Armies begin to assume some sort of organization, a Commander-in-Chief and an Inspector-General of Artillery in India having thus been established, and the artillery having been remodelled. Promotion was ordered to be by seniority, a rule not to be departed from without special sanction of the Governor of the Presidency. The European infantry does not appear, except in Bombay, to have been, up to this time, formed into battalions, but worked in separate companies; the Sepoys, although in some cases supplied with arms, and disciplined to some very small extent, being little better than peons, that is to say, an inferiorly armed police, destined, however, soon to assume bolder proportions, and take their share in many a hard-fought field. It is also worthy of remark that the force of Sepoys was commanded by their own officers, native gentlemen of position, and wore their own native costume. A Major Goodyear was appointed to command in Bombay, on a salary of £250 a year.

In the same year that witnessed the appointment of the first Commander-in-Chief, is recorded the first instance of disaffection among the Sepoys. The Mahometan commander of the native troops of Tellicherry was discovered to be in treacherous correspondence with Mons. Dupleix, and to have formed a plot by which the Sepoys under his command were to desert to the French. He

---

* Broome's *History of the Bengal Army*.

and ten other native officers were banished to the island of St. Helena, a lenient punishment for so gross a crime.*

In the month of June the French made another unsuccessful attempt to seize Cuddalore, from which they retreated, with some loss, to Pondicherry.

In August, Fort St. David was reinforced by a powerful squadron from England under Admiral Boscawen, when the siege of Pondicherry was decided upon. The force told off for this purpose consisted of—*King's Troops* from the fleet, 12 companies of 100 men each, 800 marines, and 80 artillerymen—*Company's Troops,* a European force† of 750 men including 300 Topasses, and 70 artillerymen. The Dutch factory at Negapatam supplied 120 Europeans, and Admiral Boscawen was prepared to land 1,000 seamen from the fleet. Two thousand Sepoys were also attached to the force; the latter were, however, of little use, and were used only to guard the camp. The Nabob promised a force of 2,000 horse which never joined.

The French force defending Pondicherry was 1,800 Europeans and 3,000 Sepoys.‡

As the rainy season was approaching, no time was to be lost; but several days were wasted in attacking the small fort of Ariancopang, defended by the French captain, Law. The first assault failed with the loss of 150 men; the second assault, also unsuccessful, was commanded by Lawrence in person, who was taken prisoner; but the French evacuated the works during the night, when the English took possession.

Discouraged by these failures, the English proceeded to invest Pondicherry, which they found strongly fortified; the information gained regarding the position and strength of the enemy was meagre and faulty; the Engineers were incapable; and the siege which commenced on the 30th August and terminated on the 30th September, was, in spite of the assistance received from the cannonade of the ships, an utter failure.

---

* Thornton.   † Thornton calls this force a battalion.   ‡ *Ibid.*

On the 6th October the English commenced their return march to Fort St. David, with a loss of 757 European infantry, 43 artillerymen, and 265 seamen; the Sepoys, for reasons already stated, suffered little. The French loss was estimated at 200 Europeans and 50 Natives.*

Monsieur Dupleix, naturally elated at his success, communicated it to all the surrounding Native Princes, and despatched messengers to the Mogul Court, receiving in return the congratulations of the Emperor. France had now reached a position of great power in India, when in November 1748 peace was declared in Europe, hostilities ceased, and Madras, considerably strengthened and improved, was restored to the Company on the 21st August 1749.

* Thornton.

CHAPTER V.

PROGRESS OF THE BRITISH ARMS IN INDIA FROM THE PEACE OF AIX-LA-CHAPELLE, 1748, TO THE FALL OF DUPLEIX, 1754.

In a former chapter, the first collision between the English and French forces in India was briefly touched upon, and it has been shown how in the beginning of the war the unaccountable disappearance of the British fleet, the superior activity of the French under Dupleix, the capture of Madras, and the successful defence of Pondicherry had greatly raised the *prestige* of France in the eyes of the natives, to the detriment of the importance of England.

Bombay had played but a small part in the war with France, and daily expected to share the fate of Madras at the hands of Labourdonnais. The fortifications were consequently strengthened, and the Governor and Council were much relieved to hear that a fleet, that had actually been sent against them, had been scattered by a storm.

In March 1748 they gained some small advantage over the French at Mahie, where they destroyed the ship *St. Louis*.

Bengal took no part whatever in the war, the French at Chandanagore being weak and consequently conciliatory.

With the peace of Aix-la-Chapelle, in November 1748, the sword was for a time sheathed; but the war had brought to India a European force on both sides, far greater than any that, up to that period, had been seen in Hindostan. Military ardour had been awakened, and the value of the native Sepoys as auxiliaries had, although not as yet fully developed, begun to be appreciated. The impossibility of supplying the fighting material entirely from Europe, rendered it absolutely necessary for each side to employ these native troops, so that at any rate, whatever their disadvantages, both parties suffered alike, and it still remained to be seen whether the English or French would be able to inculcate the greater degree of discipline in a body of men which, it was generally acknowledged, supplied excellent, if raw, material for a fighting force. If the Sepoys, by want of discipline, physique, and proper armament, were unable to cope with the better organized European troops, their value in guarding convoys and baggage from native attack, and saving their European companions-in-arms many of the arduous duties of an army in the field, could not be exaggerated; and for these, if not for higher reasons, they were henceforth to be largely employed.

The campaigns they were now to enter upon will be described in some detail, although a twice told tale, because they fully illustrate the successive steps by which the native Sepoy rose to the high position he now deservedly occupies.

With ambition aroused, and forces partly organized, one elated with recent success, the other burning under a sense of discomfiture if not actual defeat, it is not to be wondered that two nations, enemies from the earliest times, should be ready and willing to try conclusions by arms at the first opportunity, and should gladly seize any pretext for again drawing the sword. If with peace at home it was impossible to wage war abroad, some other means must be found; and the will being eager for the fray, the way was not long wanting.

Mahomed Shah, the Mogul Emperor, who had been forced, in 1739, to acknowledge the power of Persia under Nadir Shah, had again, in 1748, seen his dominions invaded from Kandahar by Ahmed Abdalli, the treasurer of Nadir Shah, at whose death, by assassination, the previous year, he had made himself master of all the provinces of Hindostan ceded by Mahomed Shah to the victorious Persians in 1739. Ahmed Abdalli was opposed by Ahmed Shah, the eldest son of the Mogul Emperor, with various success, but with the loss of the Vizier Kummir-ud-deen, a faithful and devoted servant of Mahomed, which event hastened the death of that weak monarch. He was succeeded without opposition by Ahmed Shah, who was acknowledged at Delhi in April 1748. Even before this event, the Mogul power was almost a thing of the past, and was daily decreasing; on all sides governors of provinces had declared themselves independent of Delhi, and had planted the seeds of civil war concerning the succession to their usurpations.

The ambitious mind of Dupleix saw in all these dissensions an easy road to power. Long continued commerce had greatly increased the cost, and consequently lessened the profits, of many of the trade commodities hitherto most valuable; besides which, to supply an increased demand, the fabric had greatly deteriorated. In all these circumstances the French Governor felt satisfied that trade was no longer worth prosecuting, and that intrigue, and possible conquest, was the quickest and easiest road to power and wealth, more becoming a great nation like France, than the humbler path of peaceful commerce. If the military power he already possessed could not be used against his legitimate enemies, the English, it might yet be employed with immense profit to help in the disputes of rival native potentates, and turn the scale in favour of the one that paid the best. His mind once made up, it did not take long to discover an object worthy of his assistance, but not before the authorities of Madras had taken the initiative in mixing themselves up with the complicated disputes of the neighbouring native states. To write even this short account of the armies of the Presidencies, without touching on the political events which actually caused their rise from a small ill-disciplined body of Europeans and badly-armed native peons, intended to guard walls surrounding valuable merchandize, to the proud position of the conquerors of Hindostan and exterminators of the French power in the great Peninsula of India, is impossible, so no excuse is needed for entering very briefly into the politics of India in so far as they affected the services of the Company's forces.

The events that induced the Government of Madras, which still had its head-quarters at Fort St. David, to use their newly-acquired and—now that the war with France was at an end—comparatively useless military forces, were briefly as follows, and are useful to these papers as showing the origin of the first expedition by land, undertaken against a native prince, and bringing prominently forward the services of Clive, the founder of the future military system of the Company in India.

As far back as 1670, the then ruler of Tanjore, being threatened with destruction by the more powerful prince of Trichinopoly, solicited the armed assistance of the Marathas under Shivaji. The assistance was granted, and the country saved from its foes only to fall a prey to the insatiable greed of the Maratha leader, who demanded so great a price as the reward of his succour, that the entire revenue of the kingdom was insufficient to defray the debt. Shivaji, therefore, seized on the Government, which he bestowed on one of his brothers, who, after a short reign, died, leaving three sons. Each of these in turn ruled for a short period and left sons, the Government finally falling to one Sanjohi, who in turn was deposed in favour of Pratop Sing.* Sanjohi presented himself to the authorities at Fort St. David, and sought their assistance for his restoration to the throne of Tanjore, assuring them that on the first signs of an advance, thousands would flock to his standard, and, agreeing to pay, as the price of European assistance, all the expenses of the expedition, which, if successful, was to be further rewarded with the cession to the Company of the fortress and territory of Devicotah.

Orme thus describes the country of Tanjore. "The Kingdom of Tanjore† extends about seventy miles from north to south, and about sixty miles from east to west. The River Coleroon bounds it to the north; the sea coast, running nearly north and south, to the east; to the south it is bounded partly by the country of Morawar; to the west, it is limited by the Kingdom of Trichino-

* Orme's *Military Transactions*.
† On the East coast of India, South of Madras.

poly and the country of Tondiman. The capital, bearing the same name (Tanjore) as the kingdom, lieth about thirty miles east from Trichinopoly."

The Government of Madras, little caring for the legitimacy of the title of Sanjohi, but eager for the possession of valuable territory capable of returning a handsome revenue, lent a willing ear to his appeal, and in the month of March 1749* despatched a force from Fort St. David, by land, under the command of Captain Cope, consisting of 430 Europeans and 1,000 Sepoys, with four field-pieces, to re-establish their *protégé* on the throne of which he had been deprived. The force had hardly taken the field, accompanied by Sanjohi, when it was overtaken by a hurricane, which destroyed its means of transport, and greatly damaged its military stores and camp equipage, so much so, that it was forced to march to and halt at Portonovo for the repair of damages.

But this was not the only loss it sustained; the fleet of Admiral Boscawen, on which it depended for the transport of many of its stores, was dispersed; two of the Company's ships were stranded between Cuddalore and Fort St. David; the Admiral's flag-ship, the *Namur*, 74 guns, sank with her crew of 750 men; and the *Apollo*, hospital ship, and the *Pembroke*, 60 guns, were also lost; a few only of the crews being saved from the disaster.† After repairing damages sustained, Cope's small force continued its march, but was disappointed in receiving no assistance from the natives of the country who were supposed to be eager to join the cause of Sanjohi. Cope, under these circumstances, determined to await reinforcements, which shortly afterwards arrived from Fort St. David, and consisted of an additional 100 Europeans and 500 Sepoys, raising his strength to 530 Europeans and 1,500 Sepoys, a not inconsiderable force for those days.

Thus strengthened, Cope advanced on the Fortress of Devicotah,

---

* At this period, the Madras European force consisted of seven companies of eighty-four officers and men, or 589 in all, and 500 volunteers formed into four companies, who were subsequently drafted into the original seven companies.— Wilson's *History of the Madras Army*.

† Orme's *Military Transactions*.

and crossing the northern arm of the Coleroon river, found himself within a mile of its walls, which he discovered to be eighteen feet high and defended with flanking bastions, or towers, and strongly held by the Tanjorine army. Being short of provisions, having but four small field-pieces wherewith to batter solid walls of brick and masonry, and seeing no prospect of being re-provisioned by the fleet, Cope determined to secure his retreat, the more so as his troops, brought face to face for the first time with the army of a native Prince, were struck with no small degree of fear when they compared the overwhelming numbers of the enemy with their own small force.

The retreat nearly proved disastrous; galled on each flank by hovering cavalry and a dropping musketry fire, a small river or tidal creek was reached, which, under the influence of the rising tide, was from seven to eight feet deep. On attempting to cross this impediment, the native coolies employed in transporting the light portion of the baggage, became panic-stricken, and, dashing into the swollen waters, perished to the number of 400 men, in sight of the army that could do little or nothing for their succour, except by dislodging the enemy from the banks with their musketry fire. With the ebb tide the stream was crossed without further opposition, and the weary troops, after a march of fifteen miles, during which they had maintained a running fight, halted for the night, and next day reached the shelter of Fort St. David.

The discomfiture of Captain Cope and his force, although it dismayed the Government at Fort St. David, did not determine it to abandon the cause of Sanjohi; another expedition on a somewhat larger scale was immediately organized, and placed under the command of Major Lawrence, the Commander-in-Chief, in person; nor was it altogether in the interest of Sanjohi that the new expedition was undertaken, but rather to wipe out the disgrace to the Company's arms, which had been forced to retire in the face of a purely native enemy; besides which, the Company's servants, always with an eye to business, were well aware that the country promised to them as the reward of success, was populated by many of the linen workers, the produce of whose looms was one of the principal manufactures valued by the Company in their trade transactions on the Coromandel Coast.

Again: the expedition and the treaty with Sanjohi had been undertaken without the authority of the Directors at home; and non-success, without any advantage to show, was certain to bring down on the authorities of Madras the resentment of their masters.

The difficulties of the land route experienced by Cope's expedition, determined the Government to despatch the force under Lawrence by sea; the mouth of the River Coleroon, although to a certain extent blocked by a sand-bar, affording an excellent harbour for the ships if once this impediment could be overcome. The force consisted of 800 Europeans,* 1,500 Sepoys, four battering cannon and six field-pieces; the Europeans and artillery were embarked on board three ships of war, and three of the Company's vessels; the Sepoys in large boats used by the natives in the Coromandel trade.†

In a few days the expeditionary force found itself close to Devicotah, but separated from that fortress by a branch of the river, on the further bank of which the siege guns (24 pounders) were erected in battery, which, by their well-sustained fire, soon rendered the breach practicable, when an immediate attack was determined on. The passage of the river was a matter of no small difficulty, and cost the British, from the fire of the enemy, thirty Europeans and fifty Sepoys.‡ Lieutenant Clive volunteered to lead the storming party, an offer gladly accepted by Lawrence, who placed confidence in that rising young soldier. The forlorn hope consisted of thirty-four Europeans and 700 Sepoys.§

Between Clive's little force and the breach lay a rivulet which had to be crossed, and four out of the thirty-four Europeans were

* Orme's *Military Transactions*.
† The European force included the detachment of the Bombay battalion. It is from this battalion, the nucleus of which dates as far back as 1668, that the late Bombay Fusiliers (now the 2nd Battalion Royal Dublin Fusiliers) claim their origin. (Vide *Records of the 103rd Royal Bombay Fusiliers*.)
‡ Orme's *Military Transactions*.
§ *Ibid*.

killed before the opposite bank was reached. Clive then advanced boldly, confident that the Sepoys were following close at the heels of the European attack. In this he was deceived; the Sepoys, a part of whom had already crossed the rivulet, waited until joined by the remainder of their companions, thus leaving a gap between themselves and the Europeans who had advanced with Clive. The enemy, perceiving their advantage, immediately detached a party of cavalry, which, skilfully handled, fell upon the rear of the advancing British, who, before they could turn and defend themselves, were cut down almost to a man, twenty-six of their number being killed. Clive himself escaped narrowly, and retired on the Sepoys whom he found drawn up on the rivulet bank hesitating to advance. Lawrence, seeing the ill success of Clive's attempt, immediately determined to attack with the whole of his European force, when the fortress was carried almost without opposition. A small force was at once detached under Captain Cope to take possession of the Pagoda of Atchaveram, five miles south-west of Devicotah, which was at once surrendered to the British by the attendant Brahmins who alone occupied it; but it was shortly afterwards attacked by a force of 5,000 Tanjorines, eager to avenge the insult offered to their gods by the seizure of their temple. The British, knowing that they could expect no mercy if obliged to surrender, fought with determined gallantry, and being sheltered behind the massive walls, suffered but little loss, and eventually drove off the enemy, who are said to have sacrificed 300 men in the attack, which they conducted with great determination.

The loss of Devicotah, and other troubles that loomed ahead, induced the King of Tanjore to offer terms; these, in spite of the promises made to the unfortunate Sanjohi, were promptly accepted by the Government of Madras; they included the cession to the Company of Devicotah, with as much land adjoining as would produce an annual revenue of 9,000 pagodas, and a pension of 4,000 rupees to Sanjohi, who, in future, was to reside in British territory, the Company's servants rendering themselves responsible for his future good conduct, by which means, from being the protectors of the unhappy prince, the Government of Madras became his jailors.*

Thus ended the first campaign conducted on land by the Company's forces against a native sovereign; it was brought to a close with but little glory to their arms, and immense discredit to their honour, being undertaken without proper inquiry into the claims of their *protégé*, whom, their object gained by the possession of Devicotah with its adjoining territory, they cast aside without hesitation and without excuse for their double dealing, more worthy of the natives against whom they fought, than of the great European Company which they represented.

In coming to terms with the Government of Madras, the King of Tanjore had other reasons than those dictated by the success of their arms; a new danger threatened, and one in which the French were partly involved through the ceaseless intrigues of M. Dupleix.

A few months after the death of the Mogul Emperor, Mahomed Shah, who, as before mentioned, had died in 1748, the Nizam-ul-Mulk, the ruler of the Deccan, passed away at the advanced age, according to Orme, of 104 years. His sons, rival claimants to the vacant Soubahship, now in reality a Government entirely independent of the Court of Delhi, at once took the field to contest the succession; Ghazi-oo-deen, the eldest son and heir to his father, was at that time at Delhi, filling an honourable and lucrative post near the person of Ahmed Shah; he at once obtained the confirmation of the Emperor to his title, which, although practically unnecessary, would at least strengthen his hand in the event of a disputed succession, especially as he was unable at once to join his Government and claim his rights. His younger brother, Nazir Jung, being on the spot, did not hesitate to seize the treasure of his father, and thus secure the favour of the army to his claims, whilst Muzzufer Jung, a favourite grandson

---

* After the fall of Devicotah, the Bombay detachment, under Captain Andrews, which had joined the Madras force in May 1747, returned to Bombay in March 1751, reduced to less than one-third of its original strength, which had been 300 Europeans and 115 Sepoys.—*Records of the Royal Bombay Fusiliers.*

of the late Nizam, prepared to dispute his uncle's pretensions. Both claimants used all the means known to Eastern diplomacy to secure the disputed succession, and at last appealed to arms.

After various vicissitudes, into which it is not necessary for the purpose of these papers to enter, the cause of Muzzufer Jung became almost hopeless, when he was unexpectedly joined by a powerful auxiliary in the person of Chandah Sahib, a soldier of fortune, who, in 1741, had been made prisoner by the Marathas at the siege of Trichinopoly, and who had ever since remained a captive in their hands. This man, at the instigation of M. Dupleix, and on payment of 700,000 rupees, was not only set at liberty by those intrepid mountaineers, but was supplied with the nucleus of an army, in the shape of 3,000 of their own men.*

During his imprisonment, the family of Chandah Sahib had lived in Pondicherry, and had been kindly and honourably treated by Dupleix, who saw in the captive chief a probable tool for his own aggrandizement. On his release, Chandah Sahib at once entertained the idea of entering into competition with Anwar-oo-deen Khan, the then unpopular ruler of Arcot, and in this ambitious scheme he was supported by Dupleix. Consequently he joined forces with Muzzufer Jung, who promised, if successful, to confirm him in the coveted Nabobship.

The combined forces, numbering 40,000 men, joined by a powerful reinforcement of 400 Europeans and 2,000 Sepoys under Mons. d'Auteuil and Bussy from Pondicherry, at once attacked Anwar-oo-deen, who, trusting to his own strength, had neither asked for nor obtained the assistance of the English Company, and who, with an army of 12,000 cavalry and 8,000 infantry, had taken up a strong position, with his right flank resting on the hill fortress of Amboor. The fight which took place on the 23rd July 1749, was obstinate, and was brought to a conclusion favourable to Chandah Sahib and Muzzufer Jung by the gallantry of the French detachment which, although twice repulsed, eventually carried the position, leaving Anwar-oo-deen dead on the field.

* Orme's *Military Transactions*.

Arcot was immediately seized, when Chandah Sahib assumed the title and dignity of Nabob, and Muzzufer Jung was proclaimed Nizam; after which, to gratify the vanity of Dupleix, the new rulers proceeded in triumph to Pondicherry, the guests and allies of France.

In the meanwhile, Mahomed Ali, a younger son of the unfortunate Anwar-oo-deen—the elder, Maphuze Khan, having been made prisoner during the late action—had effected his escape from the fatal field of Amboor, and had shut himself up in the strong fortress of Trichinopoly, and, claiming the title of Nabob of Arcot in succession to his father, implored the assistance of the British, who at first, probably disheartened by the losses in the recent Tanjore campaign, refused all aid, but subsequently adopted the half measure of sending him a detachment of 120 Europeans, thereby committing themselves to the interests of Mahomed Ali. At the same time, when they saw themselves thus virtually on the verge of another war with the French in India, the Government of Madras, at Fort St. David, agreed to the departure of Boscawen with his fleet from the Indian seas, on the 21st October 1749, although it is said that the Admiral offered to remain and render any assistance in his power,* and left a detachment of 300 Europeans to strengthen the garrison.† It is needless to say that these weak proceedings suited well the schemes of Dupleix.

At the conclusion of the ceremonials at Pondicherry, Dupleix urgently besought his new allies, Muzzufer Jung and Chandah Sahib, to march on Trichinopoly and crush Mahomed Ali before assistance could reach him; this they promised to do, but at once altered their designs and determined on a campaign against Tanjore, which promised little military difficulty, and a presumed certainty of replenishing their almost empty treasury.

This, indeed, was the threatened danger, before alluded to, that had caused the ruler of Tanjore to come to terms with the British after the fall of Devicotah.

* Beveridge's *History of India.*
† Orme's *Military Transactions.*

The King of Tanjore at once opened negotiations with his new enemies with all the skill of a native diplomatist, and protracted them until such time as he heard of the arrival of Nazir Jung (Muzzufer Jung's rival for the Soubahship of the Deccan) in the vicinity of Arcot; but in spite of negotiations and delays, the city was bombarded by the French, who, notwithstanding the fire of the Tanjorine guns, manned and fired by twenty Europeans from Fort St. David, assaulted and carried one of the gates.

This success so terrified the King that he came to terms with Chandah Sahib, and agreed to pay him seven lacs of rupees as Nabob of Arcot; to distribute two lacs of rupees amongst the French troops, and to cede to France eighty-one villages: but the news of the approach of Nazir Jung induced Muzzufer Jung to break up his camp and retire to Pondicherry. These events occurred in December 1749.

Nazir Jung had, as a matter of course, espoused the cause of Mahomed Ali, and was now at the head of an army estimated at 300,000 men, of whom 30,000 were Maratha horse under Morari-Rav, 800 guns and 1,300 elephants, and a body of 6,000 cavalry, commanded by Mahomed Ali in person. The timely arrival of Nazir Jung on the scene, at length determined the wavering policy of the authorities at Fort St. David, who now made up their minds to cast in their lot with Nazir Jung and Mahomed Ali, and despatched 600 Europeans under Major Lawrence, who reached their camp on the 22nd March 1750.*

Thus were established in Southern India two factions striving for the inheritance of the Nizam-ul-Mulk and the Nabobship of Arcot, each assisted by a European power; that is to say, Nazir Jung and Mahomed Ali,† supported by the arms of the English Company and led by Lawrence; and Muzzufer Jung and Chandah

---

* At this time the Directors at home, finding difficulty in obtaining recruits, offered a bounty of £10 to each time-expired man who would re-enlist for five years.

† This prince made over the town and lands of Mylapore, better known as St. Thomas, in the immediate vicinity of Fort St. George, to the Company in October 1749.—Wilson's *History of the Madras Army*.

Sahib, assisted by a French force under the command of d'Auteuil, and guided by the powerful and scheming brain of Dupleix.

It must not be supposed that the ambitious schemes of Dupleix met with the entire approval and sanction of the Government of France. The French King well knew the power of England, and fully recognized that, if forced into a war, the English would be slow to lay down their arms and sheath the sword; but Dupleix artfully represented that the British were bent on territorial aggrandizement in India, as shown by their recent action at Tanjore, and declared it absolutely necessary for France to counteract their rapidly growing influence, by intrigue and negotiations with the rival native potentates; consequently, whilst pretending amenability to the King and Company, he prepared to contest with England the sovereignty of Southern India.

To oppose the formidable host of Nazir Jung before alluded to, the French under d'Auteuil took up a strong position from which it would have been difficult to dislodge them, even with the assistance of Lawrence and his small British detachment, had it not been for a mutiny among the French officers, thirteen of whom threw up their commissions whilst in face of the enemy. Thus discouraged, d'Auteuil retired on Pondicherry, and Muzzufer Jung looking upon his cause as now desperate, determined to give up his person to Nazir Jung on the promise of personal safety. He was, as a matter of course, imprisoned in spite of promises, his army attacked, defeated, and scattered. Chandah Sahib, more fortunate than his weak partner in the game for power, escaped with the French to Pondicherry.

On the arrival of the disorganized French troops at the capital, Dupleix, undaunted at the reverse suffered by his arms, at once opened negotiations with Nazir Jung, whose shifty behaviour with the French ambassadors so disgusted Lawrence that he, with his small following, at once retired to Fort St. David.

In the meanwhile the French were active. In July 1750, with a force of 200 Europeans and 300 Sepoys, they seized on Masulipatam and Travadi. The latter place being within the territory claimed by Mahomed Ali, its seizure was at once resented by the British. Mahomed Ali advanced with an army of 20,000 men assisted by 400 Europeans and 1,500 Sepoys from Fort St. David, under Captain Cope, burning to recover his lost possessions. With characteristic want of energy and decision, Mahomed Ali declined to force a general action, whereupon Cope was recalled, and the French, taking advantage of the absence of the only portion of the adversary's force at all formidable, attacked Mahomed Ali on the 15th August, and completely crushed his undisciplined rabble, Mahomed himself escaping to Arcot with difficulty, where he, with a few followers, joined Nazir Jung.

Dupleix continued to pursue his advantage, and despatched a small force under the command of Mons. d'Auteuil and Bussy to seize the celebrated fortress of Gingee, situated eighty-five miles south-west of Madras, and thirty-five miles north-west of Pondicherry. This fortress, which in the hands of the gallant Marathas had for years withstood the entire force of the Mogul Empire under Aurungzebe, fell to the French with but little resistance.

Nazir Jung, at length awakened by this important conquest from a life of debauchery at Arcot, prepared to take the field. Beveridge enumerates his army at 60,000 foot, 45,000 horse, 700 elephants, and 360 pieces of cannon; it was, moreover, swelled to utter unwieldiness by camp-followers, the whole numbering probably not less than 300,000 souls.

In spite of numbers, being without assistance from the English, his heart seems to have failed him, for he despatched two trusted officers to negotiate with Dupleix, who now became imperious and extravagant in his demands. The huge army, after marching a few miles in many days, found itself overtaken by the periodical rains, and encamped between two rivers in full flood and impassable. Retreat being impossible, the Nizam granted all the demands of the French despot, but procrastination had sealed his fate. Some time before, Dupleix had managed to gain over a powerful party in the Nizam's camp, consisting of chiefs, principally Patans, who were, or pretended to be, indignant at the treatment of the prisoner Muzzufer Jung; with their aid he proposed to seize the person of Nazir Jung and place his own puppet on the throne.

Monsieur de la Touche, then in command at Gingee was, with a force of 800 Europeans and 300 Sepoys, ordered to attack the Nizam's camp whenever the traitors declared themselves ready. Early in October 1750 he set out from Gingee. Nazir Jung, who but the day before had signed the treaty with Dupleix, could not believe in a French attack, and thinking that the firing was probably some local disturbance, went in person to quell it; he was slain in his howdah by the Chief of Kurpa, one of the discontents.

On the death of Nazir Jung, the prisoner Muzzufer Jung was at once liberated by the French and proclaimed Nizam. He proceeded in triumph to Pondicherry, where he was received by Dupleix with considerable state, and duly installed in power. His treasure is said to have amounted to two million sterling in cash, and half a million in jewels. Half the treasure was to be the price of the Patan treachery, but, of course, was not forthcoming when demanded. Dupleix was made governor of all the provinces from the Kristna River to Cape Comorin, and further dignified with the command of 7,000 horse, an oriental compliment of high honour; he moreover received £200,000 in cash and some fine jewels as a personal reward, whilst £50,000 were distributed to the gallant conquerors of Gingee, and another like sum was paid to the French for the expenses of the late campaign; they also received considerable territory round Pondicherry and Masulipatam.

The reign of Muzzufer Jung was destined to be of short continuance. In January 1751 he left Pondicherry, accompanied by Monsieur Bussy in command of a French force of 300 Europeans and 2,000 Sepoys for Golconda, the discontented Patan chiefs, with their respective followings, forming a portion of his escort, and determined on his overthrow. A camp quarrel soon gave a pretext for open hostilities; a battle ensued, in which the mutinous chiefs, with the aid of Bussy's detachment, were easily defeated, but the victory cost Muzzufer Jung his life; in the heat of the action he was killed by the Chief of Kurnool in a personal encounter.

It is curious to note that the rival claimants for the Soubahship of the Deccan, Nazir Jung and Muzzufer Jung, both met their death by the treachery of the same Patan chiefs, thus showing how little reliance could be placed on the alliance and good faith of the petty states dependent on great native powers.

Monsieur Bussy, although dismayed at the untimely end of the *protégé* of France, lost not a moment in supplying his place. The choice fell on Salabut Jung, the eldest of three brothers of Nazir Jung, who were then prisoners in the camp. He at once confirmed all the grants made to the French by his predecessor, when his elevation to the vacant throne received the sanction of the now all-powerful Dupleix.

In the meanwhile the affairs of Mahomed Ali were becoming desperate; he had already lost the province of Madura, and was now threatened with a siege of Trichinopoly, his only remaining stronghold, by Chandah Sahib, his rival for the Nabobship of the Carnatic, who, contrary to the advice of Dupleix, was at the moment employing his forces in the reduction of Arcot.

Mahomed Ali, fearing the worst, had offered to resign to the French, an offer which was strongly resented by the Government at Fort St. David, who pointed out to him the madness of so suicidal a policy, which would in reality make France supreme in Southern India.

An arrangement by which Chandah Sahib should be acknowledged Nabob of the Carnatic, and Mahomed Ali retain Trichinopoly, was proposed to the French by the hesitating English, and by them refused with scornful insolence. A fresh alliance was then suggested and gladly accepted by Mahomed, who was at once furnished with a detachment of 280 Europeans and 300 Sepoys under the command of Captain Cope.

The opening act of the new campaign was an attempt by Cope to reconquer Madura with a force of 150 Europeans, 600 Native Cavalry, 5,000 foot belonging to Mahomed Ali's army, one old battering gun of native manufacture, and three small field-pieces. The attempt was gallantly sustained but failed, and Cope returned to Trichinopoly.

In April 1751, a force of mixed nationalities, consisting of 500 Europeans, of whom 50 were cavalry, 100 Caffres, including natives of Mauritius and Madagascar, and 1,000 Sepoys, with 8 field-pieces, under Captain Gingens,* was assembled with the object of attacking Chandah Sahib, who was at the time encamped near the fortress of Volconda with 12,000 horse, 3,000 Sepoys, and a strong French battalion. Captain Gingens having been reinforced with 100 Europeans by Captain Cope, and 2,000 horse and 2,000 foot by Mahomed Ali, the latter under the command of his brother, prepared for a general action on June 20th; his intention was frustrated by the disgraceful behaviour of his European detachment, which, consisting largely of foreigners, deserters from the French and Dutch, declined to face the enemy, and actually fled in terror and confusion in spite of the jeers and openly expressed disdain of the native allies.

Under these distressing circumstances retreat became a matter of imperative necessity, and was conducted in confusion until safety was gained under the walls of Trichinopoly. The whole country was now abandoned to Chandah Sahib, who, pursuing leisurely, and possessing himself of the island of Seringham (formed by the Rivers Cauvery and Coleroon), which important and easily defended position the English evacuated without firing a shot, encamped with the main body of his victorious force to the east of Trichinopoly, the walls of which were defended by Cope and 100 Europeans, whilst Mahomed Ali occupied a position to the south, and Gingens, with his disheartened troops, encamped west of the city and under its walls.

Clive is said to have been present at the disgraceful affair of Volconda, when he did his best, by personal gallantry, to give

* There was a spirit of discontent among the officers of this force, who had applied for additional allowances whilst in the field, and had been refused. The whole correspondence is published by Wilson in his *History of the Madras Army*.

confidence to the panic-stricken troops, after which he appears to have returned to Fort St. David where the Government were in despair at the non-success of their arms.

Mr. Saunders, the then Governor, a cool and shrewd-headed man, plainly saw the danger of the situation, and that if Trichinopoly fell to Chandah Sahib and the French, the ambitious designs of Dupleix would be almost accomplished and France be supreme in Southern India. He at once determined to despatch Mr. Pigot, a member of his council, with 80 Europeans, 300 Sepoys, and a large convoy of military stores as a reinforcement. Clive, who had left the military service, accompanied this force in his civil capacity of commissary. The convoy and its guard reached Trichinopoly in safety after crossing a difficult country, and defeating a hostile chief encountered *en route*.

Clive again returned to Fort St. David, and again set out with a small reinforcement for Trichinopoly (he having at this period rejoined the army with the rank of captain), which was augmented from Devicotah by a detachment of 100 Europeans, 50 Sepoys, and one field-piece under Captain Clarke, who, as senior officer, assumed command. This detachment reached Trichinopoly in safety after a successful skirmish with a French force near to the fortress of Coilady.

In August 1751, Clive, who once more found himself at headquarters, represented to the Government of Fort St. David, that, in spite of all efforts to reinforce Trichinopoly, the army of Chandah Sahib out-numbered that of Mahomed Ali by ten to one, and that the French mustered 900 Europeans at least against the English 600. Clive now proposed a diversion by an attack on Arcot, at the time garrisoned by about 1,000 of the enemy. His suggestion was adopted and every effort made to collect a sufficient force, so much so, indeed, that the garrison of Madras was reduced to 50 men and that of Fort St. David to 100. In spite of all efforts, 200 Europeans, 300 Sepoys, and 8 field-pieces, were all that could be mustered, and with this insignificant following Clive set out for what ultimately proved a career of victory.

On the 31st of August 1751, Clive entered Arcot in triumph almost without resistance, and at once prepared for the siege which he anticipated and hoped for, as a relief to Trichinopoly. His first act after fully provisioning his position, was to follow up his recent success by an attack on the late garrison, which he discovered encamped some few miles from Arcot; twice he engaged the enemy with partial success, and finally dispersed them in a night attack made on the 14th of September. About this time he was strengthened by the timely arrival of two 18-pounder guns, a few Sepoys, and a convoy of military stores.

On September 23, the anticipated siege by Chandah Sahib commenced. He had drafted 4,000* men from Trichinopoly, and was assisted by 150 French, and 3,000 Natives, collected in the neighbourhood, the whole under the command of his son Rajah Sahib. With this force the city was at once occupied, Clive retaining the Fort. Determined to dislodge the enemy from the streets, a sortie of the garrison was ordered; it failed with serious loss of European life, 14 men being killed, and 16 wounded, besides Clive's only artillery officer.

The garrison, already greatly reduced by sickness, was quite insufficient for the defence of the walls, which in many places were in a ruinous condition, and were of considerable extent; 126 Europeans and 200 Sepoys only, could be mustered against the army of the besiegers, numbering quite 10,000, of which, however, only 150 Europeans and 2,000 Sepoys could be called really effective, the remainder being composed of a rabble of undisciplined peons and irregular cavalry. Both stratagem and hard fighting were resorted to; but still the siege continued, and on the 24th October, the French opened a battery, which soon dismounted one of Clive's valued eighteen-pounders, and made a practicable breach in the rotting walls. In retaliation, the British with immense exertion, succeeded in mounting a big gun, throwing a ball of 72 lbs. weight, said to have been transported to Arcot by Aurungzebe, with 1,000 yoke of oxen: it burst at the fourth discharge. An attempt to reinforce Arcot

* Monsieur Law in his narrative says 5,280 men.

with 100 Europeans and 200 Sepoys from Fort St. David, under the command of Lieutenant Innes failed, when Clive opened negotiations with the Maratha Chief, Morari Rav, who, with a force of 6,000 men, was hanging about the neighbourhood in the hope of plunder. He accepted the proposed alliance in terms flattering to the bravery of the English, and soon after arrived in the vicinity of Rajah Sahib's camp, where he captured a convoy of ammunition.

In the meanwhile, further efforts were being made to relieve Clive. Major Kilpatrick was despatched from Madras to assume command of Lieutenant Innes' detachment, which was further reinforced. Rajah Sahib, made aware of Kilpatrick's advance, and of the Maratha alliance, determined on an assault before assistance could arrive, and on the 14th November delivered his attack at two breaches, which, according to Mill, were defended by eighty Europeans and 120 Sepoys only, the behaviour of both being beyond praise. The attack failed with the loss to the enemy of at least 400 men, and, during the night, Rajah Sahib raised the siege, which had lasted for fifty days. The following evening Kilpatrick arrived with his detachment, too late to share in the glory of the gallant defence.

Clive did not lose a moment in following up his hard-won success. Leaving Kilpatrick with a slender garrison in Arcot, he, with 200 Europeans, 700 Sepoys, and three field-pieces, marched on Timery, which at once surrendered. He next, with the assistance of 600 Maratha Horse, engaged the French, numbering 300 Europeans, 2,000 Native Cavalry, and 2,500 Sepoys, at Arnee, gaining a complete victory, and capturing Rajah Sahib's treasure chest containing a lac of rupees.

His next feat was the siege and capture of Conjiveram from the French, after which, having re-garrisoned Arcot with 200 Europeans and 500 Sepoys, he returned in triumph to Fort St. David.

No sooner had the British force retired, than Rajah Sahib began to ravage the country, an act that induced the Government to again assemble a small force which was again entrusted to Clive; it consisted of 380 Europeans, 1,800 Sepoys, and six field-pieces, a formidable force in the hands of so skilful a commander. The enemy, numerically stronger, could not be induced to risk an engagement, their object being the capture of Arcot by treachery, they having gained over two native officers of the garrison, who had promised to open the gates to a night attack; the plot was discovered in time and, happily, failed.

Shortly after this event Clive came up with the enemy, vastly superior in artillery, at Coverypauk; by a skilful rear attack he captured the French guns, and gained a decisive victory, the fruits of which, besides many French prisoners, being nine field-pieces, three mortars, and the surrender of the fort of Coverypauk. In this action, Clive was assisted by a detachment from Bengal, consisting of a full company of European infantry, made up to 100 men, who afterwards went to Trichinopoly, and were finally incorporated into the Madras army.*

Being recalled to Fort St. David, Clive, *en route*, had the immense satisfaction of destroying the town of Dupleix-Futteh-abad, where the French Governor had erected a monument with a pompous inscription in French, Persian, and several native languages commemorating the treacherous victory over the unfortunate Nazir Jung in 1750.

The conduct and success of Clive in his late campaign, was highly appreciated and commended by the Government of Fort St. David, and his fame spread throughout southern India, so much so, indeed, that friends and foes shared the belief in his invincibility; even the hardy Marathas expressed their opinion that Clive's soldiers, European and native, were made of sterner stuff than those with whom they had before come in contact. Clive appears to have possessed an extraordinary power over the native mind, which enabled him to gain, not only the admiration and respect of his troops, but also their affection. Ever ready to face the greatest danger in person, he was, on account of many hair-breadth escapes, looked upon as invulnerable, and they willingly entered into the most desperate enterprises under his command, feeling confident

* Broome.

that his boldness in attack and skill in all the tricks of war would assuredly lead to ultimate victory.

Meanwhile, the siege of Trichinopoly by Chandah Sahib and his French allies continued. The latter had a battery of two eighteen-pounder guns 2,000 yards from the city walls on the east side, in position at a place known as the French rock; another on the banks of the Cauvery, which had taken the form of a regular redoubt; and a third on the Island of Seringham which commanded the north gate of the city. These batteries were badly placed and did but little damage. The cannonade returned by the British was little more effective than that of the French, much time and ammunition being expended in a useless artillery duel.

Mahomed Ali casting about for fresh allies soon discovered one in the Regent of Mysore (the reigning Rajah being at the time an infant) who, in October 1751, furnished a few men. His contingent was followed by an army of 8,000 foot and 12,000 cavalry, 4,000 of whom were Marathas, under Morari Rav, who had formerly assisted Clive.

The Mysorean alliance was soon followed by one with Tanjore, which State supplied 3,000 horse and 2,000 foot. The affairs of Mahomed Ali now assumed a more healthy complexion, but the inactivity of the English garrison gave cause for discontent to their native allies, and it was strongly suspected that the Maratha chief was actually in secret correspondence with the French.

But reinforcements were on their way from Fort St. David, which were eventually to turn the tide of success completely to the side of the British. Major Lawrence, lately returned from leave in England, was advancing in command of 400 Europeans, 1,100 Sepoys, and eight field-pieces, assisted by Clive, who was his second in command. In March 1752 he reached the outskirts of Trichinopoly, where, after a narrow escape of being surrounded by the French under Monsieur Law, he was joined by a detachment of 200 Europeans and 400 Sepoys from the garrison, and a great part of Mahomed Ali's army.

The French attempt to oppose the advance was defeated with loss, and the victory would have been more decisive if the native allies had played their proper part in the action; but they remained inactive and sulky under Morari Rav and other Chiefs. The advent of Lawrence and Clive, his recent defeat, and another attack delivered the same night, although only partly successful, so disheartened Monsieur Law that he retreated to the Island of Seringham, in spite of the protests of Chandah Sahib, and so, with the loss of a great portion of his baggage and military stores, virtually raised the siege.

Their recent successes determined the British to try bolder measures. It was decided that the army should be divided into two divisions, under command of Lawrence and Clive, to act south of the Cauvery and north of the Coleroon respectively. The risk of the enterprise was fully recognized, for it was well understood that the defeat of one division would probably result in the destruction of both; but with characteristic courage the risk was accepted.*

In April 1752, Clive set out with 400 Europeans, 700 Sepoys, 3,000 Marathas, 1,000 Tanjorine horse, two heavy guns, and six field-pieces, and took possession of the pagodas of Samiaveram on the high road to Ootatoor. In the meanwhile, a reinforcement, under Monsieur d'Auteuil, consisting of 120 Europeans and 500 Sepoys, was advancing to the assistance of Monsieur Law, who detached a small force to attack Samiaveram. This attack, in reality a surprise, was for a time successful, and Clive had more than one narrow escape for his life, but the French were ultimately defeated; with the loss of 700 Sepoys and some European prisoners.

The immediate effect of this defeat of Law's detachment, was to induce d'Auteuil to retreat to Volconda, after abandoning the greater part of his stores, where he shortly after surrendered to Clive. These reverses had such an effect on the native allies that they gradually deserted the cause of Chandah Sahib, and

* In 1752, the number of disciplined Sepoys considered sufficient for the protection of the Madras possessions by the Court of Directors was 1,300 men, *i.e.* Fort St. George 600, Fort St. David 600, Fort Davi Cotah 100, all over that number were maintained at the cost of Mahomed Ali. Wilson says they could not have numbered less than 3,000, including the garrisons of Trichinopoly and Arcot.

2,000 horse, and 1,500 of the best Sepoys joined the victorious British.

Monsieur Law, blockaded in Seringham, depending as it did on d'Auteuil's force entirely for stores and assistance, surrendered to Lawrence on the 31st May 1752, whereby 820 French, and 2,000 Sepoys became prisoners of war, and 11 heavy guns, mostly eighteen-pounders, 20 field-pieces, 4 mortars, 2 petards, with plentiful ammunition, and some stores fell into the hands of the victors, and Chandah Sahib was delivered over to the tender mercies of the Commander of the Tanjorine army, who, in spite of promises of protection, put him to death; thus ended the career of a brave soldier, and Mahomed Ali at last reigned, for the moment, supreme as Nabob of the Carnatic without a rival to his claims.

Before these successes could bear fruit, a fresh difficulty arose. It appeared that Mahomed Ali in soliciting the alliance of Mysore and the Marathas, had promised to both, as the reward for their aid, the territory and city of Trichinopoly, of course without the smallest intention of keeping faith with either; nor, indeed, would the British have allowed him to pursue such a course, although, according to Dr. Nolan, Lawrence, foreseeing difficulties in the future, advised that the claims of the chiefs should be considered, or that their persons should be seized. A hollow truce was patched up with the discontented and deluded allies, and a force of 200 Europeans and 1,500 Sepoys was left as a garrison to prevent the city falling a prey to the Mysoreans or Marathas. The necessity for this course greatly weakened the little army needed to complete the subjugation of the Carnatic, which, in June 1752, set out, consisting of 500 Europeans, 2,000 Sepoys, and 2,000 Native Horse to undertake a task needing far greater numbers for its proper completion.

Volconda immediately acknowledged Mahomed Ali; but Lawrence, whose health had broken down in consequence of the hardships and anxieties he had undergone, was forced to give up the command of the force, which he left to Captain Gingens, and retired to Fort St. David for rest. At this time the Government was again established at Madras.

Dupleix, disheartened but not confounded by recent French reverses and the death of Chandah Sahib, soon began new intrigues which were greatly assisted by the tortuous policy adopted by Mahomed Ali in his behaviour to the Chiefs of Mysore and of the Marathas, who had sworn vengeance. These latter now received encouragement from the crafty Dupleix, who, at the same time, proclaimed a son of Chandah Sahib, Nabob of the Carnatic. He had, moreover, another puppet to his hand, Salabut Jung, who, it will be remembered, had succeeded Muzzufer Jung as Nizam, and was, at the moment, at Golconda under the protection of Monsieur Bussy, who, in command of a French battalion and 5,000 Sepoys, did with him what he pleased. The pay of these men had for various reasons been in arrears, when Bussy insisted on territory, the annual revenue of which was (including that of Masulipatam already ceded) £855,000, being made over to the French Company to ensure regular payment of the troops. This territory consisted of the Northern Circars, and, with Masulipatam, made the French masters of the coast for 600 miles, from Medapilly to Juggernaut, and virtual masters of the Deccan.*

Gazi-oo-deen, who was the true heir to the Nizamship, and who had been formally acknowledged by the Mogul Emperor, now appeared on the scene, and had reached Aurungabad, where he had entered into an alliance with the Maratha Peshwa, Balaji, who, however, did not hesitate to desert him and join the cause of Salabut Jung, on the promise of substantial reward. The death of Gazi-oo-deen removed the only obstacle to the succession of the French *protégé*. Here, then, Dupleix had two trump cards, Salabut Jung and the discontented chiefs of Mysore and of the Marathas, which, if properly played, might yet win the game, the stake of which was the supreme power in Southern India, and the expulsion of the British.

Affairs were in the state described, when Mahomed Ali, puffed

* Mill's *History of India*.

up with recent successes, due entirely to his English allies, determined, against the advice of Lawrence, to wrest Gingee from the French. Assisted by a British force of 200 Europeans and 1,150 Sepoys, he set out; the expedition failed utterly, and the French gained a decisive victory at, or near, Vicravandi. A hasty retreat now ensued, which brought the disheartened and defeated troops into the territory of Fort St. David ; when Dupleix immediately reinforced the much elated French, who, mustering 450 Europeans, 1,150 Sepoys, and a body of 500 well-disciplined horse, appeared under the walls of the Fort.

The previous year, the Company at home finding the greatest difficulty in procuring recruits, had ordered the purchase of 600 slaves in Madagascar, and had raised two companies of Swiss troops, numbering 8 officers and 231 men; these had arrived in Madras in 1752.* The Government of Madras, anticipating trouble at Fort St. David, after the defeat of the expedition against Gingee, despatched one company of Swiss by sea to reinforce the garrison ; the whole company was captured by a French cruiser, and taken as prisoners of war to Pondicherry. Curiously enough, this was deemed by the Government of Madras a gross violation of treaties, because the two nations were not at war, but only fought on the sides of rival native claimants for power. Dupleix naturally replied, that he saw no difference between his seizing the company of Swiss troops at sea, and the English making prisoners of Monsieur Law's force at Seringham.

Lawrence was at once despatched by land with the remaining Swiss company to the relief of Fort St. David, where he found himself in command of 400 Europeans, 1,700 Sepoys, and 4,000 of Mahomed Ali's troops. In August 1752, he, by stratagem, induced the French to accept battle at Bahoor, when the latter were completely routed, not, however, before the French and English had met at the point of the bayonet, when the former gave way. In this action the French commander, Monsieur de Kerjean, 13 officers and 100 Europeans were made prisoners, a

* Wilson's *History of the Madras Army.*

great number being killed. The French, besides, lost all their artillery, ammunition and stores; the English loss was 4 officers, and 78 men killed out of the European force of 400.*

In September 1752 Clive was again in the field with 200 European recruits, and 500 almost undisciplined Sepoys. In the face of the greatest difficulties he reduced the fortress of Covelong and Chingleput, after which exploits a visit to England, to recruit his shattered health, became absolutely necessary, after an absence of ten years. Dr. Nolan well says that he had indeed done much for his country in India; during the absence of his friend Lawrence, he had redeemed the military reputation of England, and humbled Dupleix, and he and Lawrence together had saved the Carnatic from becoming practically a French province, at least for a time.

Whilst Madras was taking the most active part in the affairs of Hindostan, Bombay was by no means idle or without its troubles; the force at Tillicherry, consisting of some 600 Europeans, of whom 500 were Topasses, had encountered the French in September 1751, and had been compelled to retreat. The small town of Edicote was, however, successfully defended against repeated attacks, and the enemy repulsed with heavy loss. A dispute having arisen between the Mogul's representative, the Siddee, and the Bombay authorities, regarding the appointment of a native Governor for Surat, a force of 200 Europeans and 400 Sepoys was sent there to support the British Agent. Affairs came to a crisis in March 1752, when the Siddee commenced hostilities by opening his batteries on some of the British Sepoys: a European detachment took the battery, and spiked the guns. On the 3rd April the British took the initiative, and attacked the Siddee's forces with a detachment of 60 Europeans and some Sepoys; the latter behaved badly, and the Europeans had to retreat with a loss of 37 men.† After repeated attacks on the Siddee's defences, the British became themselves besieged in their factory, and, being

---

* Wilson's *History of the Madras Army.*
† *Records of the Royal Bombay Fusiliers.*

betrayed by one Cojah Latiff, who admitted the enemy into the factory, had to accept the mediation of the Dutch, who, early in April, secured a cessation of arms, and on the 14th of the same month peace was concluded. In the same year 160 European recruits were received besides a company of Swiss.*

To return to Madras; the shifty behaviour of Mahomed Ali regarding the reward to be paid to the Mysorean and Maratha Chiefs, for their assistance in the late campaign, had induced them to cast aside their late ally and to enter into open alliance with Dupleix. A desultory war was the consequence, which, with French assistance, was waged at Trichinopoly, in which the small English garrison under Captain Dalton suffered some losses, and was after a time reduced to famine owing to the scandalous behaviour of a brother of Mahomed Ali, who, representing the Nabob, had sold for his own advantage the stores on which the garrison depended for their support. The city was fortunately relieved in May 1753 by the indefatigable Lawrence, who, however, found himself surrounded with difficulties and dangers.

The French, again established on the Island of Seringham, mustered 450 Europeans, 1,500 Sepoys, 3,500 Maratha horse, 8,000 Mysore horse, and 16,000 Mysore infantry. Against this formidable array, Lawrence could only show 500 Europeans and 2,000 Sepoys. With a force so superior in numbers, the French and their Allies, under the command of Monsieur Astruc, were able to cut off all communication with the surrounding country, and consequently provisions again began to fail. A brilliant affair with the French on the 26th of June, at the Golden Rock, near Trichinopoly, in which Lawrence, with 300 Europeans and 500 Sepoys, defeated nearly the whole of the allied forces, enabled him to supply the city with food for two months' consumption, and to himself march away with the greater portion of his force into the

---

* *Records of the Bombay European Fusiliers,* and letter from the Surat Agent to the Government of Bombay. The Swiss mentioned were probably artillery; for Wilson says that in 1752 the Directors revised the artillery establishment, and that in 1753 Madras received a whole company of artillery, composed entirely of foreigners, principally Swiss.

territories of the Chief of Tanjore, for the purpose of securing the assistance of that potentate. In this, he was fortunately successful, and again advanced on Trichinopoly, reinforced by 170 Europeans and 300 Sepoys from Madras, besides 3,000 Tanjore horse and 2,000 foot. On the 9th August was fought a battle near the Golden and Sugar Loaf Rocks, three miles south-west of Trichinopoly, which position, strongly held by a French detachment, was stormed by a party of the English grenadiers assisted by 800 Sepoys, whilst Lawrence, with the remainder of his force, attacked the main body of the French under Monsieur Brenier, who had superseded Monsieur Astruc, utterly routed them and forced them back to Seringham.

Both forces now received considerable reinforcements; 237 Europeans and 300 Sepoys joined Lawrence, whilst Brenier received no less than 400 Europeans, 2,000 Sepoys, six field-pieces, and a large body of Maratha horse.* Undeterred by disparity of numbers, Lawrence, on the 21st September, again attacked the enemy, strongly posted at the Sugar Loaf Rock, three miles southeast of the city. His victory was again complete, Monsieur Astruc and 100 Europeans being taken prisoners. The French lost, besides 100 Europeans killed, 11 pieces of cannon and all their tents, ammunition, and baggage; the English loss being 40 Europeans killed and wounded. Lawrence followed up his success by storming the fort of Weycondah, situated three miles west of Trichinopoly, on the 23rd September. On this occasion the British sepoys particularly distinguished themselves, meeting those of the French at the point of the bayonet, slaughtering many, and obliging 400 to lay down their arms; and in October, a small force of 40 Europeans and 200 Sepoys, sent from Madras, defeated, near Trepatti, a disturber of Mahomed Ali's government at the head of 5,000 men. After these severe reverses the French remained inactive at Seringham, and permitted Trichinopoly to be re-provisioned with stores sufficient for six months, when Lawrence, not wishing to consume what he looked upon as his

* Beveridge's *History of the British Empire in India.*

supply for the rainy season, removed the greater portion of his little army to the Tanjore frontier where supplies were plentiful.

In November, the French, having received a further reinforcement of 300 Europeans, 200 Topasses, and 1,000 Sepoys, determined, during the absence of Lawrence, to take the city by assault. On the 27th of the month the attempt was made, and, owing to the English neglecting the duty of guarding the point of attack, very nearly proved successful, but was ultimately repulsed with slaughter, the French losing 400 Europeans; that is to say, 1 officer and 40 Europeans killed, and 8 officers and 364 Europeans taken prisoners.*

In January 1754, Dupleix and the Government of Madras opened negotiations for peace; the terms demanded by both sides were such as to render the negotiations useless, and the war was continued with aggravated intensity.

In spite of continued reverses, the ever active Dupleix managed to supply his forces at Seringham with ample reinforcements. Early in 1754 the French mustered 600 Europeans, 400 Topasses, 6,000 Sepoys, and 30,000 Maratha and Mysore troops, against 600 Europeans and 1,800 Sepoys commanded by Lawrence, the Chief of Tanjore having failed to supply any further contingent in aid of the cause of Mahomed Ali. The great disparity of number was, in February, increased in favour of the French, by a serious disaster that befell the English, who lost to the enemy a convoy valued at many thousands of pounds, laden with necessaries for the garrison, and guarded by 8 officers and 180 Europeans and 800 Sepoys, all of whom were killed, wounded, or taken prisoners. These numbers included 100 of the European grenadiers, whose courage, as Orme remarks, had decided every victory—a loss soon after partly repaired by the authorities of Madras, who sent 180 men to replace the victims of the former fight. It is worthy of notice that the Mysore horse that took part in this action on the side of the French, were commanded by Hyder Ali, who was destined

---

* Wilson-Orme puts the killed at 37 and the prisoners at 360.

for years afterwards to be a thorn in the side of the English in India.

During the many actions that had taken place at and near Trichinopoly, the loss of English officers in proportion to the men had been so great, that the Government of Madras found itself obliged to apply to Bombay for officers, several of whom volunteered and did good service.*

In the month of May 1754, Captain Calliaud in command of 120 Europeans, 500 Sepoys, and 2 field-pieces, having started from Trichinopoly to meet and escort a convoy of provisions, unexpectedly found himself opposed by a French force of 250 Europeans, 1,000 Sepoys, and 4,000 Mysore horse; an action ensued, both sides being strongly reinforced, until the French, numbering 700 Europeans, 5,000 Sepoys, 50 European cavalry, and 10,000 Mysore horse, gave way before a little force of 360 Europeans, 11 troopers, and 1,500 Sepoys, commanded by Lawrence.† The victory was decisive, and the French, who had lost 200 Europeans and 300 Sepoys, fled with precipitation to their old position on the Island of Seringham. The English loss was also severe, being 72 Europeans killed, 6 officers and 48 men wounded, and 150 Sepoys killed and wounded.

During the same month the Government of Madras, at its wits' end for troops, applied to Bombay for every man that could be spared. The call was promptly responded to, and two companies of the European battalion, 100 Topasses from Tellicherry, and fifty from Anjengs, besides Sepoys, divided into three companies, were collected, in all 750 men. Of this number, 450 were men of the European regiment, viz.:—200 English, 100 Swiss, and 150 Topasses. The force sailed in May, and arrived at Madras in June. On the 7th June, 400 of the Bombay Europeans, that is to say, half European and half Topasses, in battalion, with 300 Sepoys‡ proceeded with Maphuze Khan, Mahomed Ali's brother, to Tanjore;

---
* *Records of the Royal Bombay Fusiliers.*
† Orme's *Military Transactions*
‡ Orme says 500 Sepoys.

but as he delayed his advance, Captain Forbes, who commanded the force, left him and joined Lawrence, who was encamped at Atchempettah on the 15th August.* Thus reinforced, Lawrence commanded 1,200 Europeans (including Topasses), 3,000 Sepoys, and fourteen field-pieces, with which once again to try conclusions with the French on the plains of Trichinopoly.†

On the 16th of August 1754, the French army under Monsieur Maisin, numbering 900 Europeans, 4,000 Sepoys and 10,000 Mysore cavalry, the latter under Hyder Ali, was found in position eastward of Trichinopoly; an indecisive action ensued in which the French lost 100 Europeans and the English eight only, as well as some carts which formed a portion of the baggage train; these latter fell to Hyder Ali and the Mysore horse, who thought more of plunder than of taking part in a regular action. The enemy, who again retired to Seringham, could not be induced to risk another battle, and the rains setting in, hostilities ceased; the British going into cantonments at the Warriore pagodas.‡ On 11th October a cessation of arms was proclaimed between the French and English, which was to last three months; and Lawrence, having returned to Madras, had the gratification of receiving a Royal Commission of Lieut.-Colonel, and a sword set with diamonds, valued at £750, as an acknowledgment of his field services. Clive was similarly rewarded.

The events that led to the cessation of arms were as follows:— The recent campaigns had not only been costly in men and money but had greatly affected trade; moreover, the British Government, at peace with France in Europe, interfered, and opened negotiations with deputies sent from Paris; so little progress was however made, that, to bring matters to a speedy conclusion, the Home Government prepared for war and equipped a strong squadron for India. This spirited action had the desired effect and determined the policy of France; terms were at once arranged and a French

---

* *Records of the Royal Bombay Fusiliers.*
† Orme's *Military Transactions.*
‡ *Records of the Royal Bombay Fusiliers*

Commissary appointed to carry out the settlement of affairs in India.

Aware that Dupleix would be most unwilling to act in the cause of peace, and that he would probably throw every impediment in the way of an adjustment of difficulties, the French Government and Company decided to supersede him. Monsieur Godehen was accordingly appointed in his place, and arrived at Pondicherry in August 1754, armed with supreme power to act for France in India.

Mill, in his *History of India*, defends the conduct of Dupleix during his Governorship; there can be no doubt that he was a man of immense ability, ambitious for his own and his country's glory, and that sooner than face war in Europe he was sacrificed by the French Government. There can also be no doubt that, by his schemes and intrigues, he involved the French in a sanguinary war, with all the consequent sacrifice of life and vast expenditure.

Monsieur Godehen brought with him from France 1,200 troops, of whom, according to Orme, 600 were Hussars, a powerful reinforcement that might have turned the scale of events in his favour, had it not been for the arrival off the coast of Admiral Watson with three ships of the line and one sloop, carrying a reinforcement of 1,000 British. This timely arrival gave the Government of Madras a preponderance of power, and so much determination was shown by the authorities in England to further increase the forces in India, if necessary, that Monsieur Godehen found himself compelled to give in on all points.

Two of the most important clauses of the treaty were, firstly, the recognition of Mahomed Ali as Nabob of the Carnatic; and secondly, the restoration to the Nizam, by France, of the 600 miles of coast line and vast territory already mentioned.

Thus, in October 1754, ended the second phase of the war with France in India; but peace was not destined long to endure. To quote the words of Dr. Nolan in his *History of the British Empire in India*:—

"The French had placed themselves in such a position that they must go on in a career of conquest and intrigue, until the thrones of the Indian Chiefs were at their disposal, or sink into mere traders, craving permission to traffic, and in constant danger of losing all chance of mercantile success, in consequence of the superior trading capacity which the English and Dutch everywhere displayed; the roots of French diplomacy had so spread and fastened among the courts of southern India, that there they must remain, unless cut out by the sword. The English eventually found that solution of the difficulty the only one, and did not shrink from undertaking the laborious task."

With the fall of Dupleix the power of France was on the wane, although she fought hard to recover it; her efforts and her failures will form the subject of another chapter, which will deal with the third campaign against the French and their native allies, and the further progress of the Sepoys in the art of war.

CHAPTER VI.

THE PRESIDENTIAL ARMIES.

IT is a pleasure to commence this chapter by recording the gallant behaviour of the Sepoys on several occasions in the campaigns described in the last chapter. Major Lawrence spoke highly of their conduct during the attack on Cuddalore by the French in 1748; at the defence of Arcot, 1751; and at the battle near Volcondah in the same year, when the European troops retired in panic, their behaviour was also excellent, and Orme praises them for being very well to the front at the second battle of Volcondah, in 1752, under Clive. At the siege of Trichinopoly in 1753, and at the repulse of the night attack in November of the same year, they also fought gallantly,* and many instances of personal bravery and devotion on the part of native officers have been placed on record; the names of Subadahr Sheik Ibrahim, and Subadahr Meer Munsoor are particularly brought into notice by Colonel Wilson in his *History of the Madras Army*. In the *Quarterly Review*, January 1818, No. XXXVI., in a paper by Sir John Malcolm, the story is told, how, at the siege of Arcot, provisions being very low, the Sepoys requested Clive to give the European soldiers all the rice remaining in store, contenting themselves with the water in which it had been boiled, an act of devotion that cannot be too highly praised. Strange to say, Malcolm quotes Orme as his authority for events that happened during the siege, and Orme does not mention any want

---

* Wilson's *History of the Madras Army*.

of provisions; indeed, according to his account, there was a sufficient supply when the siege was raised. Wilson alludes to this, and says, that from the tenor of Clive's correspondence, it may be asserted that the garrison at no time suffered from famine; hence he concludes that the incident did not occur at Arcot; but that does not prove that it did not occur at all.

The reinforcements brought out by Admiral Watson in 1754, as mentioned in the last chapter, consisted of 700 men of the 39th* Regiment under the command of Colonel Adlercron (who, by reason of seniority, superseded Lieut.-Colonel Lawrence in command of the army), 40 men of the Royal Artillery, and 200 European recruits belonging to the Company;† the fact is interesting, as it establishes the date of the first appearance of the royal troops in India since the arrival of the Bombay Regiment in 1662, although the service for which they were originally intended was that of marines on board the ships of war. The arrival of the King's troops brought into force the Mutiny Act (27th Geo. II.) On the 1st September 1754 the garrison of Madras was paraded in the presence of the Governor and Council, and the Act of Parliament for the punishment of mutiny and desertion, and for the better discipline of the Honourable Company's forces was duly read; after which the officers were asked if they were willing to serve on the terms of the Act, to which they returned an affirmative reply. Agreeably to the Act, all men were enlisted in England for His Majesty, and were transferred to the Company's service previously to embarkation.

In the eighteenth century treaties appear to have been as easily evaded as they are at the present time. The treaty signed in 1754 by Mr. Saunders on the part of England, and Monsieur Godehen as the representative of France, distinctly laid down that the rival Companies were in future to abstain from interference in

---

* Now the 1st battalion Dorset Regiment. According to the *Naval and Military Magazine*, March 1827, this regiment had served at home as a marine battalion for five years prior to its despatch to India (Broome).

† Orme.

the affairs of the various native Powers. The ink was hardly dry when this particular clause was treated as a dead letter by both parties.

Early in 1755, Mahomed Ali, finding himself free from French aggression, and caring little for the Mysorean force that still occupied Seringham, in hopes of obtaining possession of the much coveted Trichinopoly, determined on an expedition to Madura and Tinnevelly, for the purpose of collecting arrears of revenue, and applied to the English for assistance. In defiance of the treaty obligations of 1754, this was immediately granted, and 500 Europeans, among whom were included the detachment of the Bombay European Regiment, and 2,000 Sepoys, under Lieut.-Colonel Heron, were despatched to join his forces. Madura and Tinnevelly surrendered without opposition, and the surrounding country professed submission, more nominal than real. The fortified pagoda of Coilgoody was successfully carried without loss, and some booty belonging to the temple was secured, after which 200 Europeans and 500 Sepoys were detached to reduce the fort of Nelli Cotah, forty miles south of Tinnevelly, which place they reached in a march of eighteen hours, and immediately stormed with complete success.* On the 22nd May the whole force returned to Madura, and on the 23rd, on its way to Trichinopoly, was attacked by one of the Polygars of the Colleries in the densely wooded pass of Nuttum, who looted the baggage and carried off the idols and treasure taken from the Coilgoody pagoda. The force reached Madras in November, when the Bombay detachment embarked for their own Presidency, having lost 123† Europeans out of the number sent to Madras in the previous year.

In the meanwhile the French disregarded the treaty of 1754 after the example of the British. Salabut Jung was, with Bussy and his French battalion, marching against Mysore, to enforce arrears of tribute, whilst Balaji Rao threatened the frontier at the head of a Maratha force. This double danger induced the Mysorean

* *Records of the Royal Bombay Fusiliers.*
† *Ibid.*

commander to evacuate Seringham and hasten to his own country; thus at length leaving Trichinopoly free. At this period the whole of the Sepoys of the Madras establishment were commanded in chief by Mahomed Issoof, a gallant soldier who had greatly distinguished himself under Lawrence, by whom he was brought forward, being promoted by the Government of Madras in 1754. Early in 1756 a disturbance having broken out in Tinnevelly, Mahomed Issoof was sent to assist Maphuse Khan, who had been left in charge by his brother, Mahomed Ali, the Nawaub. He was entirely successful in reducing the Polygar chiefs for a time. It is interesting to note that at this period of Indian history much trust and confidence was placed in native commanders, for besides Mahomed Issoof, it is recorded by Orme that in an action near Tinnevelly, fought on the 21st March 1756, against the Polygars of Madura, 1,000 of the Company's Sepoys were commanded by Jamaul Sahib. The victory was complete, the enemy losing 2,000 men. The conquest of the Polygars having been effected, Maphuse Khan marched to Madura, where his troops mutinied and detained him on account of arrears of pay due. They, moreover, hauled down the British colours and turned the garrison, consisting of three companies of British Sepoys, out of the fort,* and Madura was again lost.

The course of history now renders it necessary to revert to the military proceedings of the Government of Bombay. The depredations of Toolaji Angria, the descendant of Kanhoji Angria, whose exploits have already been described,† had determined the Government of Bombay, in conjunction with the Marathas, as long ago as 1751, to undertake his destruction; but the intention was not carried out until 1755. In March of that year the Peshwah Balaji Rao (Toolaji having failed to pay the customary tribute) requested the promised assistance of the British for the extermination of this ocean pest. The request was promptly acceded to, and on the 22nd March, Commodore James, the commander of the

* Wilson's *History of the Madras Army.*
† Chapter IV.

Company's naval forces, left Bombay in the *Protector*, 44 guns, accompanied by a smaller ship of 16 guns, and two bomb-vessels, and was shortly afterwards joined at Chaul, by the Maratha squadron, consisting of seven grabs and sixty gallivats carrying 10,000 men.*

It was agreed that the enemy should be attacked both by sea and land, the latter to be undertaken by the Maratha force, their guns being worked by a detachment of James' European gunners. On the 2nd of April operations commenced against Severndroog, one of the pirates' strongholds, and the adjacent forts of Gora, Futtehdroog, and Connoidroog, when, the Maratha land attack being of the feeblest, the Commodore determined to try the effects of bombardment from the sea. This had the desired result; the land batteries surrendering on the 3rd, and Severndroog on the 4th April 1755,† without any loss on the side of the British. The next attack was directed against the island of Bankot, six miles to the north, which surrendered without resistance. For these exploits the Commodore was rewarded with a gold medal and 1,000 Rs.; and the British force, naval and military, received two months' pay as a gratuity. All the fortresses enumerated above were, as by previous agreement, handed over to the Marathas, Bankot to be kept for the English until they should be prepared to occupy it. The Marathas, delighted with these successes, offered 200,000 Rs.‡ to the British if they would continue the conquest and attack the fortified position of Dabul; but the offer, greatly to James' disappointment, was declined. In the following May the Marathas were assisted in an unsuccessful attack on Ratnagiri, on the coast south of Bombay, and in October the British occupied their recent conquest, Bankot.§

Toolaji Angria, after the fall of Severndroog, took refuge in the strong fortress of Gheria, situated on the sea-coast 170 miles

---

* *Bombay State Papers*, Professor Forrest.
† *Ibid.*
‡ Beveridge.
§ *Bombay State Papers*, Professor Forrest.

south of Bombay, which owing to exaggerated reports was supposed to be impregnable.

In the meanwhile Admiral Watson, with his fleet, finding himself without occupation on the Coromandel coast, by reason of the treaty concluded with the French, in the beginning of November sailed for Bombay. There he found a considerable force assembled, recently arrived from England, destined, in alliance with the Peshwah Balaji, to attack the Nizam's fortress of Aurungabad, in retaliation for his support of French designs. The expedition which had been arranged in England previous to the signing of the Treaty of 1754, had to be abandoned. It was, therefore, determined to use the strong force at hand for the utter extinction of the Angria, so well commenced by Commodore James.

Clive arrived from England in the *Streatham* in time to take part in the expedition;* he rejoined in India with the rank of lieutenant-colonel in the King's service, and with the appointment of Deputy Governor of Fort St. David,† and by virtue of his seniority assumed command of the land forces.

In February 1756 the expedition started for Gheria; in addition to a powerful naval force under Admiral Watson, Clive commanded 800 Europeans, 600 Sepoys, and a company of the King's Artillery.‡

Commodore James in command of the Company's fleet had previously rendered good service by reconnoitring the enemy's position, which he found to be very strong, but by no means impregnable. The fortifications were placed on a sea-washed precipice fifty feet high, and consisted of a double wall flanked with

---

* Mr. Gleig, in his *Life of Clive*, says he brought with him six companies of artillery.

† Some historians call him Governor of Fort St. David, but in a letter of remonstrance regarding a certain court-martial, dated Bombay, 15th April 1756, addressed to the Honourable Richard Bouchier, Esq., the Governor and Council, Clive distinctly announces his rank and dignities in these words, "and considering the rank I bear of Lieut.-Colonel in His Majesty's service, of Deputy Governor of Fort St. David, and of a member of the Committee of this place." (See Dr. Nolan's *History of the British Empire in India*, vol. vi. p. 240).

‡ *Bombay State Papers*, Professor Forrest. Beveridge says 1,000 Sepoys.

towers,* to the north of which was the harbour, where lay the pirate fleet. The land attack, it was again arranged, should be conducted by the Maratha army under Ramaji Punt, to whom Toolaji in vain offered terms on the approach of the British fleet. The fort having been summoned to surrender by Watson without effect, next day the bombardment commenced from 150 cannon, from the broadsides of the fleet and several mortars, when, having sustained the fire for some hours, the Angria guns were silenced. Clive then landed with the troops and prepared to take the place by storm, as it was feared that the Marathas would be beforehand with them, and so seize on any treasure that might be stored in the fortress; that this was their intention seems to be proved by the fact of the Maratha commander offering the British officer in command of the advance picket 80,000 Rs. to allow him and his troops to get in.

The bombardment being renewed the next day the fort surrendered to Clive, who took possession of 200 guns, six mortars, quantities of stores, and money to the value of £120,000, the whole of which was divided among the British troops to the exclusion of their Maratha allies, and was afterwards a fruitful source of dispute among the English commanders. Sir John Malcolm in his *Life of Clive* censures " that spirit of plunder and that passion for the accumulation of wealth which actuated all ranks."

Thus were the Angria pirates crushed with, at the end, little trouble. Gheria was subsequently, after many disputes between the Marathas and the Bombay Government, given over to the former, according to a previous agreement.

In April 1756, Clive, with Admiral Watson, sailed for Madras, where they arrived in May, and Clive soon after took up his appointment at Fort St. David on the 20th June 1756, a date memorable as that on which Calcutta and its garrison fell victims to Surajah Dowlah, the Nabob of Bengal.

For many years the English in Bengal had flourished in regard

* Beveridge

to their trade under the just and mild rule of Ali Verdy Khan the Nawaub of Bengal. Unlike their countrymen in Madras they had not interfered in the affairs of the native states, nor had they come to any open rupture with the French company, whose head-quarters and factory were at Chandernagore some miles higher up the river Hoogly than Calcutta, and not far from the Dutch factory at Chinsurah. In 1753 Ali Verdy Khan, growing old, had appointed his grandson, Suraj-ad-Dowlah, more commonly known as Surajah Dowlah, heir to the Nabobship of Bengal. The boy being of a perverse and cruel disposition grew up infamous and profligate, and when quite a young man had been guilty of rebellion against his benefactor, of secret assassination and open murder. On the death of Ali Verdy Khan in April 1756 Surajah Dowlah took possession of the Government of Bengal, and filled many of the highest appointments with the worthless companions of his pleasures, by the removal of the trusted administrators of his grandfather. Among others deprived of office was Meer Jaffir Khan the paymaster-general, who, although subsequently reappointed, never forgave the insult. The young Nabob immediately proceeded to fill his treasury by the open robbery of his relatives and also demanded a large sum from Rajbullut, Deputy Governor of Dacca, who in alarm removed his family and treasure to Calcutta. Surajah Dowlah had from his earliest youth looked upon the English at Calcutta with hatred. In them he saw a growing power likely to prove dangerous if permitted to expand, and he, not unnaturally, although as it ultimately proved unwisely, determined to be rid of them. A pretext for quarrel was easily found. He demanded that the family and treasure of Rajbullut should be given up, a demand that was refused by Mr. Drake the Governor of Calcutta; this was the first cause of offence. As rumours of a war with France were rife, the fortifications which had been allowed to fall into a disgraceful state of disrepair, the very cannons sent out in former years for defence, lying dismounted and uncared for under the walls, were strengthened. The Nawaub ordered Mr. Drake to stop the work and to demolish that which had already been done; non-compliance with this order filled him with fury, and led to the war which caused his downfall and early death.*

Determined to chastise the rebellious British, the Nawaub assembled an army and marched a detachment of 3,000 men against the factory of Cossimbazar presided over by Mr. Watts, and garrisoned by twenty-two Europeans and twenty Topasses.

On the 1st June the Nawaub with the whole of his army arrived. The place was utterly indefensible, and at once capitulated, the garrison being sent as prisoners to Morshedabad, whilst Mr. Watts and one of his Council were detained in the Nawaub's camp. Mr. Drake, alarmed for the safety of the settlement, despatched daily letters to Mr. Watts instructing him to express to the incensed Nawaub his willingness to comply with all his demands; to these letters no reply was returned. In the meanwhile the defences of Calcutta were neglected, and the Nawaub continued his advance. Under these circumstances intimation of the distressed condition of Calcutta was despatched to Madras and Bombay, and assistance asked for, although it was well recognized that none could be expected to arrive under two months. Application was also made to the Dutch at Chinsura, and the French at Chandernagore. The Dutch declined to interfere, whilst the French, who had previously supplied the Nawaub on his advance with 200 barrels of gunpowder, insultingly intimated that if the English would evacuate Calcutta they might take refuge in their settlement.

Thrown on his own resources, Mr. Drake now showed some activity. Defences were hastily improvised, provisions were collected; the Sepoys were augmented to 1,500; a militia was enrolled and mustered 250 men, among whom were many Armenians and Portuguese, but on these little reliance could be placed; whilst the regular garrison consisted of 264 Europeans only, of whom but 174 were English.

The British now took the initiative. To secure retreat in case of disaster it was deemed necessary to gain possession of the native

* Stewart's *History of Bengal.*

port of Tanna on the Hoogly, five miles below Calcutta, which commanded the narrow channel leading to the distant sea. The native garrison was easily dislodged, on the 13th June, by a small force, (sent in four armed vessels) who spiked the guns, instead of preserving them for future defence.

On the 14th June, the British detachment was in turn attacked by 2,000 men of the Nawaub's army, and forced to retire with its ships to Calcutta.

On the 15th June, Surajah Dowlah reached Hoogly, and transported his army to the Calcutta side of the river.

On the 16th June, the attack on Calcutta commenced. Stewart thus describes the fortifications: "The factory or fort was situated on the bank of the river; its length from east to west was 210 yards; its breadth on the south side was 130 yards, and on the north only 100 yards; it had four bastions, mounting each ten guns, but the curtains were only four feet thick, and the terrace which was the roof of the store-rooms, formed the top of the ramparts; the gateway on the eastern side projected and mounted five guns; and along the bank of the river was a line of heavy cannon, mounted in embrasures of solid masonry, so that the place might have made a long defence against such an enemy, had not the houses of the principal Europeans, and the church overlooked and commanded the fort."

On the 17th of June the enemy made an attack on the east side of the town, broke into the Company's bounds in large numbers, set fire to the bazaar and took possession of the native quarters.

An attack on the outposts of the fort was delivered on the 18th of June, and before evening all the outer defences were in the hands of the enemy, in spite of many gallant attempts to resist their overwhelming numbers. The defenders of the lost batteries included several of the civil servants, and Orme particularly mentions Messrs. Charles Smith and Wilkinson, who, being separated from their comrades, fell into the hands of the enemy, but not before the former had killed five men with his own hand, when he succumbed to his wounds. Mr. Wilkinson then surrendered, and was immediately cut to pieces.*

On the evening of the 10th June it was decided to send the European women on board the Company's vessels lying off the fort. This was accordingly done under the direction of two members of the Governor's Council, and a party of the militia who not only declined to return to their duty, but actually deserted their comrades and dropped down the river to Govindpore, three miles below the fort, an example followed by all the other vessels, leaving the garrison without means of escape, except by one vessel lying higher up the river, in the event of disaster which now appeared almost certain.

On the 19th June the enemy succeeded in occupying the Church, the Governor's house, and another building commanding the fort, and dire confusion reigned within the walls of Calcutta. An attempt was made to embark the Portuguese women and children, but the remainder of the militia and others hastening to escape at the same time caused overcrowding of the boats, several of which were upset and many persons drowned. It is painful to relate that the fugitives included the Governor, Mr. Drake, who had hitherto shown coolness under fire, Captain Minchin, the commander of the troops, four members of Council, four commissioned officers of the regular army (Grose says three), many civil servants, and 100 soldiers and militia. The garrison now reduced to 190 men (for the Sepoys, or rather the armed peons, had deserted at an early period of the siege), fell under the command of Mr. Holwell, and gallantly repulsed many vigorous assaults, but the fort commanded on all sides was no longer tenable. The last hope of escape rested in the Company's ship *St. George*, already mentioned as lying higher up the river, which, coming to the assistance of the distressed garrison, struck a sandbank and remained hard and fast. Signals were exchanged with the vessels

---

* Very full descriptions of the siege of Calcutta are to be found in Orme and Broome.

near Govindpore, which were still in sight, but as Broome well says, to the eternal infamy of those on board, not an effort was made to render any assistance, and for this cowardly and inhuman conduct there can be no palliation.

On the morning of the 20th June the Nawaub renewed the attack with vigour, and the small garrison was further reduced by twenty-five men killed and seventy wounded, whilst others broke into the spirit stores, and became hopelessly intoxicated. Under these circumstances capitulation became unavoidable, and was offered by Mr. Holwell, but no reply was vouchsafed. At noon the enemy ceased firing, and the weary garrison hoped for terms, but at 2 P.M. the bombardment recommenced. At 4 P.M. an officer of the Nawaub, the bearer of a flag of truce, was seen approaching, and the order was given to cease firing. A parley ensued, during which the enemy treacherously forced the Eastern Gate, and cut down the palisades of the south-west bastion, and attempted to escalade the southern side of the fort. In the meanwhile, some of the soldiers, worn out with fatigue, tried to escape by the western gate, but the enemy rushed in and the fort was lost. Further resistance being impossible, the troops laid down their arms. The victorious Nawaub entered the fort an hour afterwards, and Mr. Holwell and other principal Europeans were brought before him with their hands bound. Surajah Dowlah ordered them to be unloosed, and on the word of a soldier promised them protection; he then took his departure, and the unhappy prisoners were shortly after confined in the common dungeon of the fort, generally known as the Black Hole, and used for the punishment of refractory soldiers. The story of the horrors of the night have been so frequently and well told that little need here be said except that the chamber was but eighteen feet square, and had two small windows barred with iron on the leeward side, and even these were obstructed by a low verandah which kept off every breath of air. In this chamber, at the hottest season of the year, 146 persons, including one lady, were thrust. Scenes of unparalleled suffering ensued, and on the morning of the 21st June, twenty-three only emerged alive.* Bad as he undoubtedly was, it is but fair to say that it is generally accepted that Surajah Dowlah was unaware of what was occurring in the fort, as in spite of the agony of the unhappy prisoners the native officer of their guard refused to disturb the Nawaub who had retired to rest. The miserable remnant of the garrison were set at liberty, and allowed to join their comrades at Govindpore. In Orme's words, "Here their appearance, and the dreadful tale they had to tell, were the severest reproaches to those on board, who, intent on their own preservation, had made no efforts to facilitate the escape of the rest of the garrison; never, perhaps, was such an opportunity of performing an heroic action so ignominiously neglected; for a single sloop, with fifteen brave men on board, might, in spite of all the efforts of the enemy, have come up, and anchoring under the fort, carried away all those who suffered in the dungeon."

Meanwhile the Nawaub's army was employed in plundering Calcutta, where, however, comparatively little was found. The fugitive English reached Fulta, a town with a market near the sea, and the station of all the Dutch shipping. Here they were joined by the agents and junior servants of many out-stations, and employed their time in mutual recrimination.

Surajah Dowlah, in his ignorance, believed that he had exterminated the English, and never imagined that his late actions could induce an invasion of his territory from Madras or Bombay. He consequently failed to follow up his success, and instead of pursuing the Calcutta fugitives, he allowed them to remain unmolested at Fulta. To perpetuate the memory of his victory he

---

* Broome's *History of the Bengal Army*. He quotes from Orme. The following is the list of officers who perished: Captains Clayton, Buchanan, and Witherington; Lieutenants Bishop, Hop, Blagg, Simpson, and Bellamy; Ensigns Piccard, Scott, Hastings, and Wedderburn; also Ensigns Coles and Dumbleton of the Militia; 74 non-commissioned officers and privates of the regular forces and militia. This list, with the 23 who survived, leaves 35 persons unaccounted for, they were probably civilians and merchants. The survivors included Messrs. Holwell, Court, and Burdet, Ensign Walcott, the only officer who escaped, and thirteen men of the regulars and militia. The lady, Mrs. Carey, also survived.

ordered the name of Calcutta to be changed to Alinagore, meaning the Port of God, and on the 2nd of July left the city.

Whilst these events were occurring in Bengal the French were losing ground in the Deccan. In May 1756 Mons. Bussy, who had so long ruled Salabut Jung, the Nizam, was with the whole of his troops, at the instigation of the Nizam's Prime Minister, dismissed from the service of that potentate. Mons. Bussy, with his force consisting of 600 Europeans in battalion, 5,000 well-disciplined Sepoys, a well-appointed train of artillery, two troops of hussars, and one of dragoons, retired to Hyderabad (Deccan), escorted on his march by a considerable Maratha force. He reached Hyderabad on the 14th June, after a march of considerable danger and difficulty, and soon after found himself besieged in his position at Charmaul, a walled garden near Hyderabad, by the army of his former *protégé*, Salabut Jung, who, moreover, had now thrown himself into the arms of the British at Madras, the latter receiving his propositions and request for assistance with the greatest possible pleasure as affording them a most favourable opportunity of striking a blow at French influence in the Deccan. Salabut Jung was at once assured that troops would be despatched to his assistance, and 300 Europeans and 1,500 Sepoys were on the point of taking the field when, in the middle of July, the news of Surajah Dowlah's advance on Calcutta was received from Bengal. It was at once recognized that to save the Bengal possessions from utter destruction, every man who could be spared from the Coromandel force would be required; and the expedition to assist the Nizam was consequently, with much regret, abandoned. Four hundred and fifty men, mostly Europeans, under the command of Major Kilpatrick were at once shipped on board the Company's vessel *Delaware*, and sailed for Fulta on the 20th of July.

On the 5th August full details of the capture of Calcutta were received with feelings of horror and resentment at Madras.

On the 15th June, the very day on which the first news of the difficulties in Bengal reached Madras, the French had detached a force of 500 Europeans and a train of artillery from Pondicherry to the assistance of Bussy.

The troops maintained by the English and French on the Coromandel coast were at this time nearly equal, and consisted of about 2,000 Europeans and 10,000 Sepoys; but the French force was weakened by the 500 men detached to the assistance of Bussy, nor had they any squadron in the Indian seas to oppose to that of Admiral Watson; but letters from England, received in August, informed the Government of Madras that war with France at an early date was considered inevitable, and that the French were preparing to send a fleet of nineteen ships-of-war, and 3,000 troops, from Brest to Pondicherry.

Under these circumstances the question arose, which was the more important course to adopt, to assist Salabut Jung and crush French influence in the Deccan, or to regain the Company's possessions in Bengal, punish Surajah Dowlah and retrieve the national honour? It was plain that to try both would be to separate the force and to court disaster; on the one hand the firm establishment of French influence in the Deccan meant future trouble, on the other hand it was recognized that the loss of the Bengal investments and revenue for even three years meant ruin to the Company. It was finally determined to undertake the expedition to Bengal.

The consequence of this decision was that Salabut Jung, after a war that had lasted some months, became reconciled to Bussy, and the French found themselves again virtually masters of the Deccan.

The resolution of the Government of Madras to despatch an expedition to Bengal was communicated to Admiral Watson, who consented to it. Many days were, however, spent in discussions as to the disposal of captures that might be made by the squadrons, and as to who was to command the expedition; what should be his authority in military operations and in negotiations with the Nabob; in what relation he ought to stand to the Government of Calcutta on its re-establishment, &c. &c.

After much discussion it was decided to entrust the command of the expeditionary force to Clive, as Lawrence was suffering severely from asthma, and Colonel Adlercron was inexperienced in Asiatic warfare. The Government of Madras wisely invested their well-tried and gallant servant with independent powers in all military matters and operations, and instructed him to prosecute the war with vigour so as to return with the troops to Madras in six months time. They, moreover, furnished him with ample treasure, and empowered him to draw bills on the Presidency. It was further determined that Mr. Drake, the ex-Governor of Calcutta, should be entrusted with all power in civil and commercial matters. A sloop of war was despatched to Fulta with the cheering news of the intended expedition for the subjugation of Surajah Dowlah.

On the 16th October 1756 the fleet set sail from Madras Roads. It consisted of the *Cumberland*, 70; the *Kent*, 64; the *Tyger*, 60; and the *Salisbury*, 50; the *Bridgwater*, 20 guns; a fire-ship, three of the Company's ships, and two smaller vessels to act as transports. The troops embarked were as follows :—

Detachment 39th Regiment	250
Madras Europeans	528
Madras Artillery Company	109
Lascars	160
Sepoys	940

12 field guns and one howitzer.

Another detachment of 250 Sepoys embarked on the 28th October.* Admiral Watson hoisted his flag on the *Kent*, and Clive sailed with him; Admiral Pocock hoisted his on the *Cumberland*. Clive's instructions were to attack Surajah Dowlah in his capital itself, if necessary, if he would not come to terms and make full reparation for all injuries he had inflicted. He was also to capture Chandernagore from the French, provided war was declared with France during his absence in Bengal. It should be here mentioned that Clive does not appear to have been in command of the detachment of the King's 39th Regiment which Colonel Adlercron stipulated should act as marines only, as will be made

---

* Wilson's *History of the Madras Army*

more clear in the account of the capture of Calcutta. There was also much friction between him and Admiral Watson not of a personal nature, but rather as regarded the authority of Clive, the Admiral being inclined to support that of Mr. Drake and the Calcutta Council.

Before following Clive in the campaign in Bengal, it will be convenient to describe the events that occurred in southern India during the remaining months of 1756, which can be done very briefly as they were not of any remarkable military character or importance; indeed, Madras had been so denuded of troops, that any expedition on a large scale in the Coromandel was rendered impossible. What troops remained were mostly at Trichinopoly, under the command of Captain Caillaud, but were unable to do more than protect that city, as towards the end of October news was received that war with France had been declared in Europe. The French occupied their old position on the island of Seringham, but no hostile proceedings appear to have been taken before the close of the year 1756, although the French force was superior to that of the English, and amounted to 530 Europeans and 1,500 Sepoys.

Shortly after the Company's troop had been turned out of Madura, as before mentioned, the Polygars became very troublesome, but sufficient troops were not available to coerce them. Although more than one attempt was made to secure the rendition of Madura by negociations, they ended in failure. On the 1st December Mahomed Issoof, in command of about 1,500 Sepoys and six field pieces, defeated, at Gangadoram, about twenty miles north of Tinnevelly, a Polygar army of 10,000 men, of whom 1,000 were cavalry. This was the only affair of any importance that occurred in southern India before the close of 1756.

The squadron carrying the expeditionary force to Bengal did not arrive at Fulta until the 15th of December, having encountered heavy weather in the Bay of Bengal.* On that day the *Kent* and

* The officers of the 39th Regiment were:—Captain Grant in command, assisted by Captains Eyre Coote, and Weller; Lieutenants Waggoner, Corneille, Carnac;

the *Tyger* reached their destination, and on the 20th December were joined by all the other vessels of the squadron except the *Cumberland*, 70 guns, and the *Marlborough*, one of the Company's ships. Their absence caused considerable anxiety, as the *Cumberland* carried 300 of the European troops, and nearly all the field artillery had been shipped on board the *Marlborough*.* Kilpatrick's detachment had reached Fulta on-the 2nd of August, but before the arrival of Admiral Watson's fleet, one half of the 230 men originally sent from Madras, had fallen victims to the deadly climate, and of the remainder 30 only were fit for duty ;† but many were so far recovered before hostilities commenced, that they were all able to take part in the campaign ; the little force was, moreover, strengthened by seventy volunteers, embodied at Fulta.‡

The following facts connected with the march to and recapture of Calcutta are taken from Clive's journal of his proceedings, forwarded by him to the Government of Madras.

On the 16th December the European troops disembarked from the *Kent* and *Tyger*, and the Sepoys from the transport *Walpole*, where they were found by Kilpatrick's detachment. On the 22nd they were joined by the troops disembarked from the *Salisbury* and *Bridgewater* ; the whole force remained in camp until the 27th December, when, pursuant to the decision of a council of war, they re-embarked, and the fleet proceeded up the river towards Budge-Budge. Two field-pieces with eighty artillerymen, under Captain Barker, followed the fleet in boats, and seven companies of

---

Ensigns Jorke, Donnellan, and Broadbridge. The officers of the Madras Infantry were :—Captains Gaupp, Pye, Fraser ; Lieutenants Campbell, Rumbold, Adnet ; Ensigns Knox, MacLean and Oswald. Captain Briggs was A.D.C. to Clive ; Mr. Walsh was Paymaster to the force (Broome).

* Wilson's *History of the Madras Army* put the Europeans on board the *Cumberland* at 250. Broome says the *Cumberland* carried 300 Europeans, of whom 90 belonged to the 39th Regiment, and the latter would appear to be correct, as Orme distinctly states that 90 men were subsequently landed for the defence of Vizagapatam, and 100 at Madras, leaving 90 men only on board belonging to the 39th Regiment.

† Orme. Mr. Ives, Medical Officer of the *Kent* in his voyage and narrative says 30 men only remained alive, and that 10 only were fit for duty.

‡ Malcolm's *Memoirs of Lord Clive*.

Sepoys, commanded by a native officer, Keser Singh, proceeded by land, keeping the ships in sight.

On the 28th December the whole force, with the exception of the King's troops, disembarked at Myapore and joined the seven companies of Sepoys under Keser Singh, and at 6 P.M. marched northwards with the object of gaining the road leading from Budge-Budge to Calcutta, and thus cutting off the enemy's communications with the latter place, which was garrisoned by 3,000 men under the Governor, Monick Chund, whilst the Nawaub's army was advancing from his capital, Moorshedabad. The road was gained with the greatest difficulty by forced marches during the night, the troops, and guns dragged by the men, passing over tidal creeks and deep morasses. From a private letter of Clive's addressed to Mr. Pigot, the Governor of Madras, it appears that Clive objected to this dangerous land march, and requested Admiral Watson to send the troops in his boats to the very spot which they afterwards reached. The request was, however, not entertained.*
At 8 A.M. on the 29th the force entered the Calcutta road, about three miles north of the fort of Budge-Budge. At 9 A.M. the European Grenadiers and all the Sepoys were detached towards the fort, whilst the remainder held the road. The force having reached Budge-Budge, found that the King's troops, under Captain Coote, had landed and had silenced the enemy's fire. During this time the Europeans formed in battalion, and the company of European volunteers had been posted on the road, and feeling excessively fatigued, were allowed to rest and quit their arms. According to Orme, no precautions against attack were taken. They were surprised by Monick Chund at the head of 1,800 men. The skirmish lasted an hour, during which time the battalion lost one officer and nine men killed, and eight men wounded, the guns, moreover, were for the moment abandoned, but were subsequently recovered by the volunteers.† The enemy is said to have lost fully 200 men, four officers, and one elephant. Clive then recalled the Grenadier company and the Sepoys detached to

* *Malcolm's Memoirs of Lord Clive.* † Orme.

Budge-Budge, and ordered the pursuit of the enemy, who were by that time in full retreat towards Calcutta and Hoogly, twenty-three miles above Calcutta, and adjoining the Dutch settlement of Chinsura. At noon the whole force marched on the fort, which, in the meanwhile, had been battered by the guns of the fleet; but no breach had been made. The troops being greatly fatigued, it was determined to storm the fort at daybreak on the 30th December; the party told off for the purpose being the King's troops, the Grenadier company of Europeans, and 100 seamen. At 8 P.M. a drunken sailor having wandered into the fort, found that it had been abandoned, when the whole party entered in confusion, and Captain Campbell was accidentally shot by one of the seamen or Sepoys.* In the fort were found 22 cannon, 33 barrels of powder, and some grain. After destroying the walls and spiking the guns, the European troops disembarked on the 30th December; whilst the Sepoys, again under the command of Keser Singh, advanced by the land route, keeping the fleet in sight. The artillery was again embarked in large boats. On the 31st December the ships proceeded up the river.

At 10 A.M. on the 1st January 1757 the fleet came in sight of Tanna near Calcutta, and at 2 P.M. arrived abreast of the fort, which they found evacuated by the enemy. At 3 P.M. the fort, together with the small fort of Alighur opposite, was occupied by seamen of the ships. In these forts were found 31 guns of 24 lbs., 13 smaller cannon of sizes, and a small quantity of ammunition.

On the 2nd January, at six in the morning, the European troops of the Company under command of Clive landed and joined the Sepoys, and at 8 A.M. advanced on Calcutta with two field-pieces. The enemy abandoned their batteries as the troops approached.

---

* Mr. Ives tells us an amusing story of this affair. The sailor's name was Strahan. That day he was had up before Admiral Watson for irregularity and severely reprimanded, and threatened with the "cat." He remarked: "Well, if I am flogged for this 'ere action, I will never take another fort by myself, as long as I live, so help me God." He was not punished, and lived for many years after on a pension; the height of his ambition being to be a cook on board a fast vessel.

At 10 A.M. the fleet came up abreast of the fort, and opened fire. The enemy made a show of resistance, and by their fire killed nine men on board the *Kent*, and seven on board the *Tyger*,* but soon deserted their guns, and escaped by the eastern gate. At 11 A.M. Fort William was in possession of Captain Coote, and a detachment of the King's troops and seamen. Clive on arriving with the Company's Europeans and Sepoys naturally desired to assume command of the fortress, when, to his astonishment, Coote produced a commission from Admiral Watson appointing him Governor of Fort William in the King's name. Clive remonstrated with Watson, but without avail, and the dispute threatened serious consequences, when the matter was arranged on the 3rd January by the admiral landing, and handing over the fort and all stores and goods found therein to representatives of the Company. It is clear from private letters from Clive to Mr. Pigot that Mr. Drake and the Bengal Council greatly resented the independent powers entrusted to Clive, and desired that he would consider himself subordinate to themselves, a position that Clive declined to accept. Admiral Watson supported the demands of the Council, and this was the cause of friction between the two commanders and of the slights that Clive was made to endure.

The greater part of the merchandise belonging to the Company was found intact in Fort William, it having been put aside as the Nawaub's share of the plunder; but all private property had been removed or destroyed, and most of the best houses had been demolished or damaged by fire. Thus many of the Company's servants found themselves reduced to ruin, the only means remaining to them being the ridiculously small pay received from the Company for their services.

The 21st January was employed in mounting the guns on the ramparts, and repairing the defences and preparing for the expedition. The force consisted of the King's troops, 200 seamen, the Company's Europeans and 200 Sepoys, which, at 8 P.M., embarked on board the *Bridgewater* and several small vessels for

* Orme.

the purpose of following up the success of the 2nd January by an attack on Hoogly. The command of this expedition was entrusted to Major Kilpatrick, who was accompanied by Captain Coote. The *Bridgewater* having grounded on a sandbank, the expedition was delayed some days, and did not arrive before Hoogly until January 10th. The fort was found to be garrisoned by 2,000 men, and 3,000 more lately arrived from the Nawaub's army held the town, but retreated as the Europeans landed from the ships. The latter bombarded the fort until the evening when, the breach being hardly practicable, it was determined to storm at daybreak on the 11th. A false attack on the main gate drew off the enemy's attention from the breach, which Coote, with a few Europeans, some seamen, and a body of Sepoys, stormed, losing three Europeans and ten Sepoys killed, before the place was fully gained.

It was during the attack on Hoogly that news of the declaration of war with France in Europe reached the authorities at Fort William. Fearing that the French, who had a force of 300 Europeans and a train of artillery at Chandernagore would at once join the Nawaub, the Council at Calcutta determined to try negotiations with the latter, but all efforts were unavailing, and the Nawaub continued his advance on the city. Strange to relate, far from joining forces with the Nawaub, the French refused their assistance, and proposed to the British that the two nations should agree not to molest one another during the continuance of the war in Europe.*

In the meantime the English at Calcutta were preparing for the Nawaub's expected attack and had established a fortified camp about one mile to the north of the town, and half a mile from the river, from which position it was Clive's determination to oppose the enemy's advance. Clive, moreover, had made up his mind to the important step of training the Sepoys under his command who had hitherto fought in companies, generally under their native leaders, and forming them into regular battalions with European

* Orme.

officers. He raised some 400, men with due care to physique and military qualifications. These men he dressed and armed in a manner somewhat similar to the European troops. The battalion was possibly recruited from among the Madras Sepoys; the officers, according to Williams, being selected from the Madras detachment. The corps thus raised was called by the natives *Lall Pultun*, or the Red Battalion; *Pultun* being a native corruption of the word platoon, itself derived from the French *Peloton*, being a detachment of about thirty men. The battalion was officered by one captain, two subalterns (Europeans), who acted as field officers, assisted by a sergeant-major and several sergeants also European; there was a native commandant, who took post in front with the captain, and a native adjutant who remained in rear with the subalterns. The battalion consisted of ten companies, two being grenadiers, each company had a subahdar, 3 jamadars, 5 havildars, 4 naiks, 2 tom-toms or drummers, 1 trumpeter, and 70 sepoys with two colours, one bearing the subahdar's device, the other, belonging to the grenadiers, having the Union Jack in the upper corner. This is the first mention of a Sepoy battalion.

On the 30th January the Nawaub's army crossed the river ten miles above Hoogly, and on the 3rd February his advance guard appeared before Calcutta. During the afternoon of the same day the enemy in force began to entrench themselves in a large garden about a mile and a half south-east of the British camp. A skirmish ensued, in which two artillerymen and three Sepoys of Clive's force were killed.

On February 4th the main body of the Nawaub's army appeared; Surajah Dowlah himself being present. He took up his headquarters in a large garden, situated in the north-east portion of the Company's territory, and within the Maratha ditch, belonging to a native merchant, one Omichund, who previous to the attack on Calcutta by the Nawaub had enjoyed the confidence of the Company's servants, with whom he had large dealings. His guns not having yet arrived, the Nawaub intended to amuse the English with negotiations until he was ready to attack. This fact having been made known to Clive, he determined to take the initiative and attack the Nawaub's camp.

On the morning of the 5th February Clive set out with 650 Europeans formed in battalion, 100 artillerymen, 600 sailors from the fleet, 800 Sepoys, and some 6-pounder field-pieces. The order of march was remarkable, for the Sepoys led, 400 Sepoys forming the advance guard, followed by the European battalion, after which came the remainder of the Sepoys. In rear were the guns and Lascars carrying the ammunition, and guarded by the seamen who also dragged the guns. A portion of the Nawaub's army was encamped within the Maratha ditch, and near Omichund's garden, but the greater part was spread over the country without any particular order. A very thick fog, common in the cold season in India, enabled the British to advance to the walls of the garden with but small opposition, but with the loss of some ammunition accidentally exploded, which caused momentary confusion. A charge of Persian cavalry was gallantly awaited, fire being withheld until the troopers were within thirty yards of the line, when one discharge was sufficient to drive them back in confusion, and with considerable loss.

The fog continued to thicken, and in an attempt to gain the rear of the enemy's position the troops found themselves in confusion, and under the fire of two heavy guns loaded with grape. The fire of these guns, at 200 yards distance, killed and disabled no less than twenty-two of the European force at the first discharge. The line was at once extended, and the troops ordered to make for the high road leading across the ditch into the Company's territory. Before this could be accomplished, many rice fields had to be crossed, where the labour of dragging the guns under a heavy fire became excessive, and the advance was further impeded by the fire of two additional guns mounted a quarter of a mile to the south. Two of the field-pieces had to be abandoned. At 9 A.M. the fog cleared, and the British force did not reach the road until 10 A.M., when they were attacked in front and in rear by large bodies of cavalry, which, however, were always gallantly repulsed.

Clive, seeing the exhausted condition of his troops, determined to abandon the attack, and at noon reached Fort William, having suffered the very serious loss of 27 Europeans, 12 seamen, and 18 Sepoys killed; 70 Europeans, 12 seamen, and 35 Sepoys wounded. The killed included 2 captains (Pye and Bridges) of the Company's service, and Mr. Belcher, Clive's secretary. The enemy's loss was estimated at 22 officers, 600 Sepoys, 4 elephants, besides many horses and draught bullocks. Strange to say, the unsuccessful British attack was viewed in quite a different light by the Nawaub, who, looking upon it as an act of remarkable intrepidity, prepared to retreat, and actually moved his army three miles away, and opened negotiations with Clive.

On the 9th February a treaty very favourable to the British was concluded, by which all former grants were confirmed, and all the factories and plunder restored. Permission was also given to fortify Calcutta in whatsoever manner the English should consider expedient. But whilst the negotiations were in progress Surajah Dowlah opened communications with Mons. Bussy in the Deccan, and invited him to join forces and extirpate the British from Bengal. On the 11th February the Nawaub, who had now entered into an alliance offensive and defensive with the British, moved his army further to the north, and Clive employed Omichund to sound Surajah Dowlah, whether he would resent an attack on the French settlement of Chandernagore. Having received no positive injunction to the contrary, Clive made up his mind to prosecute the enterprise. On the 18th the British crossed the river a few miles above Calcutta, but the attack was for a time deferred by the positive orders of the Nawaub.

Early in March the good news reached Clive that Commodore James had arrived in the river with three ships conveying three companies of the Bombay European Infantry,* and one of Artillery as a reinforcement from Bombay, and that the *Cumberland*, 74

---

* Orme. The *Records of the Bombay Fusiliers* says that two companies of the battalion, 400 strong embarked on the 29th October 1756, and it took them four and a half months to sail round India.

guns, so long looked upon as lost, and which carried 250 European infantry, had arrived off Balasore.

Thus powerfully reinforced, the attack on Chandernagore was no longer to be delayed, in spite of the Nawaub's objections, and the Bombay detachment having joined, hostilities commenced against the French on March 14th.

Chandernagore was strongly fortified, although a portion of the defences, commenced at the first news of the declaration of war in Europe, was as yet incomplete. It possessed many heavy guns, 24- and 32-pounders. The fort was about 130 yards square, with 4 bastions, each mounting 10 guns, and the garrison consisted of 600 Europeans and 300 Sepoys; of the former 300 only were regular troops, the remainder being composed of the merchants, inhabitants, and seamen of the trading ships. Several vessels had been sunk in the channel of the river, with the object of preventing the approach of ships of war. The French had obtained promises of assistance from Surajah Dowlah, but Omichund succeeded in bribing the Native Commandant of Hoogly to withdraw his forces on the approach of the British. The troops under Clive entered the French territory from the west and by the high road leading to the north face of the fort. On the first day of the attack the French retired from all their advanced batteries with the loss of the guns of one battery, which they spiked.

On the 16th of the month the English opened fire from their batteries and the bombardment continued with activity, with the loss of some 20 men, European and Sepoys, until the 23rd, on which day it was determined to attack with the ships which, with the assistance of a French deserter and a plucky reconnaissance conducted under a heavy fire, had managed to find a navigable passage between the sunken vessels. Admiral Pocock, finding that it would not be possible to bring the *Cumberland* up the river in time to join in the assault, embarked in his barge, and, rowing day and night, reached the scene of action a few hours before the attack and hoisted the flag on board the *Tyger*.

The *Tyger* was detailed to bombard the N.E. angle of the fort, the *Kent* to act against the ravelin before the middle of the curtain, and the *Salisbury* against the S.E. bastion,* the land batteries, two in number, supporting the naval attack on the bastions with five 24-pounders. The *Kent*, coming within 50 yards of the enemy's guns to take up position, was for a moment thrown into confusion by the fire of the enemy, which swept the deck, wounding Captain Speke, the Commander, and mortally wounding his son, a midshipman. In the confusion that ensued the Captain's order was misunderstood, and the cable allowed to run out to its full length, whereby the ship passed her position opposite the ravelin, and brought up beyond the S.E. bastion, the position to be occupied by the *Salisbury*, which thus remained out of action. The *Kent* was exposed to the fire of the S.E. bastion as well as to that of the S.W. bastion.

The cannonade on both sides was kept up with great fury, the ships losing heavily as every shot told; but the land batteries, fortunately, drew off a certain amount of the fire. At 9 A.M. the fort held out a flag of truce. Captain Coote, of the 39th Regiment, and Lieutenant Brenton, the only officer of the *Kent* unwounded, were sent on shore to open negotiations, and at 3 P.M. the fort surrendered, several officers and some 70 men escaping northwards in hopes of joining the Nawaub's army.

The terms of the treaty were simple: all civilians were permitted to depart with their clothes, the officers were granted parole, the European troops became prisoners of war, and the Sepoys were allowed to return to their homes. Many of the Europeans subsequently enlisted under Clive.

The British loss had been very severe, as the French defence had been most gallant under their Governor, Monsieur Renault, and Monsieur Deviques, commander of the French ship *Sainte Contest*, who took charge of the artillery and directed its fire with coolness and ability. The loss of the land attack was on the day of assault comparatively small, one European only being killed and 10 wounded; the total loss during the siege being but 40 or

* Orme.

50 killed and wounded, Europeans and Sepoys. It was, however, far different on board the ships of war; the *Tyger* lost Mr. Phillips, the Master, and 14 men killed, Admiral Pocock, Mr. Pater (mate), beside Midshipmen Wilkinson, Thompson, and Cribble, and 41 men wounded. On board the *Kent*, the 1st Lieutenant Perrean was killed. Mr. Hey, 3rd Lieutenant and Midshipman Speke were mortally wounded; Captain Speke; the Commander, Mr. Staunton, 2nd Lieutenant, Mr. Barnes (Purser), Mr. Lister, Admiral's Secretary, and Midshipmen Marriot and Wood were severely wounded; 37 men were killed and 74 wounded; three of the lower deck guns were dismounted, and the gallant ship received six shots in her masts and 142 in her hull.*

† The Soubah had, at any rate, been consistent in forbidding in the most peremptory terms any attack upon the French. An Afghan invasion, news of which reached Bengal about the time of Surajah Dowlah's retreat from Calcutta, had greatly disturbed the intriguing mind of the young despot. Eastern flattery had assured him that any foreign attack from their old western enemies must, although ostensibly delivered against Delhi and the tottering Mogul Empire, have for its real object the invasion of Bengal. In the contemplated attack on North-Western India there was some degree of truth; the invasion of Bengal, however, might be looked upon as chimerical. Under these circumstances the Nawaub knew not which way to turn; his deeply-rooted hatred for the English, although he had good reason to acknowledge their power not only in arms but in diplomacy, pointed them out as the most valued allies. The news of the constant success of the British arms in native alliance against those of the French in Southern India, had by this time reached, with many exaggerations, to Bengal. The very fact of the apparent French weakness, confirmed by their defeat at Chandernagore, pointed them out to the

* Broome's *History of the Bengal Army*; also Orme, who does not, however, give all the names.

† From here was written by me from Colonel Rivett-Carnac's dictation, from his memory without notes. I believe facts and dates are correct.—SOPHIA RIVETT-CARNAC.

native mind as allies valuable in spite of their comparative weakness, provided always that the handful of British could, with their aid, be extirpated from Bengal; because they themselves would be more easily coerced when the time arrived, and they would suffer the same degradation as their more powerful adversaries, and thus render Bengal free from the hated foreigner.

CHAPTER VII.*

CHANDERNAGORE—PLASSEY—CHINSURAH—OPERATIONS IN
BENGAL.

AFTER the disposal of his native as well as European opponents, nothing could have been better than the dauntless Clive's attack on the French, and capture of Chandernagore. It was indeed a glorious victory, and it brought out the character of our greatest early Indian soldier and statesman in a clearer light than ever. The distinguished Captain who had carried on so many struggles against French supremacy in the Madras Presidency, making us frequently wonder how he had not exhausted nature as well as glory long before he came to succour Bengal, did a really valuable service against his old enemies at this time by dispossessing them of Chandernagore. When, on the 14th of March 1757, hostilities began, it was little thought by the proud but gallant French in India that in nine days the capture of the place would be effected, or that the fort would hang out a white flag and capitulate—ringing the death-knell of supreme French power in the East.

The assistance of a "French deserter" at the conclusion of this remarkable siege—which gave rise to the severest struggle in which the English had yet been engaged in India—has already been alluded to.† The story is short, but interesting. It has been

---
* Here begins the continuation of Colonel Rivett-Carnac's narrative, which will be chiefly devoted to the operations of our Indian armies.
† Page 184.

frequently hinted that the loss of Chandernagore arose from treachery; and that the English corrupted the French soldiers or officers. This report arose from the following circumstances:— The French Governor, to prevent the progress of the English ships, had blocked up part of the river by sinking boats, but had left one narrow channel open, which was known to but few. One Terreneau an officer in the French service, disgusted for some cause with Renaud (" Renault"), the Governor, went over to Clive and pointed out the channel to him. This man afterwards made a little money in the English service, and sent some of it home to his aged father in France; but he returned it with contempt, as coming from a traitor. This so affected Terreneau that he hung himself with his own handkerchief at his own door.*

On no other occasion of Clive's brilliant career can it be more truly said than after Chandernagore, "that the views of no statesman of the times (if we except Burke, who is an exception to everything) contain more political and practical foresight directed to Indian affairs." So wrote his famous biographer, Sir John Malcolm; and preceding this decisive opinion of the great Indian " Political," comes another highly deserved eulogium, which is even more true at the present time:—" India has produced many illustrious men both in his time and since; but none of them has yet obscured or equalled the fame of Clive."† The nearest approach to him in " practical foresight" is probably to be found in four most able and successful Viceroys—the Marquess Wellesley, Marquess of Dalhousie, Lord Lawrence, and the Marquess of Dufferin and Ava. Among strictly military statesmen and soldiers might also be mentioned the "lion-hearted" Outram, and the admirable Sir Henry Lawrence. It is the doing of so much good work single-handed, with such strong opponents as Dupleix, Bussy, perfidious Nabobs, and even perfidious European acquaintances at home and in India, which sheds such a peculiarly bright lustre over Clive's character. The Navy and Army in India could certainly not have

* Marshman.
† Sir John Malcolm's *Life of Robert, Lord Clive*, vol. iii.

found two fitter instruments to re-establish the interests of the East India Company in Bengal than Admiral Watson and Colonel Clive; and the Presidency armies may well be proud of them. Bombay, with the exception of the attack on Gheriah (the pirates' stronghold to the south of the Western Presidency), saw or heard but little of Clive; his immortal work was all done in Madras and Bengal; but the "heaven-born General" no doubt owed a portion of his success to the gallant Bombay European Regiment, of which two strong companies and a company of Artillery from the same Presidency served at Chandernagore, and eventually at Plassey. Again, with reference to this siege, it may be interesting to state, what is not generally known, that while Calcutta was found unable to stand for two days the assault of so contemptible a rabble as the Viceroy's army, it required all the resources of European strategy, and the assistance of three men-of-war, besides a large land force (under Clive) to reduce the Bengal Paris of the East to submission.* And it is well said that if the infuriated Nabob had turned his arms against the French settlement, he would have been obliged ignominiously to raise the siege, and would probably have been pursued by the French to his own capital; and the foundation might then have been laid of a French monarchy in Bengal,† if not of a French Empire in India.

A sum of £130,000 was acquired by the fall of the French capital, and it paved the way for the destruction of the Nabob of Bengal. By the capture of Chandernagore (Fort D'Orleans) Clive's steady resolution to extinguish all European influence in Bengal, except that which he himself directed, was fully carried out; and, as has been well remarked, "it inflicted a blow on the prosperity of the French from which they never recovered."

The palmy days of Chandernagore extended only from the arrival of Dupleix to its capture by the English, during a period of little more than thirty years. As the star of England rose on

---

* Chandernagore is about twenty miles above Calcutta, on the right bank of the Hooghly.

† *Calcutta Review*, No. VIII. (1845); "Notes on the Right Bank of the Hooghly."

the horizon of India, that of the French declined.* There was no lack of "political and practical foresight directed to Indian affairs" to produce such a happy consummation; so why should there be such a general indifference to, or neglect of them, one hundred and thirty years from the fall of Chandernagore, under the present Queen Empress? It is difficult to reconcile the fact of the lamentable want of interest felt on the production of the last Indian Budget in the House of Commons, concerning upwards of one-sixth of the human race, with the glowing terms in which the Marquess of Dufferin and Ava spoke at Belfast (September 19, 1889) of our Indian Empire.

The noble Marquess, on being entertained to a dinner, said of India: "The history of the world did not exhibit a more splendid example of the way in which the material and moral condition of a vast congeries of nationalities might be elevated and improved than did our Eastern Empire." Alluding to the governing capacities of his countrymen—an important subject in these Home-Rule days of would-be Governors—Lord Dufferin, having at the commencement of his speech spoken of the mighty dead—those illustrious Ulster men—who had served England and India so well during the great Mutiny, for the preservation of the Empire, remarked, with a touch of humour which even the highly gifted Sheridan might have envied, that we could never get on without Irishmen. Not only our Indian but our Colonial Empire plainly showed that "Irishmen had a positive genius for governing, if not themselves, at all events other people!" Just before this pleasant sally, his Lordship had cited the names of various illustrious Irishmen, emphatically declaring that both Ireland as a whole and Ulster as a province had imparted a vast amount of ability, industry, and valour into the Indian Military and Civil Service. The present Viceroy was a Kerry man, and the Governor of Madras was a Burke of Mayo†;

---

* "Notes on the Right Bank of the Hooghly," by the late distinguished J. C. Marshman, C.S.I., who founded *The Friend of India*. He was son of Dr. Marshman, the famous missionary of Serampore, and in all local matters was one of the strongest contributors to the *Calcutta Review* in its most palmy days.

† Brother of the admirable Viceroy, the Earl of Mayo, who was assassinated at Port Blair, in February 1872.

while the Commander-in-Chief of the Queen's armies in India, Sir Frederick Roberts (Bengal Artillery), the victor of Candahar, was an Irishman. Sir Frederick and Clive would have done well together; at least, so far as energy or a determined nature in the way of conquest was concerned.

Every well-wisher of India may, even at the close of the nineteenth century, with justice exclaim: Would to God we had more statesmen with political and practical foresight directed to Indian affairs!

Having, as above, digressed to our Indian governors, suggests a return to Chandernagore, where reigned by far the greatest French governor who ever came to India, who threatened to reduce Madras and Calcutta to their original state of fishing towns,* and consequently the local terror of our early Presidential armies—M. Dupleix, or Le Sieur Dupleix, as he was styled by the French; a character to which, during the early portion of an Indian career, we gave some attention after visiting scenes immortalised in history by French energy and enterprise in the East.

The motto of this extraordinary Frenchman—this would-be Great Mogul—was simply: "When France is contented with her Indian possessions, the East will remain at peace!" just as used to be said —but what shrewd journalists tell us cannot be affirmed now— "When France is contented Europe is tranquil." The story of Dupleix's admirable administration of Chandernagore has been often told, but the French governor far from sufficiently appreciated. The would-be Paris of India was under his direction from 1730 to 1742; and he increased its prosperity beyond all precedent. From being an extensive merchant, he had improved the trade of the town by his vast energy and private enterprise; and he had no fewer than twelve ships of his own, with which he traded to every port in India. "During his government," writes Marshman, "two thousand brick houses were built at Chandernagore, and the influence of the French was greatly extended in Bengal."

* Orme.

This extraordinary man, who so evidently wished to extinguish our Presidencies of India—governors, writers, soldiers, and all—at one fell swoop, had the good fortune to possess an excellent father, who was a Director of the French Company (as before stated, founded by Colbert in 1664), and in 1720 the accomplished son had come out to India, with the titles of " Premier Conseiller du Conseil et de Commissaire des Guerres."* In 1742 Dupleix was promoted to the government of Pondicherry (Madras Presidency), and proclaimed Governor of all the French settlements in India. Thus the French in both Madras and Bengal had the full advantage of his political sagacity and government, before which all the wretched attempts of France in our day to found a sort of Eastern Empire sink into nothing. His fall (1754) has been already related; and the amiable, industrious historian of the Madras Artillery gives as one chief reason for such a catastrophe—his removal from Pondicherry—his "mixing up European and Asiatic politics together."

Of such a man as Dupleix it is scarcely credible to read—after being informed that at the Saidabad factory, where he lived a long time, he was the Louis Philippe of the French interests in Bengal, his great aim being to raise French power through the influence of French commerce—that with all his attention to business he indulged in frivolity, having (we presume during his "griffinage") been seen in the streets of Chandernagore with a fiddle in his hand and an umbrella over his head, "running half naked with some other young fellows and playing tricks at every door."† This is apt to remind us of Cowper's adventurous Frenchman in the last century, with "his lass, his fiddle, and his frisk," laughing "the sense of misery far away."

Doubtless his mad companions little thought that their *pro tem.* frivolous comrade would one day gain twenty lakhs of rupees (£200,000) in India, and originate French private trade in the

---

* See also page 117 of the present narrative.
† *Calcutta Review*, 1846, " The Banks of the Bhagarathi."

country. But so he did, as well as taught us how to conquer and partly keep India with its own inhabitants.*

By readers fairly well up in the history of the French in India—and we are afraid they are very few—Lord Macaulay's intense admiration for Dupleix is easily understood, for it is really well deserved. There could not possibly be a more correct estimate of the talents and experiences of the great Franco-Indian political than what is given in the immortal essay on Lord Clive; and the student of Indian history should ever bear in mind that "the man who first saw that it was possible to found an European empire on the ruins of the Mogul monarchy was Dupleix." And "he clearly saw that the greatest force which the princes of India could bring into the field would be no match for a small body of men trained in the discipline and guided by the tactics of the West." Again, "he saw that the natives of India might, under European commanders, be formed into armies such as Saxe or Frederic would be proud to command." It is good, also, to reflect on a statement by the discriminating historian and essayist, in these days when Englishmen are apt to think too little of what the Queen-Empress and her Indian Empire owe to Madras, especially while the great commercial companies of Europe had long possessed factories in Bengal, and the French were settled, as they still are, at Chandernagore, that "the servants of the Company at Madras had been forced by Dupleix

---

* "Look there, sir," said the sailor Governor of Pondicherry to the present writer (1845-46), who was paying his respects at Government House during a brief residence among the French in India, pointing to a marble bust of Dupleix at the end of the room; "there is the man who taught you how to conquer India with its own inhabitants. You are, of course, aware that Clive took his idea of the Native soldier (Peon) entirely from this clever Frenchman." The conversation had turned on the Afghan political exploits of Lord Ellenborough, and our wonderfully constituted Bengal native army; for no one ever dreamt then that, in another twelve years, such a large mutinous crew would nearly ruin our power in Hindustan. There has been nothing like it in the world's history. The Bengal army in particular went on increasing till 1857, when the grand explosion took place; so what (with a few European troops) served our purposes, and those of others in the East, during early European conquests, was no longer to be relied on. And it is curious to note how, after the Mutiny (as if out of compliment to Clive, who won his first glories in Madras), the order of faithfulness to British rule in the Presidency native armies was clearly seen to run—Madras, Bombay, Bengal.

to become soldiers and statesmen, while those in Bengal were still mere traders, and were terrified and bewildered by the approaching danger."* Returning to Clive; he knew well that war had broken out in Europe between the English and French. At Chandernagore, before the siege, the French had as many European troops as Clive had under his command; and we cannot help admiring the foresight of the great British leader in being well assured that Calcutta could not be safe while the French kept so large a garrison at their chief post. He was consequently anxious to free himself entirely from the Nabob before proceeding to attack the French. Clive and Admiral Watson, however, held firmly to their plans, as is well known to readers of Indian history; and both distinguished fire-eaters were quite contented with the order to attack which they found in Suraj-ood-dowlah's words, " Whatsoever you think right, that do." It should be kept in mind that both the Admiral and Clive were expecting Bussy with a great army. "Is it to attack you? Is it to attack us?" asked the Admiral. "I see but one way," he wrote. "Let us take Chandernagore, and secure ourselves from any apprehension from that quarter, and then we shall assist with every man in our power, and go with you even to Delhi," he said to the Nabob, "if you will."

Admiral Watson appears to have resembled our Commodore Lambert during the Second Burmese War. Watson had written, just before the last remarkable reply, to the Nabob, saying that the troops which he expected had arrived, and that he would kindle such a war in his country that all the water in the Ganges would not put it out. We recollect our Commodore (1852) remarking to a Burmese "Admiral," that if he brought his ship any nearer to the *Fox* or the *Serpent*, he would blow him out of the water! Such was the good old style of being decisive with our enemies.

It is somewhat difficult to understand why the French did not

---

* Essay on Lord Clive—*Critical and Historical Essays,* vol. iii., p. 144.

attack the Presidency town, destined to become so famous, nearly twenty years before; for, as stated in the "Notes" before quoted, so far back as 1740, while Calcutta was in a state of comparative insignificance, Chandernagore had risen to great opulence and splendour under the most enlightened and energetic administration the French have ever had in India. "It was in the mansion on the banks of the river," writes the graphic Calcutta reviewer, "on the site of which stands the present Government House, that Dupleix contemplated the establishment of a French power in the country, and determined himself to lay the foundation of it; but Providence had otherwise determined the destiny of India." It is also said that travellers who visited Chandernagore between the peace of 1763 and the commencement of the French Revolution in 1793, reported that every effort to restore its former splendour proved unsuccessful. The chief aim of the French being the establishment of a political power in India, when all their schemes had been defeated by the genius of Clive they sunk into comparative insignificance, and were outstripped in the race of commercial enterprise by their hard-working, plodding neighbours, the Dutch.

It is curious to notice that, during the French Revolution of 1792 and 1793, the infection of revolutionary principles extended even to the distant possession of Chandernagore. The French populace determined to enact on a small scale the proceedings of Paris, and revolutionize the Government. When they had succeeded in obtaining possession of the public authority, the Governor fled to his country house at Giretty.* When it was announced that the mob of Paris had proceeded to Versailles and conducted the King as a prisoner to the capital, the mob of Chandernagore are said to have gone to Giretty and brought back the Governor in triumph to the town, where he was subjected to much

* The French Garden of Giretty—where stood the famous house in which the French governors were wont to show their hospitality, and the Dutch from Chinsurah, and Clive, Verelst, Warren Hastings, and Sir William Jones, from Calcutta, had all been magnificently entertained—is about one-third the extent of the great Barrackpore Park, the tasteful country seat of the Governors-General, founded by the Marquess Wellesley.

indignity. He was at length released by the English Government, who sent a party of soldiers to put down the revolution; and soon after, formal possession was taken of the town on the declaration of hostilities in Europe.

The latter event is alluded to in the following brief summary of the ups and downs of the French in India, when, after Chandernagore, they had ceased to give our presidencies and their armies any anxiety:—In 1763, Pondicherry, Karikal, Mahé, and Chandernagore were restored to the French; but with a very limited territory. Yanaon was likewise restored. Pondicherry partially regained its former splendour, but was retaken by the English in 1778, and again given up to the French, with their other possessions, by the treaty of peace of the 20th of January 1783. These possessions fell again, after a few years, into the hands of the English; and Pondicherry, on the 20th day of August 1793, ceased to be a French capital.

At the peace of Amiens, in 1802, the French possessions were again restored; but, on the 11th of September 1803—that memorable year in which Bonaparte was making such vast strides to universal power—Pondicherry, with a garrison of only 152 European soldiers, capitulated, and passed, for the fourth time, into the hands of the English. The beautiful little city, like Niobe, now began to weep for her children. The treaties of 1814 and 1815 replaced the French in possession of their East Indian establishments (now considerably reduced by former stipulations), which consist of mere points widely separated from each other, situated on the coasts of Coromandel, Orissa, Malabar, and in the interior of Bengal. Their population used to be about 195,000, of which less than one thousand were Europeans.

It would be useless to deny that the presence of the French in the Bengal and Madras Presidencies during so long a period has had a strong, though indirect, influence on the action of our Presidency armies in India. Forty-four years ago it was said, with reference to Chandernagore and its capture by the English in 1793, that though it was restored twenty-two years after, it had since that time existed as a French establishment without any object, political or commercial; and the only advantage it conferred on the parent state consisted in the patronage of an overgrown establishment. While the affairs of the Danish Serampore had been managed with great ease by two European civilians, the administration of Chandernagore embraced no fewer than ten European officers. The same anomaly was visible on the coast, in the settlement of Pondicherry, which contained an establishment of officers altogether disproportioned to the size of the territory or the requisitions of public duty.* It is interesting to relate that the famous Talleyrand's forethought procured the restoration of the three hundred chests of opium from the British Government for the support of the settlement of Chandernagore, which privilege was effected at the Congress of Vienna.

The French at home condemned the political measures of Dupleix with about as much reason as he would have had in questioning the proper government of France. The English Company encouraged Clive—"Encourage Ensign Clive," they said at the beginning of his marvellous career—and all his bold adventures, leaving the fate of India entirely to the bravery and wisdom of their servants in the East—by far the most prudent plan at such a period. Clive wisely took advantage of the neglect of Dupleix by his countrymen. The keen eye of the rising soldier and statesman saw how well the clever Frenchman understood how to form an army of natives, and make mere puppets of princes: to do these well formed the grand secret of firmly establishing European power in India.

Earl, afterwards Marquess, Cornwallis, having defeated various schemes of the French to resuscitate their power, sailed for England in 1793. In the Hyderabad dominions and the Mahratta territories, nevertheless, Frenchmen were still plentiful. It was one of the first steps in the policy of that admirable and determined statesman, the Marquess Wellesley, as will be seen hereafter, to order the Nizam of Hyderabad, his ally against

* *Calcutta Review*, No. VIII., p. 510.

Tippoo Sultan, to dismiss all French officers from his service. This was obliged to be done by force of arms; and, in 1798, the commanders of the Nizam's army—French officers who had ruled fourteen thousand men—were compelled to leave India for France. The troops were immediately officered by the British. Nothing could have been wiser than this active measure by Lord Wellesley. Had it not been carried out, the English might have had some difficulty in becoming the heroes of Seringapatam in May 1799. The French had even become popular instructors as far north as the magnificent cities of Agra and Delhi; and to prevent their leaguing with the Mahrattas, or any other shifting native power, at such a period, must always be considered as an admirable stroke of policy. It appears strange that Scindiah, the Mahratta chieftain, should have regarded the French attached to his army with a jealous eye. Even Monsieur Perron, his great coadjutor, was not to be trusted. Scindiah probably fancied that, French power having fallen, French self-interest would now be the ruling principle; and it is impossible to imagine that Perron was much grieved, in a political point of view, when Lord Lake annexed the cities of Agra and Delhi to the dominions of the English East India Company. The chief power of the Mahrattas fell in 1803.

The Presidency armies were, as we know, kept well alive by all such important transactions. Before proceeding with further operations in Bengal, succeeding Chandernagore, it may be well to relate that, in 1871, after writing a sketch of Pondicherry (Pont-dechiré, like our Pontefract, and styled by the natives Puducheri) and the French in India, public attention was drawn to a fair little isle, though hardly "the fairest isle breathed on by Heaven," one of the British Possessions in Europe, which Campbell has made immortal in his wild but beautiful poem of " The Death-Boat of Heligoland." The subject of purchase of the French possessions in India long occupied our attention—particularly during the Franco-German war—and the exchange of Heligoland having come forward in the above year prompted us to say a few words on the subject, in connection with the French in India, for a repetition of which a slight digression may be pardoned:

By the treaty of peace between Great Britain and Denmark, Heligoland is ours "in perpetuity." It is a small island in the German Ocean, opposite to the mouth of the Elbe, about nine miles in circumference. "Heligo's Isle," then, had been attracting attention; and the first week in June (1871) the rumoured cession of Heligoland to Germany brought forth some remarks from Sir J. Hay in the House of Commons: "It would be in the recollection of the House that at the time the treaty of peace between France and Germany was in progress, a statement appeared in the newspapers that Pondicherry was about to be ceded by France to Germany; and within the last few weeks statements had been made in some of the German papers that Heligoland was to be added to Germany." Viscount Enfield informed the gallant member that no proposal had been made for the cession of Heligoland to Germany. But, although no correspondence had yet passed on the subject, it was quite possible that the occupation of this island had for some time been an important subject with the acute and far-seeing Prince Bismarck—before, on account of Prussia's triumph over Denmark; and now, more than ever, since the Emperor and his Chancellor had become lords of the ascendant. Of Pondicherry it was said, in February 1871, that it was to have been exchanged for Heligoland. Although it would seem to be politically necessary for us to retain the island, yet, we wrote, for the sake of our gaining Pondicherry, and, of course, all the French settlements in India, the bargain might have been struck. But since it had been officially stated that Germany did not intend to acquire through peace with France any possessions in India, Asia, or any Transatlantic country whatever, it seemed to be our bounden duty to negotiate at once for the French possessions in India. "If 'German unity,'" we wrote, "is ever to be advanced by the possession of Heligoland, why not British in the East by Pondicherry? We must avoid even the shadow of the possibility of revolution and disorder through the agency of any European Power in Hindustan. And no European Power should have any influence there save our own."* Chandernagore is first mentioned as a French settlement in 1700, just seventeen years after M. Martin founded Pondicherry (1683), destined to play such an important part in the Madras Presidency. There is little more of interest to be related of Chandernagore, except, perhaps, that it used to have two Catholic churches. The fine old church of St. Louis, we read, on which four pieces of cannon were mounted in the siege of the town in 1757, was demolished during its progress. A magazine in rear of it was afterwards fitted up as a church, in which for many years divine service was performed. Churches in India have frequently been put to strange uses, as, in the above instance, converting one into a battery; while the construction of at least one sacred edifice has a touch of humour about it not often surpassed in the history of ecclesiastical architecture. Mr. Marshman, of Serampore, has told us, regarding the church at Chinsurah—where we shall arrive with a Presidency army in due course—that it stands immediately above the ghât at the entrance of the town from the south, and was the joint gift of Mr. Sichterman and Mr. Vernet. Sichterman erected the steeple, with a chime clock, in 1744, and Vernet added the church twenty-four years afterwards; thus reminding us of the popular remark that the Frenchman invented the frill, and the Englishman added the shirt.† We are afraid that this, or a similar assertion, is entirely applicable to colonial progress among more than one of the great European Powers. A portion of the force employed against Chandernagore has already been named; but the Presidencies of India, at any period, have never sent forth to war, or included in their armies, two finer corps that the 1st Madras and 1st Bengal European Regiments. It was in the

---

* *The French Possessions in India: Reasons for an Endeavour to Purchase them, &c. In a Letter to His Grace the Duke of Argyll, K.T., Secretary of State for India* (1871). It may be here also mentioned that in 1883 there was a rumoured purchase of Chandernagore. It was said that the Government of India were in treaty with the French for the purchase; but nothing was known for certain on the subject.

† "Notes on the Right Bank of the Hooghly."

year 1755 that the Madras Artillery and the 1st Madras European Regiment were first regularly incorporated, the sepoys regimented, and the pay established. "It appears quite clear," writes Colonel P. R. Innes, "from Colonel Clive's Diary, despatched officially to the Court of Directors in February 1757, that 'the Bengal European Regiment' was organised by him on, or immediately prior to, the 22nd December 1756; for he noted that, on that date the Grenadier and the Artillery Companies, from the *Salisbury* and *Bridgewater*, in which vessels they had arrived from Madras, joined the battalion which was in the camp. The 'battalion' referred to must have been the 'Bengal European Battalion,' which he had just formed; for there was no other battalion in the camp, or indeed with his army."*

Two strong companies of the Bombay European Regiment and the detachment of Artillery from that Presidency, being reinforcements which left Bombay in October 1856, did not arrive on the scene in Bengal till February 1757. The Bombay European detachment was, after the battle of Plassey, incorporated with the Bengal European Regiment. The detachment of Madras Artillery was also incorporated with the Bengal army,† as if prophetic of the huge Bengal Presidency swallowing up to some extent the minor ones and their armies in times to come!

We must not leave Chandernagore without recurring once more to the French garrison; and Major Innes's recent excellent work on the Bengal European Regiment seems to contain the best account of it which has come under our notice. It consisted of 146 European Infantry, 300 Sepoys, and about 300 Militia formed from amongst the European inhabitants of the town; and there were, in addition, a number of French sailors, drawn from the ships lying under the guns of the fort. With reference to the number of European Infantry, the Major has noted:—"Various authorities place the French garrison at a much higher figure; but

---

* *History of the Bengal European Regiment, now the Royal Munster Fusiliers*, pp. 16 17.

† Begbie's (General P. J.) *Services of the Madras Artillery*, vol. i., p. 88.

Malleson "—the well-known colonel, and probably our greatest living light in Anglo-Indian literature and research—" who has examined the old records at Chandernagore, ascertained they only had 146 French Infantry in the garrison." Again, the English force consisted of the Bengal European Regiment, the detachments of the Bombay and Madras European Regiments; these, after leaving sufficient men to garrison Calcutta and the outposts, amounting in all to about 700 European infantry. Besides, Clive had 150 European artillery and 1,500 Sepoys; but the most important part of the expedition was the ships of war. There were the *Kent* (64), the *Tiger* (60), and *Cumberland* (70), the detachments of the 39th Regiment (*Primus in Indis*) still acting as marines on board ship.* It will be remembered that, on the departure of the force from Madras to retrieve the fallen fortunes of the Bengal Presidency, Clive does not seem to have been in actual command of the detachment of the King's 39th Regiment, which Colonel Adlercron† stipulated should act as marines only; and this absurd arrangement, when every fighting soldier was required on land, was caused by the Madras Council refusing command of the force to Adlercron, quite unskilled in Asiatic warfare, and giving it to Clive, the only man in India except Colonel Lawrence (who, as before remarked,‡ was ill) fit for the all-important duty. Thus, as is occasionally the case in war—particularly in India— the second in command was by far the better man, which was clearly seen from the day of Clive's landing in Calcutta in command of the first real Bengal Presidency army to the fall of Chandernagore. The great event was followed up by the most decisive action against Suraj-ood-Dowlah (according to Sir John Malcolm, *Suraj-u-Dowlah*).

When Chandernagore fell, the Nabob, notwithstanding his flattering congratulations to Clive on such a successful issue,

---
* *History*, &c., p. 42.
† Commander-in-Chief, whose complete independence of all local authority was "one of the anomalies of the times."
‡ P. 173.

marched a large army to Plassey, which he interposed between the English and his capital. Clive, affecting alarm at the attitude thus assumed, kept his troops together in and about the new conquest. Of course, Clive had as little confidence in the Nabob as the Nabob had in him. And now the time for action arrived. In spite of all their care, "a suspicion of the fidelity of Meer Jaffier and his colleagues" had been roused in the mind of Suraj-ood-Dowlah.

The Admiral with his ships and Clive with his troops had gone back to Calcutta. Chandernagore was garrisoned chiefly by sailors and a few sepoys. In the arrangements for his advance, Clive ordered all the troops which could be spared to march from Calcutta, " on the 12th of June, leaving only some sick Europeans and Sepahis to guard the French prisoners."* On the 13th the army, with 150 sailors, marched, the English troops, with one field-piece and ammunition, being towed up the river in 200 boats and the sepoys marching along the right bank.

"The English army," writes Major Innes, "on the 16th June reached the town of Pulti, about twelve miles from the Nawab's fort of Kutwah. The governor of this fort was believed to be in league with Mir J'affar Khan's party†; but when Major Eyre Coote, with an imposing force, including a detachment of the Bengal European Regiment, summoned the garrison, the Governor refused to surrender. Major Coote, first opening fire, despatched a body of Europeans, who effected a passage across the river, when the enemy, firing some buildings adjoining the fort, took to flight."

The Madras and Bombay European regiments also assisted in this smart affair, which ended in the British occupation of the town and fort—hardly so important as the materials for carrying on war and the possession of " a very large supply of grain and a considerable quantity of military stores, as well as fourteen pieces of artillery." Clive, then, was now within a few miles of the plains of Plassey. He had received a letter from Meer Jaffier, which

* Innes. See *History*, p. 54. † To dethrone the Nabob.

gave an account of his "reconciliation with the Nawab, and how he had sworn to assist him against the British; but he concluded by saying that the purport of his engagement with the English must be carried out."* Truly, the character of Meer Jaffier, which Lord Macaulay has drawn so strongly and vividly, is one of the most extraordinary in Indian or any other history; and if he did nothing else, he was the cause of teaching us the value, in the foundation of our Indian Empire, of a really good Presidency army, and of such a military genius to lead it as Robert, Lord Clive. Meer Jaffier was an adept in the art of serving two masters. The Nabob, too, was a very strange compound; but no Indian official of his time could see through him so well as Clive. The grand art of governing men will ever consist in seeing through them; after a fashion it may be, but still they must in some way penetrate into the very cranny of their natures. We recollect, many years ago, after the Southern Mahratta war, asking a brother officer what was his impression of Outram. "His eye was everything," was the reply; "he looked as if he *could see through you!*" And this was also the case with the "Iron Duke," Sir Charles Napier, and other brave and independent military leaders.

Sir John Malcolm has clearly given the sentiments Clive had formed of the Nabob's character and policy. In a private letter to Mr. Pigot, Governor of Madras, written a month after the fall of Chandernagore, he gives a vivid description of the Nabob's character and "of the motives and feelings which he supposes to agitate his weak and vacillating mind at a period critical both for himself and for the Company's establishment in Bengal." Notwithstanding his signing articles of peace, from his tyranny, cowardice, and suspicion, no dependence could be had upon him. "No consideration," wrote Clive to Mr. Pigot,† "could induce him to deliver up the French. It is true he has ordered them out of his dominions, and they are at some distance from his capital;

---

* *History*, p. 55.   † 30th April 1757.

but he has retained them secretly in his pay, and has certainly written to Monsieur Delegrit and M. Bussy to send men to his assistance. One day he tears my letters and turns out our vakeel (agent), and orders his army to march; he next countermands it, sends for the vakeel, and begs his pardon for what he has done." Twice a week he had threatened to impale Mr. Watts.* In short, he was a compound of everything bad, kept company with none but his menial servants, and was "universally hated and despised by the great men." Clive next informs the Madras Governor of "a conspiracy going on against him by several of the great men," and that there can be neither peace nor security while such a "monster" reigns. The proofs that Clive's conclusions were just are to be found in various documents, but particularly in the letters from Mr. Watts and in the communications made by the Nabob to the French officers Bussy and Law (the French agent at Cosimbazar, who enjoyed pre-eminent influence at the Moorshedabad Durbar), some of which were intercepted at the time, and others found after the battle of Plassey.† In the now famous "Memoirs" there is no more interesting or amusing passage than that in a letter to M. Bussy, February 1757, where the Nabob observes:— "These disturbers of my country, the Admiral and Colonel Clive (Sabut Jung), whom bad fortune attend! without any reason whatever, are warring against Zubat-ul-Toojar (M. Renault), the Governor of Chandernagore. This you will learn from his letter. I, who in all things seek the good of mankind, assist him in every respect, and have sent him the best of my troops that he may join with them and fight the English; and if it become necessary, I will join him myself. I hope in God these English, who are unfortunate, will be punished for the disturbances they have raised. Be confident; look on my forces as your own. I have wrote you before for two thousand soldiers and musqueteers under the command of two trusty chiefs. I persuade myself that you have already sent them, as I desired; should you not, I desire you will

---

* Resident at the Nabob's Court at Moorshedabad.
† *Memoirs of Lord Clive*, vol. i., p. 208.

do me the pleasure to send them immediately. Further particulars you will learn from M. Renault."

Zubat-ul-Toojar, the title of the French Governor or Chief, is explained as meaning "the essence or excellence of merchants"; while Sabut Jung, "the daring in war," is applied to Clive, "by which title," writes Sir John Malcolm,* "he is to this day known among the natives of India." In their professions, at any rate, Suraj-ood-Dowlah had evidently a high opinion of both Frenchman and Englishman. For the Admiral he had no epithet of praise or condemnation loud enough, or he might have said that Watson, like our gallant Rangoon Commodore, was all thunder and lightning, with a dash of the earthquake in him!†

We may here incidentally mention that a namesake of the gallant Admiral, Colonel Watson, established the first dockyards in the Bengal Presidency at Kidderpore in 1780. But now let us proceed to the famous battle which did so much for other peaceful triumphs in India. At length Clive marched down with his army to Plassey. The troops were set in motion early in June 1757. The scene of the celebrated and decisive battle which fixed the destiny of India, or gave us an Indian Empire, is thus graphically described: "Following the tedious and shifting windings of the river (the Bhagirathi), we come to the field of PLASI (Plassey), so called from Palasa, a tree counted very holy; Sir W. Jones states that there was a grove of these trees at Plasi formerly, and they were to be seen at Kishnagur in Jones's time. Of the famous mango grove, called Lakha Bag, from there having been a lakh ‡ of trees in it (this tope was about a mile to the east of Ramnagar Factory), all the trees have died or been swept away by the river, excepting *one*, under which one of the Nawab's generals, who fell in the battle, is buried; the place is called by the natives *Pirha Jaya*, and is held sacred by the Hindus and Musalmans, but particularly by the last.

* 1835-36.
† We believe this, or something like it, was said by an American at Rangoon of Commodore Lambert.
‡ 100,000.

"This grove was 800 yards long and 300 broad; it existed at the time of the battle; there is only one tree left.* The river has so changed its course as to have swept away everything which was on the surface at the time the battle was fought; as late as 1801 there were 3,000 mango trees remaining, and the place was notorious for dakoits, who lurked in jungles there." An English traveller of 1801 thus writes about Plasi :—" The river, continually encroaching on its banks in this direction, has at length swept the battle-field away; every trace is obliterated, and a few miserable huts, literally overhanging the water, are the only remains of the celebrated Palassi." Murders and "dakoitis" were formerly very common in the neighbourhood of Plasi, the jungly state of the country affording shelter to marauders of every description; it is now a cultivated plain.

There is always something melancholy to the reflective mind in wandering over what has once been a field of battle. We have had this feeling in Europe as well as in Asia. Visiting Waterloo many years ago, it was impossible not to feel the utter desolation of the place, when knowing that "glorious war" had once so revelled there. The infantry squares, the cavalry charge, and the horse artillery—

Rivalling lightning's flash in ruin and in speed!

Napoleon, with his wonderful command of masses of men; and the Iron Duke's pathetic exclamation of, "Would to God that night or Blucher would come!"—the entire scene at Waterloo, which secured the peace of Europe, finds some sort of a parallel in Plassey, which decided the fate of India. The intense anxiety of Clive to fall in with Meer Jaffier, who had arranged that he should separate his troops from his master (the Nabob) and join the English as they advanced; the terrible fear of the Nabob on thinking his end was nigh; the swarthy master in the art of subtlety, Meer Jaffier himself, on his caparisoned charger, darting

---

* This was in 1846. Colonel Malleson, in his *Decisive Battles of India* (note to page 61), informs us, on the authority of Mr. Eastwick, that even this last historical remnant vanished some years ago.

about, like a treacherous spectre of indecision, halting between two opinions—the masses of men wearing "the shadowed livery of the burnished sun" in motion, and the thunder of artillery on both sides, with that fearful din and confusion inseparable from Oriental warfare—all might even now come to the mind of the reflective traveller while strolling over the scene of the old grove at Plassey.

Clive marched with an army * of about three thousand men and nine pieces of artillery, and was for some days after the commencement of operations "in a state of extreme anxiety, from there being no appearance of Meer Jaffier's separating himself and his adherents from the Nabob."

The Nabob's force consisted of the flower of his army, which he concentrated at Plassey, and brought, according to one authority, 50,000 infantry, 18,000 horse, and an enormous train of artillery with him; while, as related by another, the opposing army consisted of 15,000 horse, 35,000 foot, and forty pieces of cannon.† Here was an overwhelming force bent on the destruction of our small Presidency army. As soon as the morning of the 23rd June dawned, the engagement began. According to Clive's biographer :—

At sunrise the enemy—about a mile off—now aware of Clive's march, issued from their camp in all their force with their artillery, and soon commenced a heavy cannonade. Clive, who expected a communication from Meer Jaffier, looked anxiously for its arrival; but the messenger who, on the morning of this eventful day, was charged with a note from that officer never delivered it. Still, however, Clive watched with anxiety to see his friends separate from his foes, ready to take advantage of that trepidation and

---

* According to Sir John Malcolm, Clive's force consisted of six hundred and fifty European infantry, about two hundred Portuguese troops, one hundred and fifty artillery, including fifty seamen, two thousand one hundred Sepoys, eight six-pounders, and one howitzer. With this force the British marched out of Chandernagore, on the 13th June, to measure themselves with "the entire force of a populous nation."

† The latter numbers, being the same as Clive's in his letter to the Directors, must be correct.

confusion which such movements must produce. The charge of the English forces was accelerated by one of the Nabob's principal commanders (Moodeen Khan) being killed: Clive advanced to "an easy victory."

On reaching Moorshedabad, a month after, he wrote a full descriptive letter of the battle, preceding events, and occurrences which gave rise to his success and its results, which he forwarded to the Secret Committee of the Court of Directors. The conclusion of Clive's great epistle to the Directors is well worthy of being borne in mind by all Indian administrators and by the British public, at the present time, and by generations yet unborn. It is just what might have been expected from the "heaven-born general," after such a fortunate consummation as Plassey. "I persuade myself the importance of your possessions now in Bengal will determine you to send out, not only a large and early supply of troops and good officers, but of capable young gentlemen for the civil branches of your business."

As, out of a population of 250 or 260 millions, it is quite possible—especially in these Congress days or of excess in self-government—for an inconvenient Asiatic army of 80,000 or 100,000 men, at very short notice, to assemble near any one of the three Presidencies for action, Clive's advice becomes almost as useful in 1889 as it was in 1757, although we can now procure troops by telegraph and railway from up country when required. It should be kept in mind that Clive was not only a brave and skilful soldier, but a far-seeing statesman. There is a fine passage in the *Memoirs* which touches conclusively on these points:—
"It is only by considering the circumstances in which he was placed that we can understand the hesitating conduct of Clive previous to his advance to Plassey, the defensive character of the action, and the solicitude which he showed to repress that ardour and forward spirit in those under him, which, on ordinary occasions, it was his habit and his pride to stimulate and encourage. It is obvious that his qualities as a soldier, in this short and almost

bloodless, but eventful campaign, were rendered strictly subordinate to the talents of the statesman."

In the battle of Plassey the English lost only twenty of their European troops, and fifty of their Native sepoys, in killed and wounded. With reference to Clive's "solicitude," just referred to, there is an interesting anecdote: Major Kilpatrick, observing an opportunity of attacking an advanced party under a French officer, by whom the troops in the grove were annoyed, put himself at the head of two companies and two guns, to charge. Clive, being informed of it, hastened to the spot, commanded the party back to the grove, and severely reprimanded the Major for acting without his orders. It was stated by Clive's detractors that he was asleep in a hunting-house, his head-quarters, when Kilpatrick's attack was made known to him. This assertion has been denied; but, if admitted, "it will prove no more than that this extraordinary man could give, amid such scenes, a few minutes to necessary repose."* We have read that Napoleon and the Duke of Wellington, in their wars, and General Grant (the famous American) in our time, possessed the happy knack of snatching half or even quarter of an hour's sleep when under trial and anxiety, of which neither of these heroes had more than Clive.

A pleasing incident in the battle of Plassey is thus briefly narrated:—The army of Clive had come in sight of the camp, and the cannonade had rather alarmed the Nabob. Before the armies came into contact Clive observed Meer Jaffier filing off his troops, which made him sure both of the glory and the gain: he gave the word "Forward!" The Nabob fled; his masses of men were scattered, and India was lost and won.† The story of the turban of the deposed Nabob *in esse* and Meer Jaffier is also a good one, and it appears in the pages of Marshman, Malleson, and other writers on India, the latest being Colonel Innes in his *History of the Bengal European Regiment*. As already stated, Moodeen

---

* *Memoirs of Lord Clive*, vol. i., pp. 260-61.
† Mudie's *Picture of India*.

Khán (or Meer Mudun), one of Suraj-ood-dowlah's best generals, had been killed, having lost both his legs by a cannon ball. When he was conveyed into the Nabob's tent he expired in his presence. The Nabob was now thoroughly alarmed, and began to suspect all his servants of treachery. He sent for Meer Jaffier, his once supposed faithful treasurer of the army and commandant, or commander-in-chief, and placing his turban at his feet begged, in the most abject manner, that, for the sake of his grandfather,* he would forgive him and stand by him in the hour of need. Jaffier promised to be faithful, and as a proof of it advised the Nabob to recall his troops, as the day was advanced! "To-morrow," said he, "with the blessing of God, we will draw up the troops and prepare for the battle."

Colonel Malleson writes that the Nabob reminded Meer Jaffier of the loyalty he had always displayed towards his grandfather, of his relationship to himself; "then taking off his turban, and casting it on the ground before him, he exclaimed, 'J'afar, that turban thou must defend.' Those who are acquainted with the manners of Eastern nations will realise that no more pathetic, no more heart-rending, appeal could be made by a prince to a subject. Mír J'afar Khán responded to it with apparent sincerity. Placing —in the respectful manner which indicates devotion—his crossed hands on his breast, and bowing over them, he promised to exert himself to the utmost. When he made that gesture, and when he uttered those words, he was lying. Never had he been more firmly resolved than at that moment to betray his master."† On leaving the Nabob, Meer Jaffier galloped back to his troops.

Mohun Lall, the Nabob's general, was fully engaged with the English when he received orders to fall back, which he obeyed with reluctance. His retreat damped the minds of the soldiers, and they began to fly in every direction. It was a *sauve qui peut* flight with a vengeance; and "Clive thus obtained a complete and

---

* Ali Verdi Khán.

† *The Decisive Battles of India.* By Colonel G. B. Malleson, C.S.I., (1888) pp. 66–67. London: W. H. Allen & Co.

easy victory,"* of which, from its magnificent results, the Bengal Presidency will ever have reason to be proud. One cause of the defeat of the Nabob's troops is said to have been that their matchlocks did not fire owing to the rain having wetted the powder. But Madras and Bombay also did their share of work right well, and therefore share in the laurels of the crowning conquest of India. PLASSEY is inseparable from the colours of the 1st Madras and Bombay European Regiments, as well as from the brilliant services of the Bombay and Madras artilleries. "Plassey" was the first decoration emblazoned in the colours of "The Bengal European Regiment;" and it has been inherited by "The Royal Munster Fusiliers."†

"What's in a name?" A great deal in the Army! And it is pleasing to observe, in these days of innovation, the custom held sacred of heading the lists of regiments with their victories. Among the "Line Battalions" in the Army List (1881) we find the 101st (Royal Bengal Fusiliers), or old 1st Bengal European Regiment, greeting us with a long list of immortal names :— "Plassey," "Buxar," "Guzerat," "Deig," "Bhurtpore," "Afghanistan," "Ghuzni," "Ferozeshuhur," "Sobraon," "Pegu," "Delhi," "Lucknow." And the 102nd (Royal Madras Fusiliers), the old 1st Madras European Regiment, meets our eye with "The Royal Tiger"—*Spectamur agendo*—"Arcot," "Plassey," "Condore," "Wyndewash," "Sholingur," "Nundy Droog," "Amboyna," "Ternate," "Banda," "Pondicherry," "Mahidpoor," "Ava," "Pegu," "Lucknow." [This was the regiment of Neill, the avenging angel of the great Bengal Sepoy Mutiny.]

Now Bombay comes with the 103rd (Royal Bombay Fusiliers), or 1st Bombay European Regiment, with "Plassey" and "Buxar" (with the Royal Tiger), "Carnatic" and "Mysore" (with the Elephant), "Guzerat," "Seringapatam," "Kirkee," "Beni Boo Ally," "Aden," "Punjab," "Mooltan," "Goojerat." These, with the numerous useful and brilliant services of the three Presi-

* Marshman.
† Colonel Innes.

dency Artilleries, and eventually of the Engineers,* form, with those of our Native Cavalry and Infantry, a record probably unequalled in the world's history. What Bulwer (the first Lord Lytton) styled " the nursery of Captains," could hardly fail to be proud of her Presidential Armies, with such troops and assistance from England, to fight for her interests and support.

After the battle of Plassey, Suraj-ood-dowlah mounted a camel, and marched all night with 2,000 horse. He reached Moorshedabad the next morning. But here all his former friends forsook him and fled. He remained alone and deserted in his palace. But eventually he embarked in some boats, from Bhogwangola, and proceeded up the river, intending to join M. Law, the French general, to whom he had written to come down from Patna.

After the engagement, Meer Jaffier visited and congratulated Clive on his victory. They then marched together into Moorshedabad; and Meer Jaffier took possession of the royal palace. The chief men of the city and officers of State assembled there. A Durbar was held, and Clive, rising, took Meer Jaffier by the hand, and, seating him on the throne, saluted him as Nabob of Bengal, Behár, and Orissá.

They then proceeded to the treasury. Clive received sixteen lakhs of rupees (£160,000), and the other members of council a fair share. A large gratuity was also paid to the army and navy; and 100 lakhs were paid to the Company for public losses, besides large sums to English gentlemen, Natives, and Armenians.

Vast possessions of land were given to the Company; and the French were never again to be permitted to reside in the province.

The English had, indeed, recovered their misfortunes. By order of the son of Meer Jaffier, Suraj-ood-dowlah was murdered at Moorshedabad, on the very spot where he had so often shed innocent blood.

By the treaty with the late Nabob, the English were permitted (9th February) to erect a mint, and, as already mentioned, a fort.

* Raised in or about 1770.

The first English coin of Bengal was struck on the 19th August, 1757.*

Calcutta had sought these privileges for sixty years.

We have purposely refrained from entering into details regarding the operations at Plassey, as they have been so well told by many writers, including Clive himself; but we cannot leave this most decisive battle without citing Colonel Malleson's summing up of the results, as it is so clear and masterly, and has not been equalled by any other Anglo-Indian writer of our time :—

"From the very morrow of the victory the English became virtual masters of Bengal, Bihár, and Orísá. During the century which followed but one serious attempt was made to cast off the yoke virtually imposed by Plassey, whilst from the base it gave them, a base resting on the sea, and, with proper care, unassailable, they were able to extend their authority beyond the Indus, their influence amongst peoples of whose existence even Europe was at the time profoundly ignorant. It was Plassey which made England the greatest Muhammadan power in the world; Plassey which forced her to become one of the main factors in the settlement of the burning Eastern question ; Plassey which necessitated the conquest and colonization of the Cape of Good Hope, of the Mauritius, the protectorship over Egypt; Plassey which gave to the sons of her middle classes the finest field for the development of their talent and industry the world has ever known ; to her aristocracy unrivalled opportunities for the display of administrative power ; to her merchants and manufacturers customers whose enormous demands almost compensate for the hostile tariffs of her rivals, and, alas ! even of her colonies ; to the skilled artisan remunerative employment; to her people generally a noble feeling of pride in the greatness and glory of the Empire of which a little island in the Atlantic is the parent stem, Hindustan the noblest branch ; it was Plassey, which, in its consequences, brought consolation to that little island for the loss of America, and which,

---

* Marshman. Clive's Fort William cost two crores of rupees—about two millions sterling.

whilst, in those consequences, it has concentrated upon it the envy of the other nations of Europe, has given to her children the sense of responsibility, of the necessity of maintaining a great position, the conviction of which underlies the thought of every true Englishman.

"Yes! As a victory, Plassey was, in its consequences, perhaps the greatest ever gained. But, as a battle, it is not, in my opinion, a matter to be very proud of. In the first place, it was not a fair fight. Who can doubt that if the three principal generals of Síráju 'd-daulah had been faithful to their master Plassey would not have been won? Up to the time of the death of Mír Múdín Khán the English had made no progress; they had even been forced to retire. They could have made no impression on their enemy had the Núwáb's army, led by men loyal to their master, simply maintained their position. An advance against the French guns meant an exposure of their right flank to some 40,000 men. It was not to be thought of. It was only when treason had done her work, when treason had driven the Núwáb from the field, when treason had removed his army from its commanding position, that Clive was able to advance without the certainty of being annihilated. Plassey, then, though a decisive, can never be considered a great battle."*

There is matter enough here to expatiate on, so as to form an interesting little volume of itself. Considering the numbers of Mahomedans in our Presidencies, as well as in our Presidential Armies, the fact of our being the greatest Mahomedan Power in the world, which would-be "Members for India," and others interested in our Eastern Empire would do well to "inwardly digest," is a truth worthy of thorough and attentive study; and we shall have no great or even tolerable Anglo-Indian statesmen while this gravid subject remains, as at present, neglected and unmastered. It is the very life-blood of our Indian policy; and its importance goes on increasing from year to year. Mahomedanism, like Popery, will ever be a great riddle. The latter, even

---

* *The Decisive Battles of India*, pp. 72–73.

zealous Protestants must admit, though reduced to a spiritual power only, has still the principle of life strong within her; and although the Crescent must eventually give way to the Cross, there are certainly no very strong signs at present of Islam withering away.

A well-known writer, in one of the early numbers of the *Calcutta Review,* commences a learned and brilliant article on a great "Controversy" at the time by remarking that "Mahommedanism is perhaps the only undisguised and formidable antagonist of Christianity." And Englishmen should never forget that the fourth grand era of Christianity in connection with Mahomedanism arose with the dominion of Europeans in India,* who certainly have never, to the wonder of the Turk and Persian, half improved their advantages for evangelizing the East.

Even as to moral and general conduct, England, in the eighteenth century, was fearfully neglectful of her responsibility in India; at one time our religion there was almost *nil*; and in both the eighteenth and nineteenth centuries astute Mahomedans, as well as enlightened Hindus, have too often considered us "spectacles of men without a faith," or, apparently, "infidel conquerors." Of course, all this has vastly improved in our time. Education and a tolerant Government have tended to show the people our virtues and our failings; while the stern fact remains before us of India possessing over 50 millions of Mahomedans in her population, against 187 millions of Hindus, and about 14 millions of other races, including upwards of 1,800,000 Christians.† India has truly seen Mahomedan glory and decay; and while the young student from school or college beguiles his leisure hours by reading how once the banners of Islam approached close to the Papal See, and "the Crescent, almost within sight of Imperial Rome, shone brightly upon Spain, Turkey, and Sicily," he may think that none of his creed, in Asia or Europe, ever enjoyed so much peace and security as he enjoys under the Government of the British Queen-Empress.

---

* "The Mahommedan Controversy."—*Calcutta Review,* No. VIII., 1845, vol. iv.
† The total population, in a statistical report, is given at 253,891,820.

Truly, it is difficult to fully appreciate the significance of England's being the "greatest Mahomedan power in the world," so ably brought forward by our distinguished Anglo-Indian historian as one of the magnificent results of the Battle of Plassey.

We left Meer Jaffier seated on the throne of the Three Provinces; and a more weak, cruel, and rapacious sovereign could hardly be conceived. He plundered everywhere and everybody, especially Omichund, the Hindu merchant; having been a chief party in cheating him out of thirty lakhs (£300,000), falsely promised him as an indemnity for loss at Calcutta. It is pitiful to think that, in this wretched business the great Clive was concerned, on the principle that it is fair to deceive a man who tries to deceive others. Cheated and ruined, the "Hindu friend" of the Calcutta Council went deranged—a melancholy beginning of the British foundation of power in Bengal. It was while Clive and the Council were reaping their golden harvest that the second war with the French took place in the Carnatic, and the famous, rash and unfortunate Count Lally appeared on the scene. But we must now proceed to another great victory, won by Clive's Presidency Army, over the Dutch at Chinsurah (Fort Gustavus).

It has been well affirmed that, important as the Battle of Plassey was to the English interests, there was another equally so, the battle of Biderra,* near Chinsurah (Chinsura); for, as Holwell remarks, had the Dutch gained the victory they would have been joined by the "Nawab," and "not an individual of the colony would have escaped slaughter." The struggle with the sturdy Dutch was brought about in this fashion. Clive ever kept before him the wise resolution that, as English power had been established in Bengal by force, it should be maintained by force; not allowing any other European power to have a footing in the country.

---

* This decisive battle has been admirably described by Colonel Malleson. Biderra is about midway "between Chandernagore and Chinsurah—a position commanding the road to the latter place."

In 1758, Meer Jaffier (nicknamed Clive's ass), from his weakness and misconduct, must have given serious trouble to the victor of Plassey. He had brought on no less than three rebellions, all of which had been quelled by Clive, who had also assisted Meer Jaffier in the all-important matter of the projected invasion of Behar by the Prince of Delhi, and when two powerful Soubahdars, in league with the Prince, sought a share of the lower provinces. For such great service, and being relieved from his fears, Meer Jaffier gave Clive, as a jaghire, the quit-rent which the Company had agreed to pay for the Zemindary of Calcutta, worth three lakhs of rupees (£30,000) a year. The Mogul of Delhi created Clive an Omrah, or noble of the Empire.

After various transactions, Meer Jaffier paid the Governor a visit at Calcutta, where he was received with high honours. While residing there a large Dutch armament, consisting of seven ships with fifteen hundred troops, anchored at the mouth of the Hooghly. They had evidently not come without the consent of the Nabob, who had been intriguing for some time with the Dutch at Chinsurah, with the hope of counteracting the influence of the English. These intrigues were carried on by various means, a principal actor being Khoja Wajeed, a Cashmere merchant, and former agent of the French at Moorshedabad. After the revolution, finding that his hopes from the English were not fulfilled, he determined to bring a large Dutch force into Bengal to oppose them. Mr. Bisdom, a friend of Clive's, and Governor of Chinsurah, was very anxious for the continuance of peace, while the head of another party, Mr. Vernet, would hear of nothing but war. The English, for their own sakes, had just before prevented the Dutch from having their own pilots in the river; letters had, in consequence, been sent to Batavia, and a large force asked for, which had now arrived.

Clive got out of the great dilemma with his usual dexterity; and there was only one way of getting rid of the Dutch force, and that was by destroying it. It was the action of Siva the Destroyer. The English and Dutch were at peace; but, having destroyed the

French interests in Bengal, it would have been far from politic to allow the Dutch to remain. Clive, therefore, prepared to act—to use his own phrase—with a rope ("halter") round his neck. He demanded that Meer Jaffier should instantly order the Dutch troops to depart. Clive at once saw through his tool's usual artifice for delay; so he determined that the Dutch vessels should not come up the river. Although he strengthened the works below Calcutta, he was determined not to strike the first blow. At length the Dutch came up to the fort, and at once commenced an attack, but were repulsed. They then dropped down the river, and landed seven hundred European and eight hundred Malay troops, "who marched up by land on the right bank of the river towards Chinsurah." Clive's European troops were not more than a third of those which the Dutch had now under their command. The little Presidency Army had previously been sent up, under Colonel Forde, to take position between Fort Gustavus and Chandernagore.* The Dutch army advanced, and encamped two miles south of Chinsurah.

Forde, one of Clive's best and tried officers,† knowing that the two nations were at peace, wrote for a distinct Order in Council before he attacked the Dutch. Clive received the letter, or note of demand, when playing at cards. Without quitting the table, he wrote an answer in pencil: "Dear Forde, fight them immediately. I will send you the Order of Council to-morrow." No wonder it has been said that there is nothing greater than this in all Livy. The forces met; Forde conquered the Dutch, and their ambition in India—though not of such a resolute nature as that of the French—was quenched for ever, "by the daring genius of Clive," as that of the French had previously been.

About the same time as Forde's victory, the Dutch ships in the river were captured by the English; and so Holland's great enterprise ended in smoke.

Another account of the Dutch armament, or the large fleet

---

* The Dutch settlement of Chinsurah lies within three miles of Chandernagore.
† Who had been so successful against the Northern Circars in September 1758.

which arrived from Batavia, is that it consisted of seven ships, three of thirty-six guns, three of twenty-six, and one of sixteen, with 1,100 troops, European and Malay. It was given out that the armament was intended for the Dutch settlements on the Coromandel Coast, but had been *obliged* to run up the Hooghly. A man of Clive's penetration, however, could not mistake its object, which was to take advantage of the breaking up of the Mahomedan power, and endeavour to supplant the English in Bengal.* But even setting this aside, the presence of a foreign force in the vicinity of Calcutta, of so many European soldiers, it is obvious could not be permitted.

The policy of Clive had been fully carried out. "By vigour, decision, and daring," writes Colonel Malleson, in his account of Biderra, "a danger greater than any which since January 1757 had threatened the British settlement in Bengal had been encountered and overthrown." The Colonel also is of opinion that Clive never entertained a doubt of the secret understanding between Meer Jaffier and the Dutch.

Colonel Forde, immediately after the action, invested Chinsurah (November 1759); but the Dutch hastened to make an apology to Clive. On agreeing to pay the expenses of the war, he released their ships. Soon after these events, in February 1760, he embarked for England, rich in glory and money, but with an impaired constitution, after his great labours, leaving the Government in the hands of Mr. Vansittart.†

We have already alluded to the French Governor's country house at Giretty, where, in 1775, were assembled the beauty and fashion of Chinsurah, Chandernagore, Serampore, and Calcutta. As details concerning society and manners give animation to a picture, we shall therefore conclude these few remarks on Chinsurah and the Dutch—whose Indian trade was in its most palmy state between 1770 and 1780—with the following sketch, from a description by Captain Stavorinus (February 1770), of a visit by the Dutch and

---

* *Notes on the Right Bank of the Hooghly.*
† *Outlines of the History of Bengal.*

their Director to the French Governor's seat of Giretty:—The party set off from Chinsurah at four o'clock, in six carriages, and reached the chateau at six, where they were received at the bottom of the steps and conducted into a large saloon, in which the principal ladies and gentlemen of Chandernagore were assembled. At seven, the Dutch guests were invited to witness a play in a slight building erected for the purpose. After this, a hundred ladies and gentlemen sat down to an elegant supper. The party broke up at one, and returned to Chinsurah. The entertainments at Giretty are said to have been little inferior to those of the old Government House in Calcutta, where hospitality was the rule; and, for the time, the officers of the Presidency Army, with those of the Royal Navy and mercantile services, thoroughly enjoyed themselves, and forgot they were in India.

There can be little doubt that the famous Commander-in-Chief and Governor of Bengal was as fond of dancing as any dashing young officer under him, and that he had, years before the above entertainment, figured at Giretty in the ball-room. During his furlough-life (1763), as if not yet perfection in the Terpsichorean art, we find him learning dancing in Paris "to please the French ladies "—thus becoming the daring in love as he ever was the dauntless in war. The following interesting facts regarding the elder Pitt's "heaven-born general" are still little known; and they are not to be found in Malcolm's *Life of Clive**:—Many of the French nobility, who despised all the mercantile class, contemned Clive for having been in a mercantile office; he forbade all the Company's servants in India the use of palankins, and the junior servants the use of even an umbrella; he rose early, and then executed a good part of his business, afterwards breakfasted, and then took exercise. He was rather reserved in company; he was a great enemy to interlopers, and during his government† he issued orders that all free merchants should be recalled to Calcutta and should not quit it. Clive knew nothing of the vernaculars; and he would say that if he had

---

* *Calcutta Review.*
† Shortly before leaving India in 1767.

been a linguist, he might have believed many of the lies that were told him, and would never have conquered India for us. Clive, the warrior of India, and his famous historian Orme, were appointed writers on the same day. After the battle of Plassey he proposed to the authorities the conquest of China, in order to pay off the national debt!* An East India director once asked Clive whether Sir Roger Dowler (Suraj-ud-Dowlah) was not a baronet; and this was considered as good as Lord George Bentinck's stating that if the price of sugar were raised the hundred millions of Hindustan would not be able to sweeten their tea. When Clive went home, he was exposed to various insults from civilians or military men whom he had offended in India; and once he was obliged to disguise himself three times in one day to avoid the pursuit of some of his enemies. Thus the future great benefactor of officers' widows for all time, and others who depended on the military profession, became for a season the victim of malevolence and scandal. The sense of duty in some men is so strong that the wielder of it is ever sure to make rancorous opponents; and Clive's regard for DUTY was certainly not inferior to that of the Iron Duke. Before a few remarks on Clive's Fund—one of the greatest boons ever offered to the Presidency Armies of India—we must note the principal events which occurred, as affecting Bengal, especially as a few great military operations took place, from Clive's departure for England to his resuming power in Calcutta as Governor in 1765.

In 1760 the young Prince, son of the Emperor of Delhi, Shah Allum, for the second time invaded Behar, having been amicably disposed of by Clive on the first occasion (1758). His father having been murdered, he now became Emperor. The English and Meerun, the infamous son of Meer Jaffier, marched against him. This adventurous Emperor, without power or subjects, had

* The people of Múrshidabad (Moorshedabad) expected to be plundered after the battle, and were therefore greatly surprised when no contribution was levied on them. Clive remarked that when he entered Moorshedabad at the head of 200 Europeans and 500 Sepoys, the inhabitants, if inclined to destroy the Europeans, might have done it *with sticks and stones.*

threatened Patna, which the brave Ramnarayan put in a state of defence, and wrote to Moorshedabad entreating that troops might be sent to his assistance. Colonel Caillaud, who had succeeded to the command of the army, was in command of the English troops, which, with the Nabob's soldiery, made up the force. No better argument for the substitution of British for Mahommedan rule can be found than in the facts that Meerun had already put to death two of his own officers, and decapitated two of the women of his seraglio with his own sabre. Just as Meerun was setting out on this expedition, he ordered two widows, living in obscurity at Dacca, to be put to death. The Governor of Dacca refused; but, under pretence of conducting them to Moorshedabad, orders were issued to sink them and the boats. And now comes an affecting incident, which stamps Meerun with eternal infamy:—Just as the murderers were pulling out the plugs to sink the vessels, the younger sister exclaimed, "Oh! God Almighty, we are both sinners and culprits; but we have committed no sin against Meerun. On the contrary, he owes us everything in this world." Meerun, we are informed, had the names of three hundred individuals down in his note-book for murder or execution on his return; but, fortunately, he never returned. And this was the wretched son to whom Meer Jaffier, the lazy, had deputed his power. Colonel Caillaud had requested Ramnarayan not to engage the Emperor till he could come up; but, neglecting this advice, he went out and was completely defeated. Patna was defenceless when Caillaud arrived with his troops. He wished to fall on the enemy immediately, but Meerun said the stars would not be favourable before the 22nd of February. On the 20th the Emperor attacked the united army. Meerun's fifteen thousand horse were soon broken and fled, but Colonel Caillaud steadily and boldly attacked the Emperor, and speedily routed him. The Emperor soon after emerged from the hills, and lingered about the country, having lost the chance of taking Moorshedabad. Colonel Caillaud had marched down in pursuit of him. The two armies were now in sight of each other, and the English offered battle; but, taking a sudden panic, the Emperor marched back to Patna, to which he laid close siege. Assistance was now offered him by the Governor of Púrneah. The attack on Patna was continued for nine days; and the city was just about to fall, when Captain Knox arrived with a few troops. He had been sent up by Colonel Caillaud, and had marched up from Burdwan in thirteen days. Knox fell on the Emperor's troops when they had retired to their afternoon's nap. The defeat was inevitable; and the once hope of Delhi set his camp on fire and ignominiously fled. Soon after a large army (16,000 men) from Púrneah, under the Governor, arrived, and preparations were made to attack Patna; but Captain Knox, with a small force (about 1,000) of European and Native troops, crossed the river, boldly attacked, and completely defeated him.

"This," writes Marshman, "was one of the most gallant actions fought in this war, and gave the natives the highest opinions of the English. It was on this occasion that Rajah Setabroy so distinguished himself by his bravery as to acquire the highest praise."* Clive himself could hardly have done the work better. Doubtless he read the despatch with unfeigned delight; and so more laurels were added to those already gained by the Bengal Presidency Army.

After the defeat the Púrneah Governor joined the Emperor, whose watch-words might now have been, "Save me from my friends!" Caillaud and Meerun followed his steps. The English Commander continued the pursuit, although the rains had just set in. On the night of the 2nd of July 1760, a terrible thunder-storm occurred; and while Meerun was hearing stories in his tent —after the time-honoured Oriental fashion—the lightning struck him and two of his attendants dead. Colonel Caillaud was now obliged to give up the pursuit, and to return to Patna, where he quartered his troops for the season. And so Meerun, the profligate, but the main-stay of his father's government, never returned.

Now came the distress of the English and Meer Jaffier for want of funds; and, to mend matters, Mr. Vansittart resolved to

* *History of Bengal.*

appoint the talented and energetic Meer Cossim, the Nabob's son-in-law, Deputy in Bengal. He had played his part well; for an instance, when the administration fell into disorder, and the troops surrounded the palace and became clamorous for their arrears of pay, Meer Cossim came forward and promised to satisfy them from his own purse. The English, too, had an expensive war on their hands. They had received large sums unexpectedly, and spent them without thought. In short, Clive was never so much wanted in India as when he was absent in Europe.

Meer Jaffier had sent Meer Cossim on a mission from Moorshedabad to Calcutta, where Mr. Vansittart and Warren Hastings now directed the affairs of the Company. To these distinguished statesmen his talents became at once apparent; and it was thought by the Governor that he was the only man who could give a new aspect to affairs in Bengal. Meer Jaffier objected to the appointment of a Deputy—was in consequence deposed; and Meer Cossim became Nabob of the three provinces. He was eventually invested with the government by the Emperor.

This important proceeding, as well as British reconciliation with Shah Allum, came about in a somewhat strange fashion.

As soon as the rains of 1760 were over, Major Carnac advanced against the Emperor, on the borders of Behar, and completely defeated him. After the battle Carnac offered peace, to which he very readily consented, and the English Commander paid his respects to the Emperor in his camp.

When Meer Cossim heard of this intercourse he became alarmed, and went in haste to Patna.

Although suggested by Carnac, the Nabob was too proud to wait upon the Emperor. At length it was arranged that the two parties should meet in the English factory. "A temporary throne was erected," writes the historian, "and there the Emperor of Hindustan, the descendant of Timur, a fugitive in his own dominions, took his seat. Meer Cossim entered with the usual ceremonies, and the Emperor invested him with the Soobahdary of Bengal, Behar, and Orissa, and he promised to pay twenty-four lakhs of rupees a year of tribute. The Emperor then set out towards Delhi, and Carnac accompanied him to the banks of the Kurumnassa. On taking leave of him there, the Emperor offered to grant the English the dewanny of the three provinces whenever they might desire it."*

We should have noticed that, as considerably affecting the Presidency Army at this period, there was an innate desire on the part of Meer Cossim—feeling that all real power in the country remained with the English—to deliver himself from subjection to the Council of Calcutta. And the only way to do this was by force. He therefore determined to improve his army, and placed at its head an Armenian, a native of Persia—Gurghin Khan, or Gregory Khan. The Nabob's army was to be disciplined after the model of the English; but, strange enough, this Oriental military genius, once a mere seller of cloth, and now a Commander-in-Chief, steadily pursued the plan of making his master independent of the English. He manufactured muskets, cast cannon, trained up artillerymen; and the army he commanded was considered the best Native army ever seen in Bengal.

To facilitate his plans, and keep away from the all-searching eye of the English, which Clive, though absent, still kept busy, Meer Cossim forsook Moorshedabad, and made Monghir his capital. It was there that the Armenian general established his gun manufactory, and the reputation of the town for its muskets was to be traced to the scientific talent of the young Armenian—Gurghin Khan.†

The year 1761 was an unimportant one in Bengal; but, in 1762, disputes arose between Meer. Cossim and the English on the subject of duties as affecting private trade. Both civil and military officers had now begun to engage in the latter; but while Clive remained in the country they paid the same duty as the native merchants.

They now resolved to become free-traders in the strictest sense, by paying no duties at all.

* Marshman. † *History of Bengal.*

Fierce debates in the Calcutta Council took place, till at length private free-trade seemed to become as important a matter as the conquest or keeping of Bengal.

Meer Cossim wanted money, and was obstinate to the last in the subject of all duties. And so the authority of the Nabob's Government was destroyed, the native merchants were ruined, and the English gentlemen made "very large fortunes."

The revenues of the Viceroy being diminished, although he had large sums to pay his masters, was of no apparent consequence whatever.

Warren Hastings, of the Council, said, with at least some justice, " that there was no reason why a sovereign Prince, like Meer Cossim, should not do good to his own subjects." The chief of the Dacca factory said that such " language was more fit for a Nabob's Agent than for a Member of Council." To this Hastings replied, that " none but a rascal would hold such language."

Thus were civilities exchanged in the Bengal Presidency Council nearly one hundred and thirty years ago.

At length it was resolved to send Mr. Amyatt and Mr. Hay to Meer Cossim to insist on his laying the former duties (which he had just taken off) on the Native trade. At first there was a chance of success; but Mr. Ellis, the violent chief of Patna, destroyed all hopes of peace. He (1763) surprised and took the city of Patna. But the town was soon re-taken by the Viceroy's troops, and Mr. Ellis and all the Europeans were placed in confinement. Meer Cossim now knew from this affair at Patna that war was inevitable; and he proceeded to take his vengeance at leisure. Amyatt, when near Moorshedabad, *en route* to Calcutta,* was killed in a scuffle.

When news of Mr. Amyatt's death, and of the confinement of Mr. Ellis and his companions, reached Calcutta, the Council, notwithstanding the opposition of Mr. Vansittart and Warren Hastings, determined on instant war.

* Mr. Amyatt had been dismissed by the Nabob at the interview at Monghir, leaving Mr. Hay as a hostage for his own officers who were in custody.

"Oh, for an hour of Clive!" was muttered by not a few Europeans in Bengal, on learning the resolution of the Council; for the Bengal Presidency Army was still indeed very small.

There is no finer or truer passage in Sir John Malcolm's most excellent *Life of Lord Clive* than where it is said of him, on sailing from India (25th February 1760), that he left a blank that could not be filled up. "It appeared" (to use the strong and expressive language of a contemporary observer) "as if the soul was departing from the body of the Government of Bengal."* Such was the vast intrinsic power evinced by the once " merchant's clerk," who had so raised himself to celebrity.†

The majority of the Calcutta Council had ordered the English army to take the field. At the same time they determined to raise Meer Jaffier, for the second time, to the throne, on his agreeing to the imposition of duties on the native trade, and the private trade of the European gentlemen to be exempt. So the old man of seventy-two, scarcely able to move for the leprosy, left Calcutta, and accompanied the English army to Moorshedabad, his old capital. Meer Cossim had taken the utmost pains to discipline his troops, and, as before remarked, they were the best that any Native prince in Bengal ever possessed; of course, all owing to the great military talent of his General-in-chief, Gurghin Khan, the Armenian. The war, however, did not last long; owing to discord among the Viceroy's generals, his troops were defeated at Cutwa on the 19th July 1763, and on the 24th the English, after storming the lines constructed for the defence of the city, took Moorshedabad. A distinguished officer who commanded the troops, Major Adams, at length discovered the Soubahdar with his whole force drawn up (2nd August) in the plain of Geriah. The troops are said to have presented the aspect of a European army. They were brigaded, clothed, and accoutred in the English style, and "supported by a fine train of artillery." There were 20,000 horse and 8,000 foot; but to oppose this force Major Adams—a

---

* *Memoirs of Lord Clive*, vol. ii, p. 143.
† Lord Brougham, in *Lives of Eminent Statesmen*.

Sir Charles Napier of his day—had only 3,000 men. The Major led them on most gallantly, however; the assailants carried everything; and the native warriors fled, abandoning all their artillery and provisions.

Colonel Malleson has described the battle of "Ghériah"[*] in his usual graphic style, telling us that the village, about a mile distant from the scene of action, gave its name to the plain. We learn also that Major Adams, assisted by Major Carnac, placed his Europeans, composed of the 84th and Bengal European Regiment (the present Royal Munster Fusiliers), in the centre, "with three battalions of sipáhis on each flank, the guns in the intervals, and one battalion of sipáhis as a reserve. The action began with a discharge of artillery from both sides. Under cover of this, the infantry advanced, and the European troops, in the centre, were soon engaged" with the enemy. This additional triumph of the Bengal Presidency Army was immediately followed up by a really decisive battle. Meer Cossim had thrown up a strong entrenchment at U'ndwah Nálá, near Rajmahl, and thither his troops now retreated. During these transactions he had remained at Monghir; but he now resolved to join his army. Before leaving Monghir, in a fit of brutality, the Nabob put to death all his native prisoners, including Rajah Ramnarayan, the former Governor of Patna. He was drowned in the river "with a bag of sand"; and two wealthy bankers (*setts*) were brought out and thrown from a tower of the Fort of Monghir into the river. The boatmen as they passed along, says Marshman, continued long after to point out the spot where the unfortunate men perished. After these vile murders, Meer Cossim joined his army at U'ndwah Nálá. Early in October the English attacked his camp, and completely defeated him. This entrenched camp on the U'ndwah was so strongly enclosed between the river, the mountains, and a swamp, that its reduction detained

---

[*] This spelling of "Gh" would seem to be generally applied to Gheriah, the pirate Angria's stronghold, south of Bombay, already alluded to. It is thus spelt by Malcolm, Macaulay, Gleig, and other writers. The battle in the plain of Bengal, above noticed, is spelt by Marshman, Innes, and others, "Geriah," which we have adopted.

the army nearly a whole month. One historian writes: "In the end it was surprised and carried; after which Meer Cossim never again attempted to face his adversaries in the open field." But for a full and vivid description of this battle, we must refer our readers to the pages of Malleson,* who thus sums up the grand result:—

The battle of the U'ndwah Nálá "was one of the most glorious, one of the most daring and most successful feats of arms ever achieved. It was, in every sense of the word, a most decisive battle. Adams did not merely defeat the army of Mír Kásim, he destroyed it. The blow had been so great that a rally henceforth was impossible. In one morning, with an army 5,000 strong, of whom one-fifth only were Europeans, Adams had stormed a position of enormous strength, defeated 40,000 and destroyed 15,000 men, captured upwards of a hundred pieces of cannon, and so impressed his power on the enemy that they had no thought but flight."

And again, as regards the hero of the war: "In little more than four months Major Adams had begun and brought to conclusion a campaign which did more than confirm the advantages which Clive had gained for the country by the victory of Plassey."† We must now retrace our steps in the drama. A day or two after Meer Cossim's defeat at U'ndwah Nálá, he retired to Monghir; but finding he was unable to oppose the English army, which was in pursuit of him, he fled with his troops to Patna. The English gentlemen, it is said, who had fallen into his hands, he dragged along with him. The second day after leaving Monghir, his army was encamped on the banks of the Rewah. Suddenly there was a commotion in the camp; everyone seemed eager to cross the river; then some men were seen carrying a dead body across the fields to be buried. It was the body of the General-in-Chief, Gurghin Khan, and it was "the Nabob's pleasure." Three or four Moguls had rushed into his tent, towards the close of the day, and put him to death. The Nabob had been told that his able and scientific General was a traitor. "Within twenty-four hours after," writes

---

* For full account see *Decisive Battles of India*, p. 161-164.
† *Ibid.*, pp. 171-172.

Marshman, "Georghin, the Armenian General, was a corpse."* Meer Cossim now fled in haste to Patna. Adams immediately marched and laid siege to Monghir, which the Soubahdar had (as before stated) made his capital, and which was now found strongly fortified. After nine days of regular operations the place capitulated, which threw the Indian chief into a dreadful paroxysm of rage, and he found that he must leave Patna and quit the country. His hatred towards the English being intense, he resolved, before he left, that all his prisoners should die. He had already given notice that on the advance of the British troops he would murder all his captives. A former sergeant in the French service, now serving Meer Cossim, became the executioner. He proceeded with a file of soldiers, who fired upon the defenceless men, and put them all to death, with the exception of Dr. Fullarton (or Fullerton), who was spared on account of his medical skill. Forty-eight English gentlemen, including Mr. Ellis, Mr. Hay, and Mr. Lushington —members of Council—and a hundred and fifty soldiers, fell in this terrible massacre at Patna; perhaps only equalled by that at Cawnpore during the great Sepoy Mutiny of 1857.

Patna fell into the hands of the English on the 6th of November 1763. At the investment the garrison had been reinforced with 10,000 men, and the defence supported by strong bodies of irregular cavalry. There was a vigorous resistance; the garrison took one of the English batteries and blew up their magazine, yet in eight days a breach was effected and the place taken by storm.† Meer Cossim fled to the Soubahdar of Oudh for protection; and thus ended a short and decisive war, well conducted, and adding greatly to the glory of the Bengal Presidency Army, as well as to that of the British name throughout the presidencies of India.

After the flight of Meer Cossim there was great discontent among the British forces. At the Soubahdar of Oudh's court the fugitive Viceroy of Bengal was well received; but Sujah Dowlah had then a still more illustrious refugee, one who bore the mighty name of the Great Mogul. Sujah, with a view to his own interest,

* *History of Bengal.* † *History of British India.*

undertook to support the Viceroy's cause; and at length these three distinguished personages marched, with united force, to attack the British army. Our troops were then very ill prepared to sustain so formidable an encounter.

We read that the troops, composed in a great measure of foreigners and sepoys, complained that, after such a series of brilliant victories, they were left not only without reward, but suffering severely from the climate and scarcity of provisions. The later days of batta, prize-money, and good rations were yet far distant; so no wonder at the discontented state of our forces. They broke forth into open mutiny; numbers even separated from the main body. Major Carnac, who had now assumed the command, not feeling himself in a position to undertake offensive operations, waited the attack in his camp near Patna. The soldiers, when engaged in battle, it is pleasing to relate, forgot their mutinous propensities, and only thought of duty. The utmost steadiness prevailed, and, after a protracted conflict, they completely repulsed the enemy, though, from extreme fatigue, they could not follow up a pursuit. Sujah Dowlah was obliged to retreat into Oudh.

In May 1764 Major Hector Munro assumed command. He was a bold and enterprising officer, and was determined to follow up the advantages gained by his predecessors. He firmly resolved to put down a spirit of insubordination which began to lurk in the Native army. A battalion of sepoys having left the camp soon after he had joined, he ordered them to be pursued and brought back, when he had twenty-four of the ring-leaders "blown from the mouth of a cannon." No disposition to mutiny was thenceforth manifested.

It may be safely affirmed that had there been one Clive and a few Hector Munros during 1857, the great Indian mutiny would have been far sooner stamped out. But too long peace is apt to produce—especially in India—a foolish security, and consequent serious danger, for which we must ever be prepared, recollecting Clive's immortal words: "We won India by force, and must ever

be prepared to keep it by this stern, yet unavoidable, auxiliary!"*
"Globe-trotters" and so-called "peace-makers" may argue to the contrary; but, in fact, the latter possess a more ready and dangerous food for war than the well-conducted and well-disciplined regiments of the Queen-Empress.

On the 23rd of October Munro met the troops of Oudh at Buxar, and completely defeated them. During retreat they lost an immense quantity of stores, and 130 pieces of artillery. The Emperor had already made overtures to Major Carnac, which he did not think proper to accept; these he now renewed, complaining that Sujah Dowlah had treated him with indignity. Major Munro gave a favourable answer, and only delayed the final acceptance of his proposals till they should receive the sanction of the Presidency, which was readily granted. The Mogul now marched under the banner of his allies. An arrangement was made with the Vizier after the victory. As for Meer Cossim, to whom Oudh had given an asylum, he was eventually plundered of his treasures and allowed to escape. Throughout the Bengal Presidency, and especially in the army, it is well said that, "by his barbarities," about as atrocious as any to be found in Indian history, "he forfeited the interest which his spirited conduct and hard treatment would otherwise have excited." The Nabob never troubled Bengal again.

Meer Jaffier, having been raised to the throne a second time, as was to be expected, found it impossible to pay the sums which he had promised to the English. He was now well advanced in life. The leprosy gained ground on him, and he expired at Moorshedabad in January 1765, at the age of seventy-four. The Delhi Emperor should have appointed his successor, but, as he had neither means nor authority, the English did as they pleased. The members of Council, as usual, received large sums of money from Nujun-ood-dowla, the son of Meer Jaffier;† and so they made him Nabob. Thus, as in English history we read of King-makers, so in Indian we have had Nabob-makers, who too often "fleeced" their poor kings of a day.

* *Memoirs.* † By Munny Begum.

It may be well to conclude this chapter—which we have greatly diversified, in order to excite a love of Indian history and geography among students of the present generation, subjects far too much neglected in educational work—by remarking that the fugitive Meer Cossim, from his retreat in the interior of his dominions, obtained the aid [of a body of Mahrattas under Mulhar Rao, and of Shazee-ud-deen, who were once the most powerful adherents of the Mogul throne. With such mighty auxiliaries he hoped to make another stand against the victorious English. But Sir Robert Fletcher, who held the temporary command, laid siege to Allahabad (1765), which, as soon as a breach was effected, surrendered. Carnac, now raised to the rank of General, succeeded him, and advanced to attack the army of the Vizier (of Oudh), which was completely defeated, and the prince compelled to abandon all his dominions. In this, what has been styled "a splendid British campaign," the Bengal European Regiment was ever to the front, and Major Innes has done wisely in giving at the beginning of his work a table of "War Services," of more than usual excellence. The dates of the various actions fought may be seen at a glance, from the capture of the Fort of "Baj-Baj" (Budge-Budge), re-capture of Fort William, Calcutta, and capture of the Fort of "Hugli" (1757), down to the siege and capture of Lucknow (1858), numbering over eighty actions, battles, expeditions, sieges, and other brilliant operations.* The Madras and Bombay

* After perusing such a list of services, few will be disposed to quarrel with the author of the *History of the Bengal European Regiment* (the Royal Munster Fusiliers) for putting on his title-page, "How it Helped to Win India." From one hundred years of glory we take the following facts:—Battle of Plassey, 1757; Battle of Condore, 1758; Occupation of Rajahmundri; Capture of the French Position at Narsurpore; Storm and Capture of the French Fortress of Masulipatam; Relief of Patna, 1759; Defeat of the Dutch at Chandernagore; Battle of Bederra against the Dutch; Defence of Patna, 1760; Defeat of the Emperor of Delhi at Belkoss; Relief of Patna; Battle of Beerpore; Battle against Shah Alám and the French at Suan, 1761; Battle of Manjee, 1763; Kutwah; Geriah; Capture of the Fortified Position at Suti; Storm and Capture of U'ndwah Nálá; Capture of Monghyr; Siege and Capture of Patna; Defence of Patna, 1764; Battle of Buxar; Assault of the Fort of Chunar; Storm of the Nawab Vizier's Camp near Benares; Capture of the Fortress of Allahabad, 1765; Capture of the Fort of Chunar; Action at Karrah; Battle of Kalpi; Battle of Kutra, 1774; Battle of Patuta,

Presidency armies also, in the services of their first European regiments, with the admirable and devoted artillery and engineers of the three Presidencies of India, in like manner furnish immortal rolls of victories won, the actions in them affording bright examples of Anglo-Indian and Native heroism and devotion, not excelled in the histories of the ancient and modern world.

1781; Capture of the Fort of Bridge-ghur, also in that year. The regiment now went again to the Madras Presidency, to be employed in the " war against Haidar Ali in the Carnatic."

CHAPTER VIII.

ORIGIN AND PROGRESS OF OUR INDIAN ARTILLERY—LORD CLIVE AND THE ARMY.

LOOKING at the progress which has been made in Artillery science, as well as in the quantity and quality of the material in our day, it is interesting to go back upwards of two hundred and fifty years and think of the artillery of that army which, "originating in a few gunners' crews and factory guards," had, before the Bengal Sepoy Mutiny, "swollen to that gigantic and well-disciplined host known as the Company's army."*

At the Armegon factory, on the coast of Coromandel, in 1628, the garrison consisted of twelve pieces of ordnance and twenty-eight soldiers, of what arm does not appear, but it seems probable that they were trained as Infantry, and also "to work the guns in time of need." Mr. Day, the enterprising mercantile chief of the factory, must have had the greatest confidence in his artillery, as we thus find as many guns as a few more than half the number of the garrison. When, in 1640, he removed the factory to Madrasnapatam, just thirteen years before Fort St. George (Madras) was raised to the rank of a Presidency, he was employed in the very natural and useful work of raising a fortification; and, in 1644, the early inhabitants of Madras must have hailed with joy the landing of thirty recruits and a considerable number of

* Begbie's *History of the Services of the Madras Artillery* (Madras 1852).

ordnance and military stores, with the promise of twenty more "recruits" in the following year.*

Even sixty-seven years after this, we find the grand deficiency with the artillery to be in draught cattle, of which there were none available for the attack on the fort of Budge-budge, already narrated; and, in consequence, the two field-pieces and a tumbril with the force were drawn by the troops themselves. Even Clive, who could fight with anything, complained (January 1757), not only of the want of draught cattle, but of the guns being "mounted on wrong carriages, with neither tubes nor portfires!"† Now, at the close of 1889, we all know of the splendid equipment of our batteries of artillery in India, and read with pride and satisfaction that our Indian Artillery for the ensuing year is fixed at 12,375, with 6,578 horses.

Truly, in such an all-important matter as Artillery draught, when in a country swarming with bullocks (as has sometimes been the case at later periods), there were none available, toil, in the strictest sense, has built on toil, and age on age improved!

Colonel Carnac has already remarked on the formation of companies in our Indian Artillery; but we now hope to present a few more interesting notes on its origin and progress.

While writing this "Continuation," Alexander III., Czar of Russia, has just celebrated the introduction of Artillery into Russia five hundred years ago. It may, therefore, be pardonable to remark, that as the Czar believes the Artillery branch of the Russian Army would distinguish itself, in case of need, as highly in the future as it has done in the past, the same may be said of the Indian Artillery, which, long before it came directly under the Crown, had attained a state of great perfection.

The first company of Bengal Artillery, we are told, was raised in 1749; the orders were received, it is believed, from Bombay, then the chief presidency. A company was ordered, at the same

---

* In 1690-91, a company of European Artillery and a troop of horse constituted a part of the garrison of Fort St. George; and in the same year Fort St. David, near Cuddalore, was built.

† Begbie thinks their equipment may have been left on board the *Salisbury*.

time, at each presidency, in the Court of Directors' general letter of 17th June 1748. A copy of the warrant for that at Madras will be found in the *Artillery Records* for October 1843, and for Bombay, in one of a series of papers entitled "Three Years' Gleanings," which appeared in the E.I. *United Service Journal* in 1838; the entire warrants are too voluminous for insertion. A similar one was most probably sent to Bengal, but all records perished when Calcutta was taken. Admiral Boscawen was requested to supply such aid in raising the companies as he could spare from the fleet, for gunners; and the master gunner was appointed to the Bombay company. The companies were to be completed as early as possible, and all the gun-room's crew, who were qualified, were to be included.

The "gun-room's crew" appears to have been the denomination given to a certain number of men set apart for the duties of the artillery; their officers were called gunners, gunner's mates, &c., and combined the magazine duties with the more properly called duties of artillerymen.

The new company was to consist of one captain, one second captain, one captain-lieutenant, and three lieutenant fireworkers; four sergeants, four corporals, three drummers, and one hundred gunners. This list slightly differs from that already given.* There is also a discrepancy in the dates of formation of the Bengal and Madras artilleries, as well as in the pay of the companies. In a Minute of Council, dated Fort St. George, 1755, it is written:—"Artillery Companies, conformably to the Orders of the Hon'ble the Court of Directors in their Letter dated 15th December 1752." Here the captain receives £200 per annum, the first lieutenant £100, and the second and third £90. The sergeants received 2s., and the gunners 1s. 6d. a day.† But let us return to Captain Buckle.

In an old and rather curious volume of travels in India, entitled

---

* Page 121. In the list of salaries, Captain Buckle puts down the "Captain and Chief Engineer at" £200 per annum.

† Begbie.—Captain Buckle has a Captain, Lieutenant, and Director of Laboratory at £100 per annum.

Account of the Trade in India, by Charles Lockyer, published in 1711, and relating to a period a little antecedent to this date, we find a notice of the "gun-room crew" at Madras, with the rates of pay received by the different grades.

"The garrison," he writes, "consists of about 250 European soldiers, at ninety-one *fanams* (£1 2s. 9d.) per month, and 200 topasses, or Black Mongrel Portuguese, at fifty or fifty-two fanams a month. The 'gun-room crew' is about twenty experienced Europeans to manage the guns, at 100 fanams per month. The Captains are paid fourteen pagodas per month, Ensigns ten pagodas, Sergeants five pagodas, and Corporals the same pay as the gun-room crew. Chief gunner of the inner fort, fourteen pagodas; gunner of the outworks, twelve pagodas; and their mates in proportion." These rates of pay appear to be sufficiently liberal, seeing that, at that time, the Governor had only £200 per annum salary, and £100 gratuity; the councillors had from £100 to £40 per annum. Senior merchants drew £40, junior merchants £30, factors £15, and writers £5. There were in those days at Madras, "two ministers" at £100 per annum each; one surgeon at £36; two assay masters at £120; one judge at £100; an attorney general at fifty pagodas (gratuity) per annum; and a scavenger at £100. The scavenger, it would seem by this, ranked above the Attorney General! and, as we are told that "lawyers are plenty, and as knowing as can be expected from broken linen-drapers and other cracked tradesmen, who seek their fortune here by their wits," we cannot be surprised that the legal dignitary was in no very high repute.

"This by way of digression," as Mr. Lockyer says at the end of a passage, which is much more to our purpose. He complains that the European soldiers were a shabby-looking, stunted set of men, because the Company would only enlist Protestants. "I wish," he says, "for the honour of the English nation, they would decline sending such diminutive, dwarfish, crooked recruits as of late have gone to supply their settlements. To say no better could be had in time of war is an evasion my own experience proves altogether light; for since 'tis no matter what country in Europe they are of, let but three captains be sent to Ireland, in less than three months they could raise a regiment of picked fellows, who would be able to do them service; besides, they look like men, which is enough for them at Fort St. George. Objecting to their religion looks like partiality; for the topasses in India are all of the same principles. The Queen's officers list none but Protestants to serve in her troops, wherefore the country is quite overrun with lusty men who are ready to starve for want of employ." This exclusiveness continued to a much later date.

One more passage, however, must we give from the old volume before us, if only to show how little change the character of the European soldier in India has undergone in a period of nearly a century and a half. "New House is the soldier's lodging and scene of many a drunken frolic. It fronts the main guard and has a strong battery on the other side against the river. One company at a time sleeps in it, of whom a corporal and two soldiers walk the streets every hour in the night to suppress disorders and apprehend any who cannot give an account of themselves. *Pay-day comes once a month, when they'll be sure to have the enjoyment of the few fanams left them by their creditors; their debts, if within due bounds, are all cleared at the pay-table.* Every one keeps his boy, who, though not above ten years old, is procurer and *valet de chamcre* for seven or eight fanams a month." One need not look for a more accurate description than this of the European artilleryman of the present day. Fortunately our artillery *officers* of the present day are very different from the occasional pictures we find of them in the writings of the last century. Let us see what they were when Colonel Pearse took command of the corps. According to Captain Buckle, on the death of Major Kindersley, 28th October 1769, Lieutenant-Colonel Pearse succeeded to the command of the regiment, and, as its organisation is much indebted to that officer, it is fortunate that we are able to quote from letters to his early friends his record of the state in which he found it:—

"When I first came into command of the corps I was astonished at the ignorance of all who composed it. It was a common practice to make any midshipman who was discontented with the Indian ships an officer of artillery, from a strange idea that a knowledge of navigation would perfect an officer of that corps in the knowlege of artillery. They were almost all of this class, and their ideas consonant to the elegant military education which they had received. But, thank God, I have got rid of them all but seven!"

We are still further informed:—The strange idea above referred to appears to have affected the Home Government at a still earlier period, as, on the first formation of Artillery companies, "such assistance as the fleet could spare" was given. To this idea are we indebted for many terms which have hung about the corps till the present day. Our tindals, lascars, serangs, cossibs, all came from the naval nomenclature, and their etymology would most probably be found in the Portuguese dialect, which has retained its influence on shipboard. From the same fountain of "English (not) undefiled" must have been drawn the "bankshall," a name by which our gun-sheds are known throughout the regiment, but a term of considerable mystification to the uninitiated.*

Various improvements were effected by Colonel Pearse, especially in the *matériel* of the Corps of Bengal Artillery. The "Scientific Corps" now formed as important a part of the social circle in India as it did in the Presidency army. The *Calcutta* reviewer of Captain Buckle's *History* happily selected a passage for his readers, in which there is a picture of the artillery officers in regimentals, and a glimpse of certain social usages during the reign of Warren Hastings:—

"At this time the head-quarters of the regiment were quartered in Fort William, moving out during the cold months to a practice-ground at Sulkeah, nearly opposite the western mouth of the Circular Canal; the powder-works were between the canal and

---

* *Calcutta Review*, No. XXIV., December 1849: Review of Captain Buckle's *History of the Bengal Artillery*. This famous military work, after the death of its gifted and lamented author, was edited by J. W. Kaye, late lieutenant Bengal Artillery, founder of the *Calcutta Review* (May 1844), and eventually Sir John Kaye, K.C.S.I., F.R.S.

Cossipore. The dress of the regiment consisted of a blue coat faced with scarlet, and cut away in the fashion of the time; white cloth waistcoat and breeches, with buckles at the knees, and gaiters, or half-spatterdashes, as they were called; red leathern belt, with swivels; black silk stock, buff gloves, and regimental hat, supposed to be a plain cocked hat, in the fashion of George the Second's time. The hair was worn greased, powdered, and tied in a queue, false hair being substituted when the natural was not long enough."

The hours for parades, and, in fact, for everything, were early; parades were before gun-fire in the cold season; dinners were in the middle of the day, not only in private houses, but on public occasions; and invitations were given on a scale of hospitality only practicable in a small society. The orderly-book was the common channel of invitation used by the Governor-General and the officer commanding the garrison. Many such entries as the following will be found in it:—"The Honourable the Governor-General requests to be favoured with the company of officers and gentlemen belonging to the army now in the garrison of Fort William and the Chitpoor cantonment and the presidency, on Monday next to dinner, at the Court House, and in the evening to a ball and supper. The Governor-General requests that gentlemen will not bring any servants to dinner, nor their hookahs to the ball at night." Or, "Lieutenant-Colonel Wilding presents his compliments to all the officers in Fort William, staff of the garrison, and surgeons, and requests their company to breakfast, and dinner at half-past two o'clock."

The great maidán at Dum-Dum* was first used as a practice-ground in 1775. Captain Buckle gives us the following interesting details relative to the growth of that important station:—

"The Artillery, in 1775, appear first to have used Dum-Dum as a practice-ground, and to have been encamped there, when, their tents being wanted for the use of a brigade marching to Patna, they were ordered into Fort William, and their practice cut short, with

* A short march from Calcutta.

one fortnight instead of two months. In the following year, however, in December, they marched out with their tents and stores, and began the practice (as the orders record) by firing a royal salute, and after that one of nineteen guns for the Company."

It is not easy to ascertain what Dum-Dum was previous to its occupation by the Artillery. The first mention made of it is by Orme in the account of the action near Omichund's garden in 1757. He speaks of Clive crossing "the Dum-Dum road"; this road, however, was only a cutchabund, leading to Dum-Dum, the name of the place now occupied by Dum-Dum House, the origin of which building is enveloped in mystery. It is said to have been built by a Mr. (or Colonel) Home; but who he was, or the date, cannot be ascertained. Supernatural aid has been called into play; the mound on which it stands is reported to have been raised by some spirit of the ring or lamp in the course of a single night, and to this day visions of ghosts haunt the grounds.

At the practice season, the officers inhabited the house; the men's tents were pitched in the compound, and the natives' in the "Montague lines," the ground now occupied by the Nya Bazaar, called after Lieutenant Montague, the adjutant who marked them out. The name is known to the present day.

It was not until 1783 that the cantonment was marked out by Colonel Duff, who is said to have made, or rather widened, the road from Sambazar to Baraset (probably the regular road to Berhampore), and to have planted the avenue of mulseery trees now running along the southern end of the small exercising ground.

Many villages were scattered over the ground occupied by the cantonment; their sites were purchased up from time to time by Government—the last, that of Deiglak, in 1820.* Eventually the Bengal Artillery head-quarters were transferred to Meerut.

In the year 1774 Colonel James, commandant of the Madras (or Coast) Artillery, recommended that the Artillery practice-ground should be removed from Fort St. George to St. Thomas' Mount,†

---

* *Calcutta Review*, No. XXIV., December 1849.
† About nine miles from Madras.

"instead of the guns firing into the sea" as had hitherto been the custom; and so the Mount became the permanent head-quarters of the Madras Artillery.

The reduction of the Golundaz (Native) battalions of Artillery, in 1779, is particularly noticed by Captain Buckle in his work, and, it has been considered, with much justice and effect.

The danger of teaching the natives of India the use of artillery was, at the time of which we write, seriously apprehended. But it is useless to consider such apprehension "absurd." The Sikh invasion of British India and the Sepoy mutiny were yet to come. Still, it may be interesting and useful to quote Captain Buckle's clear views and, in some respects, able reasoning on the subject:—

"Those who feared the native powers training up good artillerymen by means of deserters from the British service do not appear to have considered that, without the material, which is provided and kept up at a heavy expense, the best artillerymen would be useless; and that, although artillerymen are *taught* the preparation of stores, still very few have that intimate knowledge, which only results from constantly handling and making them up, and which is in reality found in a much greater degree in the magazine workmen—a class who come and go at their pleasure—and appear to be little thought of, although the practical information they could carry to an enemy would be worth more than hundreds of mere well-drilled artillerymen.

"The Court of Directors, however, must be excepted; for, in their warrant (17th June 1748), they direct that 'no Indian, black, or person of a mixed breed, nor any Roman Catholic, of what nation soever, shall, on any pretence, be admitted to set foot in the laboratory, or any of the military magazines, either out of curiosity, or to be employed in them, or to come near them, so as to see what is doing, or contained, therein.' And to such an extent did this fear then carry them, that another paragraph runs: 'And if any person belonging to the company of artillery marry a Roman Catholic, or his wife become a Roman Catholic after marriage, such person shall immediately be dismissed from the company of artillery, and be obliged to serve the remainder of his time in one of the other companies, or be removed to another of the Company's settlements, to serve it out there, if the Council think fit.' And, again, in their military letter to Bombay (6th April 1770), they say: 'As it is very essential that the natives should be kept as ignorant as possible, both of the theory and practice of the artillery branch of the art of war, we esteem it a very pernicious practice to employ the people of the country in working the guns; and, if such practice is in use with you, we direct that in future you attach European artillerymen to the service of the guns, which may belong to sipahi corps, and that no native be trusted with any part of this important service, unless absolute necessity should require it.' With these views, it is not to be wondered at that the Home Government should have directed the Golundaz to be reduced; but Indian experience might even then have taught, that no more dangerous ally can be found for a native army than a large and imperfectly-equipped artillery. A native power will hardly bear the heavy *continued* expense required to keep it efficient; or, if the state should supply the means, the want of integrity in its agents will divert them from their proper course; and consequently, in the hour of emergency, the army is forced to fight a pitched battle to protect the unwieldy train of cannon, which becomes an encumbrance instead of a support; so it had been at Plassey and Buxar, and so it has been in every general action since. Assaye, Argaum, Laswari, Mahidpúr would have been avoided had there been no artillery in the native armies: unencumbered, they could have evaded the British; but the necessity of protecting their trains, and, perhaps, the confidence which their presence inspired, induced them to try the result of a battle.

"Instead of discouraging native powers from organising large parks of artillery, our policy should have been the reverse, resting confident that native parsimony and dishonesty would insure inefficiency in that branch." On this passage the *Calcutta* reviewer has some very able comments.

Captain Buckle attributes to a personal feeling against Colonel Pearse* a share in the paternity of the "obnoxious measure."

As to those days of party strife in the chief Presidency, of course, every great measure was immediately seized upon as a feeder.

And Colonel Pearse was an intimate friend and partisan of Warren Hastings, and acted as his second when he fought the celebrated duel with Philip Francis (Junius). Colonel Watson officiated for Francis, the "turbulent knight,"† as the great Governor-General styled him.

"As to the alleged reasons," we read, "for the reduction of the Golundaz, it is impossible, in these days, not to recognise the absurdity of the plea. But we are not altogether satisfied with the reasoning. The war in the Punjab (1849) has taught us that an extensive ordnance corps is not always an encumbrance and a disadvantage to a native army. But that without the material of artillery the best artillerymen would be useless, is a truth beyond the reach of contradiction. Sound policy, it appears to us, dictated that we should keep the native powers of India as much as possible in ignorance of the means of manufacturing ordnance for themselves, and render such of them as were our own allies entirely dependent upon us for the material of their artillery. They were well content to purchase our old guns; and so convinced was Lord Cornwallis of the wisdom of supplying them from our own stores, that, after the siege of Seringapatam, he presented half-a-dozen pieces of ordnance both to the Nizam and the Peishwah. They were not the most serviceable guns in his park; but the gift was appreciated, and Lord Cornwallis judged rightly, that it would have the effect, for some time to come, of diverting them from the thought of making guns for themselves, or going to other European craftsmen to make them for their use."

It is curious to note that wherever, in the East, the casting of a

---

* Inherited by Sir Eyre Coote from General Clavering.

† Warren Hastings, "in slippers," wrote :—

"A serpent bit Francis, that turbulent knight,
What, then? 'Twas the serpent that died of the bite!"

good bell is performed, the casting of a fair piece of ordnance may follow. And we specially noticed this fact during the second Burmese War, in which some handsome brass guns (cast at Ava) were used against us. And we all know that Burma, from time immemorial, has been famous for the tone, graceful appearance, and general excellence of its bells.*

The idea of the most scientific Oriental ever being able to turn out even a slight approach to an Armstrong, a Whitworth, or a Gatling gun is too preposterous to be entertained for one moment; so we may ever set our minds at rest regarding the future pieces of ordnance of Eastern nations, should they ever be compelled to cast or manufacture for themselves.†

While thus briefly considering the origin and progress of our Indian artillery—chiefly with reference to Bengal—every reader of Indian history must have observed with pride how very few have been the mishaps to, and how many the triumphs of, our artillery in action, from Plassey down to the artillery battle of Goozerat. The progress of excellence has been slow and sure, and the Bengal, Madras, and Bombay, or the Presidency Artilleries of India, have ever deserved well of the nation which reared them. Before Plassey, at Budge-Budge, where draught cattle were wanting and European gunners had to play the parts of horses and bullocks, two guns were temporarily lost, but they were soon recovered by a gallant body of volunteers. At Patna, as has already been narrated, we nearly lost a battery; but such and a few other small clouds of insignificant result appear of little consequence in history's bright and advancing prospect. Our tremendous cannonade at Plassey, against a body of 50,000 men for a whole day, combined with the bravery and endurance of Clive's small army, drawn from the three Presidencies, and the treachery of Meer Jaffier, truly

---

* See a little work on *Burma and Tonquin*, by the present writer, which also contains a popular account of Burma—" Burmese Bells," p. 35.

† Having introduced the honoured name of Armstrong (best known as Sir William), it reminds us that in the month we are writing (November) Lord Armstrong, " the revolutioniser of modern artillery," was born seventy-nine years ago.

decided the fate of India, as already shown, for we were nearly being *overwhelmed*—a military danger to which we are ever liable in India—by the enemy's vast host; and then we certainly would have lost Bengal, and probably the other Presidencies, for a time; while, without the action at Goozerat (1849), we might never have possessed the mighty Punjab, with its now famous Sikh soldiery. The glorious struggles in Afghanistan, and during the Bengal Sepoy Mutiny, also add splendour to that *ligne lumineuse* which, from first to last, has marked out the Bengal Artillery for fame; while the names of such "mighty men" who rose in the corps (each great in his peculiar province), such as Sir George Pollock, Sir Henry Lawrence, Sir John Kaye; the ever zealous and able Assistant Adjutant-General, Captain Buckle, who may be said to have died in harness while writing his history or memoirs of his distinguished regiment;* and our present renowned Comander-in-Chief in India, Sir Frederick Roberts, will secure for the Indian Artillery imperishable renown. We may yet have to chronicle a few of its brilliant achievements which live in the page of history; but we must now go back and resume our acquaintance with the great master in the art of Indian warfare and Indian administration, about to re-visit Calcutta to assume the Herculean tasks prepared for him by the Court of Directors, whom he had served so faithfully and fearlessly and well. But a word or two is here necessary to carry on the chain of our historical sketch. With Nujum-ood-dowla, Meer Jaffier's successor, the Calcutta Council formed a new treaty, and took the military defence of the country into their own hands, obliging him to appoint a manager of the civil and criminal affairs of the state. He begged that the profligate Nurdoo Koomar might fill this post; but the Council flatly refused, and Mr.

---

* This excellent and lamented officer died off Ceylon (September 1846), *en route* to England for his health, which was completely broken by the climate and hard study. The amiable and learned reviewer of his work informs us that it was one of his last expressions of earthly solicitude that the manuscript of the memoir of the Bengal Artillery, on which he had been so long and anxiously employed, should be given over to his executor, an old brother officer, to be dealt with as might seem best to him. It was Buckle's known wish that the work should be published; and so it was given into the hands of the editor, Sir John Kaye.

Vansittart wrote a long minute, detailing all the crimes of that native, and left it "for the guidance of future Governors." Mahomed Reza Khan, a relative of Ali Verdi Khan, was therefore appointed in his place.*

The Court of Directors were now aware of the evil doings of their servants in India, which were neither moral nor remunerative to the great Company. They had heard of the war with Meer Cossim and the Vizier of Oudh, and of the dreadful massacre at Patna, and naturally became much alarmed. They feared lest India should be lost, and wisely thought that there was no man so likely to save their conquests as he who had made them; so they begged Lord Clive, who had now been created a nobleman—a peer of Ireland under the title of Baron Clive of Plassey—by the King, to go out and retrieve their fallen fortunes. It is said that the Directors had not treated him after his arrival in England as he deserved;† but, with his noble sense of duty, he agreed to proceed to India as Commander-in-Chief, and Governor of Bengal, "with full powers to act." He landed in Calcutta on the 3rd of May 1765. The soul which had been so long wanting in the Presidency Council had returned at last; and impotence, or incapacity, and rapacity were forthwith to die. Although the Court of Directors had exaggerated the actual danger of things, still Lord Clive discovered there was good cause for alarm. He found the government in the utmost disorder. The good of the Company was set at nought by every well-to-do man in Calcutta; even by the great Members of Council. There was neither honour nor honesty in the government; and "the name of European," writes Marshman, "stunk in the nostrils of the people." The Court of Directors had positively ordered that their servants should take no more presents. Meer Jaffier was on his death-bed, and the Council did not choose to enter the orders on the Council books; but, on his death, made a new Nabob, and took enormous presents from him. Was ever such

---

* Marshman.

† They had even taken away the Jaghire which Meer Jaffier had given him. His right to it had been long disputed; and Mr. Pitt was very indignant at the conduct of the Directors.

rascality in a government subject to a Court of Directors heard of before! But, in the same letter stopping the presents, it was ordered that the private trade of the Company's servants should cease.

These orders the Council also defied, and got the new Nabob by treaty to agree to the old trade, as before, duty free. Clive determined, on his arrival, to carry the orders of the Directors into execution.* Sir John Malcolm says truly, that never had an individual a more arduous task of reform; but Clive came to it with great local knowledge, "with a full acquaintance of the characters of those by whom he was likely to be aided or thwarted, and with a mind determined at all hazards to execute the great work to which he had been called, almost by acclamation." The once daring ensign whom the Court of Directors wrote out to "encourage," was now a Major-General in the army, and a Companion of the Bath. The Council tried to bully him, as they had Vansittart; but Clive was made of a very different stuff. He insisted that all should sign the covenants against taking presents, and those who refused were at once dismissed. Some signed, others refused and returned home; but, as a natural consequence, all became his enemies. As if for a reward on his having put down the misconduct of the members of Government and others, on his journey to the Western Provinces, Lord Clive was, on the 12th of August, invested by the Emperor with the Dewanny (grant of all the revenues of Bengal, Behar, and Orissa), in order to make peace with the Native states and a treaty with the Nabob of Oudh (eventually concluded), as war was eating up all the revenues; this generous act being performed on behalf of the Company; and Clive promised to pay two lakhs of rupees a month (£20,000) out of the revenues to the Emperor. Clive, on meeting him at Allahabad, had asked the fulfilment of his promise before alluded to, which was now granted.† The Emperor

---

* Marshman.

† It is thought worthy of remark that, as the Emperor was a fugitive in his own dominions, he had no state pageantry with him. Before this great event of the *Dewanny*, Clive had determined to restore Sujah Dowlah of Oudh to his dominions, having conceived a favourable opinion of him on a personal acquaintance, and thinking

made over thirty millions of his subjects with two crores of annual revenue (two millions sterling) to the English. The Mahomedan historian observes on this event, that a business of such importance, which at other times would have required the sending of wise Ministers and able Envoys, and much discussion, was done and finished in less time than would have been taken up in the sale of a jackass or a herd of cattle; and this was the most important event which had happened to the English since the battle of Plassey. By this magnificent gift they became legally possessed of the three great provinces; and the Nabob of Moorshedabad dwindled to a mere cypher.*

On the 7th of September, Clive returned to Calcutta. Private trade was now interdicted, and a Commercial Society set up, and put down by the Court of Directors. Clive's Commercial Society, unlike the universal co-operative store traders of our own time, was confined to carrying on a trade in salt, betelnut, and tobacco. A large duty of 35 per cent. was to be paid to the Company's treasury, and the profits were to be divided among the whole service, civil and military. The then badly paid civilians growled apace. The military, on their small pay, became inclined to mutiny; but all discontent was of no avail, for the great Company's mandate had gone forth that their servants should not touch the internal trade of the country. Then, as has frequently been the case in our time, it was clearly found that the great expenses of the government in India had swallowed up all the revenues. And the chief source of expense, although the most necessary, was the army.

The strides in five or six years made by the Bengal Presidency army to fight the battles of Adams, Carnac, and Hector Munro—and, of course, in proportion, by the Madras and Bombay armies—are really wonderful to relate. We can hardly believe the statement of the European force in Bengal early in 1759, given by Clive a few months later to his old friend and commander, Colonel

---

he would be more formidable as an enemy, and effective as an ally, than the daring Mogul.

* Marshman.

Lawrence. He tells him of the surprise with which he had heard of M. Lally's setting himself down before Madras, "not," Clive says, "with an intent to besiege it in form, or carry on approaches; if he does, I think he must be either mad or his situation desperate; at all events, I hope it will be the means of adding fresh laurels to those already gained by my dear old friend." Orders had been given to Colonel Forde to join him with his forces, and an endeavour was being made to send a complete company of one hundred rank and file from Calcutta. Clive hoped also that Mr. Bouchier (local governor and commander-in-chief) would spare some men from Bombay. "I enclose you a short sketch," he adds, "of our strength in these parts; and, considering how much depends upon keeping up our influence in Bengal, you will say there never was a smaller force to do it with."

State of the European Force in Bengal, 6th February 1759.*

Doing Duty.	Captains.	Lieuts.	Ensigns.	Serjeants.	Corporals.	Drummers.	Privates.
Military .	6	6	9	36	29	20	314†
Artillery .	1	8	0	—	5	2	86

In a letter to General Carnac, dated 6th May 1765, Clive observes:—"Having met in Council, after some debates, the field officers were established as follows:—General Carnac, Colonel Smith, and Sir R. Barker are colonels of the first, second, and third regiments of Infantry; Sir R. Fletcher,‡ Major Peach and

* It is interesting to compare the small force here given, for 1759, with the grand armies we now possess in Bengal, Madras, and Bombay, in 1889. Of the European Army, in 1885-86, there were, in Bengal:—Royal Artillery, 261 officers 5,948 non-commissioned officers and privates, total 6,209; Cavalry, 144 officers 2,724 non-commissioned officers and privates, total 2,868; Royal Engineers, 204 officers; Infantry, 928 officers, 28,294 non-commissioned officers and privates, total 29,222; Invalid and Veteran Establishment, 9 officers, 5 non-commissioned officers and privates, total 14; Staff Corps, 445 officers; General List, Cavalry, 24 officers; General List, Infantry, 86 officers; Unattached Officers, 1 officer; General Officers unemployed, 18. Total European Army in Bengal, 2,120 officers, 36,971 non-commissioned officers and privates; total 39,091. Native Army in Bengal, 66,827. Total of European and Native Army of British India, say, 189,000.

† Whereof 140 are recruits.

‡ This gallant officer, with the first brigade, garrisoned Monghir. He also commanded the troops at the famous battle of Kalpi, 21st May 1765. Sujah Dowlah, though defeated in successive battles, and driven beyond his frontier, still held out.

Major Chapman, lieutenant-colonels; Majors Champion and Stibbart, majors." What would Clive, so contented with the ranks held by his field officers, headed by the *one* general, have done, had he been able to select from the numerous "active" generals of the present day? In his perplexity of numbers, how many would he have taken—how many passed over? Clive appears to have thought highly of Major Champion, and was anxious for his advancement.* He also writes to the General regarding Madras and Bombay: "I desired the Board would order those paragraphs relative to the power of the Committee to be transmitted to the chiefs and council of the subordinate settlements, to the commander-in-chief of the army, and to the two presidencies of Madras and Bombay, that they might know what powers the Committee were invested with." Lord Clive, Verelst, Sykes, and Sumner were clearly to have it all their own way; and no one, save "the heaven-born general," was to interfere with the army, which, beyond all question, was correct.

We must now pass on to one of the most serious events of his wonderful career, a state of mutiny, or, at least, military insubordination, in the great body whose interests he had so much at heart. Before doing so, however, it may be interesting to give a letter written by Clive seven or eight years before, or after the battle of Plassey, on the occasion of the division of the spoil among the officers of the army and navy, and the remonstrance of those of the army, for his having, in their opinion, too much favoured

---

Having collected his scattered troops, and obtained a reinforcement from the Mahrattas, he formed an army, with which he again ventured to face General Carnac. The General had great confidence in Sir R. Fletcher, and had appointed him to command the troops in the field. The battle of Kalpi was fought on the 21st of May (1765), the Mahrattas having appeared in great force on the plain, offering battle. "By a judicious manœuvre," writes Major Innes, "our Cavalry and Infantry encircled the enemy, whilst our Artillery concentrated its fire on his position with such effect that, with their front and both flanks threatened, they were forced back into a morass, and ground intersected by deep ravines, which completely crippled the movements of the Mahratta army, formed mostly of cavalry."— See *History of the Bengal European Regiment*, p. 221.

* Regarding this officer's unknown merits, Clive writes, with reference to his standing next in rank to colonel:—"Major Champion is satisfied with an assurance from me, that whatever the Directors shall order on that head shall be complied with."—*Memoirs of Lord Clive*, vol. ii., p. 320.

Admiral Watson and the fleet, which will show, in an eminent degree, the character of the man, his splendid decision, and how fit he was to quell the deadly spirit of mutiny.

"GENTLEMEN,

"I have received both your remonstrance and protest. Had you consulted the dictates of your own reason, those of justice, or the respect due to your commanding officer, I am persuaded such a paper, so highly injurious to your own honour as officers, could never have escaped you.

"You say you were assembled at a council to give your opinion about a matter of property. Pray, Gentlemen, how comes it that a promise of a sum of money from the Nabob, entirely negotiated by me, can be deemed a matter of right and property? So very far from it, it is now in my power to return to the Nabob the money already advanced, and leave it to his option whether he will perform his promise or not. You have stormed no town, and found the money there; neither did you find it in the plains of Plassey, after the defeat of the Nabob. In short, Gentlemen, it pains me to remind you that what you are to receive is entirely owing to the care I took of your interest. Had I not interfered greatly in it you would have been left to the Company's generosity, who perhaps would have thought you sufficiently rewarded in receiving a present of six months' pay; in return for which I have been treated with the greatest disrespect and ingratitude; and, what is still worse, you have flown in the face of my authority, for overruling an opinion which, if passed, would have been highly injurious to your own reputation, being attended with injustice to the navy, and been of the worst consequences to the cause of the nation and the Company.

"I shall therefore send the money down to Calcutta, give directions to the agents of both parties to have it shroffed [or banked]; and when the Nabob signifies his pleasure (on whom it solely depends) that the money be paid you, you shall then receive it, and not before.

"Your behaviour has been such that you cannot expect I should interest myself any further in your concerns. I therefore retract the promise I made the other day of negotiating either the rest of the Nabob's promise, or the one-third, which was to be received in the same manner as the rest of the public money, at three yearly equal payments.

"I am, Gentlemen,
"Your most obedient, humble servant,
"ROBT. CLIVE."

Clive's apportioning so much of the gifts of Meer Jaffier to Admiral Watson and the Fleet, there can be no doubt, shows a generous nature. The army was vastly indebted to the services of the navy for its brilliant successes; and to show that the officers then in Bengal really had this feeling, they acknowledged their error, and to their letter Clive nobly replied :—

"GENTLEMEN,
"I have ever been desirous of the love and good opinion of my officers, and have often pursued their interest in preference of my own. What passed the other day is now forgotten, and I shall always be glad of an opportunity of convincing you how much

"I am, Gentlemen,
"Your most obedient, humble servant,
"(Signed) ROBT. CLIVE." *

Seven years after, Clive was quite aware of all the odium and hostility his sudden and great reforms would bring upon him in India and in England. "But," writes his truthful biographer, "it is obvious that the knowledge of this, so far from dispiriting, only encouraged him to the great efforts he made." In a letter to Mr. Sykes, of the 29th June 1765, on the subject, he says, with amusing candour: "I fear the military, as well as civil, are so far gone in luxury and debauchery that it will require the utmost

---

* Moorshedabad, 9th July 1757.

exertion of an united Committee to save the Company from destruction."*

In an army as well as in civil society—as Clive well knew—nothing tends so much to serious disorder as dissipation. But the grand crisis was now the mutinous combinations among the officers of the Bengal army, far more difficult to manage than any abuses in the civil administration. The reduction of the military expenditure was now the "burning question."

To carry it into execution, according to the peremptory orders of the Court of Directors, it was thought advisable to reduce the allowances of the officers of the army of the Bengal Presidency. While the English troops had been employed in fighting in Meer Jaffier's name, he allowed them to draw a gratuity, which was called double batta.†

They had so long received this large allowance that they came to consider it as their right. Lord Clive, at the period of this grant, warned the army that it must be considered as an indulgence on the part of the Nabob, which the Company would not be inclined to continue. It turned out as he supposed, and the double batta was ordered to be abolished. The whole army had been formed into regiments, and, according to Clive's plan, divided into three brigades, at Monghyr, Bankipore, and Allahabad. The peace which had been established, and the regimenting the troops, offered a favourable opportunity for carrying into effect the positive commands of the Directors, and accordingly an order was issued by the Select Committee that, from the 1st of January 1766, double batta to the European officers of the army should cease, except at Allahabad, where, on account of the distance from Calcutta, the second brigade was allowed double batta so long as it should be actually in the field. At Patna and Monghyr the troops were allowed half batta when not on service, while those at the Presidency were put upon the same footing as the troops on

* *Memoirs*, vol. ii., p. 331.
† This was first introduced after the battle of Plassey.

the coast of Coromandel, who drew no batta except when marching or serving in the field.*

The story of this famous mutiny is thus clearly and succinctly told:—" Lord Clive knew that any plan of reduction would be violently opposed; but he was a man of the firmest mind, and at once issued orders that the double batta should cease. The military officers took great offence at this. They said that the country had been conquered by their arms, and that they ought to benefit by the conquest. But Clive was inflexible; he was prepared to give them a liberal allowance, but was still determined that the expenses of the army should be lessened. The officers now formed a conspiracy among themselves to oblige him to yield to their views. They carried on a secret correspondence with each other, and resolved, one and all, to lay down their commissions on the same day. As soon as the officers of the first brigade had thus resigned the service, intelligence was conveyed to Clive, and it embarrassed him not a little. He suspected that there was a general confederacy throughout the army. He had passed through many scenes of trouble, but this was the most severe trial he had yet met with. The Mahrattas (50,000) were preparing to invade the country again, and the English army was without officers. Clive, however, acted with his usual energy. He ordered up officers from Madras. Some of the Bengal officers, who had not gone so far in rebellion as the rest, retracted. The ringleaders were seized, dismissed the service, and sent back to England. By this severity he reduced the army again to obedience, and thus delivered the Government from the greatest danger which it had ever felt."†

Although he had not yet been two years in India, with that *mens æqua in arduis* of his—to which motto he is perhaps even more entitled than Warren Hastings, who came out with him in the Civil Service in 1749—Lord Clive had restored order to the Company's affairs; he had reduced the expenses; and, by the Dewanny, had increased the income to nearly two cores of

---

* *Memoirs of Lord Clive*, by Major-General Sir John Malcolm, G.C.B., F.R.S.
† *History of Bengal*, by John C. Marshman, C.S.I.

rupees a year, or two millions sterling. He had subdued a formidable rebellion in the army, which he brought into a good state of discipline. But, in those various labours his health broke down; so the great founder of the British empire in India, and, we may fairly say, the founder of the Presidency armies, was obliged to return to England. Now, even more than before, the soul was about to leave the Bengal governing body; but this time to return no more.

The blow had nearly been struck, and in a few years the commanding genius of Clive, chiefly from the worry of envious, ungrateful, and malignant foes, would be shattered, and the golden bowl, which for India was beyond all price, irredeemably broken.

Lord Clive embarked in February 1767, about ten years after he first landed in Bengal, with Admiral Watson, from Madras.

There is a fine passage in Carlyle's *Lectures on Heroes*, we think, especially applicable to Clive, who, many of our readers will admit, had nearly all the elements of a good king in him; and in his own way he did as much work, and, perhaps, generally better, than either Cromwell or Napoleon :—" The Commander over Men ; he to whose will our wills are to be subordinated, and loyally surrender themselves, and find their welfare in doing so, may be reckoned the most important of Great Men. He is practically the summary for us of *all* the various figures of Heroism."*

It is painful to think of such a mighty spirit as Clive's being eclipsed, and a violent death provoked by a rancorous pack of imbeciles, not one of whom was worthy to hold his charger while he was preparing for certain distinction on a well-fought field.

England's chief hero of the time expired on the 22nd of November 1774, in Berkeley Square, after completing his forty-ninth year.† And such is fame!

There is nothing better in the entire *Memoirs of Lord Clive* than the description of his character. A more faithful biographical portrait was never drawn; and Sir John Malcolm has done with

---

* On Heroes, Hero-worship, and the Heroic in History. Lecture VI.
† Sir John Malcolm.

pen and ink what strong painters like Dance, Reynolds, and Raeburn would have desired to represent on the canvas.*

In the following picture, the conqueror of India, the founder of the Presidency armies, comes vividly before us:—" Lord Clive was one of those extraordinary men who give a character to the period and country in which they live. His name cannot be erased from the history of India, nor from that of Britain. Born in the rank of a private gentleman, and launched out early in life into the wide sea of Indian adventure, he soon far outstript all his competitors in the race of fortune and fame. He was trained in the best of schools; a state of danger, of suffering, and activity. He could not be said to have any master in the art of war; he was, to adopt the language of the great Chatham, a 'heaven-born general'; and it was by the boldness and novelty of his measures, the impetuosity of his onset, and the imperturbable obstinacy of his defence, that he confounded his enemies, and changed the hesitating troops under his command into a band of heroes. He left nothing to chance; he foresaw and provided for everything. Victory seemed to attend him wherever he turned, and no enterprise was too arduous where he was the leader. The same success and the same renown which distinguished him in the Carnatic attended him in Bengal. From the date of the battle of Plassey, his reputation in that country was established; and all his negotiations with the native princes were from that day forward concluded more by the influence of his great name than by the energy of his determined character."

It may now be well to add that one of the grandest characteristics of Clive was charity—unaffected, genuine, practical charity. It was generosity in the highest sense; there was no hypocrisy or sham about it. It was ever deeds, not words, with him. From his cradle he was a soldier; and he loved the military profession for its own sake. On the officers and soldiers of his own army he was ever ready to bestow gifts; and, even after

---

* At the end of the third volume of the original edition (1836), it is pointed out as an *Erratum* that Sir Joshua Reynolds painted the admirable portrait which is given as a frontispiece, whereas it was by Dance, R.A., who, though not equal to Reynolds, or Raeburn, was one of the best portrait painters of his time.

Chandernagore, he lent money to a party of French officers for their expenses, although they told the conqueror they could never repay him; so he would surely be out of pocket.* He gave his dear old friend and commander a pension of £500 a year for life, advising his bankers strictly to "pay to Colonel Lawrence, or to his order." But the noblest act of his charity—unparalleled in the history of the British or Anglo-Indian Army—was the establishment of Lord Clive's Fund, from which widows whose husbands have died while serving in the latter branch of the Queen-Empress's forces derive so much benefit.

A legacy of £70,000 was bequeathed by Meer Jaffier Aly Khan, Nawab of Bengal, in 1765, to Lord Clive, and paid by his Lordship, n the year 1766, into the Company's treasury at Fort William, to run at interest at the rate of 8 per cent., as an annual fund for the support of European officers and soldiers who may be disabled or decayed in the Company's service in Bengal, and for the widows of officers and soldiers who may die on service there. 8th June 1766.

The Company extended this donation afterwards to the benefit of all invalided, disabled, or superannuated officers and soldiers, and the widows of such officers and soldiers as may die in their service in any of their settlements in the East Indies, pursuant to an agreement stipulated between them and Lord Clive in the year 1770, by which the former establishment of shares was altered to the present moieties or proportions specified as follows:—

All commissioned or warrant officers shall have half the ordinary stated pay they enjoyed while in the service.

Sergeants belonging to the Artillery shall receive 9d. per day, and such as have lost a limb 1s. per day; private men of the Artillery 6d. per day, and such as lose a limb 9d. per day. All other non-commissioned officers and private men shall receive 4¾d. per day. 23rd July 1771.† Such was the munificent gift from a true friend of the Indian army!

* To the captains he gave 1,000 rupees each.
† *Life of Lord Clive*, pp. 16–17, vol. iii. When the mutinous officers at Monghyr (1766) were informed that Lord Clive was coming, the precursors of the army, seeing their determination not to yield, remarked strongly " on their ingratitude

To some Anglo-Indians it may appear that a tinge of romance hangs around *Mutijil*,* or the lake of pearl, and the old palace whence issued the order for Clive's charitable bequest to the army. The place is thus described:—Mutijil is a lovely spot south of Múrshidabad; there are only a few arches now left of the magnificent palace erected here of black marble brought from Gaur. It was built by Suraj-ood-dowlah, at an enormous expense, in order "to indulge his vicious pleasures beyond the reach of control;" he quitted this palace in order to fight the battle of Plassey, and from the same place (1766) Clive wrote a letter making over five lakhs, bequeathed to him by Mir Jaffier, to a fund since called Clive's Fund.† "His gift of £70,000, for the support of officers and men invalided in the Company's service in India, must rank among the noblest of living benefactions."‡ Colonel Innes (late 1st Bengal European Regiment) also, in his new work, alludes to the famous bequest known as "Lord Clive's Fund," which proved a sterling boon to the Bengal army, which enjoyed its benefits for nearly one hundred years. "In 1859, the capital sum was claimed by Lord Clive's heirs on the plea that, the British possessions in India having been transferred from the East India Company to the Crown of England, the Bengal army had ceased to exist. The claim was held to be valid in law, and the amount of the fund, £50,000, was made payable to the claimants." This most philanthropic institution is now styled "The Military Fund, lately called Lord Clive's"; although, of course, it is quite distinct from the Military Funds of the three Presidencies. By the Regulations we are informed:—1. "Officers' widows will be required to sign a declaration to the effect that their husbands did not die possessed of real and personal property to the following amounts, and that they themselves do not, with what their husbands left, and from all other sources, possess, if the widow of a colonel, £4,000; a lieut.-

towards a person who had lately given up £70,000 to form a fund for invalids and widows."

* A favourite name applied to a lake in Kashmír, and another in Lahore.
† "The Banks of the Bhagirathi," in *Calcutta Review*, vol. vi., p. 441.
‡ Sir John Malcolm.

colonel, £3,000; a major, £2,500; a captain, £2,000; a lieutenant, £1,000." The pensions vary from £23 to about £114 per annum. Such, then, is the memorable fund first instituted by the charitable mind of Lord Clive, ever ready to help "the widow and the fatherless," as well as to aid the weak and restrain the strong.

CHAPTER IX.

LALLY IN THE CARNATIC—COLONEL FORDE IN THE NORTHERN CIRCARS—SUCCESSES AND REVERSES OF LALLY—BUSSY —BOMBAY.

IN connection with the work cut out for the early Presidency armies, we shall now make a retrogressive movement, and go back to Count de Lally in the Carnatic (1758). We have already briefly alluded to this clever but rash and eccentric hero of the French in India. Had Clive been in the Madras Presidency at the end of April, when he arrived at Pondicherry* with a considerable force to expel the English from Southern India, it is needless to say that, notwithstanding his energy and heroism, short work would have been made of him; but such not being the case, he gave us a vast deal of anxiety and trouble at a very critical time. Dupleix, Bussy, and Lally were the three grand French haters of British rule in India; while Clive and Watson spoke of hunting or turning out the French as if they had been so many hares or wily foxes infesting the land.

The French, with all their astuteness and talent, were never the right people in the right place in India, as they are now certainly not the Europeans we care to see at Tonquin. There, no hunters like Clive and Watson ever pursued them. When Chandernagore

* Pondichery is the spelling of Colonel Malleson—one *r*, as in "pont déchiré," the origin of the name.

was taken, Clive sought to root out the French from this quarter of India, as it was his confirmed opinion that the English and their European rivals could never have co-existence, as political powers, in Hindustan.

The Admiral was even more impressive; for, after giving the Nabob of Bengal a severe lecture for his frequent evasions, and for siding with Bussy and M. Law against us, instead of being our ally, as he promised, and assisting with his forces against the French, the gallant Admiral says scornfully:—" I have already told you, and now repeat it again, that while a Frenchman remains in the kingdom, I will never cease pursuing him; but if they deliver themselves up they shall find me merciful."*

Lally would certainly not have written to the Nabob in this style. It is more probable that, had he been a conqueror, he would have shot Suraj-ood-dowlah, or blown him from a gun (one of his favourite modes of execution); and so lost Bengal.

For generations it has been a common, and, on the whole, a fair opinion, that Clive exhibited far greater qualities as a statesman and a ruler than as a general, with the great praise, " that he never shrank from responsibility." Clive was not exactly a great tactician in the art of war; but, in our opinion, he was equally great as a statesman and a soldier. His actions and his policy just suited the times; and in no case was this more clearly shown than when he set about, from his office in Calcutta, curbing Lally, and assisting Madras in time of great need. Like "the worn war-horse," he was naturally eager for the fray, and desirous to be in Southern India once more, with a glorious battle-field before him, that he might mingle with European and Native soldiers, and lead our men on to certain victory, as he had done before in the Carnatic, for which brilliant services the Court of Directors had voted him a diamond-hilted sword. But he could not possibly leave his post in Bengal without injuring the interests of the Company. It has been justly observed that had he at this moment left the helm, the ship would have speedily foundered; the French would have

* Malcolm.

triumphed at Madras, or the Dutch might have driven us, bag and baggage, from Bengal. "But Clive remained; and taking advantage of the opening presented by the Rajah of Chicacole and Rajahmundri, who solicited the aid of the English against the French, he fitted out an expedition, under Colonel Forde (the victor of Chinsurah), and sent it to Vizagapatam to cause a diversion there, and thus indirectly to aid Madras, which was then hard pressed by Monsieur de Lally."*

The Court of Directors again had hardly used Clive well. They had appointed a Government of Rotation, or named a rotation of Governors, for the future management of their affairs in Bengal; but, although Clive had before been named as head of the General Committee, his name as Governor was omitted from the list. The Calcutta Council, however, knowing the real value of the conqueror of Plassey, urged them to make him the offer of being President of the Company's affairs in Bengal, "till a person is appointed by the Honourable Company." Clive was naturally hurt at such conduct of the Court; so he determined not to accept the high station offered. But the representations of all ranks and parties led Clive to alter his resolution. A kind and highly appreciative letter from Mr. Payne, Chairman of the Court of Directors, had much to do with altering the decision of the "heaven-born general," who now became Governor and President of the chief Presidency.

"The Court of Directors," writes his biographer, "had formed this Government of Rotation at a period when they could not have anticipated the great changes which had taken place in Bengal; that this was the case is proved by the fact of the subsequent appointment of Clive to the station of Governor the moment they heard of the battle of Plassey. They appear also to have recognised the high and disinterested motives which induced the Council to invite him to be their President."†

---

* Review of *Broome's History of the Bengal Army*— *Calcutta Review*, No. XXVIII., December 1850.

† *Memoirs of Lord Clive*, vol. i., pp. 362–63.

A well-known historian, writing on this subject, has remarked:
—"Convinced that Clive alone had sufficient authority to overcome the Nabob into the performance of his obligations, the Council (including the four gentlemen who were appointed governors) came to a resolution highly expressive of their own disinterestedness and patriotism, but full of disregard and contempt for the judgment and authority of their superiors."* But, according to Sir John Malcolm, the Court never viewed the setting aside of their arrangement in this light. It was indeed an extraordinary and unprecedented occasion.

On accepting the Government of Bengal, Clive's very first object was to assist the Presidency of Fort St. George. His view of the danger of that settlement, and the measures he adopted to afford it relief, are fully given in the pages of Orme, the contemporary historian, and no one doubted that Madras would be besieged as soon as the monsoon had sent the squadron to sea if reinforcements should not arrive before. "The preference," says Orme, "which each of the Company's Presidencies was naturally inclined to give to its own safety, as the only ground on which the property and fortunes of the whole community were established, suggested apprehensions that Madras, in the same manner as it had been treated by the Presidency of Calcutta, would, whatever might be the necessity of Bengal, detain in their own service whatsoever troops might be sent to their assistance." The destination of the force was called the Northern Circars, the country, usually known by this name, which had been ceded by the Soubahdar of the Dekhan, Salabut Jung, to the French. It runs along the seaboard from the Kistna to the Mahanuddi river, approaching, on its northern border, within two hundred miles of Calcutta. M. Bussy had been the leading spirit there, with his forces settling the country (1755); and the Nabob, before the fall of Chandernagore,† had hoped that the famous chevalier, after keeping with such a

---

* Mr. Mill, in his *History*, vol. iii., p. 244. Quoted by Sir John Malcolm.

† At that time, also, the French had several hundred Europeans at Cossimbazar, under M. Law.

strong hand the city of Hyderabad for the Soubahdar of the Dekhan, would come over and settle Bengal also.

The Marquis de Conflans, who now commanded the French force in the Northern Circars, had under him a European battalion of 500 men, with thirty or forty guns, 500 Native Cavalry, and 6,000 Sepoys. On the other hand, we are told that Colonel Forde could only muster 470 Europeans, 1,900 Sepoys—chiefly from the Upper Provinces of Bengal, trained by Clive—and six field-pieces; on the whole, a very creditable little Presidency army; while his ally, the Rajah of Chicacole and Rajahmundri, had 5,000 foot and 500 horse—a rabble that even the immortal Sir John would have disowned, and which would hardly have been allowed to march (to use Macaulay's language) " in the tail of Genseric." The sepoys under Forde were really well trained, better men, and probably better equipped, than the French native troops; "and they advanced with the prestige of victorious troops, as some of them had assisted to conquer or recover Bengal." Forde landed with his little army* on the 20th of October, at Vizagapatam; and, after some delay and much difficulty, having made his arrangements with the Rajah, he marched against the enemy on the 8th of December.

But we have left Count Lally, probably in the verandah of Government House, Pondicherry, " with his long sword drawn," ready to expel us from India. This extraordinary Frenchman is really an interesting study; but Anglo-Indian history gives us few recollections of him. We have written of him elsewhere.† The brave Lally had done his best for his masters; but it is said he was disliked by his troops, which, perhaps, was a principal cause of his reverses. Lally, in France, was considered one of the bravest yet most whimsical men in the French service. An Irishman by birth, he had worked his way up in a service open to any dauntless adventurer, fought against England, and suffered a cruel death on return to the land which had cherished him. We have also read of the famous Count, that the French Ministry fitted out an extensive

---

* Which came over in six vessels.
† *Brief View of the French in India.* Calcutta, 1847.

armament, under the command of Lally, an officer of Irish extraction who at the battle of Fontenoy had added to his many brilliant displays of personal valour by taking several English officers with his own hand. Cherishing the strongest attachment to his late master, James II., he felt also the most deadly antipathy to the people who had expelled him ; and he looked, as his highest pride, to being the chief instrument for the subversion of their Eastern dominion. On board the French vessels were 1,080 men of Lally's regiment, he himself being with them in the capacity of Governor-General of the French Settlements, fifty artillerymen, and several officers of distinction, amongst whom was Count D'Estaign. Such was Lally's energy and activity, that the day after his arrival at Pondicherry he despatched, by sunset, 1,000 Europeans and 1,000 Sepoys, under Count D'Estaign, for the reduction of Fort St. David (Cuddalore),* distant about eight miles from the French territory. Next day, firing from the English and French squadrons, under Admiral Pocooke and Count D'Aché respectively, was distinctly heard. The French naval force was 5,000 and that of the English 3,200. After an hour and a half's fighting, the French lost 500 killed and wounded, and the English 29 killed and 89 wounded, total 118. It was almost a useless naval action, which crippled both parties, without securing any great advantage to either. Although the French vessels suffered very severely, their superior rate of sailing, going three feet to one of the English, prevented their falling into the hands of the victors.†

M. de Soupires arrived from Pondicherry with a reinforcement and battering train ; and on the 1st May, Count Lally himself joined. Lally's purpose was so far served that the English squadron, damaged in its rigging, withdrew from the coast to refit, which enabled the sanguine Count to make himself master of Cuddalore, and eventually of Fort St. David. The fort, garrisoned by upwards of 2,000 regular troops, of whom upwards of 600 were Europeans,

---

* The old Fort St. David's ; purchased in 1685 by the English, from the Mahrattas, for 90,000 pagodas, or 315,000 rupees=£31,500 sterling. The English cantonment of Cuddalore was, and, we believe, is now, a very pleasant one.

† Begbie.

with 1,600 Sepoys, was placed in a state of siege, made a bad defence —Clive sadly wanted—and fell, or surrendered, on the 2nd of June 1758. All hopes of relief from the British squadron had been abandoned, as adverse winds and currents prevented its approach to Cuddalore. The French force employed against Fort St. David was 2,500 Europeans and 3,000 Sepoys.

The fall of Fort St. David alarmed the whole Presidency of Fort St. George; for the Government conceived that the French would now march against Madras; so withdrew their garrisons from Carangooly, Chingleput, Conjeveran, Cauverypauk, and Arcot, leaving only those at Poonamallee and Tripassore, as they covered a rich tract of country from the incursions of the Polygars, and, from their proximity to the Presidency, could be withdrawn on the approach of the French. The propriety of abandoning Trichinopoly was now seriously debated in Council. In short, the prospects of the Madras Presidency and its army were of a very gloomy nature indeed. The relieving Presidency for Bengal might well have been called "benighted" at this period. Fortunately, however, Pondicherry could not furnish the means of transporting by land the vast siege train requisite for operations against Fort St. George; and so long as the English held the sea, the other mode of transport was equally impracticable. Lally, therefore, turned his attention to "an easier conquest and a richer harvest."* He had found in Fort St. David a prisoner, by name Gatika, uncle of the dethroned Rajah of Tanjore, whom the British had engaged not to molest the reigning prince. Lally now set him up as the lawful sovereign, and marched on the 18th June to Tanjore to support his pretensions, leaving only 600 Europeans and 200 Sepoys under M. de Soupires for the protection of French territory.

As in the expedition against Fort St. David, Lally experienced great difficulty in procuring carriage, which made him press all the natives he could lay hands on into his service as coolies—quite regardless of caste—causing the French name to be execrated wherever this injudicious system was put in action. Although

* Begbie.

so totally repugnant to the feelings of the people, he continued to pursue this arbitrary system during his wild career in India. The art of conciliation, as practised by Clive and Wellesley, was quite unknown to Lally; and, as already hinted, he thought nothing of blowing a Brahman from the mouth of a gun if he disobeyed him. Partly owing to this arbitrary practice, the heavy guns and baggage had to be sent round by sea; and the brave regiment of Lorraine* was obliged to leave its tents behind at Cuddalore. On arrival at Devicottah, his men had been twelve hours without food.

When Lally entered the picturesque Tanjore country, the Rajah endeavoured to treat with him; but it was hopeless, owing to the extravagant demand for the immediate payment of 5,600,000 rupees with interest. At his earnest request, Captain Calliaud, commandant, had sent the Tanjore Rajah 500 of his best sepoys, 10 Madras artillerymen, and a few thousand "Colleries" (a thieving tribe) whom he had induced to enter the Tanjore service.

While the French remained at Trivalore, they swept the country of the cattle, and despatched them to the coast. "But the Colleries," says Begbie, "were more expert thieves than even the French, and managed to recapture nearly every head, selling them again, however, to the highest bidder." On the 18th July the French arrived within six miles of Tanjore, and the rajah again expressed a desire to treat. This time he paid an instalment of 50,000 rupees (£5,000). On the 29th the battering train arrived from the French settlement of Karical, which made the rajah conclude a treaty, by the terms of which he was to pay 500,000 rupees in three instalments, and furnish a force to co-operate against Trichinopoly. But, as no proper force appeared, Lally became convinced that the Tanjore rajah was playing with him in order to gain time; so he entered on a violent altercation, which terminated in a total rupture.† Captain Calliaud, who had been

---

* In September 1757, 983 men of the regiment of Lorraine, 50 artillerymen, 60 volunteers from Bourbon, 20 battering guns, some mortars, and abundance of shot and shell, arrived in the roads of Fort St. David, for Pondicherry, under the command of the Marquis de Soupires.

† Begbie.

afraid to trust any more of his men at Tanjore, on the 6th of August sent a further reinforcement of 500 of his best sepoys and "two excellent sergeants of artillery" (Madras), with twenty-seven gunners. At length, early in August, the French opened a useless fire of batteries; but everything appeared to go wrong. Cartridges for the guns, and sufficient ball ammunition were not forthcoming, without which sinews of war even Lally's bravery could do nothing. Worse than all, only two days' provisions remained in camp. On the 8th intelligence arrived of another action between the English and French fleets. The English fleet had anchored off Karical, ready for a descent; but nothing could be heard of the French. Lally deemed it prudent, therefore, to retreat, after providing for his sick and wounded. Before his departure, however, Monackjie, the Tanjore general, determined to beat up his quarters, and proceeded with a large body of horse and foot, after midnight, for that purpose. This scene of confusion, and even disaster, is thus described:—A party of the horse penetrated as far as Lally's tent; the Count was thrown down and trampled upon, but rescued.* A body of the English sepoys seized three field-pieces, which they were obliged to abandon after having lost 75 of their number in killed and wounded in the effort to bring them off. Great confusion prevailed for an hour, but in the end French discipline triumphed; and, if the French account be true that they lost only ten men, and their assailants nearly 400, Monackjie had not much reason to congratulate himself on his exploit. That night Lally, having first spiked and dismounted all his battering guns, commenced his retreat, harassed by the Tanjorines as far as Covilonil, 15 miles from Tanjore. The next march was to Trivalore, 20 miles distant, in which the not uncommon obstruction in Southern India of two adjacent rivers occurred. Had the Tanjorines taken proper advantage of these rivers, all Lally's field-artillery would have fallen into their hands; but they discontinued pursuit before they came to the first, evincing a sad want of tact and foresight in the Tanjore general.

* *Services of the Madras Artillery*, p. 103.

M. D'Aché, despite of all Lally's remonstrances, who wished him to try the result of another engagement, sailed with his fleet on the 3rd September for the Mauritius, leaving, however, 500 sailors—those invaluable accessories to warfare on or near a coast —and marines to act on shore. The English troops returned to Trichinopoly after the retreat of the French. Intelligence of the treaty between the Tanjore rajah and the French for an attack on Trichinopoly having reached the Presidency on the 14th August, Colonel Lawrence marched on the 18th with eight field-pieces, 620 Europeans, and 1,200 sepoys. On the 24th, after a march beyond Chingleput, Lawrence heard of the retreat of the French, and returned to Madras, where he arrived on the 31st. At this time Trevalore and Trinomallie were taken from the enemy during the French retreat, "by the Nuwab's troops." * Major Caillaud had been obliged to withdraw his outposts, including that on Seringham (at Trichinopoly), when he despatched his reinforcements to Tanjore; and the brother of Hyder Ali, who had recently been driven from it, re-occupied it with his Mysoreans.

On the return of Caillaud's detachments he was as speedily dislodged again. Caillaud was a clever "political" as well as soldier; and he knew the value of such an ejectment.

In September the intelligence of the fall of Fort St. David reached Calcutta, as well as the failure of Lally's expedition against Tanjore and the subsequent operations; and, as already remarked, Governor and President Clive preferred making a diversion in the Northern Circars to sending direct assistance to the Madras Presidency.

Colonel Forde had quitted Adlercron's regiment (the 39th), and had been invited by the Madras Government to assume the command, of course at the suggestion of Clive, who, among all his distracting cares in Calcutta, kept a steady eye on the scene of his pristine glory.

In August, the French had reduced all the small outposts in the neighbourhood of Madras, except Chingleput, which still held out,

* Begbie.

and was reinforced with three companies of sepoys under Lieutenant Airey.

On the 14th September, seven Company's ships, escorted by two men-of-war, arrived in the Madras Roads. On board these vessels were embarked 1,000 King's troops (Colonel Draper's regiment, under the command of that officer); but fifty of these had died on board the *Pitt* of the Brest fever, contracted from some French vessels. With such augmentation of strength, more sepoys could now be spared to strengthen Chingleput. The impending siege of Madras rang through the length and breadth of the Presidency. Caillaud, with all his spare troops, was ordered from Trichinopoly, the command of that important fort—200 miles from Madras—having been delivered over to Captain Joseph Smith—with Galton's, honoured names of "the rock"—whose garrison had been increased by 2,000 sepoys from Tinnevelly. Chingleput was again strengthened, and four more field-pieces sent on the 2nd October.

Lally now opened his eyes to the importance of this position—and the traveller cannot help surveying it with interest at the present day—which, twenty days before, he might have taken by escalade in open day, and now resolutely determined to march against it in force.

Intelligence of Lally's move reached the Presidency a few hours after a large convoy had left Fort St. George for Chingleput. It was resolved to take the field with 1,200 Europeans and 1,800 sepoys, by far the greatest portion of the garrison of Madras.

One half of this force marched on the 7th under Draper, with orders to halt ten miles from Chingleput, at Vandalore Choultry, the remainder being held as a reserve at St. Thomas's Mount, under Colonel Lawrence. The intelligence reached Lally; he abandoned his design, and Chingleput was safe.

We now return to Colonel Forde, anxious to measure swords (or guns) with M. de Conflans, according to Colonel Malleson, younger brother of the general who commanded at the same period the French army of Germany. According to the same authority (also quoted by Colonel Innes), the troops under the command of the General and Marquis were "the most seasoned and the best disciplined of all those who served the French Company in Southern India." The troops now marched in good earnest, and early in December came within sight of the enemy, who were encamped near Condore, about forty miles on this side of Rajamundri. The following is a graphic and animated description of this decisive battle of India, by Captain Broome:

"Colonel Forde took up his position, determined to be guided by the movement of the enemy. Condore was as far from the French camp as the old position at Chambole, but with more advantageous ground to advance upon, and with a village half way which would serve for an advanced post. M. Conflans, imagining that the possession of this village was the object of the English movement, pushed forward with his whole force to anticipate this supposed intention; and he attributed Colonel Forde's inaction, in letting him seize this post without an effort, to a consciousness of inferiority. Fearing that the English might now attempt to regain their old position, he determined upon an immediate attack, and, hastily forming his troops in line, advanced towards Condore. His European battalion was in the centre, as usual, with thirteen field-pieces divided on their flanks; immediately to the left of the battalion were the 500 cavalry, and, on either wing, 3,000 sipahis, supported by five or six heavy pieces of cannon.

"Colonel Forde drew up his force in like manner, with the European battalion in the centre, and the six field-pieces divided, three on each flank; to the right was the 1st battalion of sipahis, commanded by Captain Knox, with half of the Madras sipahis; to the left, the 2nd battalion of sipahis, commanded by Captain Lieutenant MacLean, with the remainder of the Madras sipahis; extended on either flank were such of the Rajah's troops as possessed fire-arms, and the remainder of the rabble in the rear. Captain Bristol, with his party and four field-pieces, took post with the three guns to the left of the European battalion.

"Both sides now advanced—the English steadily and deliberately, without firing a shot; the French moving more rapidly, but keeping up a hot cannonade from their artillery as they approached. When they came near, the impetuosity of the French infantry carried them in advance of their guns; upon which the English halted to receive them, and both sides commenced a fire of musketry which lasted for some minutes.

"It so happened that, when the English line halted, the European battalion was immediately in rear of a field of Indian corn, which grew so high as to intercept them from the view of the enemy; but the sipahis on either flank were fully exposed. Colonel Forde, probably with the view of leading the enemy into the very error into which they fell, ordered the sipahi battalions to furl their small colours, of which one was allowed to each company, and to lay them on the ground. This circumstance, and the men being dressed in scarlet uniform, resembling that of the Europeans, for which the French were unprepared—the English sipahis on the Madras side wearing the native dress—led them to suppose that the Europeans were divided on the flanks; the French battalion, as their line advanced, instead of moving directly forward, obliqued to the left, to engage the 2nd native battalion, which they thus mistook for Europeans. When they arrived within the distance of 200 yards, they halted, dressed their ranks, and commenced firing by platoons. Colonel Forde, who perceived their error, rode up to the 2nd battalion to encourage the men to stand; but the latter, observing the enemy's line of sipahis outflanking them to the left and gaining their rear, and being dismayed at finding themselves opposed to Europeans, began to fire in a hurried and irregular manner, and finally to give ground, retreating in the direction of the village of Chambole. Flushed with this success, the French battalion advanced rapidly, though in a disorderly manner, to follow up their advantage. Colonel Forde, who anticipated what would occur, had hastened to the European battalion, and forming them in line to the left, upon the left company, commanded by Captain Adnet, advanced and took the French in flank, just as they were clearing the field of Indian corn. As the several companies came up into their new alignment, they poured in a deadly fire of musketry upon the enemy, which did great execution. Half the French grenadiers went down at the first volley from Captain Adnet's company; and, being taken completely by surprise and thus roughly handled, the whole French battalion went about in great confusion, and hastened to regain the support of their field-pieces, which they had left nearly half a mile behind. ... The French rallied at their guns, thirteen in number, which were scattered about the plain in details, as they had been left when the advance commenced; these guns opened their fire on the English, as soon as their own troops were clear, and killed and wounded several men. Captain Adnet fell mortally wounded at the head of the leading company; but the men were not to be denied: the enemy's fire only induced them to hasten to the charge; and, forming line, they rushed on with the bayonet, drove the enemy from their guns, and once more put the French battalion to flight.

"The day, if not completely gained, was at least secured from reverse by the possession of the enemy's field artillery and the flight of their European battalion. When the European battalion advanced, its field-pieces had been left with this corps. Encouraged by this support, and the spirit of their gallant commander, Captain Knox, the sipahis, though opposed by nearly four times their own number, stood their ground nobly; taking advantage of the cover of some embankments in their front, they kept up a warm fire upon the enemy—to which the latter replied with great spirit, until they saw their own European battalion driven from the guns, and in disorderly flight, when they also began to retreat. Captain Knox now advanced with his battalion and the six field-pieces, to join the Europeans. The enemy's right wing of sipahis and the cavalry had retreated, as soon as they saw the French battalion defeated, without making any attempt to follow up the 2nd native battalion—which, having rallied, also joined the advance. Colonel Forde now determined to push on, and complete his success by attacking the enemy's camp, to which they had all retreated; and he sent to the Rajah to beg that he would advance, particularly with his cavalry, which would have been of the greatest use in following up the broken troops of the enemy; but the Rajah and all his force were cowering in the hollow of a large tank during the action, and could not be induced to stir. Colonel Forde, having made his arrangements, now advanced with his own troops; but, the ground being very bad, the guns, drawn by bullocks, were unavoidably left considerably in the rear. A deep hollow way passed along the skirt of the camp, behind which all the French troops had rallied, supported by their heavy guns, placed so as to command the line of advance. But just as the English troops had taken up their position to attack, and the leading company had stepped out to give their fire, the field-pieces came in sight—and the enemy, as if panic struck, went to the right about, and fled again in the utmost confusion, leaving their camp and the remainder of their guns in the hands of the victors; but the English following them up rapidly, many threw down their arms, and surrendered themselves prisoners. No victory could have been more complete. The enemy were totally routed and dispersed. Thirty-two pieces of artillery, including seven mortars of from 13 to 8 inches calibre, 50 ammunition carriages, a large supply of shot and shell, 1,000 draught bullocks, and the whole of the camp equipage and stores were captured; 6 French officers and 70 Europeans were killed or mortally wounded, and about 50 more slightly wounded; 6 officers and 50 Europeans, rank and file, were taken prisoners, and the loss of their sipahis must also have been considerable."*

"Thus," adds Captain Broome, "ended the battle of Condore, one of the most brilliant actions on military record; which, however, is generally but little known or mentioned in the service; and, by a strange chance, not one of the corps employed has ever received any distinction for this most important victory; whilst the 1st Madras European Fusiliers, of which not an officer or man, excepting Captain Callender, was present, have the word 'Condore' emblazoned on their colours and appointments. The corps pro-

* *History of the Bengal Army,* pp. 215-220.

perly entitled to this distinction are the present 1st Bengal European Fusiliers, the 1st Regiment of Bengal Native Infantry, and the Bengal Artillery. The 2nd Native Battalion is no longer in existence, and the Madras Sipahis present were never organised as a regular corps."

The old *Calcutta* reviewer asserts that there is a slight error, or misprint, in the above excellent description of the battle of Condore; thus the French battalion is described as obliquing to the left to engage the 2nd Native Battalion, instead of to the right, which it actually did. Such an error involves in obscurity an important movement in the action which might " puzzle a young military reader."

Colonel Innes is as indignant as Captain Broome at the omission of the distinguishing mark "Condore" from the colours and appointments of his regiment, that of a battle ranked by Colonel Malleson amongst the "Decisive Battles of India," for "it was a battle between the English and French for supremacy in India." The author of the *History of the Bengal European Regiment*, is very emphatic on the subject. He says :* "Whilst reviewing the subject of 'Decorations,' prominent reference must be made to 'Condore' having been placed on the colours of the Madras European Regiment, and inherited by the Royal Dublin Fusiliers, in place of on those of the Bengal European Regiment, which was the only British Regiment employed in the campaign in the Northern Circars under Colonel Forde, during which the memorable battle of 'Condore' and the celebrated siege of 'Masulipatam' were fought. It is a crying injustice to the 'Royal Munster Fusiliers' that it should be denied the decoration 'Condore,' to which it is clearly entitled." †

The question was submitted to the India Office for report.

* Appendix A, p. 544.

† Colonel Innes's list of services slightly differs from that before given, as in the Army List, when he says: The Decorations to which "The Royal Munster Fusiliers," as successor to the 1st and 2nd Bengal European Regiments, is entitled, are :—"Plassey," "Condore," "Buxar," "Rohilcund," "Sholingur," "Deig," "Bhurtpore," "Afghanistan," "Ghuznee," "Ferozshuhur," "Sobraon," "Punjaub," "Chillianwallah," "Goozerat," "Pegu," "Delhi," "Lucknow."

Lord Kimberley's opinion is that "The Bengal European Regiment" was present at the action at Condore, but "The Madras European Regiment" was not; and that, in his opinion, "Condore" should be placed on the colours of the Royal Munster Fusiliers.*

We should have remarked that in the battle of Condore, of the British, "Captain Adnet and 15 men of the Bengal European Regiment were killed, 4 officers and 30 men wounded, amongst the latter Mr. Johnson—political officer—serving as a volunteer with the Grenadier Company of the Bengal Europeans ; and about 100 men of the Bengal Native Infantry were killed or wounded."

The Cavalry, under Anandraz, were employed as scouts. In the pursuit of the enemy the 1st battalion and other regiments of Native Infantry were engaged, and Colonel Forde came up last with the Bengal European Regiment and "Bristol's" Artillery. This select portion of the scientific arm is thus described by Begbie : " The Rajah (as an addition to his forces) had four field-pieces worked by forty renegade Europeans, commanded by an Englishman of the same class, named Bristol. The advanced force reached Rajamundri on the morning of 10th December, and occupied the town; the French having vacated it on our approach."

The crafty Chief, or Rajah, Anandraz, appears to have given the British commander a vast deal of anxiety and trouble. Although a treaty had been made with him, he would not keep his engagements.

On this point, Colonel Innes remarks : The Chief's crafty policy became apparent when Forde was anxious to push on as quickly as possible to "Masulipatam—the principal fortress and town in the Northern Circars—where it was evident the French Army would make a desperate resistance, and gain time for the arrival of reinforcements." Anandraz wished to drive the French from his territories, " but," says Colonel Innes, " being unequal to the task, he induced the English, under false pretences, to under-

* Innes, p. 544.

take the hazardous work, hoping afterwards to starve out the victors, and derive the benefit of their conquest for himself." *

Forde waited at Rajamundri for the funds which Anandraz had promised him, and were due under the treaty. But this treaty he now ignored, and a fresh or supplementary one had to be drawn up, to the effect " that whatever sums the Rajah should furnish should be considered as a loan, and that the revenues of the districts south-west of the Godavery, which might be reduced, should be equally divided between the East India Company and the Rajah," who now agreed to assist the British in the attack on Masulipatam.

Hitherto, it is justly remarked that Colonel Forde's success was due to the "masterly precision of his strategic movements"; and, again, " Condore formed only a part—an essential one it is true— of our brilliant successes in the Northern Circars; and, considered politically, it marked the first step in the decline of French power in India, as opposed to that of the British."†

At the conclusion of the capture, M. Conflans appears to have lost his head. From his contradictory orders, confusion reigned everywhere among the French troops. At length he received a report from his principal officers that all his batteries had been captured; and he now offered to capitulate on honourable terms. But Forde would have no half measures, and said if the garrison did not surrender at once, unconditionally, he would put them all to the sword.

And so Conflans surrendered the important fortress; the British flag was hoisted in front of the French prisoners, ‡ on the parade-ground ; and on the morning of the 8th April, 1759, the town and fortress of Masulipatam passed into the hands of the East India Company.§ The district afterwards became, as it is now, one of the most important collectorates of the Madras Presidency.

---

* *History of the Bengal European Regiment*, p. 81.

† *Ib.*, p. 80.

‡ Placed under a guard of 100 Europeans and 200 sepoys, with two field-pieces.—*History*, p. 91.

§ For details of the operations in the Northern Circars, see the graphic pages of Colonels Malleson, Innes, and others.

The same may be said of another Circar, to which there is an interesting little piece of history of a later period attached.

The relations between the Madras Government and the Soubahdar of the Dekhan, Nizam Ali, had been somewhat confused—not an uncommon occurrence in the early days of our Indian history. This prince having dethroned his brother, Salabat Jung, made over to him the province of Guntoor, one of the Northern Circars, which the dethroned soubahdar found difficulty in reducing to order without calling in the aid of the English. Now Nizam Ali did not wish the bond of union between his brother and the English to be drawn very tight. He therefore forbade their marching to the assistance of Salabat Jung, and was very angry when they disregarded his prohibition. He was pacified, however, by a promise that they would assist him against any other enemy that might attack him; and, in consideration of that engagement, he confirmed the Mogul's deed, brought about by Clive, by which the rest of the Northern Circars became a province of Madras.*

After the capture, Masulipatam and the adjacent districts were ceded to the British; and Forde continued in command. The brave little army in the Northern Circars was broken up; and the Right Wing of the Bengal European Regiment, which, as such, had been greatly distinguished during the operations, returned to its own Presidency.

Colonel Forde, it is said, saw that the taking of Masulipatam was the main object of the campaign; and, like a good general, he sacrificed everything to gain that vital point. One hundred and twenty pieces of ordnance were found in the fort, and a large supply of military stores, which were of great value to the English. The conduct of our troops in the assault was admirable; the sepoys "emulated the Europeans," and much of our brilliant success was attributable to their gallantry.

Salabat Jung, and, doubtless, the combined army of M. du Rocher, and the Dekhan troops, were astonished and surprised at

* *British India.* Edited by the Rev. G. R. Gleig, M.A., late Inspector-General of **Military Schools.**

the fall of the place. Probably, Salabat Jung thought that, had his old friend, counsellor, and captain, M. de Bussy,* been there, there would have been a different tale to tell; but, considering that it was a British foe they had had to deal with, he thought no more on the subject. He re-advanced to within fifteen miles of the fort; but finding it impossible to re-take it, he concluded a treaty with the English, and hastily retraced his steps, his presence being urgently required in his own dominions, in consequence of the preparations that had been made by his brother, Nizam Ali, to seize the subahdari. Thus everything fell out as Colonel Forde had hoped and anticipated. The most effectual aid was given to the English cause by the capture of Masulipatam, and the French interests in that part of the country were entirely destroyed. We must pass over the rest of the gallant acts of this detachment; but we give our readers Captain Broome's admirable summary of the effects of this expedition, which returned to Bengal in March 1760 :—

"Thus terminated this brilliant expedition, during which the troops obtained all the objects contemplated, diverted the attention and means of the French from the prosecution of the war at Madras, gained one glorious and complete victory in the field, took one of the strongest forts in that part of India, captured upwards of 200 pieces of cannon, acquired a most valuable and extensive tract for the Company, drove the French completely out of the Northern Provinces, and destroyed their influence at the court of the Nizam; and all this, in the face of a superior force of regular troops, and in spite of difficulties and obstacles of the most serious nature. Viewed under all the circumstances attending it, and the results

* The better to strengthen his hands on opening his arduous campaign, Lally had recalled M. de Bussy from attending on Salabat Jung, Soubahdar of the Dekhan. The key-stone of his government was now gone. On account of this impolitic step, various rajahs and petty chiefs at once rose against Salabat, and one of them had captured Vizagapatam, which we eventually re-took. During his full command of the Circars, this town had originally been reduced to one factory by Bussy. Lally in ordering him to quit the court of the Soubahdar, was anxious to unite his forces, to reduce Madras, and attack our new settlements in Bengal. The parting of M. de Bussy from Salabat is given at page 81 of Colonel Malleson's admirable work :—*Decisive Battles*, Kondúr and Machhlípatanam.

obtained, this may be considered one of the most successful and important expeditions ever undertaken by this army, although the details have been slightly passed over by historians generally."*

Of course, while his great lieutenant, Forde, was assaulting Masulipatam, Clive was not idle in Bengal. When was Clive ever idle? Certainly never in India. But we have given so much space to the Chief Presidency that we must at once return to Lally.

While military operations were being carried on in the Northern Circars, Count Lally with his whole force was advancing to the siege of Madras.

Captain Joseph Smith, Commandant of Trichinopoly, under orders from the Presidency, equipped 2,000 sepoys of his garrison, and sent them with a couple of field-pieces across the Coleroon, under the command of Usoff Cawn, on the 21st November, to act on his rear. On the 29th November, the French army advanced from Conjeveram, along the high road towards Madras; a large detachment, under the command of M. de Soupire, being sent along the banks of the Palaur river, with orders to halt between the river and Chingleput.†

On the 4th December, Lally in person reconnoitred Chingleput. He had the audacity to do so within musket-shot; but, finding it impracticable, save by regular approaches, he committed the dangerous error of leaving it hanging in his rear.

On the 12th December, the enemy marched from St. Thomas's Mount, and their European cavalry came suddenly upon a choultry on the Triplecane road, garrisoned by three companies of sepoys, who fired a volley and fled to join the main body. But Lawrence's field-pieces, commanding the road, opened upon the cavalry, and compelled them to quit their position, on which they galloped up the St. Thomé road, with the view of gaining the Triplecane bridge; but they were again met with a fire from artillery " from behind a barrier thrown across the road, on which they retreated out of range."

* *Calcutta Review*, No. XXVIII.. December 1850.
† Bogbie's *Services of the Madras Artillery*, vol. i., pp. 109-110.

The main body of the French had advanced, cannonading as they went along, to which Lawrence replied with his six field-pieces; and, at length, calling in his outposts, he gradually retired within the walls of the fort. The cannonade had occasioned some loss to English as well as French. Simultaneously with this advance, 300 Europeans, with two 12-pounders, had been despatched under Lieut.-Colonel Murphy—an Irish officer in the French service—against Poonamalee. This officer summoned Ensign Crowley to surrender; and of course he refused, on which the guns were employed till night-fall in the attempt to effect a breach. But little or no effect was produced on the stone walls of the fort; and Crowley, with the pluck of a Clive, marched his sepoys out at midnight by an unguarded point, and reached the north part of Black Town by daybreak, where his 300 men were joined by the 200 who had constituted the garrison of Tripasore. With the arrival of these the British muster-roll stood thus:—the European military, including the officers, 64 topasses (Portuguese), and 89 Caffres, incorporated in the companies, amounting to 1,758 men; sepoys, 2,220; amongst the Europeans were 24 mounted troopers; "the Nawaub's rabble of horse," 200. The European civil inhabitants of Madras amounted to 150, who were told off, irrespective of rank, to serve out stores and provisions to the garrison.

On the morning of the 14th the French troops were in motion. At length the whole French army appeared in the southern parts of the town, Lally's regiment taking up their quarters on the beach, and Lorraine, with the battalion of India, on the rising ground to the west. A number of natives of Black Town, we learn, who, with their usual apathy, had remained in their houses till the last moment, now came crowding upon the glacis, requesting admission to the fort, but were refused. These people reported that the French were plundering in all directions, and intoxicated themselves with all the liquor that they could lay their hands on; and, in fact, parties of them could be seen from the fort, staggering in every stage of intoxication.* Colonel Draper proposed that advantage

* Begbie.

should be taken of their helpless condition to attack them; and 500 of the best men were accordingly draughted for that purpose, and marched under his command, followed by two field-pieces, at 11 A.M., out of the western ravelin, 100 more following shortly afterwards under Major Brereton as a support. Eventually, a very hot fire, both of guns and musketry, commenced on both sides, and lasted for twenty minutes, but with constantly increasing effect from the French, whose numbers augmented every moment. Draper, apprehensive that the arrival of Lally's regiment might cut off his communication, directed the retreat to be beaten, but the drummers were now nowhere to be found; and the consequence was that a party of 100 men, of whom 80 were grenadiers, who were in a large enclosure, were ignorant of the measure until too late. The enemy pressed upon the retreating column so closely that the two field-pieces had to be abandoned, while the men in the enclosure surrendered themselves as prisoners. Lally's regiment, which now came up, would have annihilated the detachment, but fortunately it was too drunk to act with effect, and the remainder made good their escape in great disorder to the fort.

After various sallies, on the 28th December another was made from the fort, with no other result than that of the interception of a despatch from Pondicherry; and the year closed with the completion of two batteries of the enemy, called respectively, "Lorraine's and Lally's batteries."

We could not in the space allotted to us narrate even a small portion of the events connected with the famous siege of Madras. Suffice it to say that Lally and Bussy deemed it expedient to carry it on for upwards of two months, under very great difficulties.

The garrison, already alluded to, was commanded by Governor Pigott, and the veteran Colonel Lawrence; and it made the most gallant defence. The blockade was terminated, to the intense satisfaction of the Madrassis, by the appearance, on the 16th February 1759, of an English squadron with 600 fresh troops. When this fleet hove in sight, the French army, without waiting their commander's orders, began to retreat precipitately, and Lally had not time to execute his "cruel purpose" of leaving the Black Town in ashes. And thus the siege of Madras, which had lasted sixty-seven days, was raised. The proud, energetic, daring, but too rash Lally was destined to return vanquished to Pondicherry; but still the old Irish fire in him was far from extinguished. After their defeat by Colonel Coote at Wandewash, which was essentially an artillery battle, and in which General Bussy was taken prisoner (January 1860), on our reconquest of the Carnatic, it had been evident that French dominion in India was fast drawing to a close. "Their general," writes the historian, "has acknowledged that if, after their late successes, our countrymen had marched direct upon their chief city, they might have become masters of it in a few days." Having obtained repeated reinforcements—keeping up a succession of Presidency armies—which the enemy looked for in vain we were enabled to close in around Pondicherry, and make preparations for its actual siege.

Lally, by high promises, obtained an auxiliary force from Hyder Ali, now master of Mysore; but his troops soon departed, after witnessing the manifest weakness of their French allies. In a state of desperation, the brave Lally made a spirited midnight attack on the British camp; but after carrying some important posts, he met with a final repulse.

By the end of September 1760, Pondicherry was closely blockaded by sea and land. The horrors of starvation set in, and all was terror and dismay. War in itself is bad enough, but famine in war is far more terrible.

On the 27th November, the French commander insisted on expelling the native (or black) inhabitants of Pondicherry. To the number of 1,400, they were thrust out of the gates; but as they relieved the garrison, enabling them to hold out for a longer period, they received no sympathy at first from the besiegers. The unhappy creatures wandered about the glacis picking up roots and plants to eat, and imploring either an entrance to the city, or a passage through the army. After a week the British commandant, Colonel Coote, humanely gave leave to the whole to retire into the country, which they did in the most exhausted state, and nowhere to look for refuge. However, we read that they were extremely grateful even for this chance of preservation.

On the 12th January 1861, the trenches were regularly opened. The enemy had only provisions for two days left. At length, on the 14th, came deputations, " one from Lally, and the other from the governor and council." The latter asked some favourable terms for the inhabitants; " but, as matters stood," writes the historian, " everything rested with the discretion of the conquerors, who, however, promised to act with consideration and humanity."

Colonel Coote (the famous Sir Eyre) entered Pondicherry on its surrender—Lally and his garrison having become prisoners of war. Three days after, the defeated French general, held by the Brahmans to be the scourge of Southern India, set sail for France. And thus ended the stormy military career of one of her most extraordinary, bravest, and ill-used sons.

It is impossible to view with sufficiently deep execration the vile treatment Lally received from his countrymen on arrival in Paris. But, after the disgraceful treatment awarded to Dupleix and La Bourdonnais, who had done so much to establish French power in India, it was quite to be expected. However, in the case of Lally, there was murder as well as ill-treatment and man's ingratitude to the full. He was accused of ruining French affairs in India, and of high treason; and although, doubtless, he did some harm to the former from his native Irish impetuosity, or blind and headlong zeal, of the latter he was certainly not guilty. Rashness and imprudence were characteristics of the age in which he worked, especially in India. Among the French there, the great Bussy alone had little, if any, of these qualities;* and, through a miracle, he had been well treated on leaving India, and on reaching the French capital. Lally, on his arraignment, was removed from the Bastille to a humbler prison. He was denied the aid of counsel,

---

* Next to him may be ranked La Bourdonnais, best known as Governor of the Mauritius (Isle of France), the scene of Bernardin St. Pierre's beautiful tale of " Paul and Virginia."

"according to the ungenerous practice of France." The Parliament pronounced sentence of death, against which two of their most humane and distinguished members protested, and which Voltaire, in his eloquent indignation, pronounced to be a judicial murder. The ever magnanimous biographer of Clive, Sir John Malcolm, says well: The Count Lally was the victim offered by the Ministers of France to an incensed public. The principles of justice and the feelings of humanity appear to have been alike violated by this act, which a philosopher of France (Voltaire) truly denominated, at the period of its perpetration, "A murder committed with the sword of justice." Before this, Sir John, quoting Orme, the historian, informs us: "When Lally heard his sentence, he threw up his hands to heaven, and exclaimed, 'Is this the reward of forty-five years service?' and snatching a pair of compasses, which lay with maps on his table, struck it to his breast; but it did not pierce to his heart. He then gave loose to every execration against his judges and accusers. His scaffold was prepared, and his execution appointed for the same afternoon. To prevent him from speaking to the spectators a large gag was put into his mouth before he was taken out of prison, whence he was carried in a common cart, and beheaded on the Grève. He perished in the sixty-fifth year of his age." This foul murder, by a pack of biassed Government administrators, would never have been perpetrated had the French Government put Bussy, in the place of Lally, in supreme military command at the most critical period of French political and military action in India. There is no act more grievous to a distinguished soldier than supersession; and when the superseded officer, from general to captain, is well known and appreciated, such an act of useless despotism may be fatal to that army. On this point, according to Sir John Malcolm, how different was the conduct of the great Chatham! When the troops of his sovereign were ordered to India to support the national interests, he at once decided that neither Lawrence nor Clive should be superseded in their command.* And what was the consequence?

* *Memoirs of Lord Clive*, vol. ii., p. 30.

The two experienced local captains, between them, conquered Southern India and Bengal for all time.

We cannot part with Lally and Bussy—who threatened the very existence of our two Presidencies and their armies—without a few more remarks. There can be no doubt that Clive viewed Lally as a distinguished man, and able—if not very excellent—soldier. When he first became an actor in the wide Indian theatre of war, the "heaven-born general" writes of him, as if implying some slight doubt as to his real rank:—" Although M. Lally is a colonel in the Irish Brigade, I do not find any of that corps have come out with him." And again, with his usual foresight: "The capture of St. David's ought to add nothing to our apprehensions of his succeeding in future enterprises." So Clive wrote to his friend Mr. Pigot, Governor of Madras. And again, after the famous siege:—" Your defence of Madras," Clive observes in a letter to Mr. Pigot of the 21st August 1759, "and your foiling a man of Lally's rank, will certainly gain you much honour at home; but what affords me most pleasure is the principal part you have acted in this famous siege. I always said my friend (Colonel Lawrence) would shine whenever an opportunity offered."

It is well affirmed by Sir John Malcolm that the delight of Clive was heightened by his warm feelings of friendship towards those who had so nobly supported the reputation of the service of Fort St. George, to which he had a pride in belonging; and to none of these friends had he greater pleasure in writing than to Governor Pigot.*

Too much cannot be said in praise of Bussy. He appears to have had the happy knack of thoroughly understanding and

---

* This distinguished Anglo-Indian of the old time appears to have been a remarkable man. We have briefly alluded to him in another work. In those days, or in the earlier years of the Presidencies, the commissions of Governors also bore the title of Commanders-in-Chief. Arriving in Madras, 1737, he became Governor in 1755, and embarked for England in 1763. As the Right Hon. Lord Pigot he became Governor for the second time in 1775, when he was placed under arrest by the Madras Council, and detained at St. Thomas' Mount in 1776; allowed to return to Garden House for change of air in April 1777, and there died on 20th May 1777. Was ever distinguished Governor so treated before?

gaining the favour of great Indian princes, on which, after all, the secret of good government in India so much depends. In this respect, among the French in India, he was the Metcalfe, Munro, or Malcolm of his time. He seems to have ever had the words of Clive to Mr. Payne, the Chairman of our Court of Directors, before him: "It cannot be expected that the princes of this country, whose fidelity is always to be suspected, will remain firm to their promises and engagements from principle only." It is absolutely necessary, therefore, to keep up a strong force. At a later period he wrote to the Court, the practical wisdom of which may have in our future Indian policy to be more fully appreciated than at present: "Either the princes of the country must, in a great measure, be dependent on us, or we totally so on them." On this Sir John Malcolm remarks that Clive's clear and practical mind puts the question on its real basis; and there is no other alternative. Bussy must have thought likewise. Lally was deaf to Bussy's good advice.

On one occasion, when it was thought prudent to put Basalut Jung, brother of the Soubahdar of the Dekhan, on the throne of the Carnatic, he being a warm supporter of the French, Lally precipitately proclaimed the son of Chunda Sahib Nabob, who was quite useless, as an ally.

The influence of Bussy at Salabat Jung's court was truly wonderful. With his followers we read that he dictated or directed every movement; and surely France had reason to be thankful to a man who had been the chief means of giving her a territory on the coast of Coromandel and Orissa, including the Northern Circars, of some hundreds of miles in extent, and yielding, with what she already possessed, a revenue of some £800,000.

It is curious to observe, while Bussy was at the height of his power (1754-55), and Dupleix had ceased hoping one day to become Great Mogul, that "the heads of the two European presidencies" (as they are styled by the historian), under instructions from home, were ordered to bring their differences to a termination. They began by examining the titles by which each held their respective possessions from the native powers, especially the Mogul; but the English alleging that the documents produced by the French were forged, proposed to reject this mode of arbitration, and determined to use actual force alone in settling their differences. The Indian war became a theme of interest in Europe; commissioners were sent out, and such was the state of affairs when Godheu, the French envoy, arrived at Pondicherry to succeed Dupleix.

Five or six years after these events, Bussy was made prisoner at the battle of Wandiwash (January 1760), but, writes Clive's biographer, "was instantly released by Colonel Coote, from respect for his character, and as a return for that kindness and consideration which he had invariably shown to English prisoners." The Nabob Muhamed Ali wrote to Governor Pigot that the capture of M. Bussy "was of itself equal to any victory, and suggesting the propriety of his being sent to him, when he would take great care of him!" Soon after this occurrence he returned to France, "leaving behind him a name as fondly cherished by the natives of India as by his countrymen."

Bussy's courage and conduct as a soldier were not less conspicuous than his great qualities as a statesman; and they stood high before the genius of Dupleix, appreciating his character, sent him into the Dekhan.*

We cannot better conclude these few remarks on this distinguished Franco-Indian statesman and soldier than in the words of Colonel Malleson, in one of his brilliant chapters on the *Decisive Battles of India*, while alluding to French influence in the Dekhan, that such influence was maintained " by the presence at Haiderábád of a considerable body of French troops, commanded by an officer of rare intelligence and capacity, the Marquis de Bussy."†

It is like proceeding from Romance to Reality, with both of which Indian life abounds, when we take a stride from M. Bussy to

---

* *Memoirs of Lord Clive.*
† *The Decisive Battles of India*, p. 77.

Bombay. A good deal has already been said about Bengal and Madras; but, latterly, not much concerning the famous Western presidency of India or its capital. The chief reason for such indifference must be on account of its good behaviour, or being the least troublesome of the three Presidencies, either with regard to its trade or its army. The Portuguese title, therefore, *buona baiæ* (the good bay), from which the name is derived, is decidedly well earned. In an earlier chapter, Surat and Bombay have been duly alluded to; how the latter superseded the former, on becoming the magnificent gift of King Charles to the East India Company,* and the chief seat of the now great Bombay presidency for trade. But the first measure that enabled the Company to get the sovereign power which they sought was a rebellion at Bombay, the commandant having declared that he held that island for the King. The Company had the power of keeping their own servants in subjection, and of defending themselves; so they removed their seat of government to Bombay, prepared to contend with Arungzebe himself, as they had hitherto done with the Moguls and Mahrattas collectively.

While the settlement of Bombay was taking place in India, a remarkable man—Sir Josiah Child—was discoursing upon Indian trade in Europe. This most energetic and distinguished of all the Company's supporters and the interloper's enemies was giving a fresh impulse to the notion of the value of Indian commerce. Sir Josiah did this towards the end of the seventeenth century; and this impulse, to which the fair and gentlemanly, and always business-like Parsís have given such a commercial charm in Bombay in the nineteenth century, has gone on steadily increasing till the present time.†

* See pp. 45-46.

† We find in the *Selections* (1887) that measures were so far back adopted for the encouragement of trade in Bombay (1671); the prices of horses procurable in Bombay for the cavalry; of Captain Richard Keigwin appointed first commander of the Bombay Cavalry; of the situation of Bombay in an excellent latitude and the excellence of its harbour; of the instructions from the Company to make Bombay "an important port" for the exportation and importation of goods; of the probability of the French attacking it, and the measures taken to defend Bombay against the French. Such and many other useful subjects will be found in Professor George W. Forrest's splendid volumes, to which Colonel Rivett-Carnac,

About the middle of the eighteenth century, the preparations of the troops forming the small Bombay Presidency army to defend their island against the French occupied much attention. But, with reference to the events of 1759 in Madras and Bengal, Bombay did not become seriously affected by them. There must have been a sense of security in the western presidency, unknown to the others at this time, for we find Clive's biographer writing that "the affairs of the small but important settlement of Bombay appeared as prosperous as those of Madras." Sir John Malcolm, in a slight historical retrospect, also relates how, in a distracted state of affairs, or division of authority, the Government of Bombay (1759) listened with approbation to an overture by the principal officers and merchants of Surat (who had occupied that port for a century and a half), inviting them to take the castle, to expel the Seedee (governor or chief), and on receiving an assignment, with the sanction of the officers of the Emperor of Delhi, to become the future protectors of the commerce of the port. Such events added both to the strength and the fame of the settlement of Bombay, and rendered it better able to cope with the predatory Mahrattas. "The principal chiefs of that nation, however," it is remarked, "were at this period more occupied with the affairs of the northern than of the western parts of India."* We shall conclude this rambling chapter with a few remarks on the Parsís, to which they may not object, as we have casually alluded to them, and they have so long been under the protection of our Presidential armies.

We recollect the now well-known colonial governor, Sir Henry Norman, saying at a great meeting, that to speak of Burma was to speak of Sir Arthur Phayre.† In the same manner it may be said, that to speak of Bombay is to speak of the Parsí community,

---

in the ever-laudable desire to do his work thoroughly, has already referred in this volume.

* *Memoirs of Lord Clive*, vol. ii., pp. 101, 102.

† We have lately been much pleased to behold the beautiful statue in bronze of this most distinguished Chin-Indian statesman, by Mr. Maclean, which is to adorn Rangoon.

which stands out as the most celebrated Oriental community of the time. It is unique in every way, and to it the old Roman quotation may be gracefully applied—of wearing a thousand ornaments, and in all being pleasing. It is a community of deeds, not words; of unceasing charity and benevolence, and ever-growing excellence. In a splendid work, *The History of the Parsís*, sent us from Bombay by one of their most distinguished sons (the Hon'ble. Sir Dinshaw Manocjee Petit, of Malabar Hill), we get a capital idea of this wonderfully enterprising and energetic people:—

"No authentic records exist to show the exact date of the arrival of the Parsís in Bombay, nor can we authoritatively explain what was the motive that first led them there. It seems probable that the English merchants of Surat induced some of them to settle in Bombay for purposes of trade. This much may, however, be safely affirmed, that their first settlement in that island was a little before the time when it was ceded to the British by the Crown of Portugal, as the dowry of Catherine, Princess of that country, who became the wife of Charles the Second of England, A.D. 1668. Dr. Fryer, who visited Bombay in the year 1671, says: 'On the other side of the great inlet to the sea is a great point abutting against Old Woman's Island, and is called Malabar Hill, a rocky woody mountain, yet sends forth long grass; *on the top of all is a Parsí tomb lately raised.*' The first work of the Parsís wherever they settle is to construct a tower of silence, or what Doctor Fryer calls a tomb, for the reception of their dead; and his statement that the tomb in question had been recently raised is a sufficient proof that no considerable number of the Parsís could have settled in that island prior to its cession to the English."*

Mr. Dosabhai Framji also gives the following interesting information:—

"In an account of the distinguished Parsí families of Surat the Bhavnagris may be mentioned.

---

* *History of the Parsís*, by Dosabhai Framji Karaka, C.S.I. (London: Macmillan & Co., 1884), vol. i., pp. 51, 52. Sir Dinshaw Manocjee Petit has now been created a Baronet by the Queen Empress; and we believe his last munificent act of charity to be the founding or construction of a leper hospital.

"Jamasji Framji Bhavnagri (1744) was a wealthy 'jaghirdar,' and he caused to be built at his own expense a large tank of solid stone for the use of the public at Bhavnagar.

"Another very wealthy, influential, and public-spirited citizen of Surat, who deserves mention in these pages, was Nasarvanji Kohiyar, who died in 1797 at the age of eighty. He was the agent of the Dutch factory at Surat, and carried on an extensive business in maritime insurance as the representative in his city of an eminent firm of Bombay merchants. He traded on his own account, among other countries, with Persia, which he twice visited. He was of a deeply religious nature, and his public work, which mostly took a religious form, survives to this day in a fire-temple which he established at Yezd in Persia, and for which he sent the sacred fire all the way from Surat by land, an especially hazardous and difficult undertaking in those days. He endowed this fire-temple with 'jaghirs,' and instituted in connection with it an annual religious feast which is still known as Kohiyar's Gahambar. He also built a fire-temple at Surat, and revived among his co-religionists in India the ancient Persian institution of the Jamshedi Naoroz, or the feast of the vernal equinox. Towards the persecuted Zoroastrians of Persia who sought a refuge in India, or who came there in quest of an opening for their talents, his hospitality was unbounded. Nor were his sympathies confined to his own race or creed. He was versed in the tenets of the Kabir Panth, or the philosophico-religious sect founded by the well-known Hindu reformer Kabir, for whose teaching he had a great predilection. He was well read in the Persian and Arabic languages, and he was one of the most enlightened citizens of Surat of his time."*

Mrs. Graham, in her journal of a residence in India in the years 1805 and 1806, says: "The Parsí merchant Ardeshir Dadi fed 5,000 people, besides contributing in other ways towards the support of the starving population." This recent evidence is amply borne out by that of an earlier period. The Rev. Mr. Ovington, who published an account of his voyage to Surat in the year 1689,

* *History*, vol. ii., pp. 38, 39.

has said that "the Parsís are ever ready to provide for the sustenance and comfort of such as want them. Their univeral kindness, either in employing such as are needy and able to work, or bestowing a seasonable bounteous charity to such as are infirm and miserable, leaves no man destitute of relief, nor suffers a beggar in all their tribe; and herein they so far comply with that excellent rule of Pythagoras, to enjoy a kind of community among friends."

Major Moore, in his narrative of the operation of Captain Little's detachment, says :—"The benevolence of the Parsís is not restricted to persons of their own sect. Their industry and extensive mercantile spirit have enabled many of them to amass considerable fortunes, which they spend with generous profusion in acts of charity and hospitality."* Especially during the last forty or fifty years these have been patent to all Englishmen; and we cannot think too much of the Parsí as one of the grand living agents in the prosperity of India, who has so long appreciated and enjoyed security under our Presidency armies. Whatever Mahomedan or Hindu may think of us, it is quite certain that the Parsí thinks us the best masters he could possibly have.

Mr. Gladstone, in a more general way, with his accustomed eloquence, has delivered himself (January 13, 1890) on this matter. While speaking on the subject of India, he urged that the people of England, who now had the control of the destinies of that great dependency, should deal with India on the same principles of justice as they demanded for themselves. "He believed that the natives of India would not exchange the sovereignty of this country for that of any other power." To anyone who knows India, or has carefully studied Indian history, the truth uttered by the great and versatile statesman becomes at once palpable.

But there is another argument to be considered, to say nothing of the magnificent inheritance being so long in our possession, even if we lost it to-morrow, no other European Power could keep India for a year. The nation that stood the Sikh invasion of

---

* *History*, vol. ii., pp. 265-66.

1845-46, and that severest trial, the Sepoy Mutiny of 1857, has Indian security indelibly stamped upon it; so, as Lord Dalhousie said of Pegu, we may safely repose on the assertion, that " as long as the sun shines in the heavens " the British flag shall wave over India.

CHAPTER X.

WAR WITH, AND CONQUEST OF, MYSORE—BRIEF RECORD OF
A DISTINGUISHED BOMBAY INFANTRY REGIMENT.

THE Company having obtained the firman of the Emperor of Delhi for possession of the Northern Circars, which formed part of the Kingdom of the Dekhan, under the Nizam (*lit.* putter in order) of Hyderabad, made, in 1766, a treaty with that prince, wherein they engaged to pay him annually nine lakhs of rupees (£90,000), and held a body of troops in readiness to co-operate with him for the five Circars; besides which, they ordered the Nabob of Bengal to find him five lakhs more, to be paid down, their own not to be forthcoming till they were in actual and sure possession of the Circars. The bargain that they had made in Bengal, it has been well said, " even where they had the whole revenue, might have made them pause as merchants in this one; but it did not; neither did they appear to make any calculation of the extent to which the league with the Nizam might lead them."

The renowned Hyder Ali now comes fairly on the field. The Company had been already skirmishing with him; and he had set himself up in Mysore. He was, indeed, the Mysore sovereign, and one of the most remarkable men in Indian history. Doubtless it was an unwise provision in the treaty of 1763 which gave back to the French all their old settlements in the Carnatic; for it was productive of much injury to the rising Madras Presidency. Had it not been for this piece of liberal folly, or unstatesmanlike conduct at home on our part, the British flag might now have been waving over Pondicherry—a Madras presidency Brighton, as well as a splendid depôt for cotton cloths to delight and enrich the cotton lords of Manchester for many generations!

The restless and intriguing French were no sooner restored to " as you were " in Pondicherry than they began to stir up the native powers against their British rivals; and in Hyder Ali they found a chief well suited to their purpose. By " the force of talent and unscrupulous hardihood," he had made his way to the throne. After the Nizam had quelled a mutiny of his troops with the ready money furnished by the Nabob, the new allies marched to reduce the fort of Bangalore. But Hyder had the address to detach the Nizam from the English, and to make an ally of him. The British commander, having sustained a sharp attack, was obliged to hasten to Trincomalee; and Hyder proceeded on a short plundering excursion to Madras. The Nizam offered to negotiate with us; but, not agreeing, a battle was fought near Vellore, in which Hyder and the Nizam were defeated. This brought the temporising Nizam again over to the English, who made him reduce the price of the Circars. Hyder sought for peace; but the Presidency of Madras, " who had lately, with not a little consternation, seen him at their door, waxed valiant, took the field, controlled the officers, and would have their Nabob put on the throne of Mysore."

The army, commanded by civilians, was non-effective; and it wasted the season of 1768 in unavailing trifles. At length, to the dismay of the Presidency army, Hyder dashed on by marches of forty miles a day, and showed himself with a large army of horse* so close to Madras that he could have pillaged all without the fort before the English army could have come up. Hyder stipulated for " mutual restitution and mutual aid in war," which was agreed to by the governor or president. Hyder was next attacked by the Mahrattas, and applied to the English for the stipulated assistance, which was not given; and so he became a bitter enemy of

* About 5,000.

the English, on the plea of a broken treaty. To add to our troubles, the Nizam could not be relied on. "He had no sooner reached his own dominions than a triple alliance was proposed between himself, Hyder, and the Mahrattas. Hyder was to invade the Carnatic; the Nizam the Circars; the Mahrattas of Berar were to lay waste Bengal and Behar; and the Poonah Mahrattas were to attack the British army in Gujerat." Thus a fair piece of work was cut out for each of the three Presidency armies. All the parties were quite willing to go to war where they might find plunder; but, as usual among thieves, they fell out and did not act in concert. Hyder was the only chief who went seriously to war, under the plea of the broken treaty. The Nizam made peace. The Berar Mahrattas would not come to the front; the Poonah Mahrattas were beaten; and had it not been for the diversion created in their favour by Hyder, this warlike people would have been completely subdued.

The immediate cause of the war with the Poonah, or Western Mahrattas, which originated in India Proper in 1773, is well known to the readers of Indian history. We shall, therefore, leave the eventual annexation of Rohilkund (1774) to the province of Oudh to remark that when the Mahrattas returned in 1773 from laying waste Hyder's country, they made demonstrations of moving northward. An army was accordingly marched from Bengal westward in 1778; but a portion of it was forced to capitulate the following year, though the rest passed on, reducing the greater part of the country from thence to Concan, penetrating into the very heart of Malwa. In 1780, Hyder again appeared in the Carnatic, and approached near to Madras, which occasioned the western army to retire and give up all their conquests, except a few in Bombay. The Mysore sovereign actually declared war on the 20th July 1780; and, sweeping down from his fastnesses in Mysore with swarms of horse, rushed over the plains of the Carnatic, making himself master within fourteen days of the forts of Trincomalee, Chitpett, Arnee, Gingee, Chillumbrum, Cauverypauk, and Carangooly, a complete chain of frontier British garrisons; but the possession of which now ensured his communications with the Mysore country.* Before the council of Madras had awoke from their dream of security, hordes of predatory horse had devastated the country in the immediate vicinity of the Presidency, and the smoke from burning villages arose in every direction. At length, at the close of July, the council aroused itself from its lethargy, and decided on forming a camp at Poonamallee (as the most central position), under Lord Macleod, who had by that time arrived with H.M. 73rd Highlanders. Accordingly, on the 1st August 1780, about 800 Native infantry, and 400 European infantry and artillery, were marched from Madras and the Mount to join the 73rd, then about 800 strong. St. Thomas's Mount was now the headquarters of the Artillery of the Madras Presidency.

In 1774, Colonel James, Commandant of Artillery, recommended that the practice ground should be removed to the Mount, "instead of the guns firing into the sea, as had hitherto been the custom." The recommendation was at once attended to; and so the Mount in Madras became what Dum Dum was in Bengal.

The war against Hyder Ali, in the Carnatic, was now the leading event in "the state of affairs in the Madras Presidency." The cry of Madras for assistance was nearly as loud as that from Calcutta on its capture and the tragedy of the Black Hole. The famous Bengal European Regiment was again to be in the front in Southern India, and ready to cover itself with fresh glory.†

---

* Begbie.

† In a former chapter (*Note*) we have given a list of the brilliant services of the Bengal European Regiment (Royal Munster Fusiliers) down to 1781; and now we have to chronicle the Capture of the Fort of Kurungalli; Relief of Wandiwash; Assault of Chillumbrum; Battle of Porto Novo—says Major Innes, " against Hyder Ali and the French "—second relief of Wandiwash; Battle of Sholinghur; and relief of Vellore—all in the same year. Next, the Battle of Arnee, 1782; Siege of Cuddalore, 1783; Battle of Boetura (Rohilkund), 1794; Capture of Gwalior, 1804; Battle of, and Storm and Capture of, Deig, same year; four assaults on the Fortress of Bhurtpore, 1805; Expedition to Macao, 1808; Operations in Java, 1810-17; Nepal War, 1814; Pindari War, 1817; Storm and Capture of Bhurtpore, 1826; Campaign in Afghanistan, 1838; Storm and Capture of Ghuzni, 1839; Battle of Ferozshuhur, 1845; Sobraon, 1846; Campaign in the Punjab, Battle of Chillian-

Taking a brief retrospect, we find that, in August 1778, "two European battalions of Artillery were ordered to be raised, the gunners to be selected by lot from the Bengal European regiments; at the same time, the Grenadier Companies were reduced to half their strength, the Light Companies being increased in proportion, and, on the 26th September 1779, the three regiments of Bengal Europeans were each formed into two battalions; the total strength of European infantry in Bengal being at this time about 3,000."*

We may here state that, on the 1st January 1779, Lieutenant-General Sir Eyre Coote returned to India as Commander-in-Chief at Madras.† Never was a Presidency, or its army, in greater tribulation than now, at a time when it seemed, especially after our various misfortunes, including Colonel Baillie's crushing defeat by Hyder (or, more strictly, by his son Tippoo), when the Colonel's detachment, partly through the injudicious conduct of Sir Hector Munro, was cut to pieces, and Hyder having Frenchmen attached to his army, the British became dispirited and had to retreat. Assisted by his French allies, Hyder really "out-generalled the British troops"; while the resources of the country were well-nigh exhausted, provisions scarce, and the treasury empty.

Immediately on the distressed condition of the Madras Presidency being conveyed to Bengal, Sir Eyre Coote, then Commander-in-Chief in India, left with reinforcements, in order to direct the subsequent operations in person. He arrived at Madras on the 5th November. His force consisted of 300 or 400 European infantry, 200 European artillery (Bengal), and some guns, whilst a few companies of Native infantry were drawn together from Musulipatum and Ongole. A further detachment of ten battalions

---

wallah, 1848; Battle of Goozerat, 1849; Capture and Relief of Pegu, 1852; Storm and Capture of Delhi, 1857, and minor actions during the Mutiny; and Siege and Capture of Lucknow, 1858. Certainly a grand trio is formed by this gallant corps, and the equally devoted First Madras and First Bombay European Regiments, never to be surpassed in India.

* *History of the Bengal European Regiment*, p. 254.

† Sir Eyre held this post for a short time only. He is not even down in Prinsep's List of Madras Commanders-in-Chief. He should have come between Major-General Hector Munro and Lord Macartney, K.B., also Governor, 1781-85.

of Native infantry, and twenty-two guns was expected from Bengal, where Warren Hastings, since 1774, had been the first Governor-General. According to Major Innes, the European battalion selected for this service was the 2nd Battalion of the 1st Bengal European Regiment. On the authority of one Indian historian, Sir Eyre Coote arrived with 7,000 troops, took the command, restored the spirits of the Madras army, and beat Hyder in several actions.* Hyder's army, commanded by him in person, consisted of 80,000 men, including his best cavalry; and "amongst his infantry," writes Major Innes, "were numbers of those men whose descendants may be seen to this day in the Mysore and Madras districts, running without any apparent effort their ten miles an hour for many hours consecutively. He had also a complete corps of Frenchmen, ably commanded; whilst his artillery was second to none in India." This heroic and enterprising, though unscrupulous, Mahomedan sovereign and soldier died in 1782. Tippoo, who had been more successful than his father in most actions with the British, succeeded to the throne. His attention was first called to the west part of Mysore, where General Matthews had made himself master of Canara. The unfortunate Matthews was beaten, and capitulated; but he and twenty of his officers were poisoned, and a large portion of his army massacred by order of Tippoo. The Mahrattas at length showed hostility; the French deserted, and, in 1784, Tippoo made peace, no change of territory on either side having been produced by the war.

The year 1784 has been considered a remarkable one in the

* Sir Eyre Coote, having entrusted the care of Fort St. George and the town of Madras, St. Thomé and St. Thomas' Mount to General Stuart, took the field on the 17th January 1781 at the head of "the largest force which had ever been assembled at that Presidency." It consisted of H.M. 73rd Highlanders, 600 strong; 350 Bengal, and 250 Madras, European infantry; 200 Bengal, and 200 Madras, artillery, with 62 guns; making a total of 1,600 Europeans; ten battalions of Native infantry, each 500 strong; making a total of 7,400 effective men. There were left for the protection of the Presidency under General Stuart 200 European infantry, 50 artillerymen, and 400 native infantry, and, as this force was totally inadequate, mud defences were thrown up for the protection of Black Town. Such was the way in which we defended our Indian Presidencies upwards of one hundred years ago.

history of the British since they had begun to acquire territory in India. And, strange enough, after all that had happened, they were at peace with all the native powers, which allowed the Presidency armies to take that rest to which they were so well entitled. This year is also important in the history of British influence in India as being that in which the change was made which rendered the Court of Directors in a manner subservient to a Board of Control. It is distinguished also by a change in the manner of acquiring territory, and in the conduct of our Indian armies. Hitherto the former had, though unaccompanied by fighting, been more upon the mercantile than the military system.

In the wars with Hyder and the Mahrattas but little territory had been acquired, and success had always been uncertain. "Intrigue and money," says an interesting writer,* "had done the business; and, though the natives had been made to pay, there is not much that can be said to come under the ordinary definition of military conquest. The conquests that have followed have been of rather a different character, and may be considered as a second era, as they began under Cornwallis, who was sent out ostensibly to correct the abuses of which former rulers had tolerated the existence."

As affecting the Governor and Commander-in-Chief of the Madras Presidency, it may be here stated that the close of the year 1788 was marked by "highly arbitrary and vexatious proceedings on the part of Lord Macartney towards General Burgoyne of H.M.'s Light Dragoons, and other officers, by which the discipline of the army was so materially shaken that, had not Tippoo Sultaun made peace at this juncture, matters might have worn a very unfavourable aspect." †

This Lord Macartney appears to have been able and energetic, but a self-willed and obstinate Governor. Being also Commander-in-Chief, he seems to have enjoyed proclaiming war with a portion of mankind, preferring to fight with them in Government House

* Mudie.
† Begbie's *Services of the Madras Artillery.*

to leading or assisting his army on the field. We find that his lordship came out to Madras in June 1781, and in June 1785 he resigned by letter from Vizagapatam. His first getting into hot water began at the conclusion of 1782 (the year of Hyder Ali's death). There was a grievous famine at Madras, which nearly led to a mutinous rising against the Governor, who had laid an embargo on several ships laden with rice lying in the roads, but refused to allow of the grain being sold at a moderate price. The Madras Artillery, however, remained firm to their allegiance, and the guns of Fort St. George eventually over-awed the disaffected. Early in the year Lord Macartney had fought some battles royal with one of our most distinguished Anglo-Indian soldiers, Sir Eyre Coote, whose dangerous illness arose partly in consequence of bodily fatigue, but chiefly from mental anxiety, owing to the disputes in which he was daily involved with the new Governor of Madras.*

As connected with the Southern Presidency army at the commencement of the year 1783, it may also be mentioned that Madras beheld the English army under General Stuart encamped at St. Thomas' Mount on the 2nd of January. This force consisted of the 73rd, 78th, and 101st Foot, 400 Hanoverians, the Madras European Regiment (1st Madras Fusiliers)—in all, about 1,900 Europeans, 21 battalions of native infantry, 4 regiments of native cavalry—quaintly termed by a German author *Koodry*† *sepoys*—making 11,000 native troops, and a large park of artillery, 70 guns, besides a division of 3 pounders attached to each infantry regiment. Of the native regiments (infantry), five of two battalions each belonged to Bengal. Prior to the army being put in motion, two battalions of native infantry, with a detachment from the 102nd Regiment, were detached to join a body of native infantry under Major-General Jones at Ellore, and designated the Northern Army.

General Sir Eyre Coote, on his way from Bengal, died on the 22nd April 1783 in the Madras roads, " universally regretted "—

* Begbie. † *Koodry*, the Tamil term for horse.

a great leader of men on the field, and, as one of Clive's best captains, probably ranking next to the "heaven-born general" in tact and daring.

We must now present our readers with an anecdote of the period, although it is one of a very cruel nature. One of General Stuart's objects was to demolish the forts of Carangooly and Wandiwash, the latter being that where the gallant Coote distinguished himself by besieging and taking it many years before, and which had so repeatedly changed masters. Pursuing its march, the army, especially the rear guard, suffered severely from the enemy's horse and rocket men, the loss in killed and wounded, on one day, being about 200 men. According to Begbie, quoting from a Hanoverian officer's memoirs, General Stuart offered a reward of five pagodas (a pagoda 3½ rs.. or 7s.) for every rocket-man captured. The light cavalry, having captured one of them, brought him in, bound hand and foot, sitting backwards in a cart, and having his *crime* painted in large white letters, in English and Tamil characters, on a blackboard hung round his neck. He was thus led through the camp at noon up to the gallows, where he was to be hanged, "when he obtained the *special* favour of having his sentence commuted into four hundred lashes and deprivation of his ears and nose, after which act of barbarity the poor devil (*der arme teufel*), as the Hanoverian emphatically calls him, was hunted out of the camp." Well may the writer remark that the English authors are silent on this gross violation of the rules of civilised warfare. It is difficult to believe that our countrymen, even in the last century, could have made such inhuman brutes of themselves; but, unfortunately, having perused even worse acts of barbarity in the records, with which we shall not shock our readers, we firmly believe this cruel and cowardly incident. In fact, if we are to credit history, and not look upon it as "a fable agreed upon," we are at once the most humane and inhuman nation on the face of the earth.

The death of Hyder Ali, and of Sir Eyre Coote, who had so brilliantly checked his career, left Tippoo almost master of the field in Mysore. We had made preparations to ascend the Ghauts, and march upon Seringapatam, when the officer commanding was directed to stop, and ordered to restore all his recent conquests. Tippoo had applied for two English commissioners to proceed to his camp and treat for peace; and with a courtesy which Colonel Wilks considers blameable, the Madras Government had acceded to his request. These envoys, on discovering Tippoo's proceedings with regard to Mangalore, which had been so gallantly defended for many months by Colonel Campbell, sent orders to suspend restoration. At length a treaty was concluded, founded on the basis that each party should retain his former possessions, and "that the Sultan should release such of his prisoners as had survived the cruelties with which they had been treated."*

We shall now briefly touch on the conquest of Mysore. There is certainly reason for the historian's remark, that " after this treaty Tippoo had become the most prominent personage in the political world of India." The power of Tippoo was immense; and in him Hyder seemed to live over again for the time. But the day of reckoning was nigh.

The conquest of Mysore forms one of the most interesting chapters in Indian history. In 1786, the Marquess Cornwallis arrived as Governor-General. This able statesman was to effect a complete change in our Indian policy, and to avoid, as much as possible, war with the native powers. But to show how so-called wisdom at home may become practically useless and even destructive in India, the very first efforts of the noble Marquess were directed towards the complete humbling of the power of Mysore. He knew the worth of Tippoo's treaties as well as did Lord Dalhousie, sixty-six years after, the value of those made by the Kings of Burma. The restless nature of the Mysore ruler would not allow him long to preserve the peace made early in 1784;† and

---

* *History of India.*

† From Bombay Castle, on the 17th January of the above year, we have copy of an interesting letter from Warren Hastings to Lord Macartney, Governor of Fort St. George (President and Council), regarding the Treaty of Peace with Tippoo Sultan, in which, in a rather sharp letter by the great Pro-consul, the greatest anxiety is evinced not to offend " the Maratha and other states with whom we are in friendship."

as he well knew that such an attack would bring on war, on the 29th of December 1789 he attacked the lines of Travancore, which were under British protection. Major-General Medows arrived at Madras as Commander-in-chief on the 12th February 1790, and, the army being again ordered to take the field, by the 14th March he had assembled a small force at Conjeveram, and a larger one of 15,000 men of all arms at Trichinopoly, of which he assumed command in person on the 24th May. Two days afterwards he made his first march in the direction of Mysore, it being intended that his troops, after the reduction of the Coimbatoor country, should ascend the Gujelhully pass, whilst the Bombay column—a select portion of its Presidency army—operated against its western side, and a small but efficient force, under Colonel Kelly, observed the passes leading down the Baramahal. In 1790, armies had taken the field on both sides. It should here be mentioned that the Peishwa and the Nizam both stood pledged to assist the English in the coming struggle. Even in 1786 there had been a powerful confederacy of the Mahrattas and the Nizam against Tippoo's influence and lofty pretensions, with the view of getting for themselves the new southern kingdom and the division between them of all its possessions. The first campaign was unsatisfactory. In the second, Lord Cornwallis, on the 29th January 1791, himself assumed the command, won battles and took fortresses; among other strong and important places being the town and fortress of Bangalore. To all Madras artillery officers the storming of this military position, an eventually favourite military cantonment, is an interesting historical episode. It began the second Mysore Campaign.* The centre division of General Medows' army in the first—which army had been reinforced by Bengal sepoys—may be here given. It consisted of H.M.'s 74th

Tippoo is also expected to abstain from hostilities against us and our allies, the "Nabob Nizam-ul Mulk, the Nabob Walau-Jah, and consequently against the Rajahs of Tanjore and Travancore, whose territories are dependencies of the Carnatic."—*Bombay State Papers*, vol. ii., p. 305.

* A large portion of the army had been recalled to Madras at the termination of the first Mysore campaign.

Regiment, the 3rd and 4th battalions of the Madras Europeans, a powerful train of artillery, and some native regiments; in all a force of some 10,000 strong, the whole commanded by Colonel Maxwell of H.M.'s 74th Regiment.

On the 5th February the army was put in motion, and by the 11th was near Vellore. Lord Cornwallis entered Tippoo's territories without opposition, and encamped within 90 miles of Bangalore. On the 5th March the army was encamped before the town. The following tight little force was at once detailed by his lordship for attack. One regiment from the 1st Brigade; one battalion from the 3rd; four iron 18-pounders; two iron 12-pounders; European pioneers; 400 native pioneers. "Major Maule with such officers of the Engineer Corps as he may judge necessary. Lieutenant-Colonel Moorhouse to command the Artillery of this detachment. The regiment's field-pieces to carry their limber boxes only."

On the 7th March the pettah gate of Bangalore was assaulted, and the pettah carried. There was an obstinate attempt to recover the pettah on the following day, when the enemy was repulsed with the loss of 2,000 killed and wounded. The British lost 131 killed and wounded in the two days; and amongst the fallen in the assault on the 7th was the gallant Lieutenant-Colonel Moorhouse, of the Madras Artillery. A well-deserved tribute was paid to the memory of this distinguished officer by the Madras Government. After a resolution that the remains of the gallant and devoted Anglo-Indian gunner should be publicly interred in the church of Fort St. George, at the Company's expense, and a " marble tablet fixed over his grave, with a suitable inscription in commemoration of his merits," it was resolved likewise " that a letter be written to Earl Cornwallis to inform him of this intention, and to request his Lordship will be pleased to direct that the body of the late Lieutenant-Colonel Moorhouse be moved to the Presidency as soon as the situation of affairs will admit." *

A framed and glazed print representing the death of Colonel

* Bogbio.

Moorhouse hangs (or did hang) on the walls of the old Madras Artillery mess-house at St. Thomas' Mount.

The Madras Commander-in-Chief also distinguished himself in this assault, showing his coolness, good humour, and knowledge of men, qualities so requisite in all great military leaders. Before his Madras career, the appointment of Major-General William Medows as Governor and Commander-in-Chief of Bombay had been thus announced:—" Bombay Castle, 6th September 1788. This day about noon Major-General William Medows landed from the Hon'ble. Company's ship *Winterton*, and was received by His Majesty's 71st Regiment and a party of artillery," and then "proceeded to the Government House." * The Bombay authorities were, doubtless, proud of their new Governor and Commander-in-Chief "of the town and castle of Bombay, and of all the forces and territories belonging to or under the management and control of our Presidency of Bombay aforesaid."

Among many of the old school of Anglo-Indians the quaint, despotic expressions of the East India Company, so frequently to be found in the *Records*, alone seem to excite a love and admiration of our former munificent masters. There never was such a Company before; and there never will be any approach to it again. Anglo-Indians may say reverentially, or in the spirit of Tim Linkinwater when he praised the " books " of Cheeryble Brothers : There never were, and never will be, such Letters, Despatches, and Books—such stores of knowledge concerning honourable merchants, interlopers, civil and military officers, as the books of the old " John Company," who, if he had not died after the Mutiny, could not have long survived " Limited " being written after his name—a consummation which, in these so-called days of commercial morality and general progress, would have been sure to come!

Asking pardon for this digression, we shall return to Bangalore

---

* *Bombay State Papers*, vol. ii., p 354–5. The brief extract following is from the clear but verbose document (Commission) from the Court of Directors of the " United Company of Merchants of England trading to the East Indies."

for a few minutes to relate an anecdote of Major-General Sir William Medows, K.B. We have given the little story elsewhere; but we think it will bear repetition.

It was at the storming of Bangalore (1791), just after the gallant Colonel Moorhouse had received his fatal wound, when the principal gate was almost torn in pieces by our determined troops, Lieutenant Eyre, a man of diminutive stature, forced his way through it. Medows, who preserved " an inspiring gaiety " in the midst of battle, called out: " Well done! Now, whiskers, try if you can follow or support 'the little gentleman.'" The result, of course, was, after a most gallant resistance, our eventual occupation of the *pettah* (town) of Bangalore.* While this was being carried out by our troops, it is recorded that Tippoo likewise threw in a strong corps, which renewed the contest by a heavy fire of small arms; but the British bayonet with irresistible dash soon drove the enemy through the streets and lanes, compelling them to evacuate. The loss on our side, as already stated, amounted to 131. And thus, to his great sorrow, Tippoo lost Bangalore.

After this triumph, Lord Cornwallis forced his way within sight of the Mysore capital, Seringapatam. But, having no provisions, although victorious in every encounter, he could not besiege the place; so the British commander was forced to retire to Bangalore for the rainy season. He was in hopes of obtaining supplies, and of being joined by 10,000 horse, which the Nizam had promised. When these " strange auxiliaries " arrived, however, their grotesque appearance† gave little hope of their utility. His lordship was

---

* See *Distinguished Anglo-Indians*, first series, p. 296; also Murray's *History of British India*, p. 447.

† In this motley crowd, writes the Indian historian, quoting Colonel Wilks, could be traced "the Parthian bow and arrow, the iron club of Scythia, sabres of every age and nation, lances of every length and description, and matchlocks of every form, metallic helmets of every pattern." There was a total absence of every symptom of order or obedience; every individual seemed an independent warrior, self-impelled, affecting to be "the champion whose single arm was to achieve victory"—very different from the Nizam's cavalry, in the middle of the present century, when commanded by such dashing officers as Mayne, Beatson, and Macintire.

anxiously desirous to terminate the war; and he clearly saw that this could only be effected by an advance on the capital. On again taking the field, he soon drove the enemy out of their entrenched camp, and proceeded to invest Seringapatam. To carry out this object, at the end of January 1792, the British, Nizam's and Mahratta armies effected a junction near Severndroog. Early in February the army advanced towards the capital " in three parallel columns, the battering train and ammunition carts composing the centre one, the infantry and light field-pieces the right next to the enemy, and the store carts and baggage, protected by some cavalry and strong advance and rear guards, consisting of cavalry and infantry." On the 5th the army took up a position within six miles of Seringapatam, when the Sultan's army could be descried. On the night of the 6th the British stormed the Mysore lines in three columns. General Medows, with the right column, after encountering a determined resistance, carried the left of the enemy's line; the centre, under Lord Cornwallis, did the same with the centre. On the 7th the enemy made several unsuccessful attempts to dispossess the British from the footing which they had obtained, night terminating the contest. On the 8th preparations for the siege commenced; and on the 16th the Bombay army, under General Abercrombie, consisting of four European and seven native regiments, joined the force. Already thirty-six brass and forty-four iron guns had fallen into the hands of the British, and Tippoo's loss was estimated at 4,000 killed and wounded. At length, by the 23rd, the second parallel was completed, and batteries within five hundred yards of the fort. The artillery, under Colonel Duff, was in the highest state of efficiency; and Lord Cornwallis would have shortly been enabled to open and fire from sixty heavy guns on the fort. On the 24th his lordship announced, in a General Order, that preliminaries of peace, upon terms highly advantageous to the British, had been agreed upon, and that hostilities were to cease. Tippoo's heart had failed him; and, on the 25th, his two sons entered the camp as hostages for the fulfilment of the treaty, which was definitely settled on the 19th March.

The campaign was now ended; and the troops shortly afterwards withdrew from the Sultan's territories. Even for those who have seen something of the "splendour and havoc of the East," it would have been an imposing sight to behold the promising sons of Tippoo, as they rode through a vast and motley assembly on elephants richly caparisoned, dressed in white muslin robes, having round their necks large pearls and other valuable jewels. And then, to complete the picture, the Marquess, at the request of Tippoo himself, receiving the young princes at the door of his tent. With his accustomed courtesy and urbanity he took their hands in his and led them in, when the chief vakeel (prime minister) said: —"These children were this morning the sons of the Sultan, my master; their situation is now changed, and they must look up to your lordship as their father." Doubtless the shrewd vakeel felt that he was playing a part in a splendid farce; for at heart he believed, in spite of temporary reverses, that nothing could long disturb the mighty ruler and kingdom of Mysore.

In 1793, war having broken out with France, a force, under Colonel Brathwaite, marched against Pondicherry, which surrendered on the 23rd August. In 1794 an expedition was organised against the Isle of France; but it was delayed to a later period.* The first battalion of Artillery, under Lieut.-Colonel Geils, had been nominated for this foreign service. In July 1795, a company from the 1st battalion and one from the 2nd, of Artillery, under Captain Campbell, were ordered to embark with the expedition against the Dutch settlements of Malacca, Amboyna, Banda, and Ternate, all of which fell in due course. In January 1796, the Court of Directors issued Orders for the Peace Establishment of the Madras Presidency, which included "two battalions of artillery." These, and other events, probably served to draw off attention from Tippoo's doings. No events of importance affecting Madras occurred during the next two years, although, writes Begbie, "the lowering aspect of affairs in Mysore indicated, as early as June 1798, the necessity for another campaign in that quarter."

* 1810.

By the cession of territory in the negotiations with Lord Cornwallis, Tippoo's power had been considerably weakened.

On the hostages being delivered, and a lakh of rupees paid, a serious difficulty arose about the surrender of one-half of the Sultan's dominions, which question was left in an unsatisfactory state. This, of course, did not tend to improve his temper. It is also interesting to note, at the termination of the last campaign, that the war had been conducted on truly economic principles, the extraordinary expenses scarcely amounting to two millions sterling. The prize money—different from that in the conquest of Bengal—in three campaigns amounted only to £93,500, which, after Cornwallis and Medows had given up their shares, and the Company had added a large gratuity, only allowed to a colonel £1,161 12s., and to a private £14 11s. 9d. It is also stated that the losses sustained by Tippoo during the period of hostility were estimated by General Dirom—an eminent financier and statistician of the period—at 49,340 men, 67 forts, and 801 guns.

Tippoo had sent an embassy to the Mauritius to treat with the French on the subject of driving the British out of India; but it turned out that the vain-glorious governor of the island had "not a single soldier" to give. There was also a powerful French force* and faction at the Nizam's Court of Hyderabad. The new Governor-General, Lord Wellesley (successor to Lord Teignmouth), and who arrived in Calcutta 18th May, on ascertaining how Tippoo stood affected to the British interests, issued his final orders on the 20th June 1798, for the immediate assembly of the Coast and Bombay Presidential armies.

We should have remarked, with reference to the Nizam, that Lord Wellesley wisely prevailed upon the former potentate to disarm his troops and dismiss his French officers. This was the more necessary as the French and Tippoo together were in league with the Mahrattas. Explanations were demanded from Tippoo, but without effect, and the war began.

* Or rather disciplined by the French, amounting, as stated in a former chapter, to 14,000 well-trained soldiers.

The preliminary arrangements having been made, the Bombay army, consisting of 6,420 men, of whom 1,617 were Europeans, marched from Cannanore, under the command of Lieutenant-General James Stuart, on the 21st February 1799. He was directed to protect large supplies of grain and other articles which had been collected in the Coorg territory; and the force was to await the junction of the Madras troops.

The Southern army, under Lieutenant-General Harris, had assembled at Vellore in the month of January; but it could not move towards Mysore till the middle of February. According to Wood's *War in Mysore*,* General Harris's force consisted of 5,000 Europeans (including the Bombay European Regiment, 103rd "Royal Bombay Fusiliers"), 13,900 Natives, battering train, 40 guns, light field guns 57, and howitzers 7. On the 18th of February, it was joined by the Nizam's contingent, consisting of 6,000 Company's subsidiary troops, the same number of the Nizam's own infantry, including a portion of the late French corps† (Perron's), commanded by British officers, and a large body of cavalry.

It is interesting to note that, in order to give the greater efficiency to the late French corps of sepoys belonging to the Nizam, it was divided into battalions, and the command given to Captain, afterwards Sir John, Malcolm, and H.M's. 33rd Regiment was brigaded with the Nizam's army, the command of the whole being given to the Honourable Colonel Arthur Wellesley (the future Duke of Wellington).

Colonel Beatson, in his *War in Mysore*, gives an official abstract of General Harris's force, slightly differing from, and with more detail than, the above. In this "General Abstract" we have the Grand Total :—Main Army, 20,802; Nizam's Contingent, 6,536; Nizam's Infantry (formerly French corps), 3,621; Grand total, 30,959.

* Quoted by Begbie.
† Under Lord Wellesley, the Nizam signed a fresh treaty, the leading features of which were an increase of 4,400 men to the British Subsidiary Force, and the summary dismissal of the French officers. Marquess Wellesley ratified this treaty in September 1798.

"Beatson," says Begbie, "agrees with Wood as to the ordnance."

Tippoo had at his disposal over 100,000 men, numerous guns, and, as usual, excellent cavalry. And so all was nearly ready for the grand "tug of war" at Seringapatam.

Early in March, General Harris sent a letter from the Governor-General to Tippoo, from Royacottah; commencing hostilities by capturing a few hill-forts; and a few days after the whole army had encamped at Kelamurgalum, contiguous to Royacottah, and the nearest station in British territory to the Mysore country.

Advancing towards the capital, on the 14th, the army encamped within sight of Bangalore, when, a body of 4,000 Mysore horse showing themselves, they were at once dispersed by the Field artillery. Continuing his march, the General, after sharp encounters by the way, on the 7th of April took up a final position against Seringapatam. By the 10th, a strong posting of batteries had been concluded; and the Bombay army, which joined on the 16th, took up its ground on the north side of the river Cauvery.* The Presidential armies had now a good deal of tough work before them; and we have all known from our boyhood that that they performed it "fearlessly and well."

It would be treading on the ground of well-known writers to repeat the oft-told story, yet a few remarks may be made. There is no more interesting drama in the wide range of modern history than the siege of Seringapatam and the overthrow of Tippoo Sultan, or Tippoo Saib (Sáhib) as he is generally styled. The whole life of this remarkable man is a rare study, showing the greatness and the meanness, the glory and the disgrace, the kindness and the cruelty that lurk in human nature. Ambition and superstition were also strong in him. What a grand picture comes before us, if, instead of the mock embassy, on its return from Mauritius, going through the burlesque of founding a "Jacobin Club" in the Mysore capital, and planting "the tree of liberty," surmounted by the "cap of equality," and hailing the bigoted

* Begbie's *Services of the Madras Artillery.*

Mahomedan as "Citizen Tippoo," they had come with a large French army to drive the British out of India—which would only have given more work to the Marquess Wellesley and General Harris—a picture of "Citizen Tippoo's" reception at Government House, Pondicherry, or Chandernagore, with the strange diversity of character around him, well put on the canvas by some master-hand! Another picture: the future hero of Waterloo leading, as Colonel Wellesley, his first storming party during the siege, when he drove the enemy from the entrenchments "with great spirit." And then, near the last scene of all, the principal storming party of 4,000 men, with the commanding figure of General Sir David Baird at its head—the gallant and distinguished soldier who had spent four years in the gloomy dungeons of Mysore, and of whom, when his shrewd mother heard that her son was chained to a fellow countryman, she exclaimed, "The Lord have mercy on the man that's chained to my Davie!" —the principal figure on the parapet encouraging the two divisions of his party; till at length, in the face of a heavy cannonade, British batteries covering the advance,* the forlorn hope, closely followed by the storming party, crowned the breach, and planted the British colours on its summit.† And the last picture: Sir David Baird finding the body of Tippoo—the subject of a well-known painting in the Royal Academy a good many years ago. Tippoo's dream concerning the persecution of the Christians, or some other event in his life auguring future greatness as the result of his energy and bravery had a great effect upon him.

After the capture of Seringapatam, among Tippoo's repositories, along with "treaties, State papers, and political correspondence," was found a record of his dreams and their interpretation, of which the distinguished Anglo-Indian of the olden time, Colonel (General) Alexander Beatson—who had a large share also in

---

* General Baird led on the storming party under a shower of rockets and musketry from the enemy.
4th May 1799.

concocting the plan of attack on Seringapatam—preserved some curious specimens. We can only afford space for one little dream-story, as given by a pleasant and graphic Indian historian. At one time, when Tippoo was threatened with an invasion of the Mahrattas, he dreamed that a young man came up and accosted him, who in the course of conversation proved to be a female. Hence he sagely inferred that his enemy, who at first had a manly and formidable appearance, would in battle prove "no better than women." These, and similar lucubrations, writes the historian, form a strange contrast to his display of talent on other occasions; nor can it be wondered that public measures, resting upon such conclusions, should not always have proved very prosperous.*

After the complete conquest of Mysore all future arrangements, including the appointment of an heir of the ancient rajahs, were entirely at the disposal of the British Government. The Presidency armies had done most excellent service during this long and most important war, success in which, in a great measure, preserved to us the whole of Southern India. The Rajah of Mysore, under British friendship and protection, became no insignificant member of Asiatic royalty.

In late years, our highly accomplished and versatile historian, Colonel Malleson, was, it is well known, the zealous tutor to the Rajah of Mysore, in which romantic region he won "golden opinions from all sorts of people." This reminds us of the pleasant fact that the best description of the battle of Porto Novo to be found in Indian history is from the pen of this distinguished Anglo-Indian.† This decisive battle, which gave the death-blow to Hyder Ali's schemes of conquest, was fought on the 1st July 1781; and it was not only against the great Mahomedan warrior himself, but against the French also. The English General in chief command, Sir Eyre Coote, nobly did his duty, and was well supported by his seconds, Sir Hector Munro and General Stuart.

* Murray's *History of British India*—"Conquest of Mysore."
† *The Decisive Battles of India*, pp. 222-74 (new edition).

In our brief sketch we could not especially notice this famous battle. Porto Novo is a village close to the sea, seven miles from Chellumbrum—so celebrated for its massive and splendid pagoda—and not very many marches from the famous rock of Trichinopoly. It is not enough to say that the battle of Porto Novo decided the fate of Madras.

"That battle," writes Colonel Malleson, "crushed the aggressive schemes of Haidar, forced him to act on the defensive, and paved the way after his death to the destruction of the mighty power he had created. Under his rule Maisúr had become a robber's stronghold—a stronghold the existence of which was only possible when the paramount power was inert. The British never effected a work more truly beneficial to the people of India than when they destroyed that stronghold, and, expelling the dynasty of the robber, substituted the mild sway of the Hindú ruler for the empire of the sword."

Mysore under Hyder Ali was pretty much like Upper Burma under Theebaw, a den of thieves (dacoits); and which province continued to be so a considerable time after we had wisely taken upon ourselves the overthrow of the troublesome and cruel Golden Foot.

With reference to the battle of Porto Novo, to which brilliant chapter by Malleson we would refer our readers, according to Colonel Innes, "Haidar had in his camp at this time twenty-five battalions of regular infantry, between 40,000 and 50,000 horse, above 100,000 matchlockmen, peons, polygars, and forty-seven guns, besides a corps of 400 Frenchmen. The British force, on the other hand, consisted only of 2,070 Europeans, and 6,400 Sepahís, with fifty-five field-pieces."

Sir Eyre Coote separated his army into two "lines" or divisions. "The first consisted of H.M. 73rd (71st), the Bengal and Madras European Regiments, one troop of European cavalry, two regiments of Sepahís, and thirty guns, under General Sir Hector Munro. The second 'line' or division was commanded by General James Stuart." *

---

* *History of the Bengal European Regiment (Royal Munster Fusiliers), and how it Helped to Win India*, pp. 260–61.

A DISTINGUISHED BOMBAY REGIMENT.

We shall now, having said comparatively little about the Bombay army, proceed to give an "Outline" of the "Historical Record" of the "Prince of Wales' Own Grenadier Regiment of Bombay Infantry," which may interest many of our readers as the "Record" of such a distinguished regiment of the Bombay Presidency. The volume containing the brochure is entitled *Tracts: Military*, and belongs to the India Office library. It was printed in Bombay in 1887.* There is another far more lengthy "Historical Record" published, on the first page of which appears: "The Prince of Wales' Own Grenadiers, the 2nd Regiment of Bombay Native Infantry, was raised on the 26th January 1796 as the 13th Battalion on the Bombay Establishment." According to the minor "Record":—The Prince of Wales' Own Grenadier Regiment Bombay Infantry, formerly the 2nd battalion of the 1st Regiment, was raised in 1796 at Bombay, and proceeded on foreign service to Egypt in 1801. It returned to Bombay in 1802. "As a lasting memorial of the glory acquired by the zeal, discipline, and intrepidity of the troops engaged" in this campaign, the regiment was permitted to bear on its colours the word "Egypt" with the "Sphynx."

The regiment was next engaged in 1802 and 1803 at the sieges of Baroda and Powanghur. It further served in Hindustan from 1804 to 1806, and was present at the siege of Bhurtpoor under Lord Lake, whence it was detached to Agra. It was greatly harassed both going to and returning from this place by Holkar's troops.

It then served in 1813 at the reduction of Pahlunpoor, and was engaged at the battle of Kirkee in 1817, when the Peshwa's army, consisting of 18,000 cavalry, 8,000 infantry, with 14 guns, was signally defeated. The force on this occasion was composed of 2,800 men, of whom 800 were British soldiers. For this service the regiment bears the word "Kirkee" on its colours. The regiment, however, is chiefly distinguished by its memorable defence of Koregaum on the 1st of January 1818. The history of this

* At the Education Society's Press, Byculla.

heroic event may be found in the pages of Lieut.-Col. Valentine Blacker's *Memoirs of the Operations of the British Army in India during the Mahratta War of* 1817-19, p. 179, and also of the historian, Grant Duff. The regiment, 600 strong, with 4 British officers, under the command of Captain Staunton, supported by a small detachment of British artillery, consisting of 2 officers and 27 men, with two 6-pounders, and 250 of the Poona Auxiliary Horse, suddenly found itself, after a long and fatiguing march, in the presence of the entire army of the Peshwa, estimated at 25,000 horse, with 5,000 picked infantry and two siege guns. Captain Staunton immediately took post in the village of Koregaum, and throughout the day sustained and defeated a series of the most sanguinary attacks to dislodge him. The desperate nature of this conflict may be gathered from the losses incurred in officers and men of the Grenadiers.

Two British officers and 50 men were killed, and 2 British officers and 105 men were wounded. Of the Artillery, 1 officer and 8 men were killed, and 12 were wounded. The Poona Auxiliary Horse were reported to have lost one-third in killed and wounded. So eager was the Peshwa for the destruction of this small force that he offered 20,000 rupees for the guns and 4,000 rupees for the colours of the regiment, to stimulate his troops to the attack.

To commemorate this glorious defence, the regiment was created "Grenadiers," and a monument was erected by Government, recording the names of those who fell on this occasion, inscribed as follows:—"This column is erected to commemorate the defence of Koregaum by a detachment commanded by Captain Staunton, of the Bombay Establishment, which was surrounded on the 1st of January 1818 by the Peishwa's whole army under his personal command, and withstood throughout the day a series of most obstinate and sanguinary assaults of his best troops. Captain Staunton, under the most appalling circumstances, persevered in his desperate resistance, and, seconded by the unconquerable spirit of his detachment, at length achieved the signal discomfiture of the enemy, and accomplished one of the proudest triumphs of the British Army in the East. To perpetuate the memory of the brave troops, to whose heroic firmness and devotion it owes the glory of the day, the British Government has directed the names of their corps and of all the killed and wounded to be inscribed on this monument." The corps was permitted to inscribe the word "Koregaum" on its colours, and the native soldiers were granted six months' donation batta, besides being allowed to count five years for service towards pension between 1818 and 1823. The regiment was actively employed in Guzerat against the Bheel tribes from 1825 to 1839. It was engaged on various arduous services, the most remarkable of which appears to have been a surprise and dispersion of a body of Meeanees towards the Run of Cutch, after a forced march of sixty-four miles in twenty-seven hours. In 1839 the regiment proceeded to Scinde, where it suffered severely in officers and men at the affairs of Nuffoosk and Khujjuck. Three British officers and 32 men were killed, and 68 wounded. But it was not under the excitement of active service alone that the regiment sustained its losses; it was decimated in 1841 at Kotree, and in the space of four months 4 British officers, 1 native officer, and 60 rank and file fell victims to its deadly climate. The patient endurance and fortitude displayed by the sepoy were never more conspicuous than on this occasion. The corps returned from Scinde at the close of 1841, and was shortly afterwards stationed at Sattara, from whence it was ordered to form part of the force collected for the suppression of the insurrection in the Southern Mohratta country in 1844-45. It was engaged at the storm and capture of the forts of Panalla and Powanghur. In 1857 the left flank company served in the expedition against Persia, as part of the light battalion, and for this service the regiment was permitted to bear the word "Persia" on its colours. During the eventful years of 1857-58 the Grenadiers were actively employed against local insurgents in Guzerat, and formed part of a flying column in pursuit of Tantia Topee. In connection with this period, it may be mentioned that the loyal and gallant conduct of the then Subedar Major of the regiment was made conspicuous by his having, when on leave in Hindustan, secreted and saved the life of a British officer pursued by the rebels, for which he was made Sirdar Bahadoor of the First Class of British India, and was granted a "jagheer" for life and a "khillut.'

The regiment was selected as part of the force which proceeded to Abyssinia under Lord Napier in 1868; it landed at Zoola on 4th February 1868, and was employed from that date up to the 9th May 1868 on the railway works between Koomaylee and Zoola, for which duty the regiment was broken up into two detachments, the head-quarters being generally at Koomaylee. Their services on this occasion were duly appreciated in General Orders of the Army by Lord Napier.* The regiment suffered much from the exhausting climate, and on arrival at Bombay most of the men were unfit from scurvy. A great many escorts were furnished during the Abyssinian campaign, and at its termination Lord Napier presented to the Officers' Mess a curious old brass cross engraved with a history of the Crucifixion; this cross was captured at Magdala, where it was used as a processional cross in the Cathedral Church of "St. Michael."

The regiment embarked at Zoola for Bombay by detachments on the 12th, 17th, and 23rd May 1868 respectively, and were stationed at Sattara, from whence they marched to Poona the following year.

In 1873 the regiment left India for Aden, and during the tour at that station furnished detachments to Perim and took part in the "Lahej" expedition.

On the 1st November 1875, H.R.H. the Prince of Wales landed at Aden *en route* to India and inspected the Regiment. H.R.H. remarked that he was " very pleased to find such a distinguished corps as the 2nd Grenadiers was the first to receive him on Her Majesty's Indian possessions, one that had served in Egypt, Persia, Abyssinia, had taken part in many campaigns and sieges in India, and had fought the ever-memorable battle of Koregaum."

In 1876 the regiment arrived at Belgaum, and on the 10th

* For sketch of Lord Napier's services, see Appendix A.

March of that year, Her Majesty appointed H.R.H. the Prince of Wales Honorary Colonel to the corps and bestowed on it the title of "The Prince of Wales' Own," with permission to wear "the Plumes" on colours and appointments.

Portraits of the Queen and the Prince Consort were presented to the corps by Her Majesty, and of himself and the Princess of Wales by the Prince.

In 1878 the regiment marched to Vingorla, thence by steamer to Bombay, and rail to Ahmedabad, *en route* to Nusseerabad, where in the following year they were inspected by the Viceroy, Lord Lytton, and on the last day of 1880 had new colours presented by the Governor of Bombay, Sir James Ferguson, the old colours being, at the special desire of H.R.H. the Prince of Wales, sent to H.R.H.'s residence at Sandringham.

In November 1881 the regiment marched to Rajcote, where it remained only fifteen months, starting in February 1883, by wings, on its long march *viâ* Porebunder, Kurrachee, the Indus Valley and the Bolan to Quetta, which the second wing reached in March 1883.

During the stay of the regiment in the Quetta district it furnished outposts to Goolistan, Pishin, the Quas valley (where the men built "Fort Albert," a large stone-walled redoubt), held all the Bolan posts, marched 1,000 miles through the Keran country with Sir Robert Sandeman, 140 miles to Thull, *viâ* Pui and Smallan with a Field Force under Colonel James, and finally 800 miles with Sir Oriel Tanner's Force through the Zob Valley, where the regiment was present at the action at Dowlutzaie on the 24th of October.

On the departure of the P.W.O. Grenadiers from Quetta in February, the following complimentary District Order was published by the General:—

"The Brigadier-General desires to place on record the excellent service the P.W.O. Grenadiers have performed whilst under his command and especially in the late Zob Valley expedition, where they compared favourably with regiments of the Bengal and Madras armies and did their work cheerfully and well."

The regiment marched from Quetta in February, and was overtaken by a severe snowstorm, and generally suffered through the cold weather both then and in Zob, the thermometer often registering 24° Fahr. of frost, and many baggage animals being frozen to death.

In the interval of two years, between leaving Rajcote in February 1883 and arriving at Ahmedabad in 1885, from the records it appears that the regiment marched over 4,100 miles, all musketry and drill having necessarily been suspended for that period.

In 1886 H.R.H. the Duke of Connaught was appointed Commander-in-Chief of the Bombay Army, and on the 29th of January 1887 their Royal Highnesses the Duke and Duchess of Connaught inspected the regiment, with which H.R.H. expressed himself " very satisfied." Their Royal Highnesses did the Regiment the honour of dining at the Mess, during their stay at Camp Ahmedabad, where they were the guests of Colonel James, the Commandant of the regiment.

On Wednesday, the 16th February 1887, was held throughout India the celebration of the Jubilee of Her Most Gracious Majesty Queen Victoria, Empress of India. A salute of 101 guns was fired at a grand parade of the troops. In the afternoon the "Queen's" colour of the Grenadiers with a guard of honour and the band marched to the city, taking with them the picture of Her Majesty (presented to the regiment by Her Majesty in 1876). The picture, placed on an easel surmounted by the colour, with a Grenadier havildar as sentry on either side, formed the principal object on a raised daïs at the end of the Grand Durbar Hall in the " Budhur " or palace yard in the city, where were assembled all the Rajahs, Chiefs, Talookdars and principal men of the city and surrounding country.

In honour of Her Majesty, garlands were placed on the Queen's colour by the Rajah of Patri, the descendant of the ancient kings of Gujerat, and by the Chiefs of Kote and Amod on behalf of the Talookdars, and by the " Nugger Seth," Rao Bahadur Premabhoy Hemabhoy, on behalf of the 160,000 inhabitants of Ahmedabad, all present standing, and the band playing the National Anthem.

The garlanded colour was then marched slowly down the Durbar Hall to the entrance, where it was received with a "present arms" by the guard of honour and marched home through the city to the tune of—

> "*There's a land that bears a well-known name*
> *Though 't is but a little spot.*"

On the 24th of February 1887 the battalion was reviewed by Major-General A. Carnegy, who was pleased to express himself "highly satisfied" with all that he saw of the P.W.O. Grenadiers, and promised to make a most favourable report of the corps to H.R.H. the Commander-in-Chief.

In the month of March about 30 men volunteered for temporary service in Burma. The following table gives the general state and composition of the P.W.O. Grenadiers in the year 1887 :—

Average height	5ft. 8½ in.
Average chest measurement	35¼ in.
Average age	27 years
Average length of service	8¼ ,,

Castes.

Christians and Jews	40
Seiks and Punjabis	50
Brahmins and Rajpoots	60
Mahomedans	70
Purwaries	100
Purdasies and Marwaries	200
Mahrattas	300
	820

Recruited from

The Concan and born in the regiment	500
The Deccan	80
The Central Provinces	70
Delhi	60
Oude and N.-W. Provinces	50
Punjab	50
Scind	10
	820

List of Campaigns, Battles and Sieges.

Egypt	1801
Baroda	1802
Jooria	1803
Powanghur	1803
Malwa	1804
Parich	1805
Bhurtpoor	1806
Pahlunpoor	1813
Kirkee	1817
Koregaum	1818
Akulkote	1830
Nuffoosk	1840
Kujjuck	1841
Panulla	1844
Powanghur	1845
Persia	1857
Guzerat	1858
Abyssinia	1868
Lahej	1873
Dowlutzaie-Zob	1884

CHAPTER XI.

THE BENGAL ARTILLERY—ASTONISHING MARCH TO BAMIAN—THE MADRAS SAPPERS AND MINERS.

ACCORDING to the *Calcutta* reviewer of the *History of the Bengal Artillery*, Captain Buckle investigated the long rolls of the regiment, which he found tolerably perfect, with a view to ascertain the mortality in the artillery fifty or sixty years ago,* and the result, as compared with later times, is not so unfavourable to the earlier period as might be expected :—

"It will not be uninteresting at this period to examine the casualties of the regiment, with a view to ascertaining the relative health enjoyed in those days and at present. Fortunately, the long rolls of the regiment are tolerably perfect at this period, and the following is an abstract :—

	1788.	1789.	1790.	1791.	1792.	1793.	1794.	1795.
Strength on 1st Nov.	969	980	1,176	1,155	1,162	1,083	844	755
Died	51	80	133	146	102	83	65	8
Deserted	3	6	7	11	14	10	10	65
Discharged	25	30	9	7	10	11	5	7
Invalided	26	15	21	25	35	31	15	37
Total	105	131	170	189	161	135	95	117

This gives an average of 138 casualties per annum to a strength of 1,016, or about 13 per cent. per annum—almost the same proportion of casualties as has taken place from the same causes during the last three years: their amount is 368, and the strength

---

* As the article in the *Calcutta Review* was written in 1849, it is now (1889-90) about one hundred years ago.

of the regiment in Europeans may be taken as 3,000. The average, however, of a longer period will be more favourable to modern times, as the losses during the Afghanistan war, the destructions of the 1st troop, and mortality from disease at Sukhur, all tend to swell these years beyond their predecessors."

The fluctuations in the above table are very great. "It will be seen," writes the reviewer, "that in 1788 the mortality was not much above 5 per cent., whilst in 1791 it was 12 per cent. This, we presume, is to be accounted for by a reference to the operations during the latter year in the Mysore country. The average mortality in the regiment, we believe, exclusive of war casualties, is now (1849-50) about 4 per cent."

With an anecdote or two taken at random, and a passage descriptive of the extraordinary march to Bamian, the reviewer concludes the notice of this interesting Memoir. From a narrative of the services of Lieut.-Colonel Montague, who was killed at the siege of Seringapatam in 1799, we take the following illustration of the opinion which was entertained of him by Lord Cornwallis :—

The following conversation took place between the Deputy Adjutant-General and Major Montague, as the latter passed headquarters on his march. "Lord C. has it in contemplation to give Colonel Smith the command of the artillery to be employed against Severn-drúg, and he wishes to know if that circumstance will be any impediment to your exertions." The Major replied that his lordship might rely on his utmost exertions for the public service under Smith. The Deputy Adjutant-General did not think that answer sufficiently explicit, and said, "Lord C. wished to know whether Major M. could act with more effect when independent of Colonel Smith than when under his command?" The Major answered, "that he could certainly carry a plan of his own into execution, in the same time that it would require to suggest and explain it to another." The Deputy Adjutant-General therefore concluded that Major M's. real opinion was, that he should prefer to conduct the business by himself, and informed him that "his Lordship was disposed to give Colonel Smith an opportunity of knocking down the walls of the place, where he had been so long confined in a former war; but, as it might be attended with some risk to the service, he was at length determined to appoint Major M. to command and conduct the artillery against that important place, as the capture of it was absolutely necessary to the further progress of the campaign."

There is an anecdote most creditable to the character of Lieutenant Mathison, a very gallant officer, who distinguished himself greatly both in the Nepál and the Pindarrí campaigns (1815-17-18). In the former, on one occasion when all his men were killed or wounded, he did good service by working a gun with his own hands. The following relates to the affair of Jawud, in January 1818:—" During the most severe part of this affair, a circumstance occurred truly creditable to the character of this officer, and fully substantiated by the testimony of an eye-witness. An European horse-artilleryman fell deadly wounded, and, on his comrades attempting to carry him to the rear, he entreated them to desist, adding, 'I know I must die, and I only wish to shake Lieutenant Mathison by the hand before I die.' His wish was immediately gratified; and he expired uttering 'God bless you.'"

Captain Buckle speaks of the march of the 4th troop, 3rd brigade, across the Hindu-Kúsh as "the most extraordinary ever performed by horse artillery." He had left a blank space in his manuscript for the insertion of the details of this interesting movement, and the narrative has been supplied very effectively by another writer:—

"We have now to notice perhaps the most extraordinary march ever performed by artillery, that of a native troop of horse artillery across the Hindu-Kúsh to Bamian; extraordinary both from the obstacles overcome, and the circumstance of the men of this troop being natives of Hindostan. The 4th troop, 3rd brigade, was ordered for this trip in September 1839, and, Captain Timmings having just died, it was under the command of a subaltern, Lieutenant M. Mackenzie, with whom was Lieutenant E. Kaye.

"The valley of Bamian lies about N.W. from Cabul, distant only 112 miles; but it is separated from the valley, in which the Capital is situated, by a broad belt of stupendous mountains, the highest range of which exceeds in altitude 12,000 feet. The troop entered upon its mountain road, near the village of Urghundí, and, while toiling up the first laborious ascent (steep in itself, but rendered still more difficult by huge stones and fragments of rock), it was met by Major Thomson, of the Engineers, and some other officers,[*] who were just returning from an excursion to Bamian. Major Thomson immediately declared the road to Bamian to be impracticable for guns, and that the passes in advance were still more difficult in their nature than that of Urghundí; and he said that he would, immediately on arrival at Cabul, report to the envoy that it would be useless to attempt to reach Bamian. The troop, however, continued its march, and, the passage of the Urghundí ghât accomplished, descended into the beautiful valley of the Cabul river, along the banks of which the route continued for three marches, passing Julraiz and Sir-i-Chusmeh. The road was at times difficult, being frequently in the rocky bed of the stream, and always ascending, gradually becoming steeper and more toilsome.

"The summit of the Unai pass is said to be 11,400 feet in elevation; at this great elevation, even in September, the cold was intense. The passage of the range was a work of great toil, as the ascents and descents were numerous. The summit of the range is in general a table-land, gradually sloping towards the north-west; not one continuous table-land, but intersected by numerous deep glens, running parallel to each other, with steep precipitous sides difficult to ascend or descend. On the 21st a small mud fort, named Youatt, was reached; and on the 23rd the troops, after crossing several spurs from the range just surmounted, descended to the banks of the Helmund, beyond which towered the snow-capped peaks of Koh-i-Baba.

"In consequence of the report received from Major Thomson, of the impracticable nature of the road to Bamian, the envoy had sent instructions for three guns and all the ammunition-waggons to

---

[*] Major (Colonel) Salter of the cavalry, and Lieutenant Sturt (afterwards killed action).

return to Cabul—the other three guns to halt until elephants, sent from Cabul, should arrive ; it was then intended that the three guns should be dismounted, and carried over the remaining passes on elephants. These instructions were received at Youatt; but, the neighbourhood being entirely destitute of forage, it was considered advisable to move the troop on to Gurden Dewal, on the river Helmund. Having arrived there, the troop halted, and Lieutenant Mackenzie went forward and examined the pass over the Hindu Kúsh range. This officer, having considered the passage practicable, forwarded a report to that effect to head-quarters, and requested permission to proceed with the whole of the troop. Permission was at length received, and on the 30th the march was resumed. The foot of the Irak pass was attained in three difficult marches, the ascent being constant and fatiguing. The passage was commenced immediately, nearly all the guns and carriages being pulled up by hand (the horses being taken out). At this work, the artillery and infantry soldiers, and some 200 Hazarehs, were employed during the whole day, and it was not until dark that the entire battery had reached the foot of the western face of the mountain, which was found to be considerably steeper than that up which the ascent led. On the following day the march was resumed through a deep and dreary defile, abounding in rocks, and the precipices enclosing it so steep and lofty that the sun's rays scarcely ever penetrated to its lowest depths. Through this tortuous glen the troop wound its way, until, after many an interruption from rocky ledges of dangerous descent, the small valley of Miani Irak was reached on the 4th of October, and vegetation and human habitations were once more seen. The whole of the 5th was occupied in passing the Kuski ghât, over a range of no great elevation (a spur only of the Hindu-Kúsh), but of great difficulty. The ascent was occasionally so steep (at an angle of 45°) that the men working at the drag-ropes could not keep their footing ; horses, of course, were out of the question. The ascent was, however, accomplished in the afternoon ; and the descent, by the edge of a precipice, where a false step would have ensured instant destruction, commenced. This too was effected; but night found the troop in a defile so narrow, and enclosed by such steep walls, that it seemed to be but a fissure in the mountain, caused by some convulsion of nature. Nothing further could be done till daylight. Early on the morning of the 6th of October, the troop crossed the last intervening ridge, and entered the valley of Bamian at Zohák. Next day the troop reached Bamian, and encamped close to some mud forts, which were destined now, for the first time, to become the dwelling-places of British officers and soldiers.

"This march to Bamian (1840) has been dwelt upon somewhat longer than is altogether suitable to the pages of a work of this nature, but, within a smaller space, it would have been scarcely practicable to give an idea of the service performed. It was certainly one of the most arduous undertakings ever accomplished by horse artillery." *

With this passage, descriptive of a march such as "no troop of artillery had ever before accomplished," the writer brings his extracts to a close.

Among the war services of officers of the Madras Artillery, we find a rapid march set down against those of Major (now General) J. D. Mein when serving† with the Saugor Field Division. After the battle of Banda (19th), on the 25th April 1858, at the relief of Kirwee, the Madras horse artillery and cavalry marched eighty-four miles in thirty-seven hours.—And now we may note the celebrated march of all arms to relieve Candahar, under the Bengal Artillery commander General Roberts, now Commander-in-Chief in India.

"In June 1880, Ayub Khan set out from Herat in hopes of becoming master of Kandáhár. As he neared the Helmand his orce was strengthened by the very troops which the Wali or Governor of Kandáhár had sent out to intercept him. The rout of a British brigade at Maiwand in July placed Kandáhár itself for a time in serious danger.

---

* The highest point surmounted, the Irak Pass, was 12,000 feet above the sea.
† Under that distinguished officer, Brigadier afterwards Major-General) W. H Miller, C.B.

"Happily Stewart and Roberts were both at Kábul, and they resolved between them to lose no time in relieving the weakened garrison of Kandáhár. Placing the best of his own troops under Roberts' command, Stewart sent him off in August, with a compact force nearly 10,000 strong, to make the quickest of his way to the scene of danger. In twenty days Roberts marched the whole distance of 310 miles. This feat of energy was crowned on the 1st September by the brilliant victory which Roberts gained near Kandáhár over an army well posted for defence. Ayub fled with a handful of followers back to Herat, and Kandáhár was safe from further attack."*

INCIDENTS IN THE LIFE OF GENERAL GEORGE CAMPBELL, C.B., ROYAL HORSE ARTILLERY.

There have been few more distinguished and adventurous Anglo-Indian officers in our Presidential armies than the late General Campbell, Bengal Artillery, who died at No. 1 Byng Place, Gordon Square, where he had resided for some years, on April 25, 1882,† at the ripe age of 78. A friend has sent us the following interesting matter for publication :—

On the occasion of the first meeting of the Governor-General and the Maharajah Runjeet Sing, at Rupar, on the Sutlej, in 1832, the former ordered a couple of 6-pr. guns, waggons, horses, ammunition, &c. &c., complete, to be held in readiness by the Native Troop H.A., to be presented to the Maharajah on the close of the meeting, after the review of the British troops assembled in honour of the occasion, in presence of Maharajah Runjeet Sing.

The British force amounted to some 10,000 men of all arms; while the Sikhs had a force of some 30,000 across the river, 5,000 picked men accompanying the Maharajah to the interview. The latter begged as a favour to see the Native Troop Horse Artillery

* *History of India under Queen Victoria, from* 1836 *to* 1880, vol. ii., pp. 405-6, by Captain Lionel J. Trotter.

† This correct date of death should be substituted for that given at page 191 of *Distinguished Anglo-Indians* (Second Series).

alone, put through some movements, which were carried out at a gallop, in first-rate style, under Captain Johnson, commanding.

The two guns, waggons, horses, &c., complete for service, were then presented, before both armies, by Lord Bentinck, to Maharajah Runjeet Sing, to his great delight and satisfaction. The latter remarked that he could lay a gun well, and would now put his umbrella upon the ground, and strike it with these two guns sooner than any officer on the parade. The offer was accepted, the guns loaded, and I was called out as Senior Sub. of the Troop, to open fire on the umbrella, some 500 yards in front (at a guess). This created much excitement. I loaded both guns, when the Maharajah looked over them, which act, I observed to him, was as good as a shot to begin with. He smiled and said, "That is true." The first gun fired grazed through the circumference of the umbrella, the second (elevation of which, in the smoke, I quickly lowered) struck full the middle, 4 inches below the pin which kept it open, sending it some yards to the front, collapsed like a parachute, as the ball passed through it, shivering the entire handle to fragments. The guns, instantly reloaded, awaited the Maharajah's turn, who walked up and embraced me, saying—" He dare not venture a trial where the chance of failure was so great, in presence of his army, to be beaten by a boy." He asked my name, shook me by the hand, and asked Lord Bentinck permission there to allow me to take charge of the guns to his Sikh Camp across the river; to be permitted to enter his service for one year to teach his gunners to lay a gun— as I had just done. All was sanctioned by the Governor-General, but entirely left to my option. I took the guns over, packed and repacked the ammunition, explaining all personally to himself and chiefs—and showing how all was done for various ranges, &c., till we all retired to the great Durbar of Chiefs, held in honour of the great meeting at Roopin. He made me sit on his right hand till the Durbar concluded, when he repeated his offer to enter his service, with the Governor-General's permission granted for one year. I declined firmly, as I was ignorant of the language, and might fail in giving satisfaction. He urged, his only desire was to teach his men to lay a gun as I had this morning; that he would supply me with everything, with 5,000 Rs. a month pay, with a handsome present "emam," to commence with, and the same on leaving him, &c. All in vain. He then presented me with a valuable "killut," worth some 6,000 Rs. with a bag of 1,000 Rs., for the men of the troop—and last, not least, he presented me with the umbrella, hoping I would keep it in memory of him and the good shot that day, &c. I then left the Durbar and his presence, moving to my Arab, standing to take me home. The Maharajah stealthily followed me alone, touched my arm as I was mounting, again urging his service more pressingly on me for one year, adding further increase of pay, and presents, horses, servants, food—everything necessary—and that he would send for my tents and baggage, so I need not leave him then. I remained still firm. He asked me the value of my handsome Arab. "12,000 rupees," I replied. "Well, stay with me and you shall have finer and more valuable Arabs than that!" I shook my head; he shook my hand. I dropped my sword, and galloped to camp, thanking my luck in getting away.

The "killut," according to the rule of the service, was placed at the disposal of the Governor-General, who, on this occasion, personally begged me to retain it, as well earned on parade that day.

These very two guns above mentioned were subsequently captured from the Sikhs at the battle of Ferozshah, 21st-22nd December 1845, where they came opposed, among others, to the 3rd troop 3rd Brigade H.A., then under my command as Major.

The umbrella, yellow silk, lined green, with long green fringe, diameter six feet, in good keeping, I presented to the R.A. Institute, Woolwich, in 1875, where it now rests with the two round-shot holes most apparent.

The cash, 1,000 rupees, I made over to Capt. Johnson, who saw it fairly divided among the native officers and men of the entire troop; the senior N.I. officers receiving the turbans and silk dresses comprising the "killut." The ornaments, seals, &c., I still retain, which are very handsome.

Few smarter officers ever wore the "jacket" than General George Campbell, C.B., R.A. . . . He passed all his regimental service in the Bengal Horse Artillery; and, as soldier or sportsman, none was better known in India than he.

List of Services of General George Campbell, R.A., C.B., Bengal.—First Commission, June 1823. Served in Burmese War, Horse Artillery, 1824-25-26, including siege of Donabew, actions of "Prome" "Maloon" "Pagammew" (Medal and Clasp). Gwalior Campaign, Battle of Punniar, Horse Artillery, 1843 (Bronze Star and Brevet Major). Sutlej Campaign, Horse Artillery, 1845-46—Battles of Ferozshah, &c., Sobraon (Medal and Clasp, and Brevet Lieut.-Col.). Commanded Artillery Division "Lahore," Punjab Campaign, 1848-49 (Medal). Commanded Artillery Division, Cawnpore, 1853. Commanded Artillery Division, "Agra," 1853. Commanded 1st Brigade Horse Artillery and Meerut Division Artillery, 1854. Promoted to Brigadier-General, "Rawal Pindee" Punjab, 1856. Served through "Mutiny" (Medal), 1857. Promoted to Major-General, and commanded "Benares Division" during Mutiny, 1858.* Command expired, 1863. Received Distinguished Service Pension, 1865. Appointed Companion of the Bath, 1867. Promoted to Lieut.-General, 1868. Returned to England, 1871. Promoted to General, 1874, and commanded Royal Artillery.

From Colonel W. J. Wilson's admirable *Historical Record*† we take the following notes on the

"QUEEN'S OWN" SAPPERS AND MINERS.

Each of the Presidency armies may well be proud of this useful

---

* Campbell killed his hundredth tiger in 1861 when in command of the Benares Division. He was a light-weight and a splendid horseman—rather trying to some members of the divisional staff! See also *Distinguished Anglo-Indians*, Second Series, p. 191.

† Madras 1877. Procured from the India Office Library.

and distinguished arm of the Service. On the first page of historical sketch of the Madras Corps is recorded—

> The Royal Cypher within the Garter.
> "Seringapatam," "Java," "Assaye," "Mahidpoor," "Nagpore," "Ava," "Lucknow," "Central India."
> A Company bears on its appointments a Dragon wearing an Imperial Crown, with the words "China," "Pegu," "Taku Forts," "Pekin."
> B Company, the Dragon, "China," "Pegu," "Persia."
> C Company, "Meanee," "Hyderabad" 1843, "Pegu."
> E Company, "Pegu."
> F Company, the Dragon, "China."
> G and H Companies, "Abyssinia."
> K Company, "Taku Forts," "Abyssinia."

Honorary Colonel—H.R.H. Albert Edward, Prince of Wales and Duke of Cornwall, K.G., K.T., G.C.B., G.C.S.I., Field Marshal.

The Madras "Sappers and Miners" were originally a corps of Pioneers, officered from the line. They were first raised in 1780, and were maintained until 1831, when, in conformity with instructions from the Court of Directors, the 1st battalion was placed under the command of Engineer officers, and regularly instructed as Sappers and Miners, which designation the corps has since continued to bear. The 2nd battalion of Pioneers continued on the establishment until early in 1834, when the European officers were sent to rejoin their respective regiments, and the Native commissioned and non-commissioned officers and men were incorporated into the "Sappers and Miners."

1761 to 1780.—Between 1761 and 1780 companies of Pioneers and of Miners were formed from time to time of volunteers from the European Infantry and the Native battalions, and were broken up when no longer required.

Early Services of Volunteer Pioneers and Sappers.—During the period above specified these companies were frequently employed, viz. at the siege of the Fort at Vellore in 1761 by the force under Colonel John Caillaud, commanding the army; with the expedition against the Spanish Settlements in the Philippine Islands in 1762; at the storm of the town of Manilla and the capture of the citadel on the 6th October of that year; at the siege and surrender of Tanjore in 1771, on which occasion their conduct was highly praised by General Joseph Smith; at the second siege and storm of the same place in 1773; at the siege and capture of Pondicherry in 1778 by the army under Sir Hector Munro; and at the capture of the French Settlement at Mahé in 1779.

1780.—The existence of Pioneers as a permanent branch of the army appears to have commenced in September 1780, when an order was issued directing the formation of two companies of the under-mentioned strength, viz. 2 sergeants, 3 corporals, 5 havildars, 5 naigues, and 100 Native privates. The men were dressed in blue, fifty of each company were armed with light pistols, and the remaining fifty with pikes six feet long. The havildars were to receive $3\frac{1}{2}$ pagodas each per mensem, the naigues $2\frac{1}{2}$ pagodas, and the privates 2 pagodas.

1781. *Sir Eyre Coote's Campaign.*—The Pioneers marched with the advanced guard of Sir Eyre Coote's army from St. Thomas' Mount for the relief of Wandiwash in January 1781, and were present at the battle of Porto Novo, near Cuddalore, on the 1st July. Their position on the line of march the day before the battle was determined in an order dated 29th June, from which the following is an extract:—

"One company of Pioneers to march at the head of the line, and the other to be divided among the divisions of guns in the line."

No further separate notice of the Pioneers during this campaign has been found, but there can be no doubt that they were present with the army at the battle of Polliloor on the 27th August, and that of Sholinghur on the 27th September 1781, inasmuch as Colonel Owen, of the Bengal Army, who was sent into the Chitoor hills with his brigade shortly after the battle last mentioned, and who was attacked by Hyder with nearly his whole army at the pass of Veeracandeloor, on the 23rd October, mentions a company of Pioneers, under Lieutenant Innes, as having been present at that action.

Capture of the Dutch Settlement at Negapatam.—At this time a detachment of Pioneers, under Lieutenant Abbott, was serving with the Southern Army, commanded by Sir Hector Munro, and was present at the siege and capture of Negapatam from the Dutch in October and November.

1782. *Capture of Trincomalee and Fort Ostenburgh from the Dutch.*—About the 1st January 1782 the detachment under Lieutenant Abbott, augmented by volunteers from the 9th and 23rd Native battalions, embarked at Negapatam with the expedition against the Dutch possessions in Ceylon, and were present at the capture of Trincomalee on the 5th January, and at that of Fort Ostenburgh on the 11th idem.

Sir Eyre Coote's Army.—It may fairly be presumed that the companies serving with Sir Eyre Coote's army in 1781 continued with it during the remaining operations of that year and those of 1782, viz. the relief of Vellore in November 1781, and again in January 1782; the skirmishes with Hyder on the marches to and from that place, and the battle of Arnee on the 2nd June.

1783. *Attack on the French Lines at Cuddalore.*—A detachment of the corps served with the army under Major-General James Stuart, in 1783, and was engaged in the operations against the French at Cuddalore in the month of June. Intelligence of peace with France having been received early in July, hostilities ceased at Cuddalore, and the army returned to Madras in August.

War in the South against Tippoo. Capture of Dindigul and other Forts.—During this year a force under Colonel Ross Lang, of the Madras Army, was employed to create a diversion against Tippoo by attacking his districts of Dindigul and Coimbatore, and to this force a small body of Pioneers was attached. The fort at Caroor was taken on the 3rd April, that at Averacoorchy on the

16th idem, and that at Dindigul on the 5th May. Shortly afterwards Colonel Lang was superseded by Colonel William Fullarton, of H.M. 98th Regiment, and the force was augmented to the strength of about 13,600 men, of whom about 2,000 were Europeans. The Pioneers, amounting to 147 men, under the command of Ensign Cunningham, proved remarkably useful during the continuance of the service.

Capture of the Forts at Panjalamcoorchy, Palghautcherry, &c.—They were engaged in the attack and capture of the fort at Panjalamcoorchy on the 12th August; in that of the stronghold of the Shevagherry Polygar on the 2nd September; at the reduction of the forts at Camalum, Chucklegherry, and Annamally in October; at the siege and capture of the fort at Palghautcherry on the 13th November; and the surrender of Coimbatore on the 26th idem. The services of the Pioneers at Panjalamcoorchy were thus acknowledged by Colonel Fullarton :—

"Our next object was to remove a strong hedge fronting the breach, and surrounding the whole fort, as is the practice in the Polygar system of defence. This dangerous service was effected with unusual skill by Ensign Cunningham, commanding the Pioneers, and about ten at night, with the advantage of bright moonshine, the storm commenced."

The following extract, from the report of the same officer, relates to the operations against the stronghold of the Shevagherry Polygar, at that time the most powerful of the southern chiefs, and who had on former occasions beaten off considerable detachments :—

"After reconnoitring, we found that the comby could not be approached in front. We proceeded, therefore, to cut a road through the impenetrable thickets for three miles to the base of the hill that bounds the comby on the west. The Pioneers, under Ensign Cunningham, laboured with indefatigable industry.

*　　　*　　　*　　　*　　　*

"We continued to cut our way under an unabating fire from

eight thousand Polygars, who constantly pressed upon our advanced party, rushed upon the line of attack, piked the bullocks that were dragging the guns, and killed many of our people. But those attempts were repulsed by perseverance, and before sunset we had opened a passage entirely to the mountain."

The Pioneers also proved most efficient during the march from Annamally to Palghautcherry, which is thus described by Colonel Fullarton :—

"*March through the Annamally Forests to Palghautcherry.*— From Annamally our progress became truly laborious; we had to force our way through a forest twenty miles in depth, extending thirty miles across the pass of Palghaut. Our object was to reach Calingoody, a post on the western side of the forest within fifteen miles of Palghautcherry. The frequent ravines required to be filled up before it was possible to drag the guns across them; innumerable large trees which obstructed the passage required to be cut down and drawn out of the intended track, and then the whole road was to be formed before the carriages could pass. The brigades were distributed to succeed each other at intervals, preceded by Pioneers, in order to clear what the advanced body had opened, for the guns and stores that were to move under cover of the rear division."

1784. *Peace with Tippoo.* 1788. *Guntoor Circar taken possession of.*—In March 1784 peace was made with Tippoo, and the Pioneers do not appear to have been again employed on field service until September 1788, when a small detachment under a European officer was attached to the force under Lieutenant-Colonel James Eidington, which took possession of the district of Guntoor.

1789. *Field Service in the Shivagunga country.*—In March 1789 a detachment of eighty Pioneers was sent from Trichinopoly to join the field force assembled under Lieutenant-Colonel Stuart, H.M. 72nd Regiment, for service in the Shivagunga country. It was present at the capture of Collargoody on the 14th May, and of Ranamangalum and Calacoil on the 1st and 2nd June, respectively. The following order was issued by Government on the conclusion of the service :—

"*Fort St. George*, 17*th June* 1789.

"The service for which the detachment was sent into the Shivagunga country being nearly accomplished, Colonel Stuart is desired to take the necessary measures for the return of the troops to their respective stations, excepting one battalion of native troops, which the Colonel will dispose of in the Shivagunga country in such manner as he may judge expedient.

"Government take this opportunity of returning thanks in this public manner to Colonel Stuart for his gallantry and good conduct in the command of the detachment, and they desire he will communicate to the officers and men their perfect approbation of the spirited and regular behaviour of the whole of the detachment during the service."

Campaigns of Lord Cornwallis against Tippoo.—The Pioneers served with the army under General Medows and Lord Cornwallis in the war with Tippoo during 1790, 1791, and 1792.

1791. *Storm of Bangalore.*—They were actively employed in the operations at Bangalore from the 5th to the 21st March 1791, on which day the place was carried by assault.

Their loss during that time was twenty-four killed and twenty-five wounded, being greater than that of any other individual corps engaged, with the exception of H.M. 36th Foot, which had ten killed and fifty-eight wounded. They were present at the action near Seringapatam on the 15th May, and at the capture of several hill forts in the Mysore country during the year, the principal of which were Rahmandroog and Nundidroog, the former of which fell on the 17th September, and the latter on the 19th October. The following is an extract of that part of the order issued by Lord Cornwallis, on the occasion last referred to, which concerns the Pioneers :—

"*Storm of Nundidroog.*—Although the services of Pioneers are less brilliant than those of the troops, they are of peculiar value in all such operations, and His Lordship thinks himself called upon, in justice to Lieutenant Dowse and all the non-commissioned officers and men of the Pioneer Corps, as well as to Ensign Stokoe, of the Engineers, who assisted with so much ability in directing their labours, to declare that their behaviour on this occasion has deserved his highest commendation."

Order by Lord Clyde on the Return of the Madras and Bombay Troops to their Respective Presidencies.—L Company, Sappers and Miners.—The services of this Company were mentioned by Lord Clyde, in his Order of the 28th November 1859, in the following words :—

"The Corps named in the margin, under Major-General Sir G. C. Whitlock, partook of the various operations under the direction of that officer, and have since been employed in the reduction and occupation of Bundlecund and Saugor."

* * * * *

"The whole of these troops now leaving Bengal (whether of Madras or of Bombay) have gained additional credit for the armies to which they belong, and Lord Clyde congratulates them on being about to return to their own Presidencies after a career of honourable service elsewhere."

We should here not omit to mention the very useful services of the Madras Sappers and Miners in the First and Second Burmese Wars, during the Mutiny, and in Persia, in which campaigns they contributed essentially to the success of our arms.

1860. *Second War in China.—A and K Companies.*—The A and K Companies served with the second expedition to China with the force under the command of Lieutenant-General Sir James Hope Grant, G.C.B., and were present at the action in front of the entrenchments at Sinho on the 12th August 1860, at the capture of the lines at Tongkoo on the 14th, and that of the Forts at Taku on the 21st idem. On the afternoon of that day the sappers, divided into four parties, accompanied the stormers, viz. the pontoon party under Lieutenant Pritchard, R.E., the ladder party under Lieutenant Heine, R.E., the party for removing obstacles under Lieutenant Trail, R.E., and the party with the powder-bags under Lieutenant Clements, also of the Engineers.

Surrender of Pekin.—The A Company marched with the army from Tientsin in September, and was present at the surrender of Pekin on the 13th October.

The following is an extract from the Order issued by the Governor-General on the conclusion of the war :—

" *Camp, Jubbulpore, the* 17*th January* 1861.

" His Excellency the Viceroy and Governor-General of India has much satisfaction in publishing for general information the subjoined letter, dated the 21st November 1860, from Lieutenant-General Sir J. Hope Grant, G.C.B., Commander of the Forces in China, bringing to notice the services, during the campaign in that country, of the Native troops of all arms which proceeded to China from Bengal, Madras, and Bombay.

"'The Governor-General congratulates the troops on the high testimony which they have earned for themselves from their distinguished commander by their exemplary conduct in Camp and Garrison, and by their valour in the Field."

* * * * *

" *Head-Quarters, the Tientsin,* 21*st November* 1860.

" My Lord,—Peace having been concluded with this country, and many of the Native troops serving in the Expeditionary Force being about to return to India, it becomes my duty to bring to your Excellency's notice the services of the Regiments and Corps of Her Majesty's Indian Army which have been serving during the campaign.

* * * * *

" The two Companies of Madras Artillery under Captain Hicks, and the two Companies of Madras Sappers under Captain Shaw-Stewart, rendered good and useful services in the operations which preceded and led to the fall of the Taku Forts. The latter Corps was most energetic in working without relief at the construction of the batteries, and have always shown themselves to be cheerful and willing workmen.

" (Signed)   J. Hope Grant, Lieut.-General,
" *Commander of the Forces.*"

Captain Shaw-Stewart, R.E., was recommended to favourable notice for his exertions in trench duty, and he was accordingly promoted to the rank of Major in the army from the 15th February 1861.

The other officers who served in China with the Sappers were :—
Lieutenant A. J. Filgate, Royal Engineers; Lieutenant D. H. Trail, Royal Engineers; Lieutenant H. F. Dakeyne, 22nd Regiment, M.N.I.; Lieutenant N. Swanston, 37th Regiment Grenadiers; Lieutenant M. E. Foord, 23rd Regiment L.I. Assistant-Surgeon R. E. Pearse.

Reduction of the Corps to 10 Companies.—Early in 1862 the number of companies was fixed at 10 instead of 12, and the two junior companies, viz. the L and M, were accordingly reduced. The reduction was carried out by pensioning such men as were not in every respect fit for active service in the field, provided they had completed the prescribed period of service. Short-service men considered to have established special claims on account of service in the field, were granted donations in proportion to their supposed merits. Those not having any such claims were paid up and discharged with the ordinary gratuity and travelling allowance.

Abyssinia. 1867–68. *G, H, and K Companies.*—The K Company arrived in Abyssinia on the 8th, and the G and H Companies on 12th December 1867, under the command of Major H. N. D. Prendergast, R.E., V.C., with Captain M. E. Foord as Staff Officer to the Detachment.

The following is an extract from the Report of the Commanding Engineer at the close of the campaign :—

"*G Company.*—The G Company was posted at Zoula and Kumayli during the whole campaign. The services performed by this Company on the Public Works at Zoula, on the Railway, and on the Kumayli Waterworks, have been excellent.

"The sepoys of this Company excavated a well on the Railway line 85 feet in depth, without lining of any kind, and proved themselves very skilful workmen.

"I have much pleasure in recording the good services rendered by Lieutenant Morris, R.E., commanding this Company, in superintending the water arrangements at Kumayli.

"These services have proved most beneficial to the Transport Train Establishment at that post.

"I bring to favourable notice the services of Lieutenants Prothero and Mainwaring, assistants to Lieutenant Le Messurier, who was in charge of the water-supply of the expedition.

"*H Company.*—The H Company was employed during the whole campaign on the Public Works at Zoula, and was most industrious, ever ready and willing to undertake any work required of it. Lieutenant Pennycuick, R.E., conducted his duties efficiently. Lieutenant Cunningham, R.E., was detached to Antalo, and Cornet Dalrymple was sent to the front in charge of stores.

"*K Company.*—The K Company commenced work on the Sanafe Pass after a short stay at Zoula; and afterwards, when joined by head-quarters, improved the track route between Antalo and Magdala, rendering it suitable for laden mules and elephants, and was present at the action of Arogie and taking of Magdala. Captain Elliot, N.I., commanded, Lieutenant Bird being subaltern officer."

Action at Arogie, near Magdala.—On the 10th April 1868 the action of Arogie was fought on the platform before Magdala. The K Company was on the right of the British line, and, aided by the rockets of the Naval Brigade, it prevented a detachment of the enemy from turning the flank of the 1st Brigade, and dispersed it.

Assault and Capture of Magdala.—The force that assaulted Magdala on the 13th April consisted of the 2nd Brigade, led by the 33rd Regiment, headed by the Royal Engineers and Sappers and Miners. Before an entrance was forced, Captain Elliot, Cornet Dalrymple, and Sergeant Balding had received contusions, and Havildar Kistnasamy had been severely wounded in the arm.

In Sir Robert Napier's General Order of the 22nd April 1868, he addressed the force as follows:—

"You traversed, often under a tropical sun, or amidst storms of rain and sleet, 400 miles of mountainous and rugged country.

You have crossed ranges of mountains (many steep and precipitous) more than 10,000 feet in altitude, where your supplies could not keep pace with you. In four days you passed the formidable chasm of the Bashilo, and when within reach of your enemy, though with scanty food, and some of you were for many hours without either food or water, you defeated the army of Theodore, which poured down upon you from its lofty fortress in full confidence of victory.

"A host of many thousands have laid down their arms at your feet. You have captured and destroyed upwards of thirty pieces of artillery. . . . You stormed the almost inaccessible fortress of Magdala, defended by Theodore and a desperate remnant of his chiefs and followers."

Acknowledgment of the Services of the Madras Sappers and Miners by Sir Robert Napier.—In his despatch, dated 1st June 1868, Sir Robert Napier wrote as follows:—

"The works of the Madras and Bombay Sappers and Miners, under Major Prendergast, V.C., R.E., and Captain MacDonnell, R.E., have been singularly valuable and important"; and again, "I desire to express my very high appreciation of the services of the officers commanding the several corps of the Expeditionary Force, and of the officers, non-commissioned officers, and soldiers who have served under them during the campaign."

The undermentioned officers of the Sappers were favourably mentioned in the Report of Sir Charles Staveley, viz. :—

Captain Elliot, commanding the K Company; Captain Foord, Lieutenant Bird, and Cornet Dalrymple.

Acknowledgment by the Secretary of State of the Services of the Madras Sappers and Miners in Abyssinia.—On the conclusion of the war the following extract from a military despatch from the Right Honourable the Secretary of State for India was published in the *Fort St. George Gazette* of the 4th August 1868 :—

"I transmit, for the information of your lordship's Government, a copy of a despatch which, in accordance with the command of Her Majesty, I have this day addressed to the Governor-General in Council, conveying to the Government and Army of India the thanks of Her Majesty for the service rendered by them in the conduct of the operations in Abyssinia, the termination of which in the most satisfactory manner has been recently reported to Her Majesty's Government. I especially desire to record the high sense which Her Majesty's Government entertain of the zeal and alacrity displayed in the despatch of the detachment of the Madras Sappers and Miners to take part in the expedition, and of the excellent service rendered by that body of men during the campaign, in the course of which they well maintained the high reputation of the Madras Army, no less than of the distinguished corps they represented."

1876.—In March 1876 the Sappers and Miners were distinguished by being made a royal regiment, and also by the appointment thereto of His Royal Highness the Prince of Wales as Honorary Colonel.

CHAPTER XII.

AVA, CITY OF THE NEW MARQUISATE.

TOWARDS the end of October 1888, the following announcement was published in London :—"The Queen has conferred the dignity of a marquisate upon the Earl of Dufferin, who will take the titles of Marquess of Dufferin and Ava and Earl of Ava. The title of Ava—after the ancient capital of Burma—has been assumed by Her Majesty's special command."

At this intelligence one might almost imagine the ghost of the great Marquess of Dalhousie, or during his tasting on earth a political " apotheosis rapturous," stalking forth and declaring in his own unrivalled way : "Well and gracefully bestowed. I knew exactly, when I annexed Pegu, thirty-six years ago, what the 'force of circumstances' would produce ; and with Earl Dufferin the time came, and the man !" Doubtless, the remains of the old "Secret Committee" were of the same opinion when they heard of the annexation of Upper Burma (1886). The "force of circumstances" had been decidedly fatal to the old Burmese kingdom, sweeping away in its rush the whole Burman Empire ; and neither the transcendent talents of Mr. Cobden and Mr. Bright, nor the talking and writing powers of other most able but less well-known anti-annexationists, could possibly have averted the downfall.

In the very middle of the nineteenth century the Burmese king was, after long forbearance on the part of the British Government, "weighed in the balances," and almost entirely "found wanting;" and thirty-four years after, what Lord Dalhousie, perhaps wisely, thought it imprudent to encumber ourselves with in his time, as "a useless rind," has now a fair chance, after the nearly utter extermination of dacoity, and the stronger desire of border tribes for British rule, of becoming, like his pet annexation of Pegu—that "princess among the provinces"—a flourishing and smiling land.

To those who have been interested in the welfare of the Burmese people—originally formed by union of Mongoloid tribes—since the beginning of the second Burmese war (April, 1852), the kingdom of Burma or Ava, the Burmese Army of Ava, and our "Army of Ava," then assembled at Rangoon, under the gallant old chief, General Godwin, for conquest, to say nothing of the widely-spread saying in Ashé Pyee—Burma, the Eastern or foremost country—that nothing good could possibly be found out of the province of Ava—the brief word has a strong significance about it, almost amounting to a charm. It has been well described by that most admirable Anglo-Indian General Sir Arthur Phayre—by far the greatest Chin-Indian (or Indo-Chinese) statesman England ever had.

It may first be remarked that, in A.D. 1322, great events were taking place in the then new Shân kingdom of Sagaing; events as interesting and important in their way to the Burmese race, as those which shortly after took place in England and France were to the English people under Edward the Third. The line of kings of Shân race reigned at Sagaing for forty-nine years. In the year 1364 a famous chief, with the high-sounding name of Thadomengbyâ, became the leading actor in the wide theatre which was now fairly opened in this part of Chin-India. He was indeed, in every sense, without a rival. He was said to be descended from the ancient kings of Tagaung; and, through his mother, he was grandson of a Shân king of Sagaing. And, strange enough, Sagaing was now added to his conquests. It may here be interesting to remark that the oldest city said in Burmese chronicles to have been built by Indian princes is Tagaung, on the eastern bank of the Upper Irâwadi. This may be styled the first Burmese capital, the ruins of which still exist. "Colonel Yule," writes Sir Arthur Phayre, "is of opinion that it may be identified with the Tugma metropolis of Ptolemy." (Ptolemy, as some of us know, wrote in the second century of the Christian era.) It is scarcely credible that cities such as those of which there are existing remains should have been founded independently by people in the rude condition of the Mongolian tribes, even as we see them in the present day in remote places. The tradition, therefore, as to the building of cities and the first commencement of the Burmese monarchy by Indian settlers, may be accepted as probably true. It ought to make us more interested in our highly important possession of Burma, when we consider the fact "that those Indians should have arrived by a northern or north-western route, and not have ascended from the delta of the Irâwadi, is rendered certain from the history of Pegu." And, again, in a few generations, the Indian settlers "became merged in the mass of Mongoloid tribes whom they found in the country."

Before proceeding to notice the foundation of the city of Ava, it is proper to mention, on the high authority of Sir Arthur Phayre, that "only a few of the names by which the indigenous tribes were called in the remote past are now known; but the Indian settlers gave to them, and adopted themselves, the name of Brahmâ, which is that used in Buddhist sacred books for the first inhabitants of the world. This term, when used to designate the existing people, is now written Mrâmmâ, and generally pronounced Bamâ!" And hence the European word Burma, which should never be spelt with an *h*. There is no harm in telling the world that "the people known to Europeans as Birman, Burman, or Burmese, dwell in the western region of Indo-China, which is watered by the river Irâwadi;" but the name of their country—to say nothing of the expense of an additional letter, which in these days of economists and calculators is a consideration—has no more right to the final *h* than Asia, Russia, China, or India.*

---

* See also *Our Burmese Wars and Relations with Burma*, p. 17.

Many tribes then gradually became Mrâmmû, or Burma, a corruption of the original appellation.

Let us now return to the redoubtable chief, Thadomengbyâ. His ambition prompted him at once to set about the restoration of the Burmese kingdom, which had been broken up into many fragments. Thadomengbyâ determined to found a new capital, and selected a site near the mouth of an affluent of the far-famed Irâwadi.* "The city was called Awâ, or Ava, the Pali or classical name being Ratanapura, or city of gems."† The work—commenced A.D. 1364—was carried on with great energy. Swamps were drained, golden pagodas built, and the city wall marked out; the palace, in the centre, was the "Citadel of the Defences." And no ordinary defences were required for the "City of Gems," which might have been styled the City of Jewels—the probable taste and splendour displayed by the arrangement of the gems from all parts of the country, being only outdone by a famous spectacular piece at the Lyceum, played some five hundred years after the brilliant performance of King Thadomengbyâ, and which old play-goers may recollect as one of Madame Vestris's grandest scenic displays—the Island of Jewel.

Little the conqueror thought that the city he so religiously and carefully founded would one day be called upon, by our Queen-Empress, to give a marquisate to one of the shrewdest, most accomplished, and versatile statesmen of our time, on his leaving the stage, where, like a well-graced actor, as Viceroy of India, he had, through good and evil report, so nobly and fearlessly played his part. While the building of Ava was in progress, the new king set out to subdue the country to the southward. During the campaign, Thadomengbyâ caught the small-pox, and departed on his return to Ava, ordering his queen to be put to death, that, in case of his own demise, she might not fall to his successor. He died soon after; and thus the first King of Ava, after a brief reign,

---

* Derived from *Airávati—vati* (Sans.), "like," and *aira*, "moisture"—Indra's female elephant. See *Ashé Pyee*, p. 81.

† Sir Arthur Phayre's *History of Burma*, p. 63.

ended his life by an act of cruelty, not unlike some of those which disgraced King Theebaw in our time—" the beginning of the end " of a wild career, which eventually lost him his throne and country; till at length, as already noted, old Ava was honoured with the dignity of furnishing a well-earned and appropriate marquisate. This first monarch of Ava is denounced in Burmese history as a man of cruel disposition, who altogether disregarded religion. History in King Theebaw studiously repeated itself in the latter particular; for, as well set forth by a most intelligent officer of the Royal Welsh Fusiliers during the Third Burmese War (1885-86-87), after a correct and concise account of education under the priesthood of Burma, King Theebaw was once a priest! —thus bringing to mind Shakspeare's well-known saying, that " the devil can cite Scripture for his purpose."

We now pass on to the year 1416, when a Chinese army was before Ava. With this move on the grand chess-board of Chin-Indian strife and events, comes forth a most interesting incident, which, if the like could be established in our time, would save much of the expense caused by the large armaments of Europe. Only that the two champions were pretty equal in size and strength, the incident also tends to carry our thoughts back to the days of David and Goliath. During continual war, caused by fruitless expeditions to Pegu, came this serious danger which threatened the Burmese King. Two Shân chiefs had attacked Myêdu, which was subject to Ava. The King sent a force against them, and they fled to the Chinese territory, while their wives and children were made prisoners. A Chinese army marched down to Ava, and required that the wives and children of the two chiefs should be released. According to the Burmese chronicle, the point whether they should be surrendered or not was left to be decided by the result of a battle between two champions. A Talaing (Pegu) chief, who was prisoner at Ava, was allowed to represent the Burmese side. He killed the Chinese champion, who was clad in armour, and the Chinese army then withdrew without the demand for the prisoners being enforced. Meng-Khaung, the

Burmese King, then unremittingly gave himself up to good works in the city of Ava and the surrounding country.

It may now be briefly remarked that the Burmans were, in a manner, subject to Pegu until about the middle of the 16th century. A revolution having taken place, the Burmese acquired and retained the superiority until A.D. 1740, when, the brave Peguers having revolted, a fierce civil war ensued, which was carried on with savage ferocity until A.D. 1752, when the Peguers captured the city of Ava, and completed the conquest of the whole Burmese kingdom, thus becoming masters of Ava's jewels as well as of the gold and jewels of Pegu. The King of Pegu, after many victories, returned to his own capital, and the Burmans again took up arms under the command of the far-famed Alompra—the "hunter-captain"—a man of low origin, but of a brave and enterprising character, who not only expelled the Peguers from Ava, but invaded and conquered Pegu itself, which remained subject to Burma until, from the Second Burmese War, it came under British rule.

The great Alompra, who was the founder of the historically important dynasty which was disgraced by and ended with King Theebaw, died shortly after his invasion of Siam, A.D. 1760. Both generals, Sir Arthur Phayre and Albert Fytche, give very interesting particulars regarding this most distinguished Burman, quite worthy of attention, though not of our worship, in the study of Eastern heroes. Remarking on this famous captain in the introductory pages of *Our Burmese Wars*, the writer was led to observe that it was during Alompra's reign that the British Government was first brought into political relationship with the King of Ava or Burma (p. 8). Had his descendants served their country as faithfully and well as he did, it is quite certain there would have been no Marquess of Dufferin and Ava in 1888, or as little chance of such a title as of an Earl of Bankok, or even a Duke of Pekin! There was really something of William Wallace or William Tell about Alompra. It may be interesting to give a few particulars of the doings and sayings of this famous national hero, who, as will have been seen, flourished when there seemed every likelihood of the rule of the Talaing King being established in Upper Burma, or the upper country, to distinguish it from Pegu, the lower or southern region.

Before the fall of Ava, Uva Râjâ, brother of the Talaing sovereign, had issued a proclamation, summoning the administrative officers in the country north of the city to submit and swear allegiance to the King of Pegu. Alompra (or more properly Alamghprâ, signifying " embryo Buddha," a title which the patriot hero assumed)* " dared to disobey and ventured to resist." Although in a subordinate position, it is stated among the narratives of his career that he was of royal race, and that signs and wonders in heaven and earth, which took place at his birth, had foreshadowed his future greatness. The intense nationality of Alompra was remarkable. It presents a noble contrast to the hollowness of many professed patriots, in Europe as well as in Asia, at the present day. His native village, of which the name is unknown, was situated about sixty miles north of Ava—a few miles from the west bank of the Irâwadi. The village became famous as the home of the Muthsovo or hunter-captain, " as being the scene of his successful resistance to the invader, and eventually the capital of the kingdom." From the beginning of the national troubles, he was determined to resist the Talaing or any other invader; and Sir Arthur Phayre, in his admirable history—a perfect monument of Indo-Chinese research—relates that when his father and mother entreated him to submit, he declared that he could never swear allegiance to a Talaing king, adding: "When fighting for our country, it matters little whether our band is large or small; it is, rather, important to have a few comrades with true hearts and strong arms to will and work." On this brief speech Sir Arthur Phayre remarks:—" These noble words are a key to his conduct in the early part of his career, before success and irresponsible power had roused selfish ambition and hardened his heart."†

* Sir Arthur Phayre.
† *History*, p. 150.

Alompra, then, was no exception to the general rule in every country that heroes, or rather public men, as well as angels have fallen, and may yet fall, through ambition. It should have been remarked that, on Alompra's conquering the whole of Pegu, with the intuitive genius of a true conqueror he founded the now well-known modern seaport of Rangoon, which, as styled elsewhere, is the Liverpool or Glasgow of Chin-India.

About this time English envoys were sent to Alompra at Ava—one in 1755 and another in eventful 1757. General Albert Fytche has given certain details in his valuable work,* related by the two envoys, which he well considers "of singular interest." These details serve to bring out the individuality of Alompra in a surprising or wonderful degree. The first envoy described the Burmese monarch as about forty-five years of age and nearly six feet in height, "rude in his manners and hasty and vain-glorious in his temper." Doubtless his somewhat "barbarous intelligence" was of a very high order. One of his excellences appears to have been that of being able to see through, or "take stock" of, men—not an uncommon attribute among the distinguished servants who helped to build up the mighty structure of our own Indian empire. The second envoy found Alompra less boasting or vain-glorious, and consequently more sensible; but the former hunter-captain was now (1757) "brimming with curiosity." Among the "endless questions" put to our envoy by the most famous type of a Burmese monarch and warrior, no doubt causing the former to consider himself in a rather ticklish position, the following are given by General Fytche:—"Does your King [George II.] go to the wars and expose himself to danger as I do? Could you fire a cannon and kill a man at a great distance? Is there as much rain in England as there is in Burma? Why do you wear that thing (a shoulder-knot) on your shoulder? How much money does the Company pay you a month? Why do not the English tattoo their bodies and thighs as we Burmese do? Is there any ice in your country? Are the small creeks ever frozen over as they are here?"

* *Burma Past and Present*, vol. i., pp. 192-93.

Alompra's questions, it must be confessed, were brief and to the point, qualities not always observable among our public men in this often superficial and, from irrelevant questions, frequently too inquisitive age. The gallant General remarks that "the envoy answered the questions as he best could. As regards the freezing process, he stated that he had seen the river Thames frozen over, and an ox roasted whole upon the ice. This statement was received by the King and his great men with a roar of laughter; but whether they were only tickled with the story, or disbelieved it altogether, was not known."

The second envoy appears to have fared much better with Alompra than the first, with whom His Majesty of Ava was highly indignant when asked, on the part of the East India Company, if he wanted any help against his enemies. The only blot to be observed by Englishmen in this strong King of Ava's distinguished career, was the sad tragedy of the massacre of our countrymen at Negrais island. It took place shortly after the massacre or suffocation of the Black Hole which followed the capture of Calcutta; and when Alompra heard of Clive's great victories, which restored the prestige of the East India Company, he naturally became alarmed, and suspected that the English had secretly helped the people of Pegu. His fears, which, of course, had no foundation, were worked upon by French and Armenian adventurers. These unprincipled men in Burmese history kept hovering about Ava and the royal court, even down to and after 1852; and while on the field before Rangoon, in the burning month of April, an officer or soldier was anxious to gain as a trophy a Burman's dáh (sword), or a broad gilt hat, worn by the King of Ava's "Invincibles," he would be suddenly reminded that he was mortal by the approach of a round shot, well directed, and, as was stoutly affirmed, the piece laid by a scientific French or Armenian gunner.

After these few historical remarks, it may be interesting to turn very briefly to the geography of the province and city of the new marquisate. As already stated, it is believed that Ptolemy, the Egyptian geographer and astronomer, in the second century of the

Christian era, alluded to the ancient city of Tagoung, the first Burmese capital, founded about 500 B.C. And, before the middle of the nineteenth century, we have a learned Anglo-Indian Ptolemy, in the person of the Rev. A. R. Symonds,* who gives ten or twelve pages to the kingdom of Ava, a greater and more famous capital than old Padoung, and founded nineteen hundred years later.

The chapter on Ava is a remarkable one, and does the zealous head-master infinite credit; and the number of places mentioned therein, when the present or new capital, Mandalay, had no existence, warrants the supposition that he had an eye to teaching English as well as Indian gentlemen, as well as boys, Indian geography; so that there might not, in future years, be any chance of a speech such as the brilliant and jaunty veteran statesman, Lord Palmerston, once uttered to his private secretary, after receiving a long-winded deputation—that unavoidable bore of a Minister's life:—" Now, then, just hand me down that atlas, and let us see where the deuce all those places are!"

By Europeans the country was generally called Ava, from the common name of the capital, but by the natives themselves it was named Burma (Mrumma). The boundaries are given thus: north, Assam; north-easterly, China; east, Siam; south, Siam and the sea; and west, the sea, Arracan (Arakan), and Bengal. Some forty-five years ago, Ava had for many years been divided into the following chief provinces: Ava, Pegu, Martaban, Tavoy, and Tenasserim, of which the latter two only were subject to the British Government. The province of Ava extended to Prome, which was the southern boundary of the empire previous to the Burmese conquest of Pegu. Its principal districts were Cassay, Mogaong, Ava, and the Shan country. The principal river is the Irâwadi, which intersects the country.

It may add to the importance of the new marquisate, in a geographical point of view, if we keep in mind that Ava, so named

* M.A., Wadham College, Oxford, and head-master of Bishop Corrie's Grammar School, Madras (1845).

from the capital, constituted what was originally the whole extent of Burma proper. The country is generally described as consisting of the great valley of the Irâwadi, intersected by smaller rivers and low hills, and having mountain ranges along its northern and western sides; another cross range separating it from the Shan country. Concise as Mr. Symonds is in his descriptions, as an Indian and Chin-Indian geographer, he is even excelled by General Fytche, who gives the respective positions of Ava and Pegu in a very few words: "The northern region was known as Ava, and had a city named Ava for its capital. The southern region was called Pegu (a corruption of Bagoo), whose chief town and port was Rangoon."* In "coaching" his pupils in Indian geography—far from sufficiently attended to—it will be well for the coach of the day to make them bear these simple facts in mind, for Ava and Pegu will now become household words.

After the massacre at Negrais, diplomatic intercourse ceased with the Burmese Empire until 1795, when Colonel Symes was sent to Burma, as ambassador, by Sir John Shore, the Governor-General of India, afterwards Lord Teignmouth. The King of Burma or Ava, since his conquest of Arakan—the old battle-field of the kings of Burma and Pegu—in 1783, had been continually threatening the Bengal frontier, which made our relations with the Golden Foot of Ava of serious importance. The zealous and hard-working Colonel, who published a narrative of his mission, visited Pegu, and went up the river to the famous cities of Ava and Amarapúra (the City of Immortals). But in the opinion of General Fytche his mission was a complete failure, as he was unable to estimate the real character of the people and had the crying fault, so common among diplomatists when dealing with Eastern lands, of overrating the government and resources of the country. Nevertheless, he collected and published a vast deal of useful information regarding the Ava kingdom, for which he deserves well of posterity. His remarks on the mineralogy of the Burman

---

* The Irâwadi is navigable for ships as far as Rangoon, which is about twenty-eight miles from the sea. Rangoon is upwards of five hundred miles from Ava.

Empire alone are of great value; and coupled with the present interest attached by the mercantile communities to the Ruby Mines —of no small importance to the Indian Government as well as to the new Company—they come as landmarks, as it were, at the present time; for, in a case of this kind, it may be taken for granted that what once was, in some measure, must be now.

Coupling Ava with Amarapúra enforces the remark, made elsewhere, that Amarapúra, in lat. 21° 55′ N., long. 96° 7′ E., and Ava, in lat. 21° 45′ N., long. 96° E., have both been the capital of the Burman Empire at different times, according to the nomadic usage or caprice of the king. The capital was once nearly being established at the city of Arakan, which would inevitably have caused the annexation of Pegu and Ava in the early part, instead of the middle and towards the end of the nineteenth century. But the great Burman commander, Maha Bandoola, was quite content, in the glory of his national arrogance, to march into Arakan, provided with golden fetters, in which the Governor-General of India was to be led captive to Ava.* Fortunately, the noble Marquesses of Hastings, Dalhousie, and Dufferin—representing England, Scotland, and Ireland—were spared a humiliating march to the golden city of gems; so they had not the honour of encountering the "Lord of Earth and Air," of golden temples and golden umbrellas, and (before Gautama's chief votary) of going through various modes of worship—of kotowing, shikhoing, bending or bowing—to a monarch who considered himself so far superior to any other in the grand list of mundane monarchies. The lord of the white (or sandy-coloured) elephant also would have been glad to have exhibited the strange "sacred" beast, with the other glories of Ava, to either of the three renowned Governors-General.

History also records that when Calcutta was in danger of being approached from the Chittagong frontier, one of the Burmese generals had gasconadingly announced his intention of taking

* *Narrative of the First Burmese War.* By Major Snodgrass. London: John Murray, 1827.

possession of the town (city of palaces), preparatory to his march to England! Truly the assurance of the King and his nobles at Ava, before and during the first Burmese war (1824–25–26), was almost supernatural. It seemed as if the world were to be governed from Ava or Amarapúra. Strange enough, in all their rude notions of military science, artillery was ever their boasted arm. Bandoola himself was killed by a rocket, or a shell, at our attack on Donnabew. Regardless of human life, the Burmese *savants* were ever casting and bursting guns in the old capital. What they thought of their skill in projectiles is amusingly set forth in a little anecdote of the conclusion of the first Burmese war (February 1826). After the signing and sealing of the treaty of Yandaboo, Sir A. Campbell and Mr. Robinson (the Commander-in-chief and Civil Commissioner) took the Burman chieftains to view some of our troops and artillery. The "rebel English strangers" having astonished them with the evolutions of our infantry, some field-pieces were then brought out, and 50 rounds fired to show the rapidity of our artillery movements. Finally, some shells and rockets were thrown across the river. During the latter part of the exhibition one of the rockets exploded at the moment it left the tube, and scattered the shot around, but fortunately without doing any injury. Sir A. Campbell then drew the attention of the Burmese chiefs to the fact that we could make our shells explode at any distance we pleased. After the exhibition was ended, one of the mighty visitors, on being asked quietly what he thought of it, replied: "Oh, we can do all this much better ourselves at Ava!"*

During the second Burmese War, it was one of the writer's amusements to collect a good deal of what was said and written about the first; and, as directly pertaining to the subject of this paper, the following notes, written at Rangoon in 1855, may be interesting:—

Ava and Amarapúra.

As the British Embassy to the present (in 1855) amiable King

* From the writer's *Second Burmese War—Pegu*, pp. 304-5 (1853).

of Ava invests the above places with a peculiar interest—the Commissioner with magnificent presents for the Golden Foot, accompanied by an artist and a geologist, paying his Majesty a State visit—of such celebrated cities, it may be noted that Old Ava, the ancient capital, is four or five miles south-west from the new capital, Amarapúra, also styled "the Immortal City." Ava is divided into the upper and lower city, both of which are fortified; but the walls are now in a state of decay. Travellers describe the lower city as about four miles in circumference. The city is protected by a wall thirty feet high, with the usual deep, broad fosse. Ava was quitted by Alompra's fourth son, Minderajee Pran, who, in 1783, founded Amarapúra. What Amarapúra once was, Ava now is, for in 1824 the seat of empire was transferred back again to the old capital, and Ava is now the centre of Burman splendour, while the majestic edifices of Amarapúra are crumbling into ruins. The population is probably under 100,000. Later writers also, including Colonel Symes, wrote in a similar strain, at the end of the last and beginning of the present century, on the desolation of Ava while Amarapúra was in the height of its glory. There are numerous temples, on which the Burmans never lay sacrilegious hands, dilapidating by the corrosion of time; indeed, it would be difficult to exhibit a more striking picture of desolation and ruin than that which the forsaken capital of Ava presents—and yet it was destined one day to be the city of a marquisate! Captain Havelock,* who accompanied the mission to Ava, at the end of the first Burmese War, describes the royal palace as enclosed within a vast quadrangular wall of brick, fenced in at the distance of a few feet by a stockade of perpendicular timbers. First portal opened, an oblong court seen; a second gate, another court; right and left, stables for horses and elephants; leaves of a third portal rushed apart, then the full splendour of the palace of the Golden Foot stood unveiled.

* Afterwards the famous Sir Henry, of Lucknow, who served throughout the first Burmese War, in which served also the unrivalled sea Fielding, Captain Marryat.

At this stage, in an endeavour to bring forward sume interesting facts regarding Ava, it will not do to omit mention of a fine passage in Major Snodgrass's narrative, offering a proud reflection for the historian of British valour. Ava itself, the golden capital of the "Lord of Earth and Air," could have been easily reached; but the object was not so much to conquer a country as to teach a lesson of humility to a haughty people; and so Sir Archibald Campbell halted within four days' march of Ava, or say fifty miles from the capital. On this the gallant Major—the first writer of a narrative of a Burmese war—remarks:—"One latent feeling of disappointment alone remained. . . . We were only three marches from the capital of the despot, the source from which the war and all its lengthened misery had sprung, and from the primary cause of so much suffering and bloodshed, and it was not in the nature of a British soldier to turn his back upon the Golden City without some feelings of regret." Ava would, doubtless, have fallen to our arms; and the conquest of the capital of Alompra, as was argued by some judges who took a more general view of the case, would have had a good effect upon the whole Eastern world. Perhaps a similar feeling of disappointment took hold of many of the troops engaged in the second Burmese war, when Lord Dalhousie resolved to content himself with Pegu, leaving Upper Burma until the force of circumstances propelled us onward, which took place a good part of a century after British possession of his pet annexation.

Then came the third expedition to Burma—it can hardly be called a war—the dethronement of the savage King Theebaw, and a series of dacoity campaigns to follow up the annexation of Upper Burma, campaigns of much endurance and suffering to our brave troops, now, apparently, after a successful extirpation of so many daring and wily dacoits, approaching a successful end. We have never had so much fighting against robber chieftains and their men before in the East; and many who were steady anti-annexationists now look with pride on the British possession of Upper Burma, repudiating no longer "the force of circumstances," and ceasing to twit a prudent Government with Wordsworth's famous lines in "Rob Roy":—

> "The simple plan,
> That they should take who have the power,
> And they should keep who can."

It must strike the reflective mind that the disappearance even of such a vain monarchy as that of Ava from the political scroll of the Eastern world is no ordinary event in the history of our time. The very idea of wiping out such a once famous kingdom, however just the action, through the combined agency of a Secretary of State in London and a Viceroy in India, says much for the astonishing power of our Empire. Through Lord Dufferin (the Marquess of Ava *in esse*) the fiat went forth at the beginning of 1886, like that of Pegu, in the words of Lord Dalhousie, at the end of 1852, that Upper Burma with its 130,000 square miles was ours, irrevocable, immutable, and final. And yet, while writing these words, towards the close of 1888, there is intelligence from the old land of the Golden Foot that a belief exists among some classes of the Burmese people, that, sooner or later, the kingdom will be restored! Of course this can never be. Pegu, at least, would far sooner have British than Burman rule; and there can be no doubt that a ring of joy went through many Pegu households at the beginning of 1855, when Lord Dalhousie announced to the Burmese envoys in Calcutta, who had come to ask for the restitution of Pegu and the other conquered provinces, that (as rendered by Major (afterwards Sir Arthur) Phayre, the interpreter), "as long as the sun shines in the heavens, the British flag shall wave over these possessions."

The high-souled, chivalrous Earl of Mayo, some sixteen years ago (or not long before his lamented death), put this famous speech in another form at Rangoon:—"Arakan, Pegu, and Tenasserim are British, and British they will remain for many generations of men." It is important to note that all three Viceroys, or Governors-General, paid Burma the honour of a visit. Allusion has already been made to a British Embassy to the Golden Foot, which was a return compliment for that paid by the Burmese Envoys to the Governor-General.

The transfer of the seat of Government, from Amarapúra to Ava, has also been mentioned. In 1824, a new palace was building at Old Ava, of which the King took possession when finished; and much that was beautiful about Amarapúra was removed to Alompra's capital, which would not be a very difficult operation, the two cities (on the left bank of the river) being only five miles apart.

In August 1855, an embassy, under General Sir Arthur (then Colonel) Phayre, accompanied by a brilliant suite, including Captain, now Colonel, Henry Yule, C.B.,* the learned and highly esteemed member of the India Council, proceeded up the Irâwadi to Amarapúra, then the capital of the King of Burma. To celebrate this august occasion, the gallant Colonel (Secretary) wrote a narrative of the mission—a splendid volume, beautifully illustrated—in which will be found much interesting information. General Fytche, writing ten years ago, gives the following melancholy picture:—" Ava, the capital of the kingdom for nearly four hundred years—from 1400 to 1783—as well as Amarapúra, the late capital, only abandoned in 1860, are almost entirely deserted, and their sites overgrown with jungle." It is to be hoped that under the new and vigorous administration of Upper Burma these once famous cities will, ere many years, ring with the sound of busy men—English, Burmese, Chinese, and Indian merchants—all with " the quick pulse of gain," founding a Chin-Indian Birmingham and Manchester in Eastern Asia; and a Liverpool, in its way, has long been flourishing at Rangoon. In fact, having got rid of the selfish, monopolising King of Upper Burma, the neglected, misgoverned, and undeveloped country, where nature ever did so much, and man so little, there is no saying to what a pitch of prosperity our new conquest may attain. And, as with Lord Dalhousie in Pegu, it must ever be a pleasing thought to Lord Dufferin, the Marquess of Ava, that he endeavoured to fan the flame of a brighter day in the old kingdom during its second infancy.

* Afterwards Sir Henry Yule, K.C.S.I. This distinguished officer of the Bengal Engineers—famous also in Anglo-Indian literature—died in 1889.

To continue the slight narrative of events, it may be noted that, in 1860, the seat of Government in Upper Burma was transferred from Amarapúra to Mandalay, the present capital, so called from the hill on which it stands, and said to have been founded in 1853. The city lies about three miles from the Irâwadi; and it is stated that one of the King's motives for quitting Ava, and selecting the new site, "was to remove his palace from the sight and sound of British steamers." Except as the scene of the unparalleled atrocities of King Theebaw, and various episodes to be found in published works on Burma, there is little to interest us about Mandalay, of which Dr. Anderson, who accompanied the expeditions[*] to Western China in 1868 and 1875, writes:—"The city is built on the same plan as the old capital, described by Yule." He also mentions a remarkable incident: "When the King, in compliance with a prophecy, was crowned a second time in 1874, he made the circuit of the city in a magnificent war-boat, the splendour of which eclipsed the traditionary glory of the Lord Mayor's barge." Twelve years passed away, and Upper Burma, with Mandalay, chiefly from the combined action of Earl Dufferin and Lord Randolph Churchill (Secretary of State), became a dominion of the Queen-Empress. In Burma and India, as well as in Great Britain, education, municipal institutions (and in India delusive National Congresses), were taking the place of useless and expensive show; and a successful Viceroy of India was about returning home, as Marquess of Dufferin and Ava but not of Mandalay, from the scene of his triumphs, like another Cæsar, having played the Burmese and other games with a rare skill, to find the people of these islands, while a tranquil day had not yet broken forth in Ireland, more in earnest about public affairs than ever. From the old "City of Gems" to the precious stones and minerals of Burma, the transition is easy; but before touching on jewels, or jewellery, so much mixed up with the romance of life, a word more must be said on the stern reality of our possession of Upper Burma. Some years ago the writer had occasion to read a

[*] Under Colonel Edward B. Sladen and Colonel Horace Browne.

French view of Burma. It was originally published in the Paris *Nouvelle Revûe*, and M. Voissin, the author, with reference to Burma and Tonquin, exhibited a better knowledge of our intentions than we had ourselves. He was of opinion that as, in the interests of commerce and humanity, England was endeavouring to establish her supremacy in Burma, France should also definitely consolidate (as has since been done) hers in Tonquin. In every sense, then, the blow which we have struck in Eastern Asia redounds to the glory of Great Britain, and, of course, greatly to the honour of the existing British Government.*

* See Appendix B.

NOTES.

I.

AMALGAMATION.—BENGAL EUROPEAN REGIMENT.*—A FUSILIER ANECDOTE.

OWING to the immense interests at stake, and the vast numbers of individuals who were concerned, the process of amalgamation, commencing with the Royal Proclamation, November 1st, 1858, was not finally carried out until after a lapse of upwards of two years. During this interval serious complications arose, which at one time threatened to assume the form of a European mutiny.

The troops, with some show of justice, put forward a claim to a "bounty" on transferring their services from the Company to the Crown; but on its having been announced that the "bounty" claimed was granted all discontent disappeared, and the process of amalgamation was peaceably effected. His Royal Highness the Field-Marshal Commanding-in-Chief then issued the following general order :—

"The General Commanding-in-Chief has received Her Majesty's commands to make known to the British Army serving in India that the arrangements for consolidating the European forces of the Crown in that country have now been completed.

"His Royal Highness hails with satisfaction an event which he trusts may be conducive to the best interests of the Empire, whilst it will be of advantage to the troops whom it may concern.

---

* "Now the Royal Munster Fusiliers." In the *History* of this distinguished regiment, which "helped to win India," will be found the interesting and useful notes now given, pp. 533-535.

"He feels persuaded that the glorious deeds of arms for which the line and local troops have been ever conspicuous will not be forgotten by them now that they are about to join one united army, and that the only feeling of rivalry which will henceforth exist between the various corps will be a high spirit of emulation as regards discipline and good conduct during peace, and of gallant bearing and devotion should their services be hereafter called for in the field.

"In the name of the Army, the Commander-in-Chief most heartily and cordially welcomes to the ranks of the general service of the Crown, the officers, non-commissioned officers, and soldiers of the local services of the three Presidencies in India.

"GEORGE,
"General Commanding-in-Chief."

Lieutenant-General A. B. Roberts, C.B., who had for many years commanded the Bengal European Regiment, was appointed its Colonel; and Lieutenant-Colonel (now Major-General) F. O. Salusbury, C.B., who had served in the regiment since 1842, shortly afterwards assumed command of H.M. 101st Royal Bengal Fusiliers; and under this latter officer the regiment took a prominent part in the Umbeyla campaign, specially distinguishing itself on the 13th November 1863, when, led by Colonel Salusbury, it carried at the point of the bayonet the "Craig's picket," a difficult position in the upper heights, which had fallen into the enemy's hands. H.M. 101st Foot evinced throughout this campaign the same courage, discipline, and efficiency for which, as the "Bengal European Regiment," it had ever been prominently distinguished. On the 25th February 1862 new colours were presented to the Royal Bengal Fusiliers in substitution of the last colours of the 1st Bengal European Regiment (Light Infantry), which were handed over to the custody of the 101st Foot, by whom they were, on the 18th July 1871, with all ceremony and reverence deposited in Winchester Cathedral, where they now rest. In July 1881 a general change in the nomenclature of the regiments of the line took place; the 101st Royal Bengal Fusiliers becoming the 1st, and the 104th Bengal Fusiliers the 2nd, battalion of the "Royal Munster Fusiliers." Thus history repeats itself; the 1st and 2nd Bengal European Regiments are again united under one designation, and although its new title bears no reference to the country or service in which these battalions gained such signal distinctions, we may rest assured that the "Royal Munster Fusiliers" will ever maintain the character for loyalty, discipline, and courage inherited from its predecessor the Bengal European Regiment. We cannot part with the Bengal Fusiliers, which, with the Madras Fusiliers, Madras Artillery, and Bombay European Regiment, did so much good and hard work for the early Presidential Armies of India, without giving a little anecdote of General Godwin, at the capture and occupation of Pegu, in November 1852. The force of regimental rivalry—always laudable—could no farther go. About to storm the pagoda, our gallant chief nobly harangued the troops, in a practical style seldom surpassed. "Now," he said to the Fusiliers, "*you* are Bengalies, and *you* are Madrassies; let us see who are the best men." A deafening cheer—a rush—and all was over. Pegu had fallen; but, we trusted, only to rise in greater beauty than ever. (See *Our Burmese Wars and Relations with Burma*, page 214.)

II.

FOURTH "PRINCE OF WALES' OWN" REGIMENT MADRAS LIGHT CAVALRY.*

"Seringapatam," "Assaye," "Mahidpoor."
Prince of Wales' Plume.

Honorary Colonel

H.R.H. Albert Edward, Prince of Wales and Duke of Cornwall, K.G., K.T., G.C.B., K.P., G.C.S.I., Field Marshal.

This regiment was raised at Arcot in May 1785 as the 3rd† Regiment of Native Cavalry, and placed under the command of Captain William Augustus Younge, by whose name it was long known among the native soldiery. The nucleus of the regiment was formed of details belonging to the cavalry of the Nawaub of the Carnatic, then serving south of the river Coleroon under Lieutenant, afterwards Lieutenant-General Sir Thomas Dallas,

---

* *Historical Record*, by Colonel W. J. Wilson (Retired List); formerly of the 43rd M.N.I., Madras, 1877.—From India Office Library.

† Both the 1st and 2nd Regiments were received into the British Service in 1784.—Army List, 1848.

G.C.B., and of a party of dismounted troopers doing duty at the cavalry cantonment near Arcot.

The establishment of a regiment of Native Cavalry at that time consisted of four troops of 124 men each, officers included, viz. :—

1 Lieutenant.	8 Havildars.
1 Cornet.	8 Naiques.
2 Sergeants.	2 Trumpeters.
1 Subadar.	1 Farrier.
3 Jemadars.	97 Privates.

Staff not included in Troops.

1 Captain Commandant.	1 Trumpet-Major.
1 Native Commandant.	1 First Farrier.

Staff included in Troops.

1 Adjutant.	1 Native Adjutant.
1 Quartermaster.	1 Drill Havildar.
1 Sergeant-Major.	1 Drill Naique.
1 Quartermaster-Sergeant.	4 Line Men.

In April 1786 each of the six troops of a cavalry regiment possessed an important personage, in addition to the surgeon's assistant, enjoying the title of "Black Doctor." On the 20th June of the same year, Government determined to raise a fourth regiment of cavalry from the remaining supernumeraries and Native officers on half-pay, supplemented by a draft of seventeen men per troop from each of the existing regiments. The 3rd Regiment accordingly transferred 68 men to the new regiment, and Cornet Alexander Grant was also transferred thereto at the same time as Adjutant. Two field-pieces were attached to each regiment of European and Native infantry, or of cavalry, when commanded to take the field for service. In October 1787 the 3rd Regiment furnished five Native officers, eight havildars, nine naiques, and forty-eight privates towards the formation of the 5th Regiment (the present 1st Regiment M.L.C.), then being raised. The number of privates in each troop was at this time reduced from sixty-eight to sixty. In December of the same year, General Sir Archibald Campbell ordered a riding-master to be appointed to the Corps of Cavalry. In February 1788, standards were delivered to the regiments of cavalry for the first time, and the form of ceremony prescribed. In the same month and year, Younge's regiment became the 4th. Major Younge became fourth on the list, and his regiment was numbered accordingly. This was the last occasion upon which the extraordinary system of altering the numbers of regiments so as to agree with the seniority of the commandants was acted upon. In January 1789 a riding-master was appointed to each cavalry corps. Early in 1790 the strength of the cavalry regiments was increased to 600 privates, or 100 per cent. Early in October 1790, Tippoo moved towards Caroon with his whole force for the purpose of cutting off a detachment; but the Commander-in-Chief (General Medows) having received information of this design, moved forward in support, and Major Younge joined him in safety with his whole detachment at Cudimoody, on the river Cavery, on the 7th October. The regiment (4th) accompanied the army during the remaining operations of the campaign, and returned with it to the neighbourhood of Madras in January 1791. The regiment greatly distinguished itself in the Mysore campaign (1791) under Lord Cornwallis, who had arrived from Bengal. The Cavalry Brigade was commanded by the well-known Colonel (General) Floyd. On the 5th January 1799, Government determined to attach a proportion of Horse Artillery to each regiment of European Dragoons and of Native Cavalry. [According to Major (afterwards General) P. J. Begbie, by G.O.G., 8th April 1805, a troop of Madras Horse Artillery was raised and commanded by Captain Noble—whose name was long a household word with all Coast Artillery officers, and whose portrait, as Colonel Noble, adorned the walls of the old Madras artillery mess-house; and on the 29th of the same month (1805) two companies of Golundanze, or native artillery, were raised.*] In September 1799, orders were issued for the formation of two new regiments of cavalry, the 5th and 6th, the former to be raised at Trichinopoly, and the latter at Arcot. Drafts were made from the existing regiments, and the six regiments of cavalry were formed into two brigades, a colonel being appointed to each. The

---

* The tide of events in the Peninsula of India now chiefly bore on the Mahratta war of 1803, and the three subsequent years. The 4th Regiment was actively engaged during the Mahratta war of 1803-4, and was present at the relief of Poonah by the Cavalry Division on the 20th April 1803; it also greatly distinguished itself at the battle of Assaye (23rd September), where it charged side by side with the 19th **Dragoons**.

2nd Brigade, consisting of the 2nd, 4th, and 6th Regiments, was under the command of Colonel James Stephenson. In consequence of the increase of the establishment, Lieutenant-Colonel Thomas Dallas was posted to the 4th Regiment. On the 29th June 1800, it was directed that a 7th regiment of Native Cavalry should be raised at Arcot, to which the 4th, as usual, contributed. In May 1804, the 8th Regiment of Cavalry was raised, and the eight regiments were then formed into four brigades of two regiments each, the 4th and 8th comprising the 4th Brigade. We should have mentioned that on the 27th June 1799, orders were issued for the formation in Madras of a Body-Guard for the Governor-General, and in May 1802, it was resolved that the Madras troopers serving with the Governor-General's Body-Guard should be borne on the strength of the Madras regiments. In the middle of 1819 the designation of "Native Cavalry" was changed to "Light Cavalry," which term has been used ever since.

The Native Cavalry, stationed at Arcot, were greatly distinguished by aiding to quell the Vellore mutiny of July 1806; and their services (including those of the 4th) were fully acknowledged by the Government. In 1817, during the great Mahratta war, the 4th Light Cavalry highly distinguished itself (under Lieut. Magnay) at the battle of Mahidpoor, fought by the Commander-in-Chief, General Sir Thomas Hislop, on the 21st December.* The Regiment, as will have been seen, bears the word "Mahidpoor" on its colours and appointments in commemoration of this important event. Fighting side by side with British Cavalry, it may here be noted that, in 1813, the clothing of the Native Cavalry had been changed from red to dark blue. In 1818 it was altered by order of the Court of Directors to grey, which has been worn in Madras ever since.

The capture of the fort of Chakun was a memorable event of the year 1818, the victors being under the command of Lieut.-Colonel Deacon, Madras Establishment. Here "judgment, spirit, and decision"—the three grand requisites for taking a fort, or anything else—were exhibited in an eminent degree. "The Commander-in-Chief's approbation is also due to Captain Thew,

---

* "In August 1817," writes Colonel Wilson, "the 4th and 8th Regiments, and a detachment of H.M.'s 22nd Light Dragoons, all under the command of Major Lushington, comprised the Cavalry Brigade serving with the first or advanced division of the army of the Deccan."

commanding the Bombay Artillery, Ensign Slight, of the Bombay Engineers, employed in the service, as well as to the whole of the officers and troops of this Detachment"—one squadron 4th Cavalry, one of 8th Cavalry, 2nd battalion 17th Regiment N.I. (now 34th Chicacole Light Infantry), detachment Bombay Artillery, and Elichpoor Contingent.

Indian Regiments of Cavalry.*

It may now be of interest to note that, in 1888, there were no less than nineteen regiments of Bengal Cavalry, or twenty with the Governor-General's Body-Guard. We have already alluded to the distinguished guardians of our Indian pro-consuls of old, and our more recent Indian viceroys; but it is not generally known that the Supreme Body-Guard carries marks of distinction for field service. On the present occasion, with the uniform scarlet, and the facings dark blue, we have "Java," "Ava," "Maharajpore," "Moodkee," "Ferozeshuhur," "Aliwal," and "Sobraon." The 1st Bengal Cavalry, with yellow uniform and black facings, has "Bhurtpore," "Candahar, 1842," "Afghanistan, 1879–80." The 2nd, with blue uniform and light blue facings, "Arracan," "Sobraon," "Punjab," "Egypt, 1882," and "Tel-el-Kebir." The 3rd, with uniform drab and facings blue, "Afghanistan," "Ghuzni," "Maharajpore," "Kelat," "Moodkee," "Ferozeshuhur," "Aliwal," "Kandahar, 1880," "Afghanistan, 1879–80." The 4th, with scarlet uniform and blue facings—honorary standard, bearing a lion *passant regardant* for services in Sindh, 1844— "Afghanistan, 1879–80." The 6th (Prince of Wales's) Bengal Cavalry, with uniform blue and facings red, "Nagpore," "Panniar," "Moodkee," "Ferozeshuhur," "Sobraon," "Egypt, 1882," "Tel-el-Kebir"; Honorary Colonel, Field-Marshal H.R.H. Albert Edward, Prince of Wales, K.G., &c.

In May 1828, there were ten regiments of Light Cavalry on the Bengal Establishment. It now has five regiments of Lancers on its strength, including the 10th (Duke of Cambridge's Own) Bengal Cavalry; the 11th (Prince of Wales's Own); and the 13th (Duke of Connaught's) Bengal Cavalry (Lancers). The pleasing custom of naming Indian regiments after members of the Royal Family is now in full operation. At the end of January 1890, at a

---

* Allen's *India List*, July 1888.

grand parade, Muridki Camp, Lahore, in the presence of Prince Albert Victor, Sir F. Roberts, after some practical remarks on the use of cavalry weapons, said : He was authorised by the Queen-Empress to say that the 1st Punjab Infantry should in future be named after Prince Albert Victor of Wales.

There are now but four Madras light cavalry regiments, just half the former number; the 1st and 2nd are Lancers, and the 4th "Prince of Wales's Own" Light Cavalry. These all bear "Seringapatam" on their appointments. The 1st also "Ava," "Afghanistan, 1879-80."

Bombay has seven regiments of light cavalry, two of which, the 1st and 2nd, are Lancers. The 3rd ("Queen's Own") bears a very distinguished list of services :—"Ghuznee," "Cabool, 1842," "Hyderabad," "Persia," "Reshire," "Kooshah," "Bushire," "Central India," "Abyssinia," "Kandahar, 1880," "Afghanistan, 1879-80." In May 1828, Bombay had only three regiments of light cavalry, in addition to its two European regiments, its 26 of Native Infantry, and the Corps of Artillery and Engineers. The uniform in the Bombay Cavalry is dark green and gold, the regiments varying in the facings.

There are few more interesting or picturesque sights than Native Cavalry on parade in India; and on a field day their movements are generally, as to quickness and precision, of a very satisfactory character. In 1801-2, the effect the sight of the Bombay column of the Indian Army had on the Egyptians and Turks was, perhaps, equalled in our time, or in 1882. Of eighty years before the latter date it is written, mentioning the hero of Seringapatam, Sir David Baird :—

"The Indian Army, in very fine order, disembarked and encamped near Aboumandur. Whilst at Rhoda this army had attracted much surprise and admiration. The Turks were astonished at the novel spectacle of men of colour being so well disciplined and trained; indeed, the general magnificence of the Indian Army was so different from what they had been accustomed to see in General Hutchinson's, that the contrast could not fail of being striking. But General Baird proved to them also that his troops were not enfeebled, or himself rendered inactive, by superior comforts. Every morning at daylight he manœuvred his army for several hours, and in the evening again formed his parade. Never were finer men seen than those which composed this force, and no soldiers could possibly be in higher order."—(*History of the British Expedition to Egypt*, by Lieut. Colonel Robert Wilson.)

As before remarked, the 2nd (Prince of Wales' Own Regiment of Grenadiers) Bombay Native Infantry formed a part of the Bombay column which did so much credit to our Presidential Armies.—For some interesting Notes on the Native Armies of India, *see* Appendix C.

APPENDICES.

APPENDIX A.

Lord Napier of Magdala.

The death of Field Marshal Lord Napier of Magdala took place on Jan. 14, at his house in Eaton Square, his serious illness from influenza having been made public only on that date. His illness, indeed, was of very short duration. He was in his usual health on Jan. 11, but caught a chill in the evening, which led to an attack of influenza, with great nerve prostration. His advanced age— Lord Napier was in his 80th year—rendered such an attack extremely dangerous, and the fears of his many friends were unhappily realised by his death shortly after four o'clock on the afternoon of the 14th. The whole country has reason to deplore the loss of one who was so admirable an example of what may be accomplished by untiring energy, devotion to duty, and an indomitable spirit of enterprise.

The Right Hon. Sir Robert Cornelis Napier, G.C.B., G.C.S.I., Lord Napier of Magdala, was the son of Major C. F. Napier, of the Royal Artillery, and Catherine, daughter of Mr. Codrington Carrington, of Barbadoes. Lord Napier was born in Ceylon, in the year 1810. He was brought over to England and educated at the Military College, Addiscombe. In December, 1826, he received his commission as a second lieutenant in the Bengal Engineers. Proceeding to India, he found himself at Calcutta, to use his own language, "without friends or connections, and with nothing but his own stout heart, and his commission in his pocket." For many years his brilliant talents did not find full opportunity for their exercise. For almost a generation he was engaged in building up, bit by bit, his great reputation as a military engineer. He rendered important service in the construction of the magnificent barracks at Umballa, and in 1845 he assisted Sir Henry Lawrence in the foundation of the Lawrence Asylums, " in which hundreds of orphan children of the British soldiers in the three Presidencies are trained to habits of industry and morality."

In January 1841 Napier received his commission as captain, and having afterwards served with distinction in the Sutlej campaign he was advanced to the rank of Major. Chosen by Lawrence for the responsible post of engineer to the Durbar of Lahore, he had now an opportunity of acquiring special knowledge of the Punjab, an opportunity which he fully embraced. At the two sieges of Mooltan he acted as chief engineer, and was severely wounded. On the fall of that place, Napier accompanied General Whish in his expedition to join Lord Gough. He was present at the victory of Goojerat, being commanding engineer of the right wing of our army. He was also with General Gilbert at the surrender of the Sikh army. Napier's services having been frequently mentioned in the official military despatches, he received the brevet rank of Lieutenant-Colonel, and the war medal with two clasps for Mooltan and Goojerat.

When Colonel Napier returned to his duties as chief engineer under the Punjab Administration, he executed his long-projected plans of intersecting the country with military and commercial highways. Having provided for the efficient administration of a great province, he was summoned to Calcutta to assume the post of chief engineer of Bengal. When the Mutiny broke out, Napier acted as chief of the staff to Sir James Outram throughout the operations conducted by Havelock for the relief of Lucknow. He planned the bridging of the Goomtee river, which exercised an important influence on the operations for the overthrow of the enemy, and he was subsequently appointed to the command of the force employed to destroy the rebels reunited under Tantia Topee. The conduct of the latter undertaking, however, having been claimed by Sir Hugh Rose, Colonel Napier acted as his second in command. Napier, now Brigadier-General, gained a brilliant victory at Joura Alipore, which he followed up by the reduction of the large and strong fort of Powree. After the capture of Gwalior, he engaged in the pursuit of Tantia Topee, who was eventually taken and executed. The ribbon of the Bath was conferred upon Napier for his services during the Indian Mutiny, and he also received the thanks of Parliament.

The surrender of Pekin and the burning of the Summer Palace are events intimately associated with the names of Sir Hope Grant and Lord Napier of Magdala. In the Chinese war of 1860 he was second in command under Sir Hope Grant. In the middle of August the allied army of French and English began its march on Pekin. At the assault on the Taku forts Napier's force was chiefly engaged. Sir Hope Grant relied upon the experience of Sir Robert Napier in his measures for the capture of these formidable works. On Aug. 20 an attack was made on the Great North Fort by the British regiments of the second division, commanded in person by Napier. The day following, the fight waxed fierce, and at seven o'clock the grand magazine of the fort exploded. The defence, however, was stubbornly carried on until eight o'clock on the following morning. At this hour the storming parties—consisting of the 44th and 67th Regiments, followed by the Marines, with the pontoons—gradually closed round the rear, opened a very heavy fire on the parapet and embrasures, and in conjunction with the French effected a footing on the walls, and ultimately killed or drove the gallant defenders out of the fort at the point of the bayonet. Napier was in the thickest of the fight, and narrowly escaped death. One bullet knocked his binocular out of his hand, and another ripped open his boot. He was struck five times altogether during the assault. Sir Robert Napier followed Sir John Michel's division in the advance upon Tientsin. They remained in reserve upon the right bank of the Peiho, while Sir Hope Grant pressed forward to Pekin with the first division. Consequently, Napier was not in the action of Sept. 28 at Chang-Kia-Wan nor in the fight, some days later, which placed the allied army in position before Pekin. He was, however, sent for by Sir Hope Grant, and on his arrival with the second division the army moved forward on Pekin. The duplicity of the Chinese in the antecedent negotiations had left the Allies no option but to advance to the attack. On October 6 the Emperor's Summer Palace was taken, the French being the first to enter. As a measure of retribution for the sufferings of the European prisoners, it was set on fire by a detachment of British troops and totally destroyed. By Oct. 12 every preparation had been made for bombarding Pekin. Sir Robert Napier had brought his siege-guns into position, and the Chinese Government were informed that the cannonade would be opened on the following day at noon unless the city previously surrendered. The demands of the Allies were at length unconditionally acceded to, and the gate was thrown open to the troops.

On Feb. 14, 1861, the thanks of Parliament were voted to Sir Hope Grant, Sir Robert Napier, Admiral Hope, and others, for their services during the brief but brilliant Chinese War. Sir Robert Napier was rewarded for his services by being made Major-General and a K.C.B. He was also appointed successor to the late Sir J. Outram as a military member of the Council of India. This post he resigned in January 1865, when he was nominated to succeed Sir W. Mansfield as Commander-in-Chief at Bombay, with the local rank of Lieutenant-General. When the Order of the Star of India was instituted he was made a Knight Commander, and afterwards advanced to the dignity of a Grand Cross of that Order.

But the most remarkable military undertaking in the career of Lord Napier of Magdala was the war in Abyssinia. His successful conduct of that brief but dramatic campaign has rendered his name memorable in history. A few words will suffice to explain the origin of the war. In October 1862 Consul Cameron, who had been appointed to succeed Mr. Plowden as our representative in Abyssinia, was received by King Theodore. He was sent away with a letter for the Queen, desiring alliance against the Turks. This letter reached England in February 1863, but the Government decided not to answer it. Captain Cameron was ordered by Earl Russell to remain at Massowah, but he returned to Abyssinia in June. The following October the Rev. H. Stern, an English missionary, was beaten and imprisoned for an alleged intrusion upon Theodore. Shortly afterwards, Mr. Cameron and all British subjects and missionaries in Abyssinia were seized and imprisoned for pretended insults. The prisoners were sent to Magdala and chained like criminals. In July 1864, Mr. Hormuzd Rassam, a Chaldee Christian and first assistant British political resident at Aden, was sent on a peaceful mission to Abyssinia, Lieutenant Prideaux and Dr. Blanc being appointed to accompany him. Mr. Rassam having carried on fruitless negotiations for a year, Earl Russell appointed Mr. Gifford Palgrave on a special mission to

King Theodore. Mr. Palgrave was proceeding on his mission, when he was stopped and informed that Theodore had sent for Mr. Rassam. In January 1866, Rassam, Prideaux, and Blanc were well received by the King, and on March 12 the prisoners were released. Scarcely a month had elapsed, however, before they were again seized and imprisoned. In December 1866 Theodore received an autograph letter from the Queen, but he still did not release the prisoners. On April 16, 1867, Lord Stanley sent an ultimatum to the King, demanding the release of the captives within three months ; a second formal letter from the British Government was despatched to King Theodore; but neither of these documents arrived at its destination.

Meantime, the English Government determined to send a military expedition to Abyssinia, with the object of releasing the prisoners by force. Sir R. Napier was appointed to the command of the expedition, which was fitted out in India. The march of the army over the rocky highlands of Abyssinia was successfully and rapidly accomplished, and the troops were soon beneath the stronghold of Theodore. So little did the King relish his first engagement with the enemy that he sent Mr. Flad and Lieutenant Prideaux to the British camp with a flag of truce, in order to make terms. General Napier, however, insisted that the prisoners should be unconditionally surrendered, and the result was that they were all sent into the camp. Hostilities, however, continued, King Theodore refusing to make his own submission.

Few episodes in the history of the British army can compare, for rapid and startling effects, with the storming of Magdala. On April 13 two brigades, consisting of 5,000 men, under Sir Charles Staveley, moved forward to attack the King's stronghold. They marched along the road which led up to Fahla and through what had been Theodore's camp at Islamgee to Selassee and Magdala. As they approached the stronghold the troops opened a hot fire of shot, shell, and rockets, but this made no impression upon the gateway, which was protected by a strong stockade. The King had stationed himself here with a small band of his faithful followers, but the rest of his army had abandoned the place. The attacking troops resolutely forced their way over the stockade, and rushing into the fortress cut down the few Abyssinians, who died fighting bravely to the last. The King, nevertheless, retreated to a spot higher up, and there shot himself with a pistol before the troops could reach him. His body was found dead on the ground. There were three wounds upon him, one of which had been inflicted by his own hand. The slaughter of the enemy was great, but our entire loss was only that of ten men wounded. Thus ended one of the most brilliant and surprising of military campaigns. In an address to the army, the victorious general congratulated them on the way in which they had fulfilled the commands of their Sovereign.

The Queen despatched a congratulatory telegram to Sir Robert Napier and the army, and the news of the successful result of the Abyssinian expedition was received with the liveliest satisfaction throughout the country. On the return of General Napier, for a third time in his career he received the thanks of Parliament. Mr. Disraeli, in moving the vote, observed that happy was the man who had thrice thus been honoured by his country; and he added, respecting the expedition, that he had " transported the ordnance of Europe, on the elephants of Asia, across the mountain ranges of Africa." Mr. Gladstone, in seconding the motion, remarked that the expedition would stand upon record as a rare example among those occasions when a nation resorted to the bloody arbitrament of war, in which not one drop had been added to the cup of human suffering that forethought or humanity could spare, and in which the severest critic would find nothing to condemn.

The Queen conferred on Sir Robert Napier the dignity of a peerage, while the title of Lord Napier of Magdala, and an annuity of £2,000 per annum was granted to the new peer, to be continued to his next surviving male heir.

In 1870 Lord Napier was appointed Commander-in-Chief in India, a post which he held for the usual period of five years. On his return to England he was named Governor and Commander-in-Chief at Gibraltar, from which post he retired in 1882. In that year he was appointed a Field Marshal, and in 1886 Constable of the Tower. In the middle of 1878, when there seemed every probability of a war between this country and Russia, Lord Napier was selected for the command of an expeditionary force, and he was summoned to England to consult with the authorities of the War Office on the preliminaries of the expected campaign.

All who knew Lord Napier, says the *Times*, will bear witness to his high personal qualities. It has been pointed out by one writer that he bore a great resemblance to his old commander and friend,

Sir James Outram. "There was the same gentleness, combined with fiery valour, the same unassuming manner, coupled with a noble contempt of danger, and withal, in a not less degree, did he possess the fascination which bound to him by the ties of affection his staff and others thrown into official contact with him, no less than his personal friends." In short, in him were admirably blended those typical virtues which have made the British soldier beloved at home and feared abroad. Mr. Gladstone expressed but the general sentiment when he said in the House of Commons that "Burke would never have lamented the decay of the age of chivalry had a Robert Napier flourished in his day."

The University of Oxford conferred the honorary degree of D.C.L. upon Lord Napier of Magdala in 1878, and he was also elected a Fellow of the Royal Society. His lordship was honorary colonel of the 10th Volunteer Battalion King's Royal Rifle Corps. Lord Napier was twice married—first, in 1840, to the daughter of Dr. Pearse, of the Madras Medical Establishment. This lady, who bore him six children, died in 1849. In 1861 his lordship married, secondly, a daughter of General Scott, of the Bengal Artillery, by whom he had a family of seven children. He is succeeded in the peerage by the eldest son of his first marriage, Colonel the Hon. Robert William Napier.

The *Times*, in a leading article, says:—Great Britain loses in Lord Napier of Magdala an illustrious soldier, and one of the kindliest and most estimable of men. In the race for renown, which he was far from despising, he was often outstripped. The more rapid progress of others left no touch of bitterness on him. He never scorned to be a lieutenant because he might reasonably have expected to lead. By an experience which is almost more extraordinary, when it was his turn to go manifestly and irreversibly to the front, his ascendancy provoked no jealousy or envy. He had been nobody's enemy or maligner. His reward was to enjoy the somewhat unusual converse, and to be without detractors. Goodness and graciousness such as his are not substitutes in a campaign for professional intelligence and strategy. But in combination they become military virtues themselves. Troops believing in their chief's fortunes and abilities will let themselves be conducted to victory by a Marlborough who grudges them their bread. For one who sympathises with them, who would rather suffer than they, for whom his subordinates are all of them comrades, they will be heroic against desperate odds. Lord Napier of Magdala, if he is not to be reckoned among the foremost captains of history, had the true general's insight; and he was, moreover, an admirable English gentleman. His countrymen are proud of him, and will mourn sincerely for his death. They would be inconsolable if they did not feel that he was a type of a class of British officers. The Queen's army, both in India and at home, contains others as capable as was he, as modest and as sympathetic, as equal to the utmost demands which circumstances can make upon them, though only now and then will a conjuncture happen which, like an Abyssinian expedition, throws the light backwards along a soldier's past, and shows him to have been through the whole, potentially, as rightful an owner as was Robert Napier of the Field-Marshal's baton and of an Empire's regard.

Lord Napier had reached a ripe old age, remarks the *Standard*, and yet had not outlived his fame. The great march over the Abyssinian highlands to the heart of the mysterious kingdom of Prester John is still among the most vivid of the memories cherished by the present generation; and though the opportunity of distinction on this imposing scale came to the General when he had already passed his prime, his name was familiar for many a year after as one of the leading authorities on military policy. Of all the great men who graduated in the school of Anglo-Indian statecraft and war, none had a more honourable record than the officer who, as Commander-in-Chief in Bombay, was nominated to the command of the force to be despatched from that Presidency to secure the release of King Theodore's captives. On this the *Standard* says:—"That chapter of his life belongs to English history. With what precision and smoothness the advance to Magdala was made; how admirably contingencies had been foreseen; how waste was avoided on the one hand and a breakdown prevented on the other—all this is an old and familiar tale. It may be confessed, without disparagement to the genius displayed by the commander, that had not the mad Monarch of Abyssinia chosen to bring everything to a definite end by his act of suicidal dash, hostilities might have been prolonged in a most uncomfortable fashion, or, at any rate, the campaign would have been without its dramatic climax. But luck generally goes with good management, and everyone allows that Sir Robert Napier had fully earned his triumph by his forethought and assiduous care. The British public may be slow sometimes to discern merit that does not thrust itself upon observation; but when it is, for one reason or another, deeply interested in an enterprise, it is not niggard of rewards to the General to whose sagacity victory is due. The vanquisher of King Theodore returned to England to find that an ordeal awaited him hardly less formidable than that of leading his columns through rocky defiles and over waste plateaus."

A correspondent, "Z," writes to the morning papers:— "Through this national and irreparable loss, the opportunity is given to fill adequately the vacant place in Trafalgar Square. A *replica* of the fine equestrian statue of Lord Napier executed for Calcutta by Sir E. Boehm could probably be obtained for a moderate price. Should a subscription be opened for this purpose, I shall be glad to contribute one thousand pounds. I leave all initiative to those entitled to take it; but, in view of such subscription, I would venture to observe that Lord Napier was, above all, the friend of those who needed help, and that many of those who would most delight to give may be unable to do so as freely as they would desire. Therefore, let such memorial be made truly national by welcoming the smallest offering. Lord Napier belonged to his country alone, and on principle, as a soldier, he refused steadily to connect himself with any political party; therefore, men of all parties may conscientiously do him honour. The pedestal, if necessary, could be rebuilt."

There is a desire among military men that the remains of Lord Napier should rest side by side with those of distinguished soldiers in Westminster Abbey—notably Lord Clyde, Sir J. Outram, and Sir G. Pollock, who was Constable of the Tower from October 1871 to October 1872, and was buried at the latter date in the Abbey by the side of Lord Clyde. [Lord Napier of Magdala was buried in St. Paul's Cathedral on January 21.]

The Berlin correspondent of the *Standard* says:—The news of the death of Lord Napier of Magdala has been heard with regret in all military circles in Germany. In the German army the deceased peer was regarded as perhaps the most eminent of contemporary English generals. His achievements in Abyssinia were very highly appreciated, the details of which campaign were well known here from a German translation of Colonel Hozier's excellent work.—*Supplement to "The Overland Mail," Friday, January* 17, 1890.

APPENDIX B.

Field Operations in Upper Burma.*

No. 295, dated Simla, the 14th May 1886.

The Governor-General in Council, in directing the publication of the despatches regarding the recent operations in Upper Burma, which resulted in the capture of Mandalay and the overthrow of King Thebau, desires to place on record his cordial recognition of the admirable manner in which Lieutenant-General Sir H. N. D. Prendergast, K.C.B., V.C., and the troops under his orders, carried out the task set before them. By rapidity of movement, by skilful strategy, and by the exercise of humane forbearance, Sir Harry Prendergast has succeeded, with comparatively little loss to the force under his command, and without unnecessary bloodshed or undue severity towards the enemy, in occupying Mandalay, in capturing its King, and taking possession of the whole of Upper Burma.

For these services the warmest thanks of the Government of India are due to Sir Harry Prendergast, to the officers and men of the Naval Brigade, the British and Native Forces, the Volunteers, and the Indian Marine. They are specially due to Brigadier-Generals F. B. Norman, C.B., G. S. White, C.B., V.C., and H. H. Foord, commanding the Infantry Brigades, to Captain R. Woodward, R.N., commanding the Naval Brigade, to Colonel W. Carey, commanding Royal Artillery, Colonel G. E. L. S. Sanford, commanding Royal Engineers, Commander A. Carpenter, R.N., Indian Marine Survey, and Captain A. Campbell, the senior officer of the Indian Marine.

The Governor-General in Council also desires to record his approbation of the manner in which the various departments of the

---

* From *Tracts Military*, 663.—India Office Library.

force have carried out their duties during the campaign. The Medical Department, under Deputy Surgeon-General J. McN. Donnelly, M.D., the Commissariat and Transport Departments, under Lieutenant-Colonel A. F. Laughton and Major R. H. T. Hill, and the Ordnance Department, under Major V. C. Fisher, have proved the complete efficiency of those departments under circumstances of considerable difficulty. Lieutenant-Colonel E. W. Begbie, the Superintendent of Army Signalling, also merits the acknowledgements of the Government of India.

The Governor-General in Council is much indebted to Rear-Admiral Sir F. W. Richards, K.C.B., for the very complete and prompt manner in which His Excellency placed the whole force under his command at the disposal of the Government of India, and for the admirable manner in which the Naval Brigade was organised and equipped.

The Governor-General in Council expresses his hearty thanks to Mr. C. E. Bernard, Chief Commissioner, British Burma, Colonel E. B. Sladen, Chief Political Officer of the Force, and the other Civil officers who have assisted them during the recent operations. To Mr. Bernard His Excellency is much indebted for the valuable assistance and personal energy which so much lightened the labour of organising the force and the flotilla which carried it to Mandalay; also to Colonel Sladen, to whose tact and knowledge of the Burmese people and their language the peaceful surrender of the king was in a great measure due.

The Governor-General in Council also records his appreciation of the assistance rendered by the management of the Irrawaddy Steam Flotilla Company, and the skill shown by the commanders of their vessels.

During the operations which were being conducted in Upper Burma troubles arose on the frontiers of British Burma consequent on raids committed by lawless soldiery and dacoits. These were very promptly suppressed by the troops of the British Burma Division, who had not the good fortune to form part of the Expeditionary force. The thanks of the Government are due for these services, and specially to Major-General L. W. Buck, commanding the British Burma Division, and Mr. E. S. Symes, Secretary to the Chief Commissioner, for the very efficient measures taken by them to secure and maintain the tranquillity of the province. The labours of the troops have not yet ended, and they may still be called on to undergo privations and to perform harassing duties; but the Governor-General in Council confidently hopes that, with the aid of the Civil officers, the work of pacification and the suppression of dacoity will soon be effected.

It remains for the Governor-General in Council to place on record his gratitude to the local Governments and Army Departments for the manner in which the Expeditionary Force was organised and despatched. On the 19th October warning was given to the Commander-in-Chief in India, the Government of Madras, and the Director of Marine, that an Expeditionary Force would probably be required for Burma; and on the 21st October orders were issued for the despatch of a division of three brigades of infantry, six batteries of artillery, six companies of sappers, and a naval brigade, part of the force embarking at Calcutta and part at Madras. Embarkation took place simultaneously from both places on the 1st November, and by the 6th November the entire force had sailed from India completely equipped for service. On the 14th the force which was in course of concentration on the British Burma frontier crossed the frontier and hostilities commenced. On the 28th November, Mandalay had fallen and the king surrendered. Few expeditions have been conducted to a successful issue with such rapidity and completeness.

The Governor-General in Council desires to express his cordial appreciation of the energy displayed by the Government of Madras, the provincial Commander-in-Chief of the Madras Army, and the Departments working under their orders, for the expeditious and efficient manner in which every detail of the organisation and embarkation of the Madras force was carried out. The Government of Madras have very fully acknowledged the services of the following officers as deserving of notice, and the Governor-General in Council wishes now to add to these commendations an expression of his own appreciation of their services:—

Colonel H. P. Hawkes, Commissary-General.

Major-General S. H. E. Chamier, Inspector-General of Ordnance.

Surgeon-General I. Irvine, M.D., Medical Staff.

Surgeon-General M. C. Furnell, Indian Medical Department.

Lieutenant I. H. Taylor, R.N.R., Master Attendant.

The Governor-General in Council also desires to thank the Government of Bombay for their cordial response to the requisitions made by the Government of India, and for the rapidity with which their troops were equipped and despatched.

The Governor-General in Council takes this opportunity to thank Sir Donald Stewart, who was Commander-in-Chief in India when the Expeditionary Force in India was organised, for his co-operation and advice; also His Excellency Sir Frederick Roberts for the assistance rendered since his arrival in India. The Governor-General in Council also acknowledges the services rendered by the Adjutant-General and Quartermaster-General in India, and the Staff and Departmental officers who, under their orders, have carried out the various details connected with the organisation and despatch of the force.

The thanks of the Government of India are due to the following officers and their subordinates for the energetic part taken by them in the equipment of the force :—

Colonel I. V. Hunt, C.B., Commissary-General-in-Chief.

Colonel R. C. Low, C.B., Commissary-General for Transport.

Major-General T. E. Hughes, C.I.E., Director-General of Ordnance in India.

Surgeon-General C. D. Madden, Medical Staff.

Surgeon-General B. Simpson, M.D., Indian Medical Department.

Colonel B. Walton, C.I.E., Superintendent and Agent for Army Clothing.

Captain I. Hext, R.N., Director of Marine, for the promptitude and efficiency with which the transports were taken up and fitted; Captain G. O'B. Carew, C.I.E., Deputy Director; and Commander H. A. Street, R.N., Assistant Director.

From Major-General Sir F. D. Baker, K.C.B., Adjutant-General in India, to the Secretary to the Government of India, Military Department. No. 1465 *(camp), dated Fort William, the* 3rd *February* 1886.

I am directed by the Commander-in-Chief to submit, for the information of Government, the accompanying despatch from the General officer commanding the Burma Field Force, detailing the operations carried on by the troops under his command from the date of embarkation at Rangoon to the capture of Mandalay and the surrender of King Thebau.

2. His Excellency desires to record his appreciation of the able

manner in which Lieutenant-General Sir Henry Prendergast, K.C.B., V.C., has carried out his orders; and considers that great credit is due to him and all concerned for the rapidity with which the operations have been brought to a successful issue with so small a sacrifice of life.

From Lieutenant-General Sir H. N. D. Prendergast, K.C.B., V.C., Commanding the Burma Field Force, to the Adjutant-General in India, No. 38 L., dated Mandalay, the 13th January, 1886.

I have the honour to forward a despatch containing an account of the operations carried on by the force under my command from the date of the embarkation of the troops composing it at Rangoon until the date of the capture of Mandalay and surrender of King Thebau.

2. I have the honour to transmit with the despatch the following reports, returns, &c.

Return of casualties at Minhla and Gwegyaung-Kamyo.
Return of ordance captured.

3. My thanks are due to many for their assistance during the Expedition, and I am only awaiting the lists of those whom the Brigadier-Generals desire to bring specially to notice to submit them for the favourable consideration of the Government of India.

From Lieutenant-General H. N. D. Prendergast, K.C.B., V.C., Commanding the Burma Field Force, to the Secretary to the Government of India, Military Department. No. 39 L., dated Head-quarters, Mandalay, the 14th January 1886.

On the 12th November, having arranged the embarkation of troops and departments, and seen a considerable force on board the river steamers and flats, I left Rangoon for Prome.

2. On my arrival at Thayetmyo, on the evening of the 13th November 1885, I received a message from the Foreign Department informing me that, as the Burman reply to the ultimatum was unsatisfactory, I should advance upon Mandalay when my military preparations were complete.

3. Having heard from the Deputy Commissioner that the

Burman outposts had been strengthened on the frontier, that the villagers within British territory were alarmed and deserting their houses, and that a King's steamer with two flats had brought down a great body of soldiers to within six or eight miles of the frontier, and that the intention was to sink the flats as an obstruction, I ordered the armed steamer *Irrawaddy*, of the Indian Government, and the launch *Kathleen* to move at daylight on the 14th, to reconnoitre the river to a distance of not more than 30 miles, and to capture the King's steamer and flats.

4. On the 14th November I received His Excellency the Commander-in-Chief's orders to carry out operations with the utmost vigour and rapidity possible; and on that day the *Irrawaddy*, under command of Commander W. R. Clutterbuck, R.N., of H.M.S. *Woodlark*, and the *Kathleen*, under Lieutenant F. P. Trench, of H.M.S. *Turquoise*, found the King's steamer, with the attendant barges, near Nyaungbeumaw, on the right bank of the Irrawaddy, about 28 miles above Thayetmyo; and having accepted and returned the fire of the enemy's shore batteries at close quarters, the *Irrawaddy* cleared the decks of the steamer and flats with her machine guns, and the crews jumped overboard. The Italians, Camotto and Molinari, were among the fugitives. The batteries were repassed at very short range, and the prizes towed down by the capturing steamers. The operations were rendered difficult by the rapidity of the current opposite the batteries. Commander Clutterbuck, Lieutenant Trench, and the officers and crews of the *Irrawaddy* and *Kathleen* deserve great credit for their courage, and the Indian Marine officers and lascars serving on board the former did their duty with perfect coolness under fire.

5. The little *Kathleen*, with her crew of 16 men, repeatedly engaged the shore battery of nine guns at 50 yards' range. Her loss was one man severely wounded, namely, Robert Hutchison, gunner's mate, of H.M.S. *Turquoise*.

6. The prizes were valuable not only as an addition to the means of transport for the Expeditionary Force, but also because their loss delayed the retreat of the enemy somewhat, and prevented them from closing the channel near Nyaungbeumaw according to the plans of the Italians, which were found in one of the flats. On the afternoon of the 14th the leading steamers, containing the Bengal Brigade, anchored at Thayetmyo.

7. On the 15th November, in order to give confidence to the villagers near the frontier and to re-establish telegraphic communication between the frontier and Allanmyo, I posted two companies of the 2nd Bengal Infantry at Laingha, on the frontier, and steamed 15 miles, north of the frontier, with all troops that had come up, detail as per margin.

No. 9–1st Cinque Ports Division, Royal Artillery.

3rd Infantry Brigade, under Brigadier-General Norman, C.B., namely—
Royal Welsh Fusiliers.
2nd Regiment Bengal Infantry.
11th Regiment Bengal Infantry.

2nd Battalion Liverpool Regiment.
1st Madras Pioneers.
12th Madras Infantry.

8. On the 16th the steamers weighed anchor at daybreak, and at 9.15 A.M. a landing was effected at Zaunygyandaung, a village on the right bank, two miles below the batteries which had fired on *Irrawaddy* and *Kathleen* on the 14th. The column commanded by Colonel W. Rowlandson, of the 12th Madras Infantry, consisted of the Liverpool Regiment, the 1st Madras Pioneers, and the 12th Madras Infantry.

9. The country on the right bank consists of a series of small steep hills, covered with trees and brushwood. The landing place was selected so that the enemy could not see the debarkation.

10. Colonel Rowlandson was ordered to lead his force so as to attack the rear of the batteries and prevent the escape of the enemy. During the advance of the Infantry, the *Irrawaddy*, lying 3,000 yards below the enemy's batteries, fired occasional shells into them, to which the enemy replied, but with no effect. Nothing could be more picturesque than the advance of the Liverpool Regiment from hillock to hillock, while the batteries were kept amused by the shells from the *Irrawaddy*. The turning movement was remarkably well executed, and would have been successful had not the enemy been warned of their danger by pôngyis, or priests, who, protected by their yellow garb, had been allowed to watch the operations of our regiments.

The Burmans fled from their batteries panic-stricken. I caused the 11 guns and carriages found in the batteries to be destroyed, as they could not easily be removed; and I saw the stockade and barracks burnt. While these operations were on hand, the Mule Battery, 9–1st Cinque Ports Division Royal Artillery, and 1st Battalion Royal Welsh Fusiliers, under the command of Brigadier-

APPENDIX B. 395

General Norman, C.B., landed, and by a circuitous march reached the east face of the stockade of Singbaungwe, where it had been reported that a large force had assembled. The stockade had, however, been deserted, and was burnt. The force re-embarked late in the afternoon.

11. The leading steamers anchored that night above Taunggwen, about 34 miles above Thayetmyo, and at daybreak, on the 17th, were directed to advance to Malun and Patanago, about 6 miles on the right and left banks of the river respectively, and about 40 miles from Thayetmyo.

12. As the garrison of Gwegyaung-Kamyo were busily employed in strengthening the works there, which are on the left bank, about 44 miles from Thayetmyo, it was deemed advisable to attack at once.

The troops present were therefore told off as follows :—

1ST BRIGADE.

Liverpool Regiment.
1st Madras Pioneers.
21st Regiment Madras Infantry.
25th Regiment Madras Infantry.

Under Brigadier-General Foord, to march from Patanago, 8 miles, in order to attack the fort of Gwegyaung-Kamyo from the east.

The head-quarters with the 1st Brigade. Brigadier-General White, C.B., V.C., who arrived somewhat later, to bring up the Cinque Ports Battery Royal Artillery, and Hampshire Regiment in support of General Foord's brigade. The landing of the troops at Patanago could not be seen from the fort of Gwegyaung-Kamyo, on account of intervening hills, and the landing of the brigade at Malun could not, for a similar reason, be seen from Minhla.

13. The following troops—

12th Regiment Madras Infantry, | 2nd Regiment Bengal Infantry,
11th Regiment Bengal Infantry,

under command of Colonel T. N. Baker, of the 2nd Bengal Infantry, were ordered to march from Malun to endeavour to capture the Wungyi, or Governor-General, in his palace, west of Minhla, and were ordered to re-embark at Minhla, about 45 miles above Thayetmyo. Majors Macneill and Hill were attached as staff officers, and Commander J. Durnford, R.N., with three seamen of H.M.S. *Mariner* and three privates of the Royal Welsh Fusiliers, were attached to effect demolitions. Brigadier-General Norman, C.B., and the Royal Welsh Fusiliers had not arrived then, but he took command before evening of the brigade on the right bank.

14. The I.M.S. *Irrawaddy* and the launch *Kathleen* were directed to engage Gwegyaung-Kamyo at long ranges for two hours after the landing of General Foord's brigade, or till the British flag should be hoisted at the white pagoda of Gwegyaung, half a mile east of the Kamyo.

15. The first brigade advanced from the landing place at Patanago at 10 o'clock, and marched for about two hours and forty minutes by a narrow path over the hills and through the thick jungle to the white pagoda. Two pickets of the enemy were driven in, but no resistance was made, the pickets retiring northwards; not to the fort. The Liverpool Regiment occupied the high ground east of the fort which commands the works, and the enemy, being completely surprised by the fire of the soldiers from the east, when they were prepared for attack from the south, west, and north-west, but had not a gun bearing eastward, promptly fled by the north-west gate as the British soldiers advanced with a rush.

16. Of the 1,700 men who, under the command of Maung Sanhla Sin Bo, garrisoned the fort in the morning, only Maung Sin Hle Sin Sya, the second in command, and a lieutenant, both dangerously wounded, and two wounded soldiers, remained in Gwegyaung-Kamyo; the other wounded men were carried off. Twenty-one guns and ordnance stores were found in the fort.

17. At 11 A.M. Colonel Baker's force left Malun for the Wun's palace, and after an hour's march the skirmishers of the 12th Madras Infantry, which was the leading regiment, were suddenly checked by a heavy musketry fire from apparently thick and thorny jungle. While the 2nd Bengal Infantry turned the enemy's right flank the 12th Regiment rallied, and reinforced by the 11th Bengal Infantry gallantly broke through the thorny screen, tore over the entrenchment and breastwork of carts and bamboos which concealed the enemy, and dislodged them from the village of Yinna.

18. Thence the brigade moved towards the position which contained the palace and Minhla pagoda; the plinth of the latter was defended by field artillery and musketry; the country was difficult, and the

enemy's fire was hot; but the brilliant leading of the officers, and the dashing onslaught of the men, prevailed against the undisciplined bravery of the Burmans, who broke and fled, leaving six guns as trophies to the victors. The 11th Bengal Infantry bore the brunt of the combat.

19. The brigade then advanced on Minhla redoubt as rapidly as possible by winding paths between gardens and enclosures, the 12th Madras Infantry on the right, the 11th Bengal Infantry in the centre, and the 2nd Bengal Infantry on the left, under the fire of a 7-pounder, two wall pieces, and the musketry of the defenders.

Before the redoubt had been completely surrounded by the regiments which were trying to keep down the fire of the defenders, Lieutenant-Colonel R. J. B. Simpson, of the 12th Madras Infantry, getting together a few brave men of the 12th Madras Infantry and 11th Bengal Infantry, charged up a steep and broken ramp that led from the ground west of the work to the terreplein of the work. Foremost among the stormers were Lieutenants H. T. D. Wilkinson 12th Madras Infantry, and W. K. Downes, 11th Bengal Infantry, the former of whom was severely and dangerously wounded, receiving no less than five sword-cuts. A footing having been gained within the redoubt, supports immediately followed and a hot fire was poured into the Burmans, some of whom found shelter in the casemates, whilst others escaped by the east gate, but only to meet the 2nd Bengal Infantry, to whose fire they were so exposed that many were shot on land and the remainder, having taken to the water, were either shot or drowned in the river. Within the redoubt were taken 276 prisoners, six guns of cast iron, five brass rifled guns, and two wall pieces. The redoubt was prepared chiefly for attack on the river face. Our loss was, 1 officer killed 4 officers wounded, 3 men killed and 23 men wounded. All the wounded, British and Burman, were on board the floating hospital that night. The enemy's loss was about 170 killed and 40 wounded.

20. The navy were employed first in engaging the Gwegyaung-Kamyo for two hours, afterwards the *Irrawaddy* and *Kathleen* proceeded to attack the Minhla redoubt and a masked battery of four guns on the right bank that opened on them half-a-mile below the redoubt. The service thus performed of attracting the attention of the Burmans was of great value to the force attacking by land.

21. On the 18th the detachments shown in the margin were detailed to garrison Gwegyaung-Kamyo and Minhla respectively, and orders were given for the demolition of the former, and for the construction of defensive works for the latter.

GWEGYAUNG-KAMYO.
One company Liverpool Regiment.
Four companies 2nd Bengal Infantry.
One company Bengal Sappers.

MINHLA.
One company Liverpool Regiment.
Two companies 2nd Bengal Infantry.
Two guns Bombay Mountain Battery.

The I.M.S. *Irrawaddy, Palow, Ngawoon,* and *Kathleen,* were sent ahead to reconnoitre. The Italian officers, Commotto and Captain Molinari, surrendered to Commander Carpenter, R.N., of the *Ngawoon.*

22. On the 19th November the force advanced to Minbu, 58 miles from Thayetmyo. A barge, containing two 6·3" howitzers, was unavoidably lost.

23. On the 20th November the force advanced to Yenangyaung, 78 miles from Thayetmyo.

24. On the 21st November the force advanced to Silemyo, 115 miles from Thayetmyo.

25. On the 22nd November the force advanced to Pagan, 145 miles from Thayetmyo. The I.M.S. *Irrawdddy* and the *Ngawoon, Palow, Yunan,* and *Kathleen,* engaged the enemy's battery on a cliff at Nyaungu, were uninjured by its fire, drove the enemy from it, and having landed a party destroyed eleven guns and secured two king's steamers that the enemy had sunk; a flat that had been towed by them was found aground some miles below Pagan. These vessels would have been sunk in the channel if the enemy had had time to place them there.

Two companies Liverpool Regiment.
Two guns Bombay Mountain Battery.
No. 5 company Bengal Sappers.
Four companies 11th Bengal Infantry.

26. On the 23rd November the troops shown in the margin were landed at Pagan, and the force advanced six miles.

27. It may be well here to describe the usual formation of the force during the advance. The I.M.S. *Irrawaddy* with the *Kathleen* took up station some miles ahead to reconnoitre; the *Ngawoon,* commanded by Commander Alfred Carpenter, R.N., followed to survey and buoy the deep-water channels; then came the head-quarter steamer *Doowoon*; and, following her in succession, the *Palow, Yunan, Ananda, Ataran, Panthay, Shoaymyo, Burma, Shintsawboo, Ashley Eden, Yankeentoun, Irrawaddy*

(Irrawaddy Flotilla Company's), *Aloungpyah,* *Thooreah,* *Talifoo,* *Rangoon, Mindoon, Paulang,* and *Waikema,* in signal column line ahead at two cables distance. Owing to the difficulty of the navigation, the steamers frequently went aground, and it was not easy to keep station. Communication was maintained in a great measure by the military signallers under Lieutenant-Colonel Begbie of the Madras Army, and their devotion to duty by day and by night was most praiseworthy. Without them it would have been impossible to carry on operations with the necessary rapidity, as there were but few launches with the force, and they were in constant motion.

28. During the night the fleet was anchored in the same order at distance of one cable apart, and two armed steam launches, manned by blue-jackets, were sent a mile ahead as guard-boats with fire-grapnels and blue lights on board. Crews were also held in readiness to man all the boats of the Naval Brigade to proceed, if necessary, to their assistance with gun-cotton charges, &c., so that any floating obstacle might at once be destroyed or towed into the bank.

29. On the 24th November the Hampshire Regiment and Sappers landed at Kaunywa, 166 miles above Thayetmyo, to drive the enemy from his entrenchments and to carry off the guns from a battery that had fired on the *Ngawoon,* survey ship, the previous evening, and had been silenced by the accuracy of her fire. There were no casualties last night or this morning.

30. The force then proceeded to an anchorage near Myingyan, 180 miles from Thayetmyo, whence the enemy could be seen in considerable force at a stockade about three miles from the left bank of the Irrawaddy below Myingyan. Gold umbrellas were to be seen moving about in the stockade, and columns of soldiers, dressed some in scarlet, some in white, were evidently marching towards the river.

31. Captain Woodward, R.N., gives the following graphic description of what followed:—"The Naval Brigade, assisted by the Royal Artillery in the *White Swan,* with the *Yunan,* and a gun-barge with the *Ataran,* were ordered to engage. Fire was opened from the *Palow's* barge, and taken up by the other ships. On nearing the bank, small improvised batteries were found armed with small guns and riflemen. A hot fire was kept up for some time, the enemy retreating into the tall grass in rear of the bat-

teries. The ships slowly advanced, silencing the batteries as they proceeded. On nearing the upper end of the town, the enemy was found to be strongly entrenched and supported by a battery commanding the river. The enemy here showed a more determined resistance, and it was not until 6 P.M. that the fire slackened. During the night occasional shots were fired, and the enemy was finally dislodged and routed at daylight next morning."

32. Late in the evening the *Kathleen* returned from her station in front to the head-quarters' ship, and orders were issued for the landing of the troops on the morrow.

33. On the 25th November part of the force disembarked to dislodge the enemy, who were commanded by the celebrated Hle Thin Atwin Woon from his entrenchments; but finding that his ingeniously constructed works that commanded the river were deserted, and hearing that the rear guard had left the stockade inland, twenty guns were destroyed, and the troops re-embarked. The detachment detailed in the margin was left in the entrenchments that had been laid out and commenced during the day by the Sappers and Pioneers. The force then advanced to Yandabo, 194 miles from Thayetmyo, the head-quarters' ship anchoring opposite the tree under which the treaty of Yandabo was signed in 1826.

> Two guns Bombay Mountain Battery.
> Two companies Liverpool Regiment.
> Four companies 11th Bengal Native Infantry.
> One company Bombay Sappers.

34. At daylight on the 26th November a large flat drifted down towards the fleet; she was caught and sent to Myingyan. At 7.30 A.M. the fleet, having been delayed by fog, started and passed through a line of boats filled with stones prepared for sinking. These boats were cast adrift before the steamers towing flats advanced.

35. At 4 P.M. on the 26th November, near Nagaung, 223 miles from Thayetmyo, a Burman state barge, flying the king's flag at the stern and a flag of truce at the bow, paddled down the stream, was taken in tow by one of the steam launches, and brought alongside the *Doowoon*, head-quarters' ship. In the barge were—

(i.) Myaung Shoay-ak Myaung Atwin Wun, the Minister of the Interior.

(ii.) U-Shoay-ak Watima Wundauk.

Colonel Sladen met the envoys at the gangway, and after being presented to me they produced a note, unsigned, in a cover bearing the Royal Peacock seal, of which the following is a translation:—

"*From His Excellency the Prime Minister to the Commander-in-Chief of the English War Vessels. Dated 4th decrease of Tazaungmôn 1247 (25th November 1885).*

"1. Although the treaty negotiated at Simla was not concluded, the Burmese Government were under the impression that the former friendly conditions would still prevail, and they could not, therefore, believe that the English Government would make war on Upper Burma.

"2. The Burmese Government have always had at heart the welfare and prosperity of the English people. They have all along protected the interests of the Irrawaddy Company's teak trade, and the general interests of all British subjects.

"3. We are desirous of still further protecting British interests as far as lies in our power, both at present and in all future time.

"4. The last letter (ultimatum) forwarded by the British Government contained very important political matter, and our sovereign regrets that the time allowed was too short to allow of serious deliberation.

"5. The English Government ought to have known that the only reason why the Burmese Government in their reply to the said letter did not freely concede all the demands made was because we were not allowed sufficient time for deliberation. It must have been apparent from the tenor of our reply that the Burmese Government was desirous of remaining on terms of amity and friendship.

"6. The Burmese Government did not wholly reject the rights and privileges claimed by the British Government, and we are grieved to find that the English Government, which has always been so friendly, should in the present instance have made immediate war on us. We have simply resisted in order to maintain the reputation of the kingdom and the honour of the Burmese people.

"7. The English are renowned for their just and straightforward action in all matters (political). We look forward, therefore, with confidence to their doing what is just and proper in the present instance.

"8. The country of Burma is one which deserves justice and consideration. We believe that it will receive this consideration at the hands of the English Government.

"9. If this is granted, the kingdom of Burma need not be annexed. It is well to remember, too, that on a former occasion Her Most Gracious Majesty the Queen-Empress was pleased to declare publicly that there was no intention on the part of the English Government to annex Burma, unless such a step was necessitated on good cause shown. As no such cause exists, the Great Powers of Europe should not have it in their power to say that the Royal declaration has not been faithfully observed.

"10. In addition to the rights and privileges already granted in our reply to your ultimatum, His Majesty the King of Burma has now declared his will to concede all the other demands which were not at first allowed, because we had not sufficient time to bring them under our consideration.

"11. His Majesty the King is well disposed (in mind and heart), he is straightforward and just, and expects the English Government will act in accordance with the wishes expressed in this letter.

"12. By so doing the world will have no cause to say that the English Government have acted unjustly, or with a disregard of the rules of international law.

"13. The English Government entered our country and attacked us with a number of war vessels. We were obliged to resist. We now desire that hostilities shall cease, and we trust the English Government will meet us half-way, and enter into a treaty by which friendly intercourse may be resumed between the two great countries."

To which the following reply was sent:—

"General Prendergast begs to inform the Ken Wun Mengyi, in reply to his letter of this date, that, acting in accordance with the instructions he has received from the Viceroy and Governor-General of India, it is quite out of his power to accept any offer or proposal which would affect the movement of the troops under his command on Mandalay.

"No armistice, therefore, can be at present granted; but if King Thebaw agrees to surrender himself, his army, and his capital to British arms, and if the European residents at Mandalay are all found uninjured in person and property, General Prendergast promises to spare the King's life and to respect his family.

"He also promises not to take further military action against Mandalay beyond occupying it with a British force, and stipulates that the matters in dispute between the countries shall be negotiated on such terms as may be dictated by the British Government.

"A reply to this communication must be sent so as to reach General Prendergast by 4 A.M. to-morrow.

"By order,
"E. B. SLADEN, Col.,

"S.S. *Doowoon*,   "Chief Civil Officer,
"The 26th November 1885."   "Burma Field Force.

36. While the note was being translated, the envoys stated that the Europeans in Mandalay were uninjured. As both notes had to be translated, and copies of the letter in English and Burmese were requisite, the interview lasted about an hour. The *Doowoon*, which had been leading the column, eased speed, and allowed the fleet to pass on, so that the Burman officials could form some estimate of the British force, and might feel assured that time would not be granted for diplomacy.

37. After the interview, Colonel Sladen, with half-a-dozen sailors of the Royal Navy, boarded a king's war steamer that had been guarded by the *Kathleen* till his arrival. The envoys ordered the crew to surrender her. She flew the Burmese standard, was armed with six guns, her decks were barricaded, she had Burman soldiers on board, and was lying with steam up close to the shore. When the steamer approached, most of the soldiers deserted, but fifty-seven of them were made prisoners, and a party of the *Kathleen's* crew took possession of her and brought her up to the fleet. She is in good order, and a valuable prize.

38. The fleet anchored seven miles below Ava. Orders were issued for the attack on Ava.

39. On the 27th November the force advanced at daylight, but was delayed for an hour and a half by dense fog. After the landing-place below Ava had been sighted, the envoys again came in

their gilded boats with forty rowers, bearing a royal mandate received by telegraph, of which the following is a translation :—

"*No. 1 sent by Royal Order.*

"*From the Hlot Dau to Bo Mhu, Atwin Wun; Peu Myosa Maythit, Atwin Wun; Kyauk-Myaung, Atwin Wun; Wet Ma Sut, Wundauk; Pendalai, Wundauk.*

"When the English ships arrive you are on no account to fire on them. Let all the troops keep quiet. Publish this abroad everywhere. The King concedes unconditionally to all the demands made by the Commander of English as contained in his letter of yesterday's date. You are to let the English commander know this as quickly as possible."

40. In addition to the redoubt of Ava, the fortified walls of Ava, the Sagaing redoubt, and the redoubt of Thaybyadan, other entrenchments and batteries had been prepared, and the river had been blocked from bank to bank so that our vessels and troops might be detained under the fire of the enemy's artillery.

41. Having explained to the envoys that I could not leave a large force with artillery in my rear, I demanded the immediate surrender of the arms in Ava and the adjacent works. They considered reference to Mandalay necessary on this point; but, while awaiting the reply, the envoys accompanied me on board the *Palow* to point out the easiest place for making a passage through the barrier; and the *Palow* advanced to Ava, the other ships keeping station.

42. After a channel had been found and buoyed out by Commander Carpenter, R.N., I again demanded the arms, and when there was still delay, I signalled to the ships placed under Captain Woodward's orders to prepare to engage the batteries, and to the troops to land. On this, one envoy went on shore and at once returned with the royal mandate for the surrender of the arms.

43. Colonel Sladen went on shore at Ava with the envoys to give orders for the guns and muskets to be relinquished quietly; the Royal Welsh Fusiliers landed, and the Burmans filing past, laid hundreds of muskets, rifles, and swords at their feet; and fatigue parties of his brigade were employed by Brigadier-General Norman till after dark in carrying off guns from the batteries

and small arms from the places where they had been laid down. So at Sagaing and Thabyadan the guns and small arms were taken by Brigadier-General White and his brigade on the afternoon of the 27th, and early on the 28th all the disbanded soldiers were set free. A return of ordnance captured is appended.

44. The three redoubts were designed and built by the Italian Barbieri. Those of Ava and Thabyadan are provided with excellent casemates. Sagaing and Ava redoubts are very well placed for disputing the passage of the river at the point where the fairway is contracted by natural rocks and shoals.

45. On the 28th November the force advanced to Mandalay. No soldiery appeared, but thousands of peaceful Burmans crowded to the bank to see the fleet. In the afternoon the force marched unopposed to the palace and took charge of the gates of the city and palace. Colonel Sladen had a long interview with the King in the palace. Brigadier-General White, C.B., V.C., remained with Hazara Battery, Hampshire Regiment, and 1st Pioneers to guard His Majesty.

46. On the 29th November, at 2 P.M., accompanied by my staff and the principal Ministers of State, I visited the King in a pavilion within the precincts of the palace, and assured him that it was for the good of his country that he should leave it without delay. The Queen-mother and Queens were present during the interview. At 3.30 P.M. Thebaw and the ladies of his family were led forth from the palace through the throne room, between avenues of British soldiers, to the bullock carriages prepared to carry them to the s.s. *Thooreah*, in which, guarded by two companies of the Liverpool Regiment, and escorted by the *Ngawoon*, manned by the Royal Navy, they were conveyed to Rangoon. Brigadier-General Norman, C.B., commanded the escort, consisting of No. 9, 1st Brigade Cinque Ports Division, Royal Artillery, the Mounted Infantry Corps, Royal Welsh Fusiliers, and the 23rd Madras Light Infantry.

47. At Mandalay were captured not only 1,177 guns, 369 wall-pieces, and 6,723 stand of small arms, but also the royal dockyard, powder factory, saw-mills, gun-factory, arsenal, and powder magazine, some Crown jewellery, and more than a lakh of peacock rupees.

48. A return of casualties from all causes will be forwarded with the next despatch. The enemy's casualties included about 180 killed, 333 prisoners, and 100 wounded, but cannot be correctly estimated.

From Major-General Sir T. D. Baker, K.C.B., Adjutant-General in India, to the Secretary to the Government of India, Military Department. No. 1673 A., dated Simla, the 28*th April* 1886.

With reference to this office No. 1465 (camp), dated the 3rd February 1886, submitting a despatch from Lieutenant-General Sir Harry Prendergast relative to the military operations in Upper Burma, and to the report of Major-General Buck with regard to the operations in Lower Burma, received under Military Department No. 352 B.B., dated the 5th March 1886, I am now directed by the Commander-in-Chief to forward, for submission to the Government of India, the accompanying despatch from Lieutenant-General Sir Harry Prendergast, in which the services of the officers and troops engaged in the campaign are brought to notice.

2. The Commander-in-Chief considers that the eminent success which attended this Expedition is attributable to the able manner in which the General Officer commanding carried out his instructions, to the gallant and good service of the officers and troops engaged, and to the efficient organisation of the force.

3. The Commander-in-Chief has much pleasure in bringing to the notice of Government the excellent service rendered by the Royal Navy and Royal Marines, and their cordial co-operation, which tended greatly to the success of the Expedition.

4. In conclusion, I am directed to state, for the information of Government, that in a supplementary despatch received from General Prendergast, dated the 31st ultimo, the following officers have been brought to notice :—

Captain V. A. Schalch, 11th Bengal Infantry, for good service rendered as Brigade-Major.
Lieutenant C. P. Fendall, Royal Artillery.
Lieutenant W. H. Dobbie, 26th Madras Infantry.

From Lieutenant-General Sir H. N. D. Prendergast, K.C.B., V.C., Commanding Forces in Burma, to the Adjutant-General in India. Dated Rangoon, the 26*th March* 1886.

In continuation of my despatch dated 14th January 1886, reporting the operations of the Burma Expeditionary Force from their commencement to the surrender of Mandalay on the 29th

APPENDIX B. 407

November 1885, I have the honour to solicit a reference to my journal of operations since that date, from which it will appear that the important towns of Mogaung, Bhamo, and Shwebo have been occupied to the north of Mandalay, and the stations of Ningyan, Yemethen, Mahlaing, and Kyauksè established to the eastward towards the Shan frontier, Ava, Sagaing, Alôn, and Taungdwingyi being furnished with detachments. Several subsidiary posts have also been located in places where the presence of troops has been considered desirable.

2. The object in establishing these stations and posts has been the assertion throughout the country of our military ascendency, the maintenance of our lines of communications, the repression of dacoity, and the protection of the well-behaved inhabitants.

Though the work upon which the troops have been engaged has been of an important and arduous nature, it was not such as to render necessary special despatches from me relating to the various minor affairs which have occurred in different parts of the country.

3. The rapid success which attended the expedition to Mandalay was mainly due, firstly, to the efficient organisation of the force employed; secondly, to the very complete information on record regarding the country and its resources; and, thirdly, to the hearty and efficient co-operation of all those who were engaged in the campaign.

4. To the officers, soldiers, and sailors of the Burma Expeditionary Force my acknowledgments are due for willing obedience and cheerful discharge of duties under varied and often trying conditions of service.

Discipline has been well maintained throughout,

5. I would now submit for the favourable consideration of His Excellency the Commander-in-Chief and of Government the names of officers and others who have more specially assisted me in the conduct of this campaign:—

- Major-General L. W. Buck, commanding the British Burma Division, who most loyally co-operated with me in preparing the force for service in Upper Burma, and subsequently organized the column which operated from Toungoo.
- Brigadier-General F. B. Norman, C.B., commanding the 3rd Brigade.

Brigadier-General H. H. Foord, commanding the 1st Brigade.
Brigadier-General G. S. White, C.B., V.C., commanding the 2nd Brigade.

To each of these officers and their staff my thanks are due.

The judgment and military experience of Brigadier-General Norman, C.B., were highly valuable, and fully justified me in entrusting the command at Bhamo to him at a critical juncture.

To Brigadier-General Foord was entrusted the duty of capturing the redoubt of Gwegyaung-Kamyo.

Brigadier-General White commanded at Mandalay during my absence at Bhamo, and by his energy and determination succeeded in quelling the insurrection around Mandalay. He is an officer of high military capacity.

Colonel D. Shaw, Madras Staff Corps, commanding at Thayetmyo, protected my base at Thayetmyo by energetic action against the insurgents on the frontier.

Colonel T. N. Baker, 2nd Bengal Light Infantry, commanded effectively the column that successfully attacked Minhla on the 17th November 1885, and has since then commanded the garrison at that station.

Colonel W. Carey, R.A., commanded the Royal Artillery during the campaign. From the first organisation of the siege-train he has been conspicuous by the zeal and ability which he has brought to bear on all matters connected with his arm of the service. He contributed materially to the Intelligence Branch by publishing notes taken when he was on a visit to Mandalay a short time before the declaration of war.

Colonel P. H. F. Harris, 11th Bengal Infantry, gallantly commanded his fine regiment at Minhla, and has commanded the garrison of Myingyan since its establishment. He has shown great energy and zeal in organising flying columns for the pacification of the district, and has been well supported by the officers and men of the detachments.

Colonel G. E. L. S. Sanford, R.E., Commanding Royal Engineer to the force, has afforded me, in addition to his professional assistance, very efficient aid as Chief Engineer of Public Works after the occupation of Mandalay. As a Staff officer he is invaluable.

Colonel H. M. Bengough, Assistant Adjutant and Quartermaster-General, so organised the staff and conducted his duties that there has been no friction. He is an officer remarkable for energy, tact, zeal, and knowledge of military affairs.

Colonel W. P. Dicken, Madras Staff Corps, Commandant, 3rd Madras Light Infantry, commanded the Toungoo column, and achieved a rapid and well-merited success.

Colonel J. C. Auchinleck, R.A., has commanded the line of communication with firmness and discretion.

Colonel John Tilly, commanding the 1st Battalion Royal Welsh Fusiliers, has commanded his battalion with zeal and ability, and when entrusted with an independent command accomplished satisfactorily the duty confided to him.

Colonel W. H. B. Kingsley, commanding the 2nd battalion Hampshire Regiment, returned to his post from sick-leave at the earliest opportunity, and has ably commanded his regiment, which has done excellent service throughout the late operations.

Colonel A. A. Le Mesurier, 2nd battalion "The King's" Liverpool Regiment, has commanded his battalion throughout the recent operations, and has been successful in action as a commander of a field column.

Deputy Surgeon-General J. McN. Donnelly, I.M.D., as Principal Medical Officer of the Force, has organised and administered the very efficient hospital arrangements, afloat and ashore, to my satisfaction.

Lieutenant-Colonel W. T. Budgen, R.A., deserves credit for the good service performed by him and the officers and men of the Royal Artillery under his command.

Lieutenant-Colonel A. F. Laughton, Assistant Commissary-General, in commissariat charge. To this officer and to the officers and men of the department my acknowledgments are specially due. Owing to the numerous columns furnished by the force, the strain on this department has been unusually severe; but no instance of failure has occurred, and this can only be attributed to the untiring zeal and energy of Lieutenant-Colonel Laughton and his subordinates.

Lieutenant-Colonel J. H. Gordon, Commandant, 23rd Madras Light Infantry, deserves credit for the admirable state of the regiment which he commands, and has distinguished himself when in command of field columns.

Lieutenant-Colonel M. Protheroe, C.S.I., Deputy Assistant-Adjutant and Quartermaster-General, served on the staff; of which his ability, industry, tact, temper, and judgment made him an invaluable member, and by his knowledge and official experience has lent valuable aid to the department.

Lieutenant-Colonel R. J. B. Simpson, 12th Madras Infantry, commanded the assaulting party at Minhla redoubt, and conducted the attack on the rebels at Kado on the 13th January 1886, until severely wounded.

Lieutenant-Colonel E. W. Begbie, Madras Staff Corps, has been in charge of the Army Signalling of the Force. I have already in my former despatches had the honour to place on record the great value that the Expedition has derived from visual signalling throughout the campaign. Lieutenant-Colonel Begbie, by his sustained personal interest in and unremitting personal superintendence of the working of his department, has conduced much to the successful results attained.

Lieutenant-Colonel J. G. R. D. Macneill, Madras Staff Corps, Deputy Assistant Adjutant and Quartermaster-General conducted the duties of the Intelligence Department until wounded when acting as guide to the column at the attack on Minhla. It is to this officer's previous labours in the Intelligence Branch that I was indebted for the very complete information afforded me from the office of the Quartermaster-General in India.

Lieutenant-Colonel G. Baker, Hampshire Regiment, commanded the battalion till the arrival of Colonel Kingsley after the surrender of Mandalay, and has been twice selected for the command of detached columns.

Major F. W. Hemming, 5th Dragoon Guards, Deputy Assistant Adjutant and Quartermaster-General, took over the charge of the Intelligence Department on his joining the force, and showed zeal and activity in acquiring and formulating information.

Major (now Lieutenant-Colonel) R. F. Williamson, Royal Welsh Fusiliers, admirably commanded the detachment at the important post of Shwebo. In this command he displayed high military qualities, fought four successful actions with the rebels, and did much to secure the pacification of the district.

Major W. P. Symons, Deputy Assistant Adjutant and Quartermaster-General, has proved himself possessed of the highest qualifications for staff duties in the field and in the office, and merits recognition.

Major H. P. Law, Royal Scots Fusiliers, commanded for

some months the Taungdwingyi column with signal boldness and success.

Major R. H. T. Hill, Madras Staff Corps, as Director of Transport to the force, has rendered valuable service. Great demands were made on the Transport Department for the many flying columns despatched for the suppression of rebellion, and, thanks to Major Hill's energy and resource in organising a local transport, the wants of the Expeditionary Force have been satisfied.

Major W. B. Warner, 2nd Madras Lancers, commanded the first cavalry detachment sent to Upper Burma. He has on several occasions been selected for the command of columns, and has exhibited zeal, energy, and knowledge of his profession.

Major E. C. Browne, Royal Scots Fusiliers, personally organised a body composed of mounted Volunteers, mounted Infantry, and mounted Native Police for service with the expedition, a force which proved itself of great utility.

Major A. J. Stead, 11th Bengal Infantry, commanded the detachment at Pagan and successfully operated against the insurgents in the district.

Major E. P. Ommanny, 11th Bengal Infantry, successfully commanded a column against the enemy near Myingyan.

Major C. H. Sheppard, 11th Madras Infantry, officiated as Deputy Judge Advocate to the Force in the absence of any regularly appointed officer of that department.

Major J. E. Collins, 2nd Hampshire Regiment, for skill and energy in command of several expeditions against the enemy near Mandalay.

Major C. C. Campbell, 23rd Madras Light Infantry, commanded the expedition sent up the Chindwin to Kandat in December 1885, and showed much ability and perseverance in carrying out his mission.

Major C. W. Walker, 19th Madras Infantry, performed the duties of Deputy Assistant Adjutant and Quartermaster efficiently, both in the field and in quarters.

Captain A. R. F. Dorward, R.E., commanded the Queen's Own Sappers and Miners, and was a most efficient field engineer. He showed eminent qualifications for command when selected to command a mixed force in the field.

Captain R. L. Milne, Deputy Assistant Adjutant and Quartermaster-General is a Staff officer of merit, and deserving of recognition.

Captain D. A. A. Macpherson, Field Paymaster, has conducted the duties of his department with much ability and courtesy.

Surgeon-Major C. Sibthorpe, in medical charge of the head-quarter staff, has shown himself always ready to afford any professional or personal assistance in his power.

Captain R. O. Lloyd, R.E., owing to his knowledge of the Burmese language, was very valuable as a field engineer. He was severely wounded.

Captain W. Aldworth, Bedfordshire Regiment, has not only efficiently performed the duty of aide-de-camp, but has also given me most valuable assistance as Military Secretary.

Lieutenant G. A. Ballard, R.N., proved a most efficient aide-de-camp. His knowledge of his profession, and his willing assistance as secretary were of great advantage to me.

Lieutenant C. D. Learoyd, R.E., was a most useful Orderly Officer. His professional knowledge and skill as a surveyor enabled him to perform valuable service with detached columns.

Captain T. P. Cather, R.E., is an invaluable Transport officer, and has remarkable talent for organizing and commanding men.

The following junior officers have been brought to notice by officers commanding brigades and heads of departments in this force; and I would hope that His Excellency the Commander-in-Chief will be pleased to take them into his favourable consideration:—

Captain R. A. P. Clements, South Wales Borderers, Brigade Major; severely wounded.

Captain M. C. Barton, R.E.

Captain J. E. Preston, 12th Madras Infantry.

Lieutenant W. K. Downes, 11th Bengal Infantry; distinguished gallantry at Minhla.

Lieutenant G. L. Angelo, 23rd Madras Infantry.

Lieutenant J. A. Tanner, R.E.

Lieutenant H. E. Porter, 24th Madras Infantry, Transport officer.

Lieutenant P. M. Carnegy, 12th Madras Infantry, severely wounded.

Lieutenant W. A. Cairnes, R.E.

Lieutenant R. D. Burlton, 2nd Madras Lancers.

APPENDIX B. 413

Lieutenant P. R. Mockler, Royal Warwickshire Regiment, Transport officer.
Lieutenant W. R. H. Beresford, Royal Welsh Fusiliers.
Lieutenant H. V. Cox, 21st Madras Infantry.
Lieutenant G. H. H. Couchman, Somersetshire Light Infantry.
Lieutenant H. T. D. Wilkinson, 12th Madras Infantry; dangerously wounded; distinguished gallantry at Minhla.
Lieutenant H. L. Dodgson, 2nd Bengal Infantry.
Lieutenant R. D. Anderson, Royal Artillery.
Lieutenant R. C. B. Haking, 2nd Hampshire Regiment.
Lieutenant J. R. Dyas, 2nd Hampshire Regiment.
Lieutenant R. J. Forbes, 2nd Hampshire Regiment.
Lieutenant B. Holloway, 2nd Madras Lancers.
Lieutenant A. P. D. Harris, 11th Bengal Infantry; success in command of a detachment.
Lieutenant A. G. P. Gough, Royal Welsh Fusiliers.
Lieutenant W. A. J. O'Meara, R.E., severely wounded.
Lieutenant C. C. A. Sillery, 12th Madras Infantry; severely wounded.
Lieutenant R. A. P. Drury, Bengal Staff Corps; attached to 11th Bengal Infantry; killed.
Lieutenant H. P. Brooking, 21st Madras Infantry.
Lieutenant L. de R. Jervis, Royal Welsh Fusiliers.
Lieutenant J. H. Gwynne, Royal Welsh Fusiliers; severely wounded.
Lieutenant Q. G. K. Agnew, 4th Battalion Scots Fusiliers, Transport officer.

6. I trust the European warrant officers, non-commissioned officers and privates, and the Native officers, non-commissioned officers, and men mentioned by Brigadier-Generals commanding and heads of departments will receive suitable recognition of their services.

7. The Rev. E. T. Beatty and the chaplains of the Church of England and priests of the Church of Rome appointed to serve with the force have shown much zeal and earnestness in the discharge of their duties.

8. To Captain R. Woodward, R.N., and to the officers and crews of the Naval Brigade serving under his orders, my thanks are specially due for valuable co-operation rendered afloat and ashore with the heartiness and thoroughness characteristic of the Royal Navy.

To Captain Woodward personally I am indebted for the energy, willingness, and professional skill continuously placed at my disposal.

I would beg to endorse the recommendations of Captain Woodward of the officers and men serving under him, hoping that the services of Commander W. R. Clutterbuck, R.N., Commander J. Durnford, R.N., Commander C. J. Barlow, R.N., and Lieutenant F. P. Trench, R.N., may receive special recognition.

Commander Clutterbuck, in command of Her Majesty's I.M.S. *Irrawaddy*, in concert with Lieutenant Trench, in command of the steam launch *Kathleen*, gallantly captured a King's steamer under the fire of a battery, at the outset of the campaign; and from that time to the occupation of Mandalay, these two officers have led the van of the river fleet. Commander Durnford served on my staff until the occupation of Mandalay; and his tact, energy, and professional knowledge were of great service to me. Commander C. J. Barlow's march of 120 miles through the country, with a detachment of blue-jackets, reflects great credit on that officer and his party. The manner in which Commander A. Carpenter, Her Majesty's I.M.S. *Investigator*, conducted the duties of the river survey, is deserving of special recognition, and his labours will, I am convinced, prove to be of great practical value.

Major W. M. Lambert, Royal Marine Artillery, and the non-commissioned officers and men of the Royal Marines attached to the Naval Brigade, have lent me very willing assistance whenever possible.

9. The officers and men of the Indian Marine have worked admirably throughout the expedition, and I trust some recognition of their excellent services may be afforded to the following officers:—

Captain A. Campbell, Her Majesty's Indian Marine.
Mr. C. W. Hewett, 1st grade officer, Indian Marine.
Mr. H. S. Black, 1st grade officer, Indian Marine.
Mr. W. Chandler, 1st grade officer, Indian Marine.
Mr. G. A. Lye, 1st grade officer, Indian Marine.
Mr. G. L'E. Mathias, 1st grade officer, Indian Marine.

Captain A. Campbell, Her Majesty's Indian Marine, as senior Marine transport officer, was of invaluable service in organising and marshalling the large fleet of river steamers that conveyed the force to Mandalay.

APPENDIX B. 415

10. I would beg to tender my sincere acknowledgments to Mr. C. E. Bernard, C.S.I., Chief Commissioner of British Burma, for the hearty support and co-operation which he has extended to me from the commencement of the expedition ; and to Colonel Sladen my thanks are due for the able assistance which his extended acquaintance with Upper Burmah has enabled him to place at my service.

11. I would also wish to acknowledge the services of Mr. Kennedy, the Manager of the Irrawaddy Flotilla Company, and of the commanders and crews of the steamers of the Company, who, by their skill and willing co-operation, have contributed so much to the safety and comfort of the troops and to the success of the expedition.

12. I would solicit the attention of His Excellency the Commander-in-Chief to the special opportunities afforded by this campaign, in its latter phases, to officers of comparatively junior rank, to show the military qualities that they possess, owing to the great number of independent minor operations which have been undertaken. It has thus been possible to select a considerable number of junior officers as deserving of special notice, and I trust that each may obtain some recognition of his services.

As regards the officers of the Madras Army thus brought to notice, I would venture to invite His Excellency the Commander-in-Chief to bear in memory that the Coast Army has lately had few opportunities of seeing service, and I would very respectfully submit that the present is a favourable opportunity to give promotion to comparatively young officers who may appear to merit it, thus infusing a new life into the army without injury to the professional feeling of those who have not been fortunate enough to participate in the campaign.

[Let us now repeat Lord Dalhousie's famous words concerning Pegu, and hope that—"As long as the sun shines in the heavens, the British flag shall wave over" Upper Burma!—W. F. B. L.]

APPENDIX C.

"The Native Armies of India."*

BEFORE extracting the valuable matter on this subject, a few words may be considered necessary.

Nothing can be more gratifying to an old Indian officer than to see an interest taken at home, not only by those who have long and faithfully served the great East India Company, but by officers who have never been directly connected with it, yet have long been fully alive to the merits and advantages it possessed, in the greatest Eastern local military combination—in days gone by, commercial as well as military—the world ever saw. And well may Major-General Sir F. Goldsmid, at the beginning of a most interesting article on "The Native Armies," remark that "it is pleasant to see, on so enlightened a platform as that of the Royal United Service Institution, an attempt made to call attention to the three Presidency Armies of India, not only as they exist in figures or as a statistical fragment, but as an actual living body, capable of offence and defence, and not unlikely to be required some day to furnish proofs of loyalty and devotion."

The three lectures, or "statements," delivered respectively on the Bengal, Madras, and Bombay armies, by Major-General Gordon, General Michael, and Major-General W. E. Macleod, contained many suggestive remarks. The distinguished author of the article himself rose in the 37th Madras Native Infantry (Grenadiers), raised in that Presidency June 1800, and bearing on its colours and appointments a "Dragon" and "China." He served with the expedition to China in 1840-42, and was present at the taking of Chuenpee and Bogue Forts, on the 7th January and 25th February 1841 respectively. As a brevet-major, in June 1860, he was still serving in Sindh as an assistant to the Commissioner for Jagheer Inquiries; and eventually rose to a high

---

* Article by Major-General Sir F. J. Goldsmid, K.C.S.I., C.B., *Asiatic Quarterly Review*, vol. vi., p. 17. (1888.)

APPENDIX C. 417

position as Director-General of Telegraphs, concluding a most useful if not brilliant career, by, among his other literary labours, writing a life of the "Lion-Hearted" General Outram—a Bombay Native Infantry officer—who, as the Bayard of the Indian Army, "lived not for an age, but for all time."

"A plain, straightforward account of the Native Army of Bengal was given by Major-General Gordon, who stated his case under the ægis of a well-qualified chairman, Sir Peter Lumsden. Reducing his eight heads of exposition into three paragraphs, and interpolating an occasional note or comment, we may summarise the statement as follows:—

"1. His army, including the Panjáb Frontier Force, consists of twenty-four regiments of cavalry, sixty-four battalions of infantry, a corps of sappers and miners, and four mountain-batteries of artillery. These, with the Corps of Guides, may be considered, for the sake of lucidity, as the Bengal army proper. There are, however, besides, under the orders of the Government of India, six regiments of cavalry, twelve battalions of infantry, and four field-batteries, comprising the Haidarabad contingent, Rajputána and Central India local levies, and the Central India Horse, all, except the last-named, organised on the old irregular system, with two to four British officers attached to each corps. Two-thirds of the army of Bengal proper are recruited from Northern India and Nepál, and one-third from the North-West Provinces. Of the twenty-four cavalry regiments, three designated as 'class' are wholly Muhammadan, and two Hindú; the remaining nineteen have 'class' troops, formed separately as the regiments. In the infantry, twenty-two of the sixty-four battalions, i.e. thirteen Gurkha, five Sikh, one Dogra, and three Muzbi, are 'class,' and forty-two have 'class' companies. The sappers have 'class' companies. Of the mountain-batteries nothing is said in this respect; but, according to the *Army List*, while there is one Muhammadan among the three native officers of No. 1 Battery, there are two Muhammadans out of the three in No. 2. The cavalry regiments are numbered from 1 to 19 [as stated in Note II.] as Bengal Cavalry; of these the 9th, 10th, 11th, 13th, 14th, 18th, and 19th are Lancers; the remaining five are separately numbered as Panjáb Cavalry. Each regiment has eight

27

troops or four squadrons, with a complement of 9 British officers (including commandant and adjutant), 17 native officers, 64 non-commissioned, 8 trumpeters, and 586 sowárs. Among the native commissioned one is rissaldar major, and one native adjutant. Foot regiments are numbered 1 to 45 as Bengal Infantry; 1 to 5 Gurkhas, each with two battalions; 1 to 4 Sikh; and 1 to 6 Panjáb. There are eight companies to the battalion, and eight British officers; but as these include a commandant, two wing commanders, an adjutant and a quartermaster, there are but three left for ordinary regimental duty. Of natives there are 16 commissioned (including a subadar major and jemadar adjutant), 40 havildars or sergeants, 40 naiks or corporals, 16 drummers, and 800 privates. The Corps of Guides of the Panjáb Frontier Force consists of six troops of cavalry and eight companies of infantry, under one commandant. It has 14 British officers, and a strength of 1,381 natives of all ranks. The Corps of Sappers has six service and two depôt companies, 20 European officers, inclusive of commandant, adjutant, superintendent of park and superintendent of instruction, a warrant officer and non-commissioned officers of Royal Engineers, and a total of 1,431 natives. Each mountain-battery of six guns has with it 4 British officers of Royal Artillery, 3 native officers, 98 gunners and non-commissioned officers, and 188 drivers. A British medical officer, with native hospital establishment, is attached to every regiment. The question of reserves has not been lost sight of, and a system is now under formation providing for two kinds—active and garrison."

"General Michael's paper on the Madras army takes us back to 1758, when the local Government began to raise regiments composed of inhabitants from the Carnatic. First, companies of one hundred men were duly formed and officered; then these companies became parts of battalions, of which there were ten in 1765, and sixteen in 1767. In the re-organisation of 1796, the establishment of native infantry was fixed at eleven regiments, each of two battalions; and in 1837, the year of Her Majesty's accession, there were fifty-two single battalion regiments. Half a century later—or at the present time—the infantry of the Madras army is found to consist of thirty-two regiments only.

"A battalion of native artillery, consisting of ten companies,

APPENDIX C. 419

was formed in 1784, prior to which date native Gun Lascars had been attached to the European artillery. This arrangement appears to have been short-lived; but in 1796 there were two battalions of five companies each; and in 1837, three troops of Horse Artillery and one battalion of Foot Artillery. Now, we look in vain for the Golundáz, or native gunners, in Madras.

"Four regiments, taken over by the East India Company in 1780 from the Nawab of the Carnatic, and permanently enlisted by their new masters in 1784, may be considered as forming the first nucleus of Madras Cavalry. In 1796 the same number of regiments held good, with much the same strength in troopers, but a slight reduction in native officers; and in 1837 there were no less than eight regiments. At present the number has been reduced to the old standard of four. The Madras Sappers and Miners date from 1780, when they were called 'Pioneers' and officered from the line. In 1831 Engineer officers were appointed to command and instruct them; and under the designation which it now bears, this distinguished corps has continued for more than half a century to do credit to the presidency in which it originated. Two regiments on the strength of the Madras Native Infantry, made 'Pioneers' in 1883, may be considered, in some sense, practically qualified to act as sappers.

"The present strength of native regiments is put down as follows:—

"*Cavalry.*—9 European and 12 native officers; with 514 non-commissioned, rank and file.

"*Sappers.*—22 commissioned and 67 non-commissioned European officers; with 24 commissioned and 1,384 non-commissioned native officers, rank and file.

"*Infantry.*—9 European and 16 native officers, with 873 non-commissioned, rank and file.

"In the cavalry the proportion of Musalmans is beyond three-fourths, or 1,278 out of 1,683. Of the Sappers more than an eighth are Telingas, nearly a sixth are Christians, about one-fourth are 'Tamils,' and considerably more than a third are of unspecified caste. In the infantry, while more than a third are Muhammadans, more than a tenth Tamils, and more than three-eighths Telingas, there are not a fifteenth part Christians. At the same time it should be noted that of the higher native castes—here designated Brahman and Rajput—there is not to be found one man in thirty.

"The standard height for recruits is 5 feet 6 inches for cavalry, and 5 feet 5 inches for infantry and sappers; aged from sixteen to twenty-two. Much the same discipline is exacted from the enlisted sipáhi as in Bengal. The British commandant, whose confidential officer is the subadar major, is paramount in his regiment. Next below him in rank is the second in command, who is the senior wing or squadron commander. Wing and squadron commanders are answerable for the appearance, discipline, and officering of their half battalions or squadrons, and for the instruction of their officers, European and native. The quartermaster of a native regiment is responsible for all the public buildings used, and generally for the lines and bazár. Subadars command their troops or companies on parade, instruct them in drill, and are responsible for their order in lines and barracks, and the due intimation to them of all legitimate orders. Jemadars are the native subalterns, taking their turn of duty with the subadars as regimental officer of the day. Punishments awardable without court-martial are, with little exception, such as extra drill within prescribed limits, inflicted by the commanding officer. A prisoner has the option of being tried by European or native officers. Public quarters are not provided for the sipáhi, who pays for his hut as well as his food, and receives a grant in aid called hutting money, according to rank, on every change of station. These huts, being the property of the men, are purchased by one regiment from another on relief, at a valuation set upon them by a committee of native officers. In order to encourage the establishment, in the lines, of regimental bazárs, advances to tradesmen for the purpose are made under authority. The sipáhi is nominally allowed to have only two adult relatives living in his hut, or one adult with unmarried daughters or young male children; but much is left to the discretion of the commandant, and it often happens that the native officer or soldier has several members of his family living with and dependent on him. In the cavalry the pay is from Rs. 50 to Rs. 150 for commissioned officers not on the staff, with an allowance for carriage of Rs. 30 in the field or marching, and Rs. 50 more for a subadar major, or Rs. 17½ for a jemadar adjutant; while it ranges from Rs. 9 to Rs. 20 for rank and file and non-commissioned, with field batta from Rs. 1½ to Rs. 5, and staff allowances from Rs. 3½ to Rs. 21. For the infantry and sappers, the figures are from Rs. 40 to Rs. 100; commissioned officers, exclusive of field batta, from Rs. 7½ to Rs. 15, and staff allowances Rs. 17½ to

APPENDIX C. 421

Rs. 50; and Rs. 7 to Rs. 14 for rank and file and non-commissioned, with field batta from Rs. 1½ to Rs. 10. Promotion to the rank of native officer is usually made by selection from the non-commissioned ranks; but Government has the power (exercised in two instances only known to the lecturer) of bestowing direct commissions on gentlemen of position."

"Major-General W. E. Macleod, an officer of regimental and staff experience during an Indian service of thirty years, is the lecturer on the Bombay army. He states that when he joined in 1838, the native cavalry was represented by three regiments of regulars and Poonah Irregular horse; the artillery consisted of Golundaz. There were twenty-six regiments of regular infantry, one marine battalion, and some local irregulars. In later years the strength of the cavalry was increased by Jacob's Irregular Horse, the Guzerat Irregular, and Southern Mahratta Horse; and of the infantry by three native regular and two Baluch battalions. A Sindh Camel Corps was also raised, and the 'Aden Troop' formed from drafts of irregular cavalry. It would be somewhat foreign to the purpose of this sketch to follow General Macleod in his account of the services of particular regiments until 1844, when the withdrawal from Afghanistan has been effected and Scind annexed to British India; but we may extract a few practical paragraphs, or portions of paragraphs, illustrative of the old system, under the head of 'Interior Economy':—'Each company under a British officer was divided into sub-divisions and sections, each sub-division under a native officer, and each section under non-commissioned officers, responsible for the supervision of the men. As to the state of their arms, accoutrements, ammunition, equipment, and regimental necessaries, the cleanliness of their lines, and all matters of duty and discipline conducive to good behaviour, each section had a due proportion of 'caste' and 'country.'

"A return of 'country,' 'caste,' 'age,' 'height,' of each rank in a company (prepared by company officers) was furnished in 'one regimental form' to army head-quarters periodically.

"The periodical promotion rolls furnished by company officers received the careful scrutiny and attention of the commanding officer before the promotions were confirmed and published in regimental orders; and this scrutiny had regard to length of service; but the system which guided such promotions through the different grades from lance-naique to native officer was distinctly that of *selection*, and with regard for efficiency and a due balance of caste and nationality.

"The men's lines were subject to the supervision of the quartermaster, but each of the company authorities were responsible, through him and by constant inspection, to the commanding officer as to their general cleanliness and neatness. No strangers were allowed to live in the lines without (through the company authorities) the permission of the commanding officer.

"In the Bombay army the men were *never* separated from their arms, accoutrements, and ammunition, either in quarters, on the march, or service, except at sea, when, according to the Bombay army rules for such occasions, they were lodged in the places pointed out for the purpose by the vessel's authorities.

"'The word 'fatigue duty,' in garrison, field, or board ship, in the Bombay Native Army, included every employment under that head as performed by British regiments, and the men were detailed for it as they stood on the company roster, without any reference to 'caste or country'; and within my long experience of regimental duty I know of no 'fatigue duty' that has not been always performed by the sepoys with readiness and cheerfulness.

"The adjutant of the regiment was responsible to the commanding officer for every detail of the regiment connected with drill, duty, and discipline, theoretical and practical, and, except on holidays, was expected to be on the 'drill' (recruit) ground or parade every morning and evening. His immediate subordinates were the native adjutant, havildar major; and the staff of drill-masters (in proportion to the number of recruits) were selected by him for efficiency and smartness, and without any reference to 'caste.' Some of the old stamp of Bombay men were very smart drills and good teachers.

"Though no complete statement of the actual strength in these days of the Bombay Army under the new organisation is given, the number of infantry corps is alluded to in the following passage, referring to the possible quarters of disturbance in Western India:—

"'All these . . . may any day call forth again the services of the Bombay Native Army, which in 1838 numbered twenty-six regiments for service within the strictly-speaking Bombay limits; again, now in 1888, twenty-two regiments only, with their service extended to Scinde, Quetta, Southern Mahratta country, and Rajpootana; for, of the present thirty regiments, three Belooch and one marine battalion are, so to say, local, and *four* good old faithful regiments have, for financial reasons, been recently swept away from the Bombay native infantry.'

"Seven cavalry regiments (irrespective of the Aden Troop and Body-guard), of which two are lancers, two 'Jacob's Horse,' one is 'Poona Horse,' one light cavalry, and one so-called 'Baluch Horse.' . . . A commandant, four squadron commanders, and four squadron officers are attached to each as the European complement. The strength in natives is seventeen commissioned and 608 non-commissioned officers and troopers.

"Two mountain-batteries of native artillery; uniform dark blue and gold, with scarlet facings. Strength: four European and three native officers, with 98 non-commissioned trumpeters and gunners; drivers and others of all ranks, 208.

"Sappers and miners, of which there are four working companies and one depôt company. For these there is a commandant, a superintendent of instruction and second in command, an adjutant, an instructor in army signalling and telegraphy, five company commanders and five company officers, and five 'unattached' —all Royal Engineers. Uniform scarlet and gold, with blue facings. Strength: one warrant officer, two staff sergeants, and thirty-four European sergeants and others; fifteen native commissioned, eighty havildars and naiks, and 772 sappers, including buglers and recruit boys. Of native infantry there are twenty-six regiments, including the marine and three Baluch battalions mentioned above. Two of these are grenadiers, six light infantry, and one is a corps of rifles. Ten have red uniforms with yellow facings; four red with emerald green; four red with white; three red with black; one red with sky blue; three have dark green uniforms with scarlet, and one rifle green with red facings. Strength: one commandant, two wing commanders, and five wing officers; sixteen native commissioned, and 816 non-commissioned, rank and file, and others."

Although space prevents any more extracts from Sir Frederick's most interesting and useful essay, as regarding the Native Armies, we cannot conclude without highly recommending the entire article to our readers, and citing an excellent passage wherein, with the dignity of a Whitefield while appealing for funds to build a church, he sends round the hat to Government for a suitable building—one in keeping with the now far-famed Royal United Service Institution:—" Would it be State extravagance," he says, " to give it a habitation from the public purse worthy of the only representative society of the interests generally of the British army and navy? Would it be State economy to throw the onus of a new building upon the shoulders of naval and military officers, who, take them all in all, can hardly be classed with the wealthiest sons of this wealthy country? It is no exaggeration to say that much time is given to the discussion, by our legislators, of questions less weighty than these." The very fact of the Institution being the scene where so much light was thrown on the " Native Armies of India," alone shows its utility; for, without it, such an important subject would probably never have been brought before an intelligent public, in general ignorant of, and indifferent to, even weighty Indian affairs.

INDEX.

A.

Abyssinian War, origin of, 382; storming of Magdala (1867), 383.
Acheen, in Sumatra, E. I. Company's factory at, 24.
Adams, Maj., victor of Gheriah and U'ndwah Nálá (1763), 229-31.
Adlercron, Col., in command of Madras army (1754), 160
Adnet, Capt., killed at Condore (1758), 277.
African Company, formed 1662, 42.
Afzul Khan, murdered by Shivaji (1652), 48.
Ahmedabad, celebration of Queen's Jubilee at, 326.
Ahmed Shah, son of Mahomed Shah, succeeds his father (1748), 127.
Aislabie, appointed Governor of Bombay (1708), 106.
Akbar, Emperor, his reign, 9.
Albuquerque, Alphonso, first Portuguese Viceroy in India, 12; his conquests and death, 13
Alexander the Great in India, 6.
Ali Verdy Khan, Nawaub of Bengal, 166.
Alompra, King of Burma, his personality, 358; his early career, 357; conquers Pegu, 356; and founds Rangoon, 358; receives English envoys (1755, 1757), 358; his massacre of English at Negrais island, 359; he invades Siam, and dies, 1760, 356.
Amalgamation of Presidential Armies with the Imperial forces (1858), 370.
Amarapúra, sometime capital of Burma, 362, 363; founded by Minderajee Prau (1783), 364
Amboor, engagement near (1749), 134.
Amboyna, Dutch massacre of British at (1623), 29, 35; compensation paid for same (1654), 39.
Amery, Capt., a notorious pirate leader, 87.
Amoy, E. I. Company trade in, 74.
Anandraz, Rajah of Rajahmundri, ally of English (1758), 266, 268; his crooked policy, 280.
Andrews, Capt., commands Bombay detachment at Devicotah (1749), 133*n*.
Angria, Konoji, Admiral of the Maratha fleet, takes to piracy, 108; attacks European vessels, 109; died 1730, 110.
Angria, Toolaji, a Maratha pirate, 110; efforts for his extermination (1755), 162-64.
Annesley, Mr., President at Surat (1685), 85; seized and imprisoned by Mogul governor (1695), 86; released 1696, 87; dismissed the service (1699), 90.
Anwar-oo-deen, Nabob of the Carnatic, 117; his conduct towards English and French, 118; his army routed by the French (1746), 119; siding with the English, is attacked by the French, 120; detached from English by French intrigue, 120; defeated and killed (1749), 134.
Arabs, their early commerce between East and West, 3
Arab Mahometans in India (about 1500), 10, 11.
Arcot, taken by Chandah Sahib and the French (1749), 134; seized by Clive (1751), 142; besieged by Chandah Sahib and the French (1751), 143.
Armegon, first fortified position in India occupied by E. I. Company, 36.
Armenian merchants encouraged at Bombay and Madras, 83.
Artillery, origin and progress of Indian, 237 *et seq.*; the gun-room crew (1711), 240; description of European artillerymen, 241; reduction of

28

426   INDEX.

Artillery—*cont.*
the Native artillery (1779), 245-7; some of its successes, 248.
Artilleryman (European), pay of, under Aurungzebe, 104.
Asoka, Edicts of, 6.
Assada Merchants, or Courten's Association (*q.v.*), 38.
Astruc, Mons., in command of French on Island of Seringham (1753), 152.
Aungier, Mr., Governor of Bombay (1669), his administration, 54; deals with mutiny (1674), 72; his death (1677), 74.
Aurungabad, founded by Aurungzebe (1653), 47.
Aurungzebe, his wars with Shivaji, 47-50; attempts extermination of the English, 69; but grants another firman (1689),69; his death (1707), 102; his partition of his empire, 103.
Ava, the ancient capital of Burma, 351; founded 1364, 354; Chinese army before the city (1416), 355; captured by Peguers (1752), and retaken by Alompra (*q.v.*), 356; English envoys at (1755, 1757), 358; new palace built (1824), 367; seat of Government transferred to Mandalay (1860), 368; description of the city in 1855, 364; and in 1879, 367; its surrender to the British (1885), 403; geographical description of the kingdom, 360.
Azim Ooshan, Mogul Governor of Bengal, assists Bahadur Shah (about 1707), 103.

B.

Baber (Mahomed), establishes the Mogul Empire in India, 9.
Bagwell, Commodore, commands operations against the Maratha Pirates, 110.
Bahadur Shah, rules at Delhi, 103; dies 1712, 104.
Baboor, battle at (1752), 150.
Baird, Gen. Sir David, at storming of Seringapatam (1799), 318, 377.
Baj-Baj=Budge-Budge (*q.v.*), 235.
Bajirav, Peshwa, leader of the Marathas (*q.v.*), greatly extends his kingdom (1724-38), 111; his reply to envoy from Bombay (1739), 113-14.

Bake, Mr., Engineer and Surveyor-General of Bombay (1671), 55.
Balaji Rao, assisted by British in operations against Toolaji Angria (*q.v.*), 162.
Bamian, march of Bengal Artillery to (1839), 331.
Bandoola, Maha, great Burman commander, 362, 363.
Bangalore, storming of (1791), 309.
Bankot, Island of, taken and occupied by English (1755), 163.
Bantam, E. I. Company's factory at, 24, 36; English expelled from (1682) by the Dutch, 76; but restored, 77.
Barnet, Admiral, commands squadron in the Indian seas (1745), 117.
Bassein, in Portuguese possession, besieged by Marathas (1739), 112.
Batavia, disputed possession (1618-19), 33.
Batta, first mention of (1678), 75; question of (1766), 257.
Belasore, Company's factory established at (1661), 38, 61; taken and pillaged by the Company (1688), 69.
Bells, Burmese, 248.
Bengal, E. I. Company establish factories in (1634), 37; state of affairs in, 1620-50, 60, 61; and in 1654, 39; French first appear in (1672), 62; the Danes obtain commercial privileges in, 62; its Agent first entitled Governor (1681), 62; causes of war with the Mogul (1685), 64; struggle with the Nawab (1686), 67; trade in Bengal abandoned (1688) for a time, 69; military establishment reduced (1694), 90; Calcutta fortified (1695), 91; and made head-quarters (1703), 99; President pays tribute to Nadir Shah (1739), 114; invaded by Marathas (1742), 116; Calcutta Militia first enrolled (1742), 116; state of affairs previous to 1756, 165; Dutch power in, destroyed by Clive (1759), 220; Meer Jaffier deposed and Meer Cossim made Nabob (1760), 226; the Nabob's army improved by Gurghin Khan, 227, 229; war between Meer Cossim and the English (1762), 227-32; war with Sujah Dowlah (*q.v.*) of Oudh, 233; Nujun-ood-dowla (*q.v.*) made Nabob (1765), 234; return of Clive to (1765), 250; a Government of Rotation, 266; first English coins of, struck 1757, 215; first dockyards in, established (1780), 207; notes on Native Army of, 417.
Bengal Army, nucleus of (about

INDEX.

Bengal Army—*cont.*
1660), 61; increasing in 1683, 63; army and navy strengthened for war with the Mogul (1685), 65. 66; detachment from, assists Clive at Coverypauk (1751), 145; list of officers who perished in the Black Hole (1756), 171*n*; Bengal Regiments at the battle of Condore (1758), 279, 280; defeat of Dutch near Chinsurah (1759), 218-21; defeat of Shah Allum at Patna (1760), 224-5; battles of Geriah (1763), 230; and U'ndwah Nálá, 231; mutiny of the officers (1766), 258.
Pay of rank and file (1694), 90; strength (and officers) of, in 1759, 253; organization of, in 1766, 257; and in 1778-79, 303; strength of, in 1889, 253*n*; "Lord Clive's Fund," 262.
Bengal Artillery, first company raised in 1749, 238; state of, in 1769, 241; dress of the regiment, 243; regiment improved by Lieut.-Col. Pearse (1769), 241; practice-ground at Dum-Dum (1775), 243-4; casualties of the regiment (1788-95), 329; anecdotes of officers, 330, 334, 335; extraordinary march across the Hindu Kúsh to Bamian (1839), 331.
Bengal Cavalry, regiments of, 376.
Bengal European Regt., organized by Clive (1756), 202; list of services, 235 and *n*, 279*n*, 302*n*; notes on, 370.
Bengal Fusiliers, anecdote of, 372.
Bernard, Mr. C. E., Chief Commissioner of British Burma, 415.
Best, Capt. Thomas, commands E. I. Company's expedition (1612), 27, 31.
Biderra, near Chinsurah, decisive battle of, 218-21.
Black Hole, Calcutta, list of officers who perished in (1756), 171*n*.
Blackwell, Dr., his treachery (1694), 84.
Bombay, origin of the name, 293; early history of, 30 *et seq.*; held by Portuguese, English propose to attack (1626), 36; proposal to purchase, 41; ceded to Charles II. by Portugal (1661), 41; offered to the Company, 43; occupied by the English (1664), 44 and *n*; made over to the Company (1668), 45; Sir G. Oxinden's administration of, 51-54; threatened by the Dutch (1672), 56; growth of its importance, 70; war with the Mogul at (1687), 68; wrested from the Com-

Bombay—*cont.*
pany by Capt. Keigwin in the King's name (1683), 77; restored (1684), 79; seat of Government transferred from Surat to (1685), 80; a plague and other troubles in, 99; conquests of the Marathas threaten Bombay, 111; operations against Toolaji Angria (*q.v.*), 162; least troublesome of the three Presidencies, 293.
Defences of—in 1669, 53, 54; in 1671, 55, 56; in 1673, 71; in 1695, 85; in 1705, 101; and in 1739, 112; small forts near (1707), 105; wall round completed 1716, 107.
Military force in (1668), 45, 52; dangerous measures of economy (1678), 75; its garrison—in 1671, 54-56; in 1680, 76; in 1682, 76; in 1695, 85; and in 1706, 101, 102; European force augmented (1742), 116; notes on Native Army of, 421.
Revenues of (1667), 51; population of (1715), 106; present population of, 70*n*; the Parsís of, 295; Mint established at, 55, 73; courts of justice formed (1670), 54 and *n*; Court of Admiralty established for trial of pirates, 95.
Bombay Army, nucleus of (1668), 52; military regulations, 52; troop of horse raised (1676), 73; men enlisted for seven years, 74; unreasonable reductions (1678), 75; companies of Rajpoots enrolled (1683), 77; first regular regiment (1741), 115; first company of Artillery (1748), 239; Swiss Artillery in (1753), 152*n*; pay in 1676, 73; and in 1741, 115; mutiny among troops (1674), 72.
In engagement near Carwar (1718), 107; detachment from, takes part in expedition against Devicotah (1749), 131*n*, 133*n*; hostilities with the Siddee at Surat (1752), 151; supplies troops to Madras (1754), 155, 161; Prince of Wales' Own Grenadier Regiment of Bombay Infantry, record of services of, 321 *et seq.*
Bombay European Regiment at Chandernagore (1757), 183, 190.
Bombay Fusiliers, their origin, 131*n*; note on, 109*n*.
Bombay Infantry, Prince of Wales' Own Grenadier Regiment of, record of services, 321 *et seq.*
Bombay Light Cavalry, regiments of, 377.
Boscawen, Admiral, with fleet, assists

28 *

Boscawen, Admiral—*cont.*
the Company against the French, 123, 129, 135.
Boughton, Mr., obtains firman for the Company (1651-52), 61.
Brenier, M., in command of French near Trichinopoly (1753), 153.
Brenton, Lieut., conducts negotiations at Chandernagore (1757), 185.
Bristol, Capt., at battle of Condore (1758), 275, 280.
Britannia, derivation of, 2.
British Empire, extent, &c., 2*n.*
Brooke, Lord, reports on trade with the East (1600), 23.
Brown, Mr. Walter, attacks Maratha pirates at Gheria (1720), 109.
Bryce, Prof., M.P., his visit to India, ix.
Buckle, Capt., Bengal Artillery, his death, 249 and *n.*
Buddha, his influence in India, 5.
Budge-Budge, anecdote of taking the fort of (1756), 178*n.*
Buggesses, or Javanese soldiers, 100.
Burma, origin of the name, 353 ; its ancient capital Ava (*q.v.*), 351; civil war in (1740-52), 356; English mission to (1795), 361; English Embassy to (1855), 363, 367; capital transferred from Amarapúra to Mandalay (1860), 368.
First Burmese War (1824-26), 363, 365; Second Burmese War (1852), 352; Third Burmese War (1885-87), 355, 365; details of operations in Upper Burma (1885-6), 388 *et seq.*; with names of officers mentioned in despatches, 407; storming of Minhla, 397; engagement at Myingyan, 399; letter from the Burmese Prime Minister, 401; the surrender of Ava, 403; the British at Mandalay (1885), 405; annexation of Upper Burma (1886), 351, 366.
Burmese, anecdote of, 363.
Bury, M., conducts French expedition against Fort St. David (1746), 120.
Bussy, M., commands French troops in the Deccan (1749-51), 134, 138-40; at Golconda (1752), 149; letter of Surajah Dowlah to, 206; taken prisoner at Wandewash, 287, 292; his character and conduct, 288, 290-92.

C.

Cabral, Alvares, commands Portuguese expedition to India, 11.
Calliaud, in action near Trichinopoly (1754), 155 ; at Trichinopoly (1758), 273 ; Commander-in-Chief, at Patna (1760), 224-5.
Calcutta, Chuttanutee, the site of, 67, taken by Mr. Charnock (1690), 70 ; origin of (1695-6), 91 and *n*; made head-quarters in Bengal (1703), 99; Surajah Dowlah quarrels with English at (1756), 166 ; the attack on, 168 ; siege of, 169 ; capitulation and the Black Hole, 170 ; Clive's march to and recapture of (1756-7), 177-9.
Defences of—in 1742, 116 ; and in 1756, 167, 168; Militia first enrolled (1742), 116. *See also* Fort William.
Calicut, Portuguese first land at, 10, 11.
Cameron, Capt., imprisoned in Abyssinia (1863), 382.
Campbell, Gen. Geo., incidents in the life of, 335 ; list of his services, 338.
Carey, Mrs., survived the Black Hole (1756), 171*n.*
Carnac, Maj., in command at Patna (1763), 230, 233, xix.
Carnac, Lieut. Jacob, xix.
Carnatic, Anwar-oo-deen (*q.v.*), Nabob of, 117.
Caron, pioneer of the French in India (1672), 57.
Carr, Capt., his insulting conduct, 99.
Carwar, Company's fort and factory at, 105 ; besieged by the Dessaree (1718), 107.
Castro, Don Juan de, Portuguese ruler in India, his administration, 15.
Cavendish, Mr. Thomas, his expedition to the East (1586), 22.
Ceylon, Island of, Dutch take possession of (1656), 40.
Chancellor, navigator, attempted northeast passage to India (1553), 21.
Chandah Sahib, a soldier of fortune, supported by Dupleix for his own ends, 134, 137; victorious at Volconda, marches on Trichinopoly (1751), 141 ; besieges Arcot without success, 140, 143 ; his death (1752), 148.
Chandernagore, first mentioned as French settlement 1700, 201, 198; its defences, 184 ; French garrison of, 202; Clive's attack on (1757), 184, 188 ; English forces at, 203; story of the French deserter, 188.

INDEX. 429

Charnock, Mr., founder of Calcutta, takes Chuttanutee (1690), 70.
Child, Sir John, Governor of Bombay, appointed Governor-General (1686), 66, 80; conducts hostilities with the Mogul, 68; dies 1690, 69, 81; his character, 81.
Child, Sir Josiah, President of Court of Directors, 81; on Indian trade, 293.
Childers, Mr., M.P., his visit to India, ix.
China, Portuguese embassy to (1518), 14.
Chinese War of 1860, storming of the Taku Forts, 381.
Chingleput, fortress reduced by Clive (1752), 151; strengthened against the French (1758), 274.
Chinsurah, Dutch in, intrigue against the English, 219.
Chuprassies, why so called, 116n.
Churches in India, curiosities of, 201.
Chuttanutee, site of the present Calcutta, 67.
Circars, Northern, ceded to the French by the Nizam (1752), 149, 267; restored to the Nizam by treaty (1754), 157; campaign in (1758-59), 274, 283.
Clarke, Capt., with detachment at Trichinopoly (1751), 142.
Clifton, Capt., commands company from Marquis of Westminster's Regiment for E. I. Company (1685), 66.
Clive, Lieut. (afterwards Lord), leads storming of Devicotah (1749), 131; at Volconda, 141; with reinforcements for Trichinopoly, 142; seizes Arcot, 142; and holds it during siege, 143-4; makes alliance with Morarí Rao, 144; gains victory over the French at Arnee, 144; besieges and captures Conjiveram from the French, 144; defeats the French at Coverypauk, 145; at relief of Trichinopoly, 146; defeats French at Samiaveram (1752), 147.
Lieutenant-Colonel and Deputy Governor of Fort St. David (1756), 164 and n; with expedition to Gheria, 164; his division of loot taken there, 165; expedition to save Bengal from Surajah Dowlah, 173-5; he attacks the Nawaub's camp at Calcutta, 182; his attack on Chandernagore, 183; marches towards Plassey, 204; at the battle of Plassey (1757), 208.
Governor and President of Bengal (1758), 266; assists Madras against the French, 266; destroys Dutch power in India, 220; his return to

Clive—cont.
England (1760), 221, 223; is ennobled, 250; goes out as Commander-in-Chief and Governor of Bengal (1765), 250; invested with the Dewanny by the Mogul Emperor (1765), 251; suppresses mutiny of Bengal officers, 258; again returns to England (1767), 259
His services in India, 151; recognition of his services, 156, 214; his influence over the natives, 145; his organization of the Sepoys, 180; his administration of the Army, 254 et seq.; his reforms, civil and military, 251, 256, 258; letters to officers of Bengal Army, 255; his death (1774), 259; his character and conduct, 188, 189, 205, 222, 260, 265; his charity, 260; "Lord Clive's Fund," 261.
Cochin, ceded to English (1615), 32.
Cochin China, French endeavour to possess (17th century), 58 and n.
Coilady, skirmish with French near (1751), 142.
Cojah Latiff, his treachery at Surat (1752), 152.
Colt, Mr., President at Surat (1699), 90.
Condore, decisive battle of (1758), 275.
Conflans, Marquis de, commanding French in the Northern Circars (1758), 268; at the battle of Condore, 275; surrenders Masulipatam, 281.
Conjiveram, taken from the French by Clive (1751), 144.
Cooke, Mr., King's Governor of Bombay (1664), 44 and n.
Coote, Capt. (afterwards Gen. Sir Eyre), in the re-capture of Calcutta (1757), 177-80; at Chandernagore, 185; takes fort of Kutwah, 204; defeats French at Wandewash, 287; besieges Pondicherry (1760-61), 287; returns to India as Lieut.-General Sir Eyre Coote, Commander-in-Chief at Madras (1779), 303; at war with Hyder Ali, 304 and n; at battle of Porto Novo (1781), 319-20; died (1783), 306.
Cope, Capt., commands expedition to Tanjore (1749), 129; takes the Pagoda of Atchavaram, near Devicotah, 132; attempts to reconquer Madura (1751), 140; in campaign against Chandah Sahib, 141.
Cornwallis, Marquess, arrives as Governor-General (1786), 308; campaigns against Tippoo Sultan (1791), 309; first siege of Seringapatam (1792), 313; anecdote of, 330.

430 INDEX.

Cossimbazar, Company's factory established at, 61.
Courten's Association competes with E. I. Company (1635), 37.
Covelong, fortress reduced by Clive (1752), 151.
Coverypauk, Clive defeats the French at (1751), 145.
Cuddalore, taken by the French (1758), 269.

D.

D'Aché, Count, commands French fleet in Indian seas, 289, 273.
Dádoji Pant, guardian and tutor of Shivaji, 47.
Dalhousie, Lord, his annexation of Pegu, 366.
Dalton, Capt., in command of garrison at Trichinopoly (1753), 152.
Dance, his portrait of Clive, 260.
Danes, the, rivals of English in India (1623), 35; they procure commercial privileges from the Mogul (cir. 1676), 62.
D'Auteuil, M., commands French troops in the Deccan, 134, 137, 138; surrenders to Clive at Volconda (1752), 147.
Davenant, Mr., establishes a Court of Admiralty at Bombay for trial of pirates, 95.
Davis, Arctic navigator, made voyage to India, 21
Deccan, disputed succession in (1748-9), 133; intrigues of Duplcix, 134.
De Kerjean, M., taken prisoner at Bahoor (1752), 150.
De la Haye, M., commands French fleet, and lands in India (1672), 56, 57.
De la Touche, M., in command of French troops at Gingee (1750), 139.
Delhi, taken by Kotb-od-deen, comes under Mahometan rule, 7; ruins of ancient city at Toghlukabad, 8; taken by Timourlang, 8-9; E. I. Company's embassy to (1715), 106; sacked by Nadir Shah (1739), 114.
Deoghur, afterwards Dowlatabad, *q.v.*, 8.
D'Estaign, Count, French commander, 269.

Devicotah, storming of (1749), 131.
Diaz, Bartholomy, discovers Cape of Good Hope, 4.
Dowlatabad, formerly Deoghur, Mahometan capital transferred from Delhi to, 8.
Drake, Sir Francis, his expedition to the East (1577-80), 21, 22.
Drake, Sir Thomas, takes Batavia from the Dutch (1618), 33.
Drake, Mr., Governor of Calcutta (1756), 166, 169.
Dufferin, Lord (Marquess of), his annexation of Upper Burma (1886), 366; on India, 191.
Dum-Dum, first used as Artillery practice-ground (1775), 243.
Dungum, English factory at, plundered by Maratha Horse (1674), 72.
Dupleix, M., Governor of Pondicherry (1744), 117 and *n*; quarrels with La Bourdonnais, 119 and *n*; prefers military power to peaceful commerce, 127; sends expedition against Fort St. David (1746), 120; and attacks Nabob of the Carnatic, 120; intrigues with the Nabob and detaches him from English, 120; his success at Pondicherry, 124; his intrigues in the Deccan, 133, 137, 138; he installs Muzzufer Jung as Nizam, with advantages to himself (1750), 139; intrigues with Marathas, 149; negotiates with Madras for peace, 154; is superseded (1754), 157; his character and administration, 192-94, 196, 198.
Dupleix-Futtchabad, destroyed by Clive (1751), 145.
Dutch, the, revolting from Spain, seek trade in the East, 17; early settlements, Java, &c., 18; the Dutch East India Company (1602), 18; first Dutch factory at Surat (1617), 33; struggle with the Portuguese, 18; conflicts with English, 33; massacre of British at Amboyna (1623), 29; for which Dutch Company pay compensation (1654), 39; Dutch established in Formosa (1624), 18, 19; trade with Japan, &c. (1641), 19; extent of their possessions, 19; decline of Dutch power in the East, 20; Cromwell declares war against, 39; they threaten Bombay (1672), 563; Trincomalee taken from the Dutch by the French, 57; projected English expedition against (1683), 76, 77; British struggle with, at Chinsurah (*q.v.*), 218.

INDEX. 431

E.

East India Company, origin of, 23; in 1600, 10; their early voyages and establishments, 24-27; profits on ditto, 24, 25, 28, 31; Emperor Jehangir grants British free trade in India (1613), 27, 31; joint-stock trading (1613-17), 27, 31; second joint-stock formed (1617); Company's possessions at this time, 32; progress under protection of Mogul Emperor, 31, 32; establishment of trade in Bengal (1620-50), 60, 61; difficulties with the Dutch, 28, 29, 31; struggles with Dutch and Portuguese, 36; third joint stock subscribed (1631); Company's affairs to be regulated at home by Governor, Committee, and Court of Adventurers, 37; factories controlled by President and Council at Surat, 37; trade with Persia (1632), 37; factories established in Bengal (1634), 37; acquisition of Madrasapatam (1640), 38; war with the Dutch, 39; the new charter (Charles II.), 41; rights on the Gold Coast made over to new African Company (1662), 42; Bombay made over to (1668), 45; strength of trading fleet (1671), 56; they obtain trade privileges from Shivaji (1674), 72; important Regulations of 1675, 73; dangerous reductions at Bombay (1678), 75; the Mogul Emperor begins to oppress the Company (1682), 63; Bombay wrested from the Company by Capt. Keigwin in the King's name (1683), 77; restored (1684), 79; seat of Government transferred from Surat to Bombay (1685), 80; Soobah of Bengal causes Company's first war in India (1685), 64-66; trade in Bengal abandoned (1688) for a time, 69; a new charter granted (William and Mary), 83; their monopoly disputed in England, 86; sums spent on "gratifications," 86n; successes of pirates cause mutiny on Company's vessels, 87; depressed state of Company's affairs (1696), 87; they suffer great losses at sea by the French, 88; rivalry of a New English Company (q.v.), chartered 1698, 89, 90, 94; partial union of the New and Old Company (1702), 96, 97; complete union in 1708, 105; embassy to the Imperial Court at Delhi (1715), 106; attempts to suppress the Maratha

East India Company—cont.
pirates, 108, 109-11; missions to the Maratha rulers (1739), 113; commercial treaty with the Marathas, 114; Madras taken by the French (1746), 119; but restored (1749), 124; expeditions in Tanjore (1749), 129-33; treaty with Nizam of Hyderabad (1766), 299; Company passes to the Crown (1858), 370.
List of principal factories in 1702, 98n; ditto, maintained after reductions (1707), 105; their imports of tea, 53 and n; social condition of Company's servants (about 1703), 99; their dishonourable conduct in Bengal, 250; Clive's Commercial Society, 252; measures of self-defence, 105; re-modelling of the Artillery (1748), 121.

Edicote, defended from the French (1751), 151.

Edwardes, Mr., obtains firman for trade in Mogul's dominions, 31.

Egypt, the Portuguese destroy her commerce with the East, 12.

Elizabeth, Queen, origin of East India Company under, 23.

English in India, early history, 20 et seq.; first English expedition to India (1582), 22; East India Company's (q.v.) first factory in India, 25, 31; Emperor Jehangir grants the British free trade in India (1613), 27, 31; defeat of Portuguese fleet by British in Surat Roads, 27, 28; treaty with the Zamorin (1615), 32; treaty with Mogul Court to resist Portuguese (1618), 33; conflicts with the Dutch (1618), 33; troubles at Ahmedabad and Surat (1622), 34; Company's Agents granted power of common and martial law (1624), 35; Madrasapatam, first *independent* position of English in India, acquired 1640, 38; Madras made a Presidency (1653), 39; chief Presidency at Surat (1657), 40; occupation of Bombay (q.v.), 44; early history of Bengal, q.v., 60 et seq.; the Mogul Emperor begins to oppress the E. I. Company (1682), 63; the Dutch expel the English from Bantam, 76; the Company's first war in India (1685-87), 64-68; Aurungzebe attempts extermination of the English (1689), 69; first actual hostilities between French and English (1691), 82; Madras (q.v.) supersedes Bombay as head-quarters of Indian Government (1694), 84;

INDEX.

English in India—*cont.*
Persia applies to the English for assistance (1696), 87 ; state of affairs in 1700, 93–95 ; death of Aurungzebe (1707) and fall of Mogul Empire, 102, 103..
The three Presidencies declared separate and independent (1708), 105 ; military forces in 1708, 105 ; civil administration of the military department (1718), 107 ; quarrel with the Portuguese (1719), 108 ; attempts to suppress the Maratha pirates (1719), 108, 109–11 ; missions to the Maratha rulers (1739), 113 ; commercial treaty with the Marathas, 114.
Clive (*q.v.*) arrives in India (1743), 117 ; relations with the French (*q.v.*), 117 ; first campaign on land against a native prince (1749), 128–33 ; rival factions in the Deccan supported by the English and the French, 136 ; campaigns in Southern India (1750–51), 140 ; campaigns (under Clive, *q.v.*) against the French, 147 ; campaign with French at and near Trichinopoly (1753–54), 152–56 ; cessation of hostilities, 156 ; treaty with France, 157 ; contrary to treaty, the British again assist Mahomed Ali (1755), 161 ; treaty with Surajah Dowlah (1757), 183 ; struggles with the Dutch at Chinsurah (*q.v.*), 218 ; Madras (*q.v.*) besieged by the French, 284–7 ; gift of the Dewanny from the Mogul Emperor (1765), 251 ; war with Hyder Ali (*q.v.*) of Mysore, 301.
English East India Company, a rival to the old (London) Company chartered 1698, 89, 94 ; Sir William Norris's mission to the Mogul Court (1701), 96 ; partial union of the two Companies (1702), 96, 97 ; new company's factors deprived of consular titles (1703), 98 ; complete union with the old East India Company (*q.v.*), 1708, 105.
Exchange, rate of, in 1705, 101.
Eyre, Lieut., at storming of Bangalore (1791), 312.

F.

Fake, Corporal, executed for mutiny (1674), 72.
Famine in Madras 1782, 306.
Faulkon, Constantine, a Greek adventurer, Prime Minister of Siam (about 1683), 58.
Fenton, Mr. Edward, has charge of English expedition to East Indies (1582), 22.
Ferrokshere, Mogul Emperor, 104 ; embassy from E. I. Company to (1715), 106.
Fletcher, Sir Robert, besieged Allahabad (1765), 235 ; in command at battle of Kalpi, 253*n*.
Forbes, Capt., in campaign near Trichinopoly (1754), 156.
Forde, Col., defeats the Dutch near Chinsurah, 220 ; and invests that town, 221 ; commands expedition against the French at Vizagapatam, 268 ; in command of Madras Army, 273 ; campaign in the Circars, 274, 283.
Formosa, island of, Dutch established in (1624), 19.
Fort St. David, site purchased 1685, 269*n* ; erected 1692, 83 ; redoubt built (1697), 88 ; its garrison (1746), 119 ; French attacks on, 120 ; taken by the French (1758), 269.
Fort St. George, built about 1640, 38 ; threatened by King of Golcondah, 43*n*, 45 ; besieged by Nabob of Carnatic, 54 ; its defences—in 1683, 77 ; and 1703, 100 ; its garrison—in 1654, 40 ; in 1673, 71 ; in 1679, 76 ; and in 1690–91, 238*n*.
Fort William, Calcutta, its building (about 1700), 91, 98 ; cost of, 215*n* ; its garrison—in 1706, 102 ; and 1707, 105.
Foxcroft, Mr., appointed Agent at Fort St. George, but imprisoned by Sir E. Winter (1665), 45, 51 ; released 1668, 53.
French in India, fleet equipped for the East, 1663, 42 ; their arrival in India (1665), 43, 44 ; leaving Surat, the French take Trincomalee and St. Thomé (1672), 56, 57 ; they purchase Pondicherry and make it headquarters (1683), 57 ; their short-lived success in Siam, 58 ; they try for Tonquin, Cochin China, and Madagascar, 58 and *n*.

INDEX.

French in India—*cont.*
First actual hostilities between French and English (1691), 82; Pondicherry conquered by the Dutch (1694), 84; French capture two of the Company's ships (1697), 88; position of affairs in 1744, 117; Dupleix (*q.v.*) Governor, 117; French attack and take Madras (1746), 118; attacks on Fort St. David, 120; Madras restored to the Company, 124; the English besiege Pondicherry (1748), 123; French and English support rival factions in the Deccan, 137; siege of Arcot (1751), 143; and of Trichinopoly, 146; Northern Circars ceded to French by the Nizam (1752), 149; French defeated in battle at Bahoor, 150; joined by the Marathas, 152; war at and near Trichinopoly, 152–54; cessation of hostilities, 156; treaty with British, 157; contrary to treaty the French assist Salabut Jung (1755), 161; varying success in the Deccan, 172, 173, 180; Chandernagore attacked by Clive (1757), 184; Count de Lally (*q.v.*) in the Carnatic (1758), 264; decisive battle of Condore, 275; Masulipatam taken by British, 281; siege of Madras, 284–7; French intrigue with and assist Hyder Ali (*q.v.*), of Mysore, 300, 303; French Revolution in Chandernagore, (1793) 196; vicissitudes of fortune (1793–1815), 197; French officers of Nizam's army compelled to leave India, 199.
French East India Company formed (1664), 33, 42; established 1665, 44. *See* French in India.

G.

Gama, Vasco de, discovers sea-route to India, 1, 4; his expedition and experience at Calicut, 10, 11.
Gary, Mr., Governor of Bombay (1667), 51.
Gayer, Sir John, appointed Lieut.-Gen. and Governor of Bombay (1694), 84; troubles with Mogul governor of Surat, 86; becomes Governor and General (1695), 87; troubles with the New Company (1700), 95; is imprisoned at Surat, by order of the Mogul, 97, 100, 104.

Geriah, battle of, 229, 230*n.*
German element in Presidential Armies (1676), 73.
Ghazi-oo-deen, son of the Nizam-ul-Mulk, contests succession to the Soubahship (1748–9), 133; his death (1752), 149.
Gheria, Maratha pirates attacked at, (1720), 109; expedition against Angria Pirates at (1756), 164; its fortifications, 164.
Gillam, Capt., a pirate in the Indian seas (about 1700), 95.
Gingee, fortress of, taken by the French (1750), 138; expedition against (1752), 150.
Gingens, Capt., in campaign against Chandah Sahib (1751), 141; takes command of campaign south of Cauvery, 148.
Girotty, Garden of, French Governor's house at, 196*n.*; society at (1770), 221.
Gladstone, Mr. W. E., M.P., on our rule in India, 297; on the Abyssinian War, 384.
Goa, Portuguese at, 12, 15.
Godehen, M., replaces Dupleix at Pondicherry (1754), 157.
Godwin, Gen., in Second Burmese War (1852), 352; anecdote of, 372.
Golden Rock, near Trichinopoly, battles at (1753), 152, 153.
Goldesborough, Capt. (afterwards Sir John), appointed Commissary and Superior over all the Company's affairs in India (1692), 83, 84; his death (1695), 84.
Goldsmid, Maj.-Gen. Sir F. J., his services, 416; on the Native Armies of India, 416.
Goodyear, Maj., appointed to command in Bombay (1748), 122.
Gordon, Capt., envoy to Maratha Rajah (1739), 113.
Gordon, Maj.-Gen., on Native Army of Bengal, 417.
Governor of Presidency, first appointed 1668, 41*n.*
Governor-General of Company's settlements, first appointed 1686, 66.
Governor *and* General, original title of Company's principal officer in India, 80 and *n.*
Grantham, Sir Thomas, English Vice-Admiral (1683), suppresses Interlopers in Bay of Bengal, 77; King's representative at Bombay, 78, 79.
Greeks in India, 6.
Greville, Fulke, afterwards Lord Brooke (*q.v.*), 23

INDEX.

Guntoor, one of the Northern Circars, 282.
Gurghin Khan, improves the Native Army of Bengal (1760), 227, 229; his death, 231.
Gwalior, taken by Hoomayoon, 9.
Gyfford, Mr., Agent of E. I. Company (1683), 63.

H.

Hamilton, Dr., medical officer to an embassy, cures the Emperor Feroksbere, and obtains important grants for the Company (1715), 106-7 and *n.*
Harris, Gen., in war against Tippoo Sultan (1799), 316.
Harris, Mr., E. I. Company's Agent at Surat (1687), 68.
Hawkins, Capt., establishes E. I. Company's first factory in India, 25.
Hay, Sir J., on the cession of Pondicherry, 200.
Heath, Capt., commands E. I. Company's ships (1688), 69.
Hedges, Mr., appointed Governor of Bengal (1682), 62.
Heligoland, remarks on its exchange with Pondicherry, 200.
Heron, Lieut.-Col., in command of British forces (1755), 161.
Hindu Kush, march of Bengal Artillery across (1839), 331.
Hippon, Capt., founds first English settlement on east coast of India, 27.
Holkar, Mulhaji, sets up independent rule, 50.
Holwell, Mr., in the siege of Calcutta (1756), 169.
Hoogly, Company's factory established at (1651-2), 61 and *n.*; details of compensation demanded from Faujdar of (1686), 67 and *n.*; the New Company establish factory at (1699), 91; sacked by Marathas (1742), 116; fort taken by storm (1757), 180.
Houtman, commands Dutch expedition to the East, 17, 18.
Hyderabad, Nizam of, his rabble troops, 312 and *n.*
Hyder Ali, ruler of Mysore, 299; commands Mysore Horse against the English, 154, 156; dashes upon Madras, 300; at war with British (1780), 301; died 1782. succeeded by his son Tippoo (*q.v.*), 304.

I.

Inchbird, Capt., sent with force to aid the Sidee of Jingeera (1733), 110*n*; his operations against the Maratha Pirates, 110-11; his mission to the Maratha at Bassein (1739), 113.
India, its ancient history and literature, 5; early Arab commerce with, 3; various routes to, 21; invaded by Persians, 5; and by Greeks, 6; Tartars overthrow Greek power in, 7; Sultan Mahmood's conquests in, 7; commencement of Mahometan power in, 7, 8; Moghul Empire in, 8-10; Portuguese in (*q.v.*), 4, 10-16; the Dutch in (*q.v.*), 17-20; the English in (*q.v.*), 20 *et seq.*; arrival (1665) of the French in (*q.v.*), 44; Persian invasion of (1737), 114; decay of Mogul Empire (*q.v.*), 115; extent, &c. of British Empire in, 4 and *n.*
Indian Institute, Mr. H. S. King's fund for, ix., x.
Ingellee besieged 1687, 68.
Innes, Lieut., in command of reinforcements for relief of Clive in Arcot (1751), 144.
"Interlopers," free traders in the East so called, vi., 293; their suppression, 41; troublesome at Bengal (1684), 63; penalty for (1718), 107.

J.

Jains, origin of, 5.
Jamaul Sahib, commander of Company's Sepoys (1756), 162.
James, Commodore, commands in operations against Pirates (1755), 162; in command of Company's fleet at Gheria (1756), 164, 183.
Java, Dutch settlements in, 18; the English in, 34.
Jehangir, Emperor, his reign, 10; grants the British free trade in India (1613), 27, 31.
Justice, Courts of, established in Bombay (1670), 54 and *n.*

INDEX. 435

K.

Kalpi, battle of (1765), 25n.
Kaye, Lieut. E., with Bengal Artillery (1839), 331.
Keeling, Capt., commands E. I. Company's third voyage (1607), 25.
Keigwin, Capt., Governor of St. Helena, has command in Bombay Army (1676), 73; dismissed, 1678, 75; but again engaged, 1670, 76; wrests the Government of Bombay from the Company in the King's name (1683), 77; delivers it to King's representative (1684), 79.
Kerridge, Mr., his first commercial transactions with India, 30; obtains firman for trade in Mogul's dominions, 31.
Kidd, Capt., notorious pirate (1698), 89; seized and executed (1702), 98.
Kilpatrick, Maj., at Arcot (1751), 144.
King, Mr. H. S., M.P., his visit to, and action in, India, ix.; his fund for Indian Institute subscribed to by Maharajah of Mysore, x.
Kirkee, battle of (1817), 321.
Kirkpatrick, Maj., with Madras detachment to assist Bengal (1756), 172, 176, 180; at battle of Plassey, 211.
Knox, Capt., at battle of Condore, 275; at Patna (1760), 225.
Kohiyar, Nasarvanji, Agent of the Dutch at Surat, 296.
Koregaum, defence of (1818), 322.
Kotb-od-deen, rules at Delhi, 7, 8.
Kutwah, fort of, taken (1757), 204.

Lally, Count de—*cont.*
269; marches to Tanjore, 270; rupture with the Rajah, 271; attack on, and retreat from, Tanjore, 272; operations against Chingleput, 274; the siege of Madras (1758-9), 284-7; besieged in Pondicherry (1760-61), 287; his end, 288.
Lambert, Commodore, anecdote of, 195, 207 and n.
Lancaster, Mr. James, commands expedition to the East (1591), 23; and in 1601-2, 24.
Langford, Capt., has command of troops at Bombay (1674), 72.
Law, M., defends fort of Ariancopang (1748), 123; at siege of Trichinopoly (1752), 146-7; surrenders to Lawrence, 148.
Lawrence, Maj., appointed Commander-in-Chief (1748), 122; taken prisoner by the French, 123; with expedition to Tanjore (1749), 130; at relief of Trichinopoly (1752), 146; defeats French at Bahoor, 150; campaigns about Trichinopoly (1753-4), 152-56; defeats the French at the Golden Rock, 152; in the siege of Madras by the French (1758-9), 285; acknowledgment of his services, 156.
Lorraine, Regiment of, 271n.
Lucas, Sir Gervase, Crown Governor of Bombay (1666-67), 45, 51.
Lyttleton, Sir Edward, factor of the (rival) English Company, 89; his appointment revoked (1705), 100.

L.

La Bourdonnais, M., Governor of Mauritius (1744), 117 and n; attacks and takes Madras (1746), 118; quarrels with Dupleix, 119 and n.
Lakha Bag at Plassey, 207.
Lall Pultun, or Red Battalion, raising of (1757), 181.
Lally, Count de, Governor-General of the French Settlements, 269; his previous services, 268; at war with English in the Carnatic (1758), 264; takes Cuddalore and Fort St. David,

M.

Macartney, Lord, Governor of Madras (1781-85), 305; his vexatious proceedings, 306.
Macaulay, Lord, his estimate of Dupleix, 194.
Mackenzie, Lieut. M., in command of Bengal Artillery (1839), 331.
MacLean, Capt., at battle of Condore (1758), 275.
Macleod, Maj.-Gen. W. E., on Native Army of Bombay, 421.
Madagascar, French expedition to (17th cent.), 58 and n.

436 INDEX.

Madras, early history of the Presidency, 30 et seq.; subject to President and Council at Bantam (1640), 38; made a Presidency (1653), 39; state of affairs in 1668, 53; and in 1673, 71; declared an independent power (1687), 80 and n; supersedes Bombay as head-quarters of Government (1694), 84; precautions against French fleet (1695), 85; city attacked and taken by the French (1746), 118; restored to the Company (1749), 124; Government again established at (1752), 149; the French under Lally in (1758), 264 et seq., 270; siege of the city by French (1758-9), 284-7; war with Hyder Ali (q.v.), 301; grievous famine in (1782), 306.

Fortifications of the city in 1644, 38; defences strengthened (1684), 79; garrison of—in 1692, 83; in 1706, 102; and in 1746, 118; pay of the garrison (1676), 73; Volunteer Horse of (1665), 85; notes on Native Army of, 418.

Madras Army, strength of European force (1749), 129n; number of Sepoys in, 147; first company of Artillery ordered, 239; the gun-room crew, 240; Madagascar slaves and Swiss troops for, 150; Swiss Artillery in, 152n; strengthened with troops from Bombay (1754), 155; Royal troops and the Mutiny Act introduced (1754), 160; organization of (1755), 202; officers of the 39th Regt., 175n; and of the Madras Infantry (1756), 176; formation of Governor-General's Body-Guard (1799), 375; its services, 376; Queen's Own Sappers and Miners, notes on, 338-50; Fourth P.W.O. Madras Light Cavalry, notes on, 372.

English expedition (1749) into Tanjore (q.v.), 129; storming of Devicotah, 131; attempt to take Madura, 140; expedition against Chandah Sahib at Volconda, 141; siege of Arcot (1751), 143; campaign (under Clive, q.v.) against the French (1752), 147; war at Trichinopoly (1753-4), 152; serious British losses, 154; expedition to save Bengal from Surajah Dowlah, 173; campaign in the Northern Circars (1758), 274, 283; battle of Condore, 275.

Madras Artillery, rapid march of (1858), 334.

Madras Light Cavalry, regiments of, 377; notes on 4th P.W.O. Regt., 372.

Madras Sappers and Miners, Queen's Own, details of services, with officers mentioned in despatches, 338-50.

Madrasapatam, first *independent* position of English in India, acquired 1640, 38.

Madura, English attempt to re-conquer (1751), 140.

Magdala, the storming of (1867), 383.

Mahim, an out fort of Bombay, 85.

Mahmood, Sultan, son of Sabaktagin, his conquests in India, 7.

Mahomed Ali, son of the Nabob of Arcot, asks aid of the British, 135; gains their support, 136; defeated by the French, joins Nazir Jung (1750), 138; ready to resign to the French, still supported by the English (1751), 140; makes alliance with Regent of Mysore, the Marathas, and Rajah of Tanjore, 146, 148; defeated by French at Vicravandi (1752), 150; again helped by British contrary to treaty (1755), 161.

Mohomed Issoof, commander-in-chief of Madras Sepoys (1754-56), 162; defeats Polygar army (1756), 175.

Mahomed Reza Khan, civil and criminal manager to the Nabob, 250.

Mahomed Shah, Mogul Emperor, his power crippled by Persia (1739), 114; his dominions again invaded by Persians (1748), 126.

Mahomedanism in India, 216.

Malabar coast conquered by Portuguese, 13.

Malabar Hill, defences of (1695 and 1886), 85 and n.

Malacca, taken by Portuguese (1511), 13.

Malcolm, Sir John, in war against Tippoo Sultan (1799), 316.

Malleson, Col., tutor to the Rajah of Mysore, 319.

Mandalay, made capital of Burma (1860), 368.

Maphuze Khan, elder son of Nabob of Arcot, taken prisoner at Amboor, 135, 155.

Marathas invest Surat (1663), 43; their influence on Bombay, 46; division of the Empire, 50; besiege Surat (1703), 100; threaten Delhi (1738), 111; attack the Portuguese near Bombay, 111; commercial treaty with, by Capt. Keigwin (1684), 113; they rule in Tanjore, 128; join the French (1753), 152.

Maratha Pirates, account of, 108-11.

Marryat, Capt., served in the first Burmese war, 364n.

INDEX. 437

Martial law, Company's servants first exercising (1674), 72; royal code of, applied to Company's forces (1685), 80.
Martin, M., pioneer of the French in India, 57, 58; founded Pondicherry (1683), 201.
Masters, Mr, serves the Company (1676), 62.
Masulipatam, E. I. Company's factory at, 36; taken by the French (1750), 137; taken by British (1759), 281.
Mathison, Lieut., anecdote of, 331.
Matthews, Gen., murdered by Tippoo, 304.
Mazagon, an out fort of Bombay, 85.
Medows, Maj.-Gen. Sir W., Commander-in-Chief at Madras (1790), 309; anecdote of, 312.
Meer Cossim, made Nabob (1760), 226; war with English over trade duties, 227; the last of him, 234, 235.
Meer Jaffier Khan, offended by Surajah Dowlah, intrigues with English, 166; at battle of Plassey (1757), 208; his treachery to Surajah Dowlah (1757), 211; is made Nabob by Clive, 214; intrigues with the Dutch, 219; his death (1765), 234; his character, 205; his rule, 218; his legacy to Clive, 261.
Meerun, son of Meer Jaffier, his infamous conduct, 224; and death, 225.
Mein, Gen. J. D., rapid march of Artillery under (1858), 334.
Meng-Khaung, Burmese King (1416), 355.
Michael, Gen., on Native Army of Madras, 418.
Middleton, Capt. (afterwards Sir) Henry, commands E. I. Company's fleet (1604-6), 24; and again in 1610-14, 26.
Minchin, Capt., in the siege of Calcutta (1756), 169.
Minderajee Prau, founder of Amarapúra, 364.
Minhla, storming of, 397.
Mint, established at Bombay (1671), 55.
Mirza Raja, Subahdar of the Deccan, 49.
Mogul Empire in India, its rise, 8; reign of Akbar, 9; and of Jehangir, 10; conflict with the Marathas, 47-50; civil war in, on death of Aurungzebe (1707), 103; decay of, 115, 127.
Monackjie, Tanjore General, his attack upon Lally's camp, 272.
Monghir, siege of (1763), 232.
Montague, Lieut.-Col., killed at siege of Seringapatam (1799), 330; anecdote of, 330.

Moodeen Khan, killed at Plassey (1757), 210, 212.
Moorhouse, Lieut.-Col., at storming of Bangalore (1791), 310.
Moorshedabad, taken by British (1763), 229.
Morari Rao, leader of Maratha Horse, 136; makes alliance with Clive at Arcot (1751), 144.
Munro, Gen. Sir Hector, at battle of Porto Novo (1781), 319-20; his stern discipline, 233.
Mustees, or half-castes, 115.
Muti-jil, description of, 262.
Muzzufer Jung, son of the Nizam-ul-Mulk, claims Soubahship of the Deccan (1748-9), 133; assisted by the French, is proclaimed Nizam, 134-5; he gives up, 137; liberated by the French and proclaimed Nizam (1750), 139; his death (1751), 140.
Mysore, Hyder Ali (*q.v.*), ruler of, 299; war in and conquest of, 301, 308.
Mysore, Maharajah of, his subscription to fund for Indian Institute, x.

N.

Nadir Shah, King of Persia, invades the Punjab and sacks Delhi (1738), 114.
Napier of Magdala, Lord, obituary notice of, 379-88; in the Chinese War of 1860, 381; storming of Magdala, 383; his personal qualities, 384.
Native Cavalry, establishment of a regiment of (1785), 373; notes on regiments of, 376.
Native troops, first mentioned in garrison of Bombay, 45; regular companies of, first enrolled (1683), 77; to be enlisted from same caste (1694), 84; first enlistment of, in Bengal, 91; constitution of, in 1708, 105; first detached on service from their Presidency, 1748, 121n; confidence placed in Native commanders, 162; forbidden the use of Artillery, 245; reduction of Native Artillery, 245-7; notes on Native Army of Bengal, 417; of Bombay, 421; and of Madras, 418; pay of those under Aurungzebe, 104.
Nazir Jung, son of the Nizam-ul-Mulk, claims the Soubahship, 133; sup-

438 INDEX.

Nazir Jung—*cont.*
ported by the British, 136, 137; signs treaty with the French, 138; but is attacked by them, and killed by traitors (1750), 139.
Newport, Capt., conducts E. I. Company's expedition, 31.
Nicholson, Capt., commands fleet for E. I. Company (1685), 65-67.
Noble, Capt., raises troop of Madras Horse Artillery (1805), 374.
Norris, Sir William, ambassador to the Mogul Court (1700). 95; his mission, and death (1702), 96.
Nujun-ood-dowla, son of Meer Jaffier, made Nabob (1765), 234; makes treaty with Calcutta Council, 249.

O.

Omichund, a Hindu merchant useful to the British, 181-84; cheated and ruined, 218.
Ostend Company, for trading in the East (1717-1726), 107.
Oxinden, Sir George, President of Surat (1662), 42; first Governor of Presidency, appointed to Bombay, 1668, 41*n*, 45; his administration of Bombay, 51; and death (1669), 54.
Oxinden, Mr., attends coronation of Shivaji (1674), 71.

P.

Pagoda, value of, 41, 101, 307.
Panipat, near Delhi, battle at (1526), 9.
Paradis, M., defeats Nabob of Carnatic, 119; attempts to reduce Fort St. David (1747), 120.
Parsís, in Bombay, account of, 295; enrolled as Volunteers, vii.
Patan Chiefs, treacherous conduct of (1750-51), 138-40.
Patna, attempt to fix a factory at (1620), 60; massacre at (1763), 232; siege and storm of, 232; British victory at (1760), 224-5.

Pearse, Lieut.-Col., commands and improves Bengal Artillery (1769), 241, 247.
Perez, Portuguese ambassador to China (1518), 14.
Persia, E. I. Company's trade with, 28, 29, 31, 37; applies to the Company for assistance (1696), 87; early invasion of India, 5; Nadir Shah invades India (1737), 114.
Persian Gulf, as trade route, 13.
Peshwa, office of, becomes hereditary, 50.
Petapoli, E. I. Company's factory at, 26.
Petit, Sir Dinshaw Manocjee, 295 and *n*.
Phayre, Gen. Sir Arthur, ambassador to Burma (1855), 367; his account of Ava (*q.v.*), 352.
Phœnicians, trade between East and West, 2-3.
Pigot, Mr., Member of Council, takes reinforcements to Trichinopoly (1751), 142; Governor of Madras (1755-63), 286, 290 and *n*.
Pilaji Gaekarwar, sets up independent rule, 50.
Piplee, port of, in Bengal (1634), 37, 38.
Pirates, their successes off West Coast of India (1696), 87; under Capt. Kidd (1698), 89; the English, Dutch, and French combine against the marauders 89; flourishing in 1703, 99; and in 1705, 100; Maratha pirates (*q.v.*), 108; memorable sea fight with (1722), 109; extermination of the Angria Pirates (1756), 162-65.
Pirha Jaça, holy place at Plassey, 207.
Pitt, Mr., factor of the (rival) English Company (1699), 89; appointed to Fort St. David (1703), 98; dies, 99.
Pitt, Mr., Governor of Madras (1697), 88, 89*n*.; appointed Governor and President (1703), 98.
Plassey, description of place, 207; battle of (1757), 209; results of, 214, 215.
Pocock, Admiral, with expedition to save Bengal (1756), 174, 184; killed, 185.
Polygars of the Colleries, conquest of (1756), 161, 162; again troublesome, 175.
Pondicherry, purchased by the French (1683), 57; founded by M. Martin, 201; siege of (1748), 123; French receive considerable territory round (1750), 139; besieged by British (1760-61), 287; restored to the French (1763), 299; vicissitudes of (1793-1815), 197; remarks on its exchange with Heligoland, 200.

INDEX. 439

Porto Novo, decisive battle of (1781), 319
Portuguese discover sea-route to East, 3; land in India (1498), 4; at Calicut under Vasco de Gama, 10, 11; second expedition under Alvares Cabral, 11, 12; Albuquerque, first Viceroy, seizes Goa, 12; his further conquests, 13; conflict with Egypt, 12; embassy to China, 14; and trade with Japan, 14; extent of their power in the East (1538), 15; the administration of Don Juan da Castro, 15; decline of the Portuguese power, 15, 16; their fleet defeated by British at Surat, 27, 28; English quarrel with (1719), 108; attacked by Marathas, 111; apply to Bombay for aid (1739), 112.
Pratop Sing, rules Tanjore, 128.
Prendergast, Lt.-Gen. Sir H. N. D., commanding Burma Field Force (1885-6), 388; his account of operations in Upper Burma, 392 et seq.
President and Council, titles first assumed by Company's servants in Java (1622), 34.
Presidential Armies, organization of (1748), 122; origin and progress of Artillery (q.v.), 237 et seq.; origin of Artillery terms, 242; re-modelling of the Artillery, 121; pay of officers and men, 121-22; description of European soldiers in India (1711), 240-41; officers in Society (about 1770), 243; discontent and mutiny among troops, 232-3; mutiny of Bengal officers (1766), 257; Bombay and Madras detachments incorporated with Bengal Army, 202; notes on Indian Regiments of Cavalry, 376; standards first delivered to cavalry regiments (1788), 374; Lord Clive and the Army, 253 et seq.; transfer from Company to Crown (1858), 370; Army of British India (1889), 253 n.; questions of re-organization, xi
Honours of Plassey, 213; victories of certain regiments, 213; war with Tippoo Sultan, 308, 316; second siege and storming of Seringapatam (1799), 316.
Prideaux, Lieut., with mission to Abyssinia (1864), 382.
Prince of Wales' Own Grenadier Regiment of Bombay Infantry, record of services, 321 et seq.; state and composition of (1887), 327.
Pulo Condore, near Borneo, massacre of Company's servants at (1706), 102.
Putta-wallahs, why so called, 116n.

Q.

Queen's Own Madras Sappers and Miners, notes on, 338-50.

R.

Rajbullut, Deputy Governor of Dacca, cause of quarrel between English and Surajah Dowlah (1756), 166.
Rajpoots, companies of, first enrolled for Bombay (1683), 77.
Ramnarayan, Rajah, Governor of Patna, 224; his end, 230.
Ram-Rajah, King of Marathas (1690), 81.
Rangoon, founded by Alompra, 358.
Rassam, Mr. Hormuzd, his mission to Abyssinia (1864), 382.
Ratanapúra, or Ava (q.v.), 354.
Raymond, Mr. George, commands expedition to the East (1591), 23.
Renaud, or Renault, Governor of Chandernagore (1757), 185, 189.
Rivett-Carnac, Col. E. S., sketch of career and services, xvii.
Rivett-Carnac, Mr. James, Director, xi.
Roberts, Gen. Sir Fredk., his march to Candahar (1880), 192, 334.
Roe, Sir Thomas, Ambassador to the Mogul Court (1615), 10, 28, 32, 33.
Rolt, Mr., Governor of Bombay (1677), 74.
Royal Artillery, men of, reinforce Madras Army (1754), 160.
Runjeet Singh, Maharajah, anecdote of, 336.
Rupee, value of, in 1707, 103n.

S.

Sabut Jung, Clive so entitled, 207.
Sagaing, seat of Shan kings, 352.
Saboji, Maratha Chief, applies to Bombay for aid, 106.
Salabut Jung, placed on throne of Deccan by the French (1751), 140, 149; deserts the French and joins the English, 172.
Saldanha Bay, taken possession of by English (1620), 34.

440 INDEX.

Salsette, Islands of, taken by Marathas (1739), 112; taken from the Marathas (1774), 80.
Sambaji, son of Konoji Angria, Maratha pirate (*q.v.*), 110.
Sambhaji, son of Shivaji, 49; succeeds his father (1680), 76; commercial treaty with (1683), 79; his death, 50.
Samiaveram, Clive defeats French at (1752), 147.
Sanjohi, Maratha ruler of Tanjore, deposed, seeks aid from the English, 128; English expeditions into Tanjore on his behalf (1749), 129; sold by the English, 132.
Saris, Capt., commands E. I. Company's expedition (about 1611), 26.
Saunders, Mr., Governor of Madras, sends reinforcements to Trichinopoly (1751), 142.
Scind, E. I. Company's factory in (1635), 38.
Scotch East India Company established 1695, 86 and *n*.
Seddee, title of Mogul admirals, 68 and *n*.
Seleucus invaded India, 6*n*.
Sepoy, peons or puttawallahs so called, 115, 116*n*.; organization of (1748), 122; Sepoys in Bombay Army, 115; number in Madras Army (1752), 147*n*.; services of, in Madras establishment, 162; their value as fighting material, 126; their gallant behaviour on various occasion, 159; first instance of disaffection among (1748), 122; Clive's training and organization of, 180.
Seringapatam, capital of Mysore, first siege of (1792), 313; second siege and fall of (1799), 316.
Seringham, Island of, abandoned by English (1750), 141; French again established at (1753), 152; strength of French forces at (1754), 154.
Shah Allum, Emperor, invades Behar (1760), 223; defeated at Patna, 225.
Shah Johan, Emperor, by firman from, E. I. Company establish factories in Bengal (1634), 37.
Shahaji, father of Shivaji, 47; his death, 49.
Shahisti Khan, Mogul commander-in-chief, 48.
Shaxton, Capt., Factor of Bombay, 55; found guilty of mutiny (1674), 72.
Shillinge, Capt., takes possession of Saldanha Bay (1620), 34.

Shipman, Sir Abraham, appointed Governor of Bombay (1662), 41; ill-success, 42, 43; and death, 44.
Shivaji, his early history, 47; his conflicts with the Mogul, 37-50; seizes on Tanjore (1670), 128; his coronation (1674), 71; his death (1680), 50, 76.
Siam, E. I. Company's factory in, 27; French trade with, 58.
Silladar, a four-horse, 104 and *n*.
Sindia, Nanoji, sets up independent rule, 50.
Sion, an out-fort of Bombay, 85.
Sladen, Col. E. B., with Burma Field Force (1885-6), 389, 403, 415.
Smith, Mr. Charles, in defence of Calcutta (1756), 168.
Soarez, Lopez, Portuguese Viceroy in India, 14.
Solyman, Sultan, his fleet destroyed by Portuguese (1538), 15.
Sophie, Shah, King of Persia, grants firman to E. I. Company (1631), 37.
St. Helena, colonized (1657) and possessed (1661) by the E. I. Company, 42.
St. John, Dr., King's Judge at Bombay (1684), 79.
St. Thomé (St. Thomas' Mount), taken by the French (1672), 56; made permanent head-quarters of Madras Artillery (1774), 244.
Staunton, Capt., his defence of Koregaum (1818), 322.
Staveley, Sir Charles, at taking of Magdala (1867), 383.
Stavorinus, Capt., his description of Giretty (1770), 221.
Stuart Gen. Jas., at battle of Porto Novo (1781), 319-20; English forces in Madras under (1783), 304*n*, 306; story of the rocket-man, 307.
Stuart, Lieut. James, in war against Tippoo Sultan (1799), 316.
Suakin, E. I. Company's trade with (1645), 38.
Sugar Loaf Rock, near Trichinopoly, battles at (1753), 153.
Sujah Dowlah, Soubahdar of Oudh, opposes the British (1763), 232-34, 251*n*.
Sukaji, son of Konoji Angria, Maratha pirate (*q.v.*), 110.
Sumatra, E. I. Company established in (1691), 83.
Suraj-ad-Dowlah, or—
Surajah Dowlah, quarrels with English, 166; his attack on Calcutta (1756) (*q.v.*), 168; he again marches on

INDEX. 441

Surajah Dowlah—*cont.*
Calcutta, 181; makes treaty with British, 183; but sides with the French, 183, 186; marches to Plassey, 203; his letter to M. Bussy (1757), 206; at battle of Plassey, 208; Meer Jaffier's treachery to, 212; his flight and death, 214; his character, 205.
Surat, E. I. Company's first factory in India at, 25, 31; first Dutch factory at (1617), 33; it is made chief Presidency (1657), 40, 41; invested by Marathas (1663), 43; and attacked and plundered by Shivaji (1670), 49, 55; again raised to a Presidency (1681), 76; the seat of Government transferred from there to Bombay (1685), 80; besieged by Marathas (1703), 100; troubles at, 1706, 101, 102; hostilities with the Siddee (1752), 151.
Suree, an out fort of Bombay, 85.
Swiss troops in Presidential Armies, 150, 152 and *n*.
Symes, Col., his mission to Burma (1795), 361.

T.

Tagaung, the first Burmese capital, 352.
Taku Forts, storming of, in Chinese War of 1860, 381.
Tamerlane or Timourlang (*q.v.*), 8.
Tanjore, description of, 128; falls under rule of the Marathas, 128; English interfere in native disputes, 128; English expedition (1749) to assist Sanjohi (*q.v.*), 129; king of, comes to terms with the French, 136; French attack upon and retreat from (1758), 270–72.
Tea, first order to the E. I. Company for, 53; the Company's imports of, 53*n*.
Terreneau, story of, at Chandernagore, 189.
Thadomengbyâ, a famous Shan chief (1364), 352; founded the city of Ava (*q.v.*), 354.
Thamas Cooly Khan, better known as Nadir Shah (*q.v.*), 114.

Theebaw, King of Burma, 355; a curious ceremony at Mandalay (1874), 368.
Theodore, King of Abyssinia, war against (1867), 382.
Tillicherry, encounter at (1751), 151.
Timourlang (Tamerlane) takes Delhi, 8, 9.
Tippoo Sultan, son of Hyder Ali, succeeds his father in Mysore (1782), 304; treaty of peace with (1784), 304, 308, and *n*; campaigns against (1790–91), 309; comes to terms at siege of Seringapatam (1792), 313, 315; his sons delivered as hostages, 314; intrigues with the French, 315; second siege and fall of Seringapatam (1799), 316; his character, 317; his dreams, 319.
Toghlukabad, remains of ancient Delhi, 8.
Tonquin, the French try to establish themselves at (17th cent.), 58 and *n*; E. I. Company trade in, 74.
Toolaji, a Maratha pirate (*see* Angria).
Topasses, who they were, 52*n*; they prove their fidelity, 43*n*.
Towerson, Capt., Agent at Amboyna (1623), 34.
Trichinopoly, prince of, threatens Tanjore (1670), 128; preparations for defence of (1751), 142; besieged by Chandah Sahib and the French, 146; war at (1753), 152.
Tyrrel, Capt., commands reinforcements to the East (1683), 78.

U.

"Uncovenanted," the, vi., ix.
U'ndwah Nálá, decisive battle of (1763), 230.
United Company of Merchants of England trading with the East Indies, 98.

V.

Van Speult, Dutch Agent at Surat, 35.
Vaux, Mr., Deputy Governor of Bombay (1693), 83.
Velore, battle near, 300.
Vicravandi, French victory at (1752), 150.

INDEX.

Volconda, disgraceful behaviour of European detachment at (1751), 141.
Von Neck, Admiral, commands Dutch expedition to the East, 18.

W.

Waite, Sir Nicholas, factor of the (rival) English Company (1699), 89, 95; his treatment of the London (Old) Company's officers, 96; abuses his powers, 101; dismissed (1708), 106.
Walcott, Ensign, the only officer who survived the Black Hole (1756), 171n.
Wandewash, battle of, 287.
Warwyck, Admiral, Dutch pioneer in the East, 18.
Watson, Admiral, brings reinforcements for Madras (1754), 157, 160; with English fleet in Indian seas, 164; sent with expedition to save Bengal (1756), 173, 190; at taking of Chandernagore, 195.
Watts, Mr., President at Cossimbazar, 167; resident at Moorshedabad, 206 and n.
Wellesley, Lord, Governor General (1798), 315; at war with Tippoo, 316; his policy with the French in India, 198.
Wetwang, Sir John, English Admiral (1683), 77.
Weycondah, near Trichinopoly, fortress of, stormed (1753), 153.

Wilkinson, Mr., in defence of Calcutta (1756), 168.
Willoughby, Sir H., English navigator, 20.
Winter, Sir Edward, Agent at Fort St. George, coins pagodas (1660), 41; his extraordinary conduct (1665), 45, 51; and return to England (1669), 53.
Woodward, Capt. R., R.N., with Naval Brigade in Upper Burma, 388, 399, · 413.
Worlee, an out fort of Bombay, 85.
Wyborne, Sir John, Deputy Governor of Bombay (1685), 80 and n.

Y.

Yonge, Capt. W. A., first commandant of Madras Light Cavalry, 372.
Yule, Sir Henry, with mission to Burma (1855), 367.

Z.

Zamorin, the, or Prince Governor of the Malabar coast, makes treaty with the British (1615), 32.
Zinzan, Mr., temporary Governor of Bombay (1684), 79.

www.ingramcontent.com/pod-product-compliance
Lightning Source LLC
Chambersburg PA
CBHW022116300426
44117CB00007B/736